C0-DAC-684

Decision Support Software for the IBM Personal Computer

Raymond McLeod, Jr.

Texas A&M University

SCIENCE RESEARCH ASSOCIATES, INC.
Chicago, Henley-on-Thames, Sydney, Toronto

A Subsidiary of IBM

To Sharlotte and Glenn

Acquisition Editor   Michael J. Carrigg

Project Editor   Byron Riggan

Designer   James Buddenbaum/Design

Compositor   Total Typography, Inc.

Acknowledgments
The illustrations on pages 7, 8, 9, 11, 13, 14, 15 and 20 are courtesy of the International Business Machines Corp.

Library of Congress Cataloging in Publication Data

McLeod, Raymond,
    Decision support software for the IBM personal computer.

    Includes index.
    1. Management information systems.   2. Decision-making.   3. IBM Personal computer.   I. Title.
T58.6.M4238   1985   658.4'0388   84-20266
ISBN 0-574-21760-6

Copyright © Science Research Associates, Inc. 1985.
All rights reserved. No part of this publication may be reproduced, stored in a retrievel system, or transmitted, in any form or by any means, electronic, mechanical, photocopying, recording, or otherwise, without the prior written permission of Science Research Associates, Inc.

Printed in the United States of America.

10 9 8 7 6 5 4 3 2 1

Contents

Preface

This book is written in response to two trends—the trend to small-scale systems, and the trend to packaged software. While it is recognized that the small systems area is only one part of the computing field, it is an area one must understand to achieve "computer literacy." To understand how to use the computer, the student should include both small and large systems, and both custom programming and packaged software. This book is intended to help the student understand the two software approaches, using a small-scale computer system as the vehicle.

Why the IBM Personal Computer?

In the center of the small-scale system movement is the IBM Personal Computer (PC). It was certainly not the first small system, but the PC has achieved a degree of acceptance, especially for business applications, that none of the earlier systems achieved. The reputation of IBM as a supplier of high-quality business computers no doubt contributed to the PC's acceptance.

When an author writes a book about software, the task is much easier when he or she can address a specific computer system, such as the PC. Otherwise, too much attention has to be given to minor (but important) differences between the software versions, and the main points become obscured.

The PC is a good choice because of the large numbers of PCs and PC compatible systems in use. Also, the PC appears to offer an opportunity for longevity that is not easy to come by in the computer field. The announcement by IBM of the small PCjr and the larger PC/XT and PC/AT indicate a commitment by that organization to the PC line.

Why dBASE II, VisiCalc, and WordStar?

There may be an argument concerning the selection of the software systems discussed in this book. There are many excellent packages on the market, and the use of each could be justified. The packages tend to fall into three major groups, and this simplifies the selection process somewhat. The three areas where most of the high-quality packages can be found are data base management systems, electronic spreadsheets, and word processors. These three areas, plus the BASIC language, also provide coverage of the four major parts of a management information system (MIS) or decision support system (DSS), as we will see later.

The process of selecting a package for each area placed much weight on the current level of acceptance—the packages that have seen the widest range of adoption. The reasoning was that the schools would more likely have copies of the most popular packages, and the instructors might already be familiar with their use. Applying this logic, dBASE II was selected as the data base management system, VisiCalc was selected as the electronic spreadsheet, and WordStar was selected as the word processor.

The selection based on widespread adoption also assures that the packages are exceptionally user-friendly, as that characteristic is a necessity in a course where the student will be introduced to several packages. The packages selected for this text all meet the requirement of user-friendliness. The goal is to gain familiarity with the *categories* of software as decision support tools. It is not to become acquainted with particular *brands* within each category.

The text is organized into seven modules:

1. The IBM PC
2. Decision Support Systems Concepts
3. Procedural Programming Languages
4. Data Base Management Systems
5. Electronic Spreadsheets
6. Word Processing
7. Overview of Software for the PC

Modules 3 through 6 describe the software systems—BASIC and the three prewritten packages. Each module includes a chapter describing how that software fits into a DSS, an introductory chapter, and a more advanced chapter. You may elect to skip the chapter dealing with DSS concepts, and only cover the introductory material, or you may want to cover the concepts and the introduction but not the advanced material, and so on. And, you can cover the modules in a different sequence if you wish. For example, you may want to cover WordStar before dBASE II. Each module "stands alone." The format of the book is very flexible and can be adapted to a variety of course approaches.

The text is intended for use:

- As the only text in an introduction to computing, MIS, or DSS course where the emphasis is on student use of software.
- As a supplement to an introduction to computing (such as Bohl, *Information Processing,* 4th ed., Chicago: SRA, 1984) or an MIS text (such as McLeod, *Management Information Systems,* 2nd ed., Chicago: SRA, 1983) where the intent is to get students involved in DSS-oriented laboratory assignments.
- As the only text in a mini/micro course where the intent is to teach both small system hardware and software.
- As the only text in an IBM PC course where the intent is to teach only that system.
- As the only text in an adult short course where the intent is to update participants on small systems and small-system software.

The text is unique in two respects. First, it includes four software systems. Each of these systems is usually described in a separate book. The approach here is to cover several systems in an introductory manner, rather than a single system in depth. But, the treatment here is not superficial. As an example, the two chapters on BASIC include all of the topics that are typically incorporated into an introductory computing course—through arrays and subscripting. The main idea is to gain a working familiarity with each system, not an in-depth expertise.

The second unique characteristic of the book is that all of the material is presented in a DSS context. The intent is to show how a manager can use a small computer and a combination of a programming language and several prewritten packages as a decision support system. Neither the examples nor the overall tone of the book are geared to data processing, accounting, or clerical activities. The book focuses on management problems and how their solution can be supported by a computer-based information system. The intended audience includes both current and future managers.

A Classroom-Tested Process

During the Spring 1984 semester I used this material in a preliminary form in an introductory computer course at the University of Colorado at Boulder (UCB), where I was a visiting professor. UCB has a PC lab and emphasizes the PC in several computer courses. A classroom video monitor facilitated the demonstration of the software in class.

The experience was a complete success. The students learned the material with little difficulty, then worked ten assignments in a very acceptable manner. Class morale remained high throughout the semester. The students sensed that they were involved in a mainstream computer activity—an activity that would benefit them in not only their business careers, but their remaining academic program as well. In the beginning, there were a few who regarded the PC as a toy, but those opinions had changed by the end of the course. The result was a group of business students who not only appreciated the potential of the PC as a DSS, but were capable of performing the basic processes themselves.

Recognition of Support

This book would not have been possible without the support of a number of people. First, I recognize the assistance provided by the faculty, administration, and students at the University of Colorado at Boulder where the material was first used. Donald R. Plane, head of the Information Systems Department and now at the Roy E. Crummer Graduate School of Business, Rollins College, Winter Park, Florida, approved the approach of teaching multiple software packages in the introductory computer course. Edward J. Maes and his administrative staff at the University of Colorado at Boulder enabled me to meet some tight deadlines in getting handout material to the students. Nanci McCutcheon, Carla Williamson, and Lisa Spencer provided excellent typing support. I am especially indebted to Lisa Spencer for typing the final copy of the manuscript. And, the students who first used the material played a key role by providing many suggestions for improvements, and by showing that the material could be covered as the experiential portion of an introductory computer course.

Program language examples were provided by Professors William Fuerst, R. Wayne Headrick, Jane Carey, and Marietta Tretter of Texas AM, Professors Irvine Forkner and Robin Hill of Metropolitan State College in Denver, and by Donald Bender of Government Personnel Mutual Life Insurance Company of San Antonio. I also acknowledge the technical assistance, literature, and illustrations provided by several firms—Computer Land, Computer Works, Inc., Computer Connection, Computer Source, International Business Machines, Tandy Corp., Epson America Inc., and Statistical Graphics Corporation.

I also wish to thank Donald Lyndahl, Milwaukee Area Tech College; Dr. William Burrows, University of Washington; Dr. Paul Ross, Millersville University; and Eileen Bechtold Dlugoss, Cuyahoga Community College for their reviews of the text.

Finally, I would like to thank the people at SRA—my editor Michael J. Carrigg, and Vice President and Publisher Michael G. Crisp—who recognized the need to put this type of text into the hands of persons wishing to learn how to use the IBM PC as a decision support system.

Raymond McLeod Jr.
College Station, Texas
January 1985

Module 1
The IBM PC

1 Introduction to the IBM Personal Computer

This chapter briefly reviews the history of computing and how we reached this period when the small computer is having such an impact on recordkeeping and management, both in business and at home. As the review unfolds, the major concepts and terms of computing are presented. This material forms the important foundation upon which you will build as you gain greater familiarity with computing. Suggestions are offered as to how to learn more about small-system computing, especially the IBM Personal Computer (PC). The last part of the chapter describes the various units comprising the PC system.

How It All Began

The computer era began only some thirty years ago. In the mid-1950s, business firms and government bureaus began using the computer to process large volumes of data. The first computers were very large and were so expensive that only the largest organizations could afford them. The IBM RAMAC 305, illustrated in Figure 1.1, is an example of these early systems. But, technological innovations came rapidly, and computers gradually became smaller, faster, and less expensive.

Figure 1.1 An IBM Ramac 305

Innographics Photo

For the first ten years or so, computers were used almost exclusively for **data processing**—such as the basic accounting applications of payroll, accounts receivable, and so on. But, in the mid-1960s a new use of the computer began to receive attention. The idea of the computer as a **management information system (MIS)** captured the imagination of managers. Up until that time, managers had received some information from the computer, but the main focus was on data processing. Any information that management received was an automatic by-product of the data processing. For example, a sales manager could get sales statistics (sales by customer, sales by item, and so forth) from data that had been assembled for the billing operation. As organizations implemented the MIS concept, new computer applications were added solely for their managerial benefit.

During the 1970s the computer field continued to expand and change. A new category of small computers was introduced. These first small computers were called **minicomputers**. Although they were smaller and less costly than the larger computers, now called **mainframes**, the minicomputers often outperformed their ancestors due to their more modern technology.

The "smaller is better" trend got its biggest boost with the development of the **microprocessor**—computer circuitry on a small metal-oxide-semiconductor (MOS) chip. This chip, smaller than your fingernail, became the basis for an even smaller computer system—the **microcomputer**. The microcomputer, such as the Tandy Radio Shack TRS-80 pictured in Figure 1.2, was so small that it could fit on a desk top.

Figure 1.2   A TRS 80™ Microcomputer System

Radio Shack, A Division of Tandy Corp.

Figure 1.3   A BASIC Program

```
10   READ  R, H
20   LET  G = R * H
30   PRINT  G
40   DATA  12.75, 40
50   END
```

Today, there are three basic categories of computers, based on their size: mainframes, minicomputers, and microcomputers. The term **hardware** is used to describe the physical components of the computer. Most of the attention today is directed at the small systems. Used in business offices, they are called **small business systems**. Used by individuals, perhaps in the home, they are called **personal computers**.

While the trend in hardware was to smaller size, the trend in the programs used by the computers took another direction. A **program** is a list of instructions that tell the computer what to do. Without the program the computer is virtually powerless. A program is written for each basic application the computer is to perform, such as to print payroll checks. A firm usually develops or buys many programs so that the computer can be used in many ways. The programs are called **software**. Figure 1.3 provides an example of a very short program, written in the BASIC language, that multiplies hourly rate times hours worked to get gross earnings.

In addition to the hardware and software, you need data to process. The data is organized into a **data file** consisting of one or more **records**. Some files have thousands of records. For example, you can have a payroll file consisting of a record for each employee. The term **file** is also used to describe stored software. For example, a billing program that is stored on a disk for repeated use can be called a billing file. We will learn more about files and records later in the book.

As the MIS concept gained support among the managers, the computer specialists responded by designing systems that could provide as much information as possible. Some of these systems were mathematical models that contained hundreds and even thousands of equations. These equations were intended to represent, or simulate, the operations of the firm. Although the intent was good, many designs got out of hand and became too large and cumbersome. The systems were not easy to use, or they failed to give the manager the information that was needed. In some cases, the data was inaccurate or incomplete. Many companies scrapped their MIS efforts.

A fresh approach began in the early 1970s. A new concept, called the **decision support system (DSS)**, was much more modest in its scope. A DSS does not attempt to provide a manager with all of the information needed to do his or her job. Instead, the DSS focuses on a single problem and attempts to provide information about that problem. Since a manager is faced with many problems, a set of DSS's will be assembled. For example, a sales manager will use one DSS to help decide how many salespersons are needed, another DSS to help decide where the salespersons should be located, another to help determine how the salespersons should be compensated, and so on. The emphasis is on the word *help*. The DSS does not make the decision for the manager. The DSS only supports the manager who must provide intuition, experience, and imagination before a decision is reached that will lead to problem solution.

Some people believe that DSS replaced MIS. It is difficult to accept that idea when the term MIS is still so popular. Many businesses have MIS departments (often shortened to **IS** for **information systems**), and even vice presidents of MIS. A good way to think of DSS and MIS is to regard MIS as the overall effort in the firm to meet the manager's information needs, and to regard the DSS's as comprising the elemental parts of the MIS. It is like the MIS being a wall, and the DSS's being the bricks in the wall.

The Situation Today

The computer era has evolved through phases in both hardware and software. There are computers of all sizes, so that the smallest organizations and even individuals can afford them. And, the computers are used to process data and to provide management information.

The most popular computer today (and in history) is the IBM Personal Computer, announced by IBM on August 12, 1981. It has been estimated that approximately 500,000 PCs had been shipped by the end of 1983,[1] and that between two and three million would be shipped during 1984.[2] The popularity of the PC is based partly on the wide variety of software that has been developed for it. Special software packages are available to meet the needs of specific industries, such as real estate, and specific tasks, such as inventory control. Some of the software is available from IBM, but most has been developed by other firms. Over 1,200 programs have been written specifically for the PC.

In addition to the tailoring of software to the PC, some computer manufacturers have designed competitive hardware systems that are "PC compatible." You can use programs designed for the PC with their hardware. One example is the COMPAQ portable, manufactured by COMPAQ Computer Corporation. The PC compatibles have accounted for about 10 percent of the total sales of small, personal computers, compared to the approximately 28 percent of the market achieved by the IBM PC.[3]

So, if you learn how to use the PC, you have available (for a price, of course) a large selection of software, and if you do not have a PC available there are other systems that can process much of that software with little or no modification. While there are many other excellent computers on the market, there is no question about which one is the focal point of small-systems activity. It is the IBM Personal Computer.

1. Chris DeVoney, *IBM's Personal Computer* (Indianapolis: Que Corporation, 1983), p. 2.
2. Dennis Kneale, "IBM Says Demand and Shipments of PC Are Exceeding Company Expectations," *The Wall Street Journal* (March 16, 1984), p. 5.
3. Dennis Kneale and Alan Freeman, "Commodore Unit Signs License Accord Over IBM-Compatible Computer Gear," *The Wall Street Journal* (March 1, 1984), p. 10.

The Facts of Life

Before we get started with our discussion of the PC, there are a few things that you should know. First, there are a variety of places where you can buy a PC. IBM has approximately 73 of its own retail outlets (called IBM Product Centers) in the U.S., and approximately 53 more in other countries. IBM has contracted with Sears to sell the PC in the Sears Business Centers and with computer store chains such as ComputerLand and CompuShop. In addition, more than 300 independent retailers have been licensed to carry the product. If any of these retail outlets is in your city, you can go in and shop around.

In addition to the stores, you can buy a PC by mail order. While you are in the computer store, browse through their magazines. There are several magazines specifically for the PC, such as *PC Magazine* and *PC World*. If you buy one of these magazines and take it home, the first thing that will impress you is the huge market that has grown for products to use with the PC. You quickly get the idea that, although the computer may be inexpensive, you could drop a bundle if computing becomes habit-forming.

While you are educating yourself to the facts of life as they relate to small-system computing, keep an eye on your newspaper for computer ads. And pick up a copy of *Byte* magazine (at the computer store) and check out the classified ads. You will see the same items (including the PC itself) advertised for varying prices. Now you are getting the second basic idea. In addition to the wide variety of sources and products, the prices vary also. You can make your dollars go farther if you shop around.

But, you will quickly learn that you must speak the language if you are to be a good shopper. Let's say that you decide to buy a **diskette** (or a **floppy disk** as it is often called). The sales clerk points to a display of perhaps a dozen brands and begins to ask questions like "How many KB?" "Single-sided or double?" "Soft-sectored or hard?"

If you are interested in computing, you must get the best education that you possibly can. Take courses, read books and articles, talk with friends who are knowledgeable, and so on. You will quickly recognize that you can't learn everything, but you can learn the basics. An understanding of the basics will enable you to add more specialized knowledge as the need arises.

PC Architecture

Now that we've brought ourselves up to date on what the general situation is in the computing field, let's look at the PC.

When the first computer class was conducted, some thirty years ago, the instructor most likely drew a diagram on the chalkboard, similar to the one illustrated in Figure 1.4. The diagram is called the **computer schematic** and applies just as well today as it did to the first computer. The schematic shows the basic parts of a computer—any computer. The main unit is the **central processing unit**, or **CPU**. It houses the **primary storage** (often called **main memory**), the **arithmetic and logic unit** (the **ALU**) that performs the arithmetic and logical operations, and the **control unit** that controls all of the computer parts so that they work together as a coordinated system. In addition, there is **secondary storage** that augments the primary storage, and there are one or more input and output units. An **input unit** is used to enter data into the computer. An **output unit** displays or prints the output of the processing.

Figure 1.4   The Computer Schematic

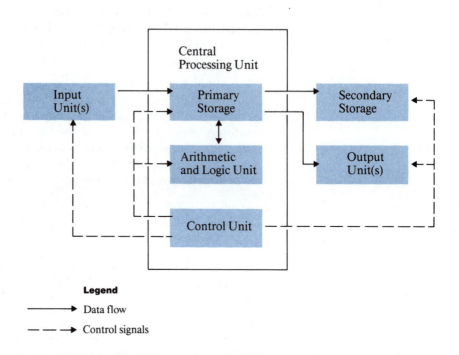

Legend

——————→ Data flow

— — — → Control signals

Although the PC is much more advanced in its technology than the first computer, its design fits the computer schematic. Figure 1.5 shows the entire system. The CPU of the PC is called the **system unit**. The system unit houses the control unit, ALU, and both primary and secondary storage. The CPU is a single MOS chip, the 8088, manufactured by Intel. The ALU is another Intel chip, the 8087. The 8087 is called a **numeric coprocessor**, or simply a coprocessor. Primary storage is also in the form of one or more MOS chips. Each chip has the capacity to store slightly over 64,000 characters. Primary storage is used to store the program as it is being executed. The secondary storage consists of one or two **diskette drives**. Each drive reads data from a rotating plastic disk into the primary storage where the data is held for processing. After processing, the data is usually written back onto the disk. In addition to data, the diskette also is used to store programs. The beauty of the diskette is that it can be removed from the system. You can insert one diskette containing a program to process inventory, perform that processing, remove the diskette, and replace it with another one containing another program—say, one to print a mailing list.

The keyboard is attached to the system unit by means of a coiled cord identical in appearance to the one found on telephones. You can move the keyboard around within a few feet of the system unit, but the normal location is just in front—as illustrated in the figure. The keyboard provides the means of entering data into the PC. It is the input unit.

Figure 1.5   The IBM Personal Computer

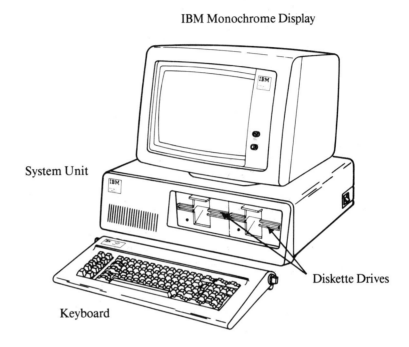

IBM Monochrome Display

System Unit

Diskette Drives

Keyboard

The television-like unit sitting atop the system unit provides some or all of the output. If you do not have a printer, all of the output must be displayed on the screen. If the unit can display only one color (green or amber on a black background) it is a **monochrome display**. If it can display all of the colors, it is a **color monitor**. We will make no distinction between the monochrome and the color units, and will simply use the term **screen**.

On some color monitors (you can buy a monitor from several sources) there are no control knobs—only an ON/OFF knob. You turn the monitor on *before* you turn on the system unit. If a computer system is composed of several units that must be individually turned on, you turn on the CPU last. This prevents a surge of electricity from rushing through the CPU as another unit is turned on. This is about the only way you can damage the PC, so don't be afraid that you will do something wrong and break it. Just remember about turning on the power in the right sequence and everything will be okay. If you forget, you probably won't cause any damage. But don't make a habit of it.

Figure 1.6   A Printer

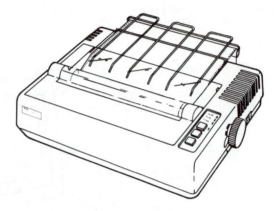

The units discussed so far comprise a complete system. All of the component parts of the computer schematic are represented. If we want printed output (called **hard copy**), however, we need a printer. Figure 1.6 illustrates one that is frequently used—the IBM Graphics Printer. It is also possible to attach printers manufactured by other firms. Printers are necessary for permanent records or output such as reports, letters, and printouts of programs.

We have described the PC in a general way. Now, let's take each unit separately and gain a better understanding of its operation.

The Keyboard

The keys in the center of the keyboard are arranged in the same pattern as an ordinary typewriter. In addition, there is a **numeric keypad** on the right (see Figure 1.7) that can be used to enter numeric data. However, the numbers can also be entered with the keys across the top. On the left are two vertical rows of **function keys**, numbered F1 through F10. These keys enable you to perform an operation by pressing a single key. For example, if you want to list your BASIC program on the screen, you must type the word LIST. By pressing the F1 key once, the word LIST is entered. The function keys can save keystrokes.

There are three keys that are not labeled with names, but with arrows. These keys are the oversized **Enter key** (just to the left of the numeric key pad), the **Backspace key** (another oversized key just above the Enter key), and the **Tab key** (just to the left of the Q key). The Enter key has a crooked arrow (↵) on it, the Backspace key has a left arrow on it, and the Tab key has both a left and a right arrow. You will give these keys, and others too, a real workout as you use the PC.

You will notice some other keys that are not normally found on a typewriter— keys labeled Del, Ins, and PrtSc, for example. We will learn what these keys do later on. For now, just understand that you enter both new programs and new data into the PC through the keyboard. Once in primary storage, the material can be stored on a diskette. Then the material can be reread into the system without keying. You just use the keyboard to get the material into the PC the first time.

Figure 1.7   The Keyboard

Primary Storage

When you enter data and program instructions by using the keyboard, they enter primary storage where the characters are stored electronically. The standard capacity of primary storage is 64 KB. The **KB** stands for **kilobytes**, or thousands of positions. Actually, the letter K doesn't mean 1,000, but 1,024. So, a 64 KB unit can store 65,536 characters, or bytes. A **byte** is computer language for character. This standard primary storage capacity can be increased up to 584 KB. The larger the capacity, the larger the programs stored can be. Some programs are so large that they require more space than the 64 KB storage system provides.

If you have read the computer ads in the newspapers, you no doubt have seen the terms ROM and RAM. These terms didn't become popular until the small-system boom. **ROM** means **read-only memory**. By read-only we mean that something is stored there, but you can only read it. You cannot write on it. The computer manufacturer records special routines in ROM that are frequently used. The ROM of the PC contains 32 KB of a version of the BASIC language, called **cassette BASIC** (we'll talk about it later), plus 8 KB of **RIOS** (pronounced rye-ose) that controls the transfer of data between the CPU and the other units. RIOS is a contraction of ROM BIOS, and BIOS stands for Basic Input/Output System. It is the seemingly insignificant RIOS that makes the PC what it is. In the Appendix, we discuss the computers of other manufacturers that are said to be "PC compatible." RIOS is the key to that compatibility. IBM copyrighted RIOS and has brought suit against two other computer firms for allegedly violating that copyright.

RAM stands for **random access memory**. RAM enables you to write your data and later read it back. RAM is what you will use to store your program and the data that it is processing. Although you can get as little as 16 KB of RAM, the minimum size for executing business programs is probably 64 KB. And, as programs have become larger, many believe that the minimum amount of storage that a business computer should have is now 128 KB. Total RAM can be expanded to 544 KB.

Figure 1.8   A Diskette

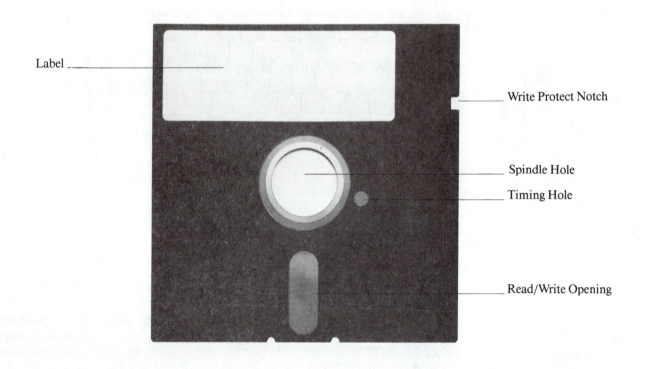

Label ——————————————

——— Write Protect Notch

——— Spindle Hole

——— Timing Hole

——— Read/Write Opening

Secondary Storage

The secondary storage system of the PC is a diskette pictured in Figure 1.8. It is a plastic disk permanently enclosed in a jacket and measures 5¼ by 5¼ inches. You do not remove the diskette from the jacket, but insert it in the drive as shown in Figure 1.9.

The large hole in the center is where a spindle fits that rotates the diskette. The oval opening in the jacket is where the read/write head in the diskette drive writes and reads the data as the diskette rotates inside its jacket. The notch on the edge of the jacket is the **write protect notch**. If you want to protect the diskette from being accidentally erased, you can cover the notch with a special sticker that comes with the diskette. This is a good practice for your programs that you read over and over. The small hole next to the spindle hole is a timing hole. There is also a timing hole in the diskette. The PC uses the timing hole to locate the starting point of data stored on the diskette. Some diskettes have several timing holes, and are called **hard-sectored** diskettes. The diskettes used by the PC have only the single hole, and are called **soft-sectored**.

It is possible to record data on both sides of the diskette, doubling its capacity. You can record about 180 KB on one side and 360 KB on two. But a diskette drive is built to handle either one side or two. The first PC diskette drives could only read or write data on one side of the diskette. These drives were said to be **single-sided**. In 1982, IBM made available a diskette drive that can read and write data on both sides. These drives are **double-sided**.

Figure 1.9   Inserting the Diskette in the Drive

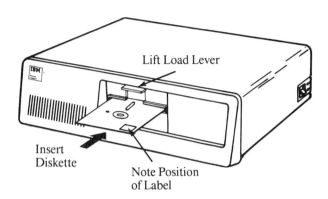

Another term that you often hear is **double-density**. This describes the manner in which the magnetic bits are recorded on the diskette. A double-density drive has the bits recorded twice as close together as a **single-density** drive. The PC drives have always been double-density. The new drives are called double-sided, double-density. The old ones are called single-sided, double-density. If you buy a PC, you should ask whether it has single- or double-sided drives.

The diskettes themselves also come in single-sided or double-sided versions. This means that the manufacturer has checked either one or two sides and verified them to be free of defects. A single-sided diskette doesn't mean that you can use only one side. Many PC owners use single-sided diskettes with double-sided drives without any difficulty. Since the single-sided diskettes are less expensive, using them may be a good way to cut costs. The diskettes typically cost $3 to $5 each, and tend to multiply like rabbits once you get the computing habit.

Data is recorded on the diskette in **tracks**, as shown in Figure 1.10. Each track is numbered and is also subdivided into several **sectors**. The sectors are similar to slices of a pie. Each sector is also numbered. The PC uses the sector and track numbers as **addresses** of data and programs stored on the diskette. So, when you command the PC to load (read) your payroll program into primary storage, the PC knows where the program is stored on the diskette.

Notice that the diskette in Figure 1.10 has nine sectors. The portion of a track within each sector can store 512 bytes. (The data is recorded in a more compact form on the inner tracks.) With nine sectors on a track, the capacity of each track is 4,608 bytes. Since there are 40 tracks on a diskette surface, one side of the diskette can store 184,320 (180 KB).

This capacity is achieved by using a recent version of the disk operating system— DOS Version 2.0, made available in early 1983. The disk operating system is a master program that controls the system. We devote Chapter 2 to that subject. The earlier version of DOS, Version 1.1, recorded data in 8 sectors. With DOS 1.1, the capacity of one disk surface is 160 KB.

Figure 1.10   Disk Tracks and Sectors

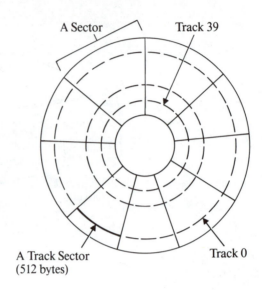

A Sector   Track 39

A Track Sector
(512 bytes)   Track 0

This difference in disk recording density is important to you as you use the PC. A disk prepared by one operating system version often cannot be used with another version without special instructions to the PC. The best procedure is to use a single operating system version on everything that you do with the PC. This is especially good practice in a computer lab where many people are using many software packages.

The Screen

The IBM monochrome display has two knobs that are used to control contrast and brightness, as illustrated in Figure 1.11. When you turn on the PC, the screen automatically comes on at the same time.

The screen can display 25 rows with 80 characters on a row. (Some computers can only display 40 characters on a row.) In addition to characters, the screen can also display graphics—pie charts, bar graphs, space ships, and the like. The graphics, especially in color, add another dimension to the ability of the PC to provide meaningful management information. You know what Confucius said about "One picture...." In order to display the graphics, you need to insert a special circuit board in the system unit; it is called a color/graphics board.

The Printer

Although your system may have a printer other than the one sold by IBM, we will describe the IBM unit. If your printer is different, your instructor (or the person who sells you your unit) can explain its features to you.

If you buy a printer, you will get a manual that tells you how to insert the paper. We will not go into that detail here. If you are using a PC in a computer lab, someone else will do that job for you.

Figure 1.11   Screen Controls

IBM Monochrome Display

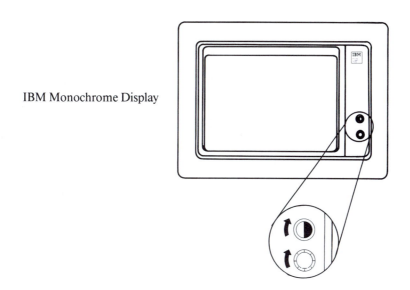

Figure 1.12 illustrates the basic printer controls. Turn the power on (before powering up the system unit), and the **Online light** comes on. This means that the printer is ready to accept data from the system unit. If you want the paper to move up, you must press the **Online key**. The light goes off, and you are now "offline."

Figure 1.12   Printer Controls

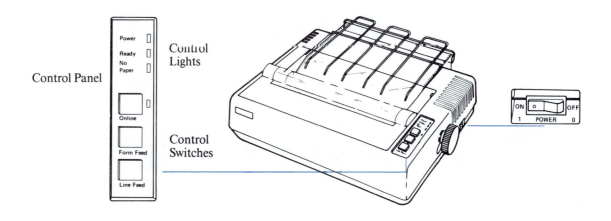

Figure 1.13　Matrix Character Patterns

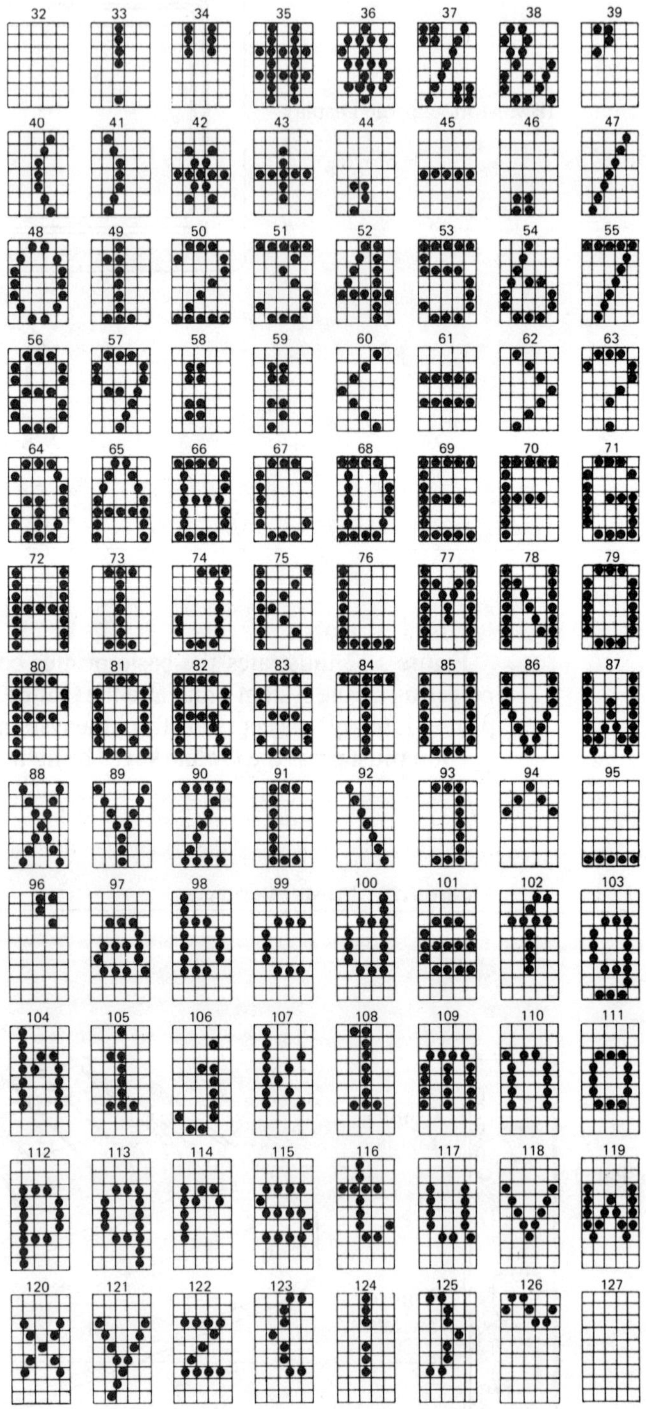

Figure 1.14   Graphics with a Matrix Printer

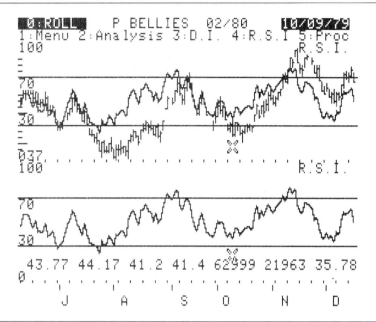

You can move the paper up a line at a time with the **Line Feed key**, or skip to the next page with the **Form Feed key**. When the paper is positioned to your satisfaction, press the Online key again.

Sometimes the printer will not feed the paper to the top of the sheet. This usually happens when someone adjusts the platen knob with the power on. To readjust the skipping, turn the printer off (after the system unit is turned off), and use the platen knob to move the paper to where the perforation is barely visible above the print head. Then turn the printer on. Test the alignment by pressing the Form Feed key with the printer offline. The paper should skip to the top of the next page. Switch the printer online by pressing the Online key and turn the system unit back on. If you are listing a lengthy program, the printing will continue from one sheet to another without skipping over the perforation. Some programs, however, are designed to make standard page breaks automatically when they print the output. You will learn how to do that in a later chapter.

The IBM printer is a **dot matrix printer**. It forms the characters and symbols by selecting a pattern of dots in a 6 by 9 dot matrix. Figure 1.13 illustrates how the letters of the alphabet appear in a dot matrix form. The dots are printed by pins as the print head moves across the paper. The print head can print moving in either direction. It is a **bidirectional printer**, printing 80 characters per second (cps).

The first IBM printer could print only letters, numbers, and special characters. In early 1983, an improved version was made available that can also print graphs. It is called the **IBM Graphics Printer**. The earlier version has been discontinued.

A dot matrix printer, including one with a graphics capability, is not a **letter quality printer**—nobody will think you typed the letter on your typewriter. It is possible to attach a letter quality printer to the IBM PC and achieve the same high quality printing as you would with the finest electric typewriter. As a general rule, a letter quality printer is more expensive and slower than one that is not letter quality.

Summary

In this first chapter, the objective has been to introduce you to the PC. The stage was set by describing briefly how the field of computing has evolved. Then you learned how the PC occupies an important place in that field. The PC can be used as a data processing system or as a decision support system within an MIS. The PC can be used by managers of small as well as large firms.

The PC is a very powerful computer—it is not a toy. Of course, a PC cannot do everything that a large mainframe system can do, but a manager using a PC as a DSS would seldom feel constrained. It is possible to perform some very sophisticated data analyses with the PC.

In the following chapters, you will learn more about the PC and what it can do. This has been an important chapter in that it has laid the foundation upon which you will build. Review the key terms that follow. If you are unclear about any of them, review those sections before continuing. As you can see from the list of terms, you have made a lot of progress in this first chapter in learning the language of computing.

Key Terms

Listed in order of introduction.

Data processing	Hard copy
Management Information System (MIS)	Numeric keypad
Minicomputer	Function key
Mainframe	Enter key
Microprocessor	Backspace key
Microcomputer	Tab key
Hardware	Byte, kilobyte (KB)
Small business system	Read-only memory (ROM)
Personal computer	Cassette BASIC
Program	RIOS
Software	Random access memory (RAM)
File	Write protect notch
Record	Hard-sectored disk
Decision Support System (DSS)	Soft-sectored disk
Information System (IS)	Single-sided drive
Diskette, floppy disk	Double-sided drive
Computer schematic	Double-density drive
Central processing unit (CPU)	Single-density drive
Primary storage, main memory	Track
Arithmetic and logic unit (ALU)	Sector
Control unit	Address
Secondary storage	Online light
Input unit	Online key
Output unit	Line feed key
System unit	Form feed key
Numeric coprocessor	Dot matrix printer
Diskette drive	Bidirectional printer
Monochrome display	IBM Graphics Printer
Color monitor	Letter quality printer
Screen	

Questions   (Do not fill in blanks in the book. Write answers on a separate piece of paper.)

1. The first computers were used almost exclusively for _____, and it was not until the mid-1960s that computers were used as a(n) _____.

2. Today the three basic categories of computers, based on their sizes, are _____, _____, and _____.

3. A _____ helps the manager make decisions to solve a single problem by providing information about the problem.

4. The most popular computer today is the _____.

5. Computers that can run programs designed for the IBM PC are said to be _____.

6. Another name for a diskette is _____.

7. The diagram that the instructor of the first computer class likely drew on the board is called the _____.

8. The central processing unit of a computer houses the _____, _____, and _____.

9. The CPU of the IBM PC is called the _____.

10. Secondary storage consists of one or two _____.

11. The screen that displays data in only green or amber is called a _____, and one that displays data in a variety of colors is called a _____.

12. When turning on the various units of the PC system, you should always turn on the _____ last.

13. A printer produces an output called _____.

14. The letters KB stand for _____ and refer to _____ of positions of storage.

15. ROM stands for _____, and RAM stands for _____.

16. The new diskette drives used on the IBM PC are _____ and _____.

17. The diskette is divided into _____ that have the same shape as slices of a pie.

18. A recent version of the PC operating system (version 2.0) permits the recording of data on the diskette in _____ sectors.

19. The PC screen can display _____ rows with _____ characters on a row.

20. A printer that prints characters as a pattern of dots is called a _____.

2 The Disk Operating System (DOS)

The computer as a decision support system is more than the hardware; the software tailors the hardware to the solution of management-type problems. There are two general classes of software—applications software and systems software. The **application programs** perform the firm's data processing tasks (such as printing payroll checks) and provide the manager with information (such as listing names of customers who are delinquent in payments). The **system programs** are provided by the manufacturer of the computer, or by special software companies. The systems software is general-purpose: it can be used by all users of a particular computer. Some of the systems software, such as the operating system, is necessary to the use of the computer. In this chapter we describe the operating system used by the IBM PC.

What Is an Operating System?

If you had started to learn about computers during their early years, you wouldn't have had to worry about operating systems. There weren't any. In the beginning, the computers executed programs under the direction of their human operator. The operator would decide which job to run next, load the punched cards into the card reader, mount the tape reels on the tape drive, and press the start button.

But, as computer users became more aware, they could see the time wasted by the comparatively slow actions of the human operator. Someone got the bright idea to let the computer control itself. The computer couldn't load card files, change tape reels, and so on, but it could do some of the operator's other chores. For example, it could determine what job to do next (using a system of priorities), it could automatically load (from tape or disk) the next program to be executed, it could keep a time record of how long each operation took, it could determine whether a user was authorized to have access to the system, and so on. For the computer to do these things it needed special programs; they became known as **operating systems**.

Whereas the operating system has relieved the user of many of the "housekeeping" responsibilities, it has added a barrier of sorts between the user and the system. The operating system is like a gatekeeper. You must go through the operating system to use the system. Some mainframe operating systems (OS) have been nicknamed "Big Oz," recognizing the omnipotent power of the software system.

It is common for the operating system to be stored on a disk—hence **disk operating system (DOS)**. Some people pronounce the term "Dee-Oh-Ess!" Others says "Dahss." Take your pick. But learning what DOS means is just half

Figure 2.1   DOS is the Outer Box

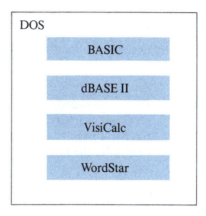

of the battle. You hear terms like **MS-DOS** and **PC-DOS**. The MS and the PC simply identify the source. MS stands for Microsoft, a computer software company that developed the operating system. IBM contracted with Microsoft for the right to market the Microsoft product under the name PC-DOS. Microsoft also sells the same product under the name MS-DOS.

PC-DOS is not the only operating system that can be used on the PC. In a review of operating systems for *PC World* magazine, Gary Kildall, who created the very popular CP/M operating system, identifies 14 separate systems.[1] And, there may be several versions of each. For example, PC-DOS has been released in versions 1.0, 1.1, 2.0, and 2.1.

PC-DOS Version 2.0 requires more primary storage space than 1.1 (24,576 bytes versus 12,400), but, as we saw in the first chapter, Version 2.0 expands the capacity of the disks. With DOS 2.0, a single-sided disk capacity increases from 160 KB to 180 KB, and a double-sided disk from 320 KB to 360 KB. All of the programs described in this text can be executed with either DOS 1.1 or 2.0.

The operating system is one area where the differences between a microcomputer and a mainframe are apparent. Both may have an operating system, but they do different things or do the same things differently. The operating system for the mainframe, for example, lets several people use the computer at the same time, a featured called **timesharing**. Only one person can usually use a micro at a time, however. The mainframe operating system will do job accounting, the micro operating system does not. There are several such differences, but they are blurring as micro operating systems become more sophisticated.

---

1.   Gary Kildall, "Operating Systems," *PC World Annual Software Review* (1983/1984): 28ff.

"A System of Boxes"

Using a computer can be likened to successively opening a system of boxes—some inside others. Figure 2.1 depicts this idea. DOS is the outer box; you must first "go through" DOS to get to an inner box. As the figure shows, DOS is the pathway to the four DSS software systems that we will address in this book—the BASIC programming language, the dBASE II data base management system, the VisiCalc electronic spreadsheet, and the WordStar word processing system. Once inside one of these four inner boxes you will find other boxes to open. We will open them later in the book as we explore the different systems.

Loading DOS

DOS is recorded on a diskette. We will refer to it as the **DOS diskette**. To load DOS into primary storage, insert the diskette in the diskette drive. If your system has two drives, they are called the **a: drive** (on the left), and the **b: drive** (on the right.) Put the DOS diskette in the a: drive.

If the computer is not on (if the screen is dark, check the power switch to see if it is in the OFF (down) position), you must turn it on. Turn on the units in the following order (1) color monitor, (2) printer, and (3) system unit. Figure 2.2 shows where the system unit power switch is located.

If the computer is already on, you have to prepare it to receive your commands. You do that by **booting the system**. You may have heard of the expression "pulling yourself up by your own bootstraps," which means to do everything for yourself. During the early years of the computer, a specially-designed punched card, called a bootstrap card, was used to load the programs into the computer's storage. That is no doubt the origin of the term that is used with today's generation of microcomputers.

Figure 2.2   The System Unit Power Switch

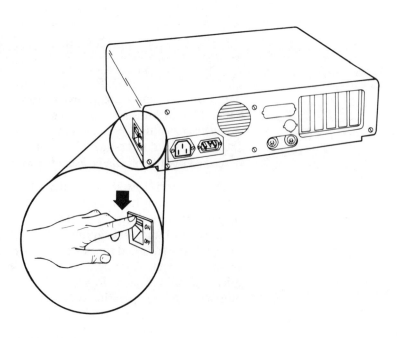

You boot the system by pressing three keys on the keyboard with the system turned on. The three keys are (1) Control (Ctrl), (2) Alternate (Alt), and (3) Delete (Del). Hold the Control and the Alternate keys down with your left hand and press the Delete key with your right. You will learn several commands that require you to press more than one key. Usually, the Ctrl key is one of the keys.

When you boot the system you hear a clicking sound as the PC reads DOS from your diskette. This sound is accompanied by a red light that blinks on next to the diskette drive. Never try to insert or remove a diskette when the red light is on— wait until it goes off and the clicking sound stops.

On the screen, DOS asks you for the date. This date will be used when you save files on the diskette as an aid to you in keeping your files current. Often you will end up with several versions of a file (such as a program to which you have made a series of changes) and you will want to know which version is the most recent.

Type one or two digits for the month, a dash or a slash, one or two digits for the day, a dash or a slash, and two digits for the year.

Examples: 10-31-85
             1-3-86
             07/19/87

After you type the date, press the Enter key. The Enter key is the jumbo sized one on the right with the crooked arrow (↵) on it. Any time you want to enter something into the PC, first type it, and then press Enter. This causes your data to enter primary storage. DOS next asks for the time. You can bypass this if you prefer by simply pressing Enter.

When DOS wants you to enter information, it prompts you. The messages that it prints on the screen are called **prompts**. After you satisfy the date and time prompts, DOS displays the **DOS prompt (A>)**. Anytime you see this on the left margin of the screen, you know that the PC is in the DOS mode. You are "in DOS." This means that you have gotten inside the DOS box in Figure 2.1. To get into an inner box, such as BASIC, you must respond to the DOS prompt by typing the name of the box, such as **basic**. To get into **dBASE** II, you type dbase, and so on. You can type either upper or lowercase letters for all of these DOS commands; the PC treats them the same. We will use lowercase letters. To type all uppercase letters, press the Caps Lock key. It is a **toggle key**; that means if you press it a second time you are in the lowercase mode; a third time returns you to uppercase, and so on.

The DOS File Directory

DOS maintains a **directory** of files that are recorded on the diskettes. You already have several files on the DOS diskette and they are listed in its directory. If you add files to the diskette, their names will be added to the directory. You give each file a name, such as PAYROLL. If you delete files from the diskette, their names are removed from the directory. To obtain the directory, type **dir** in response to the DOS prompt.

DOS prints a line for each file, identifying (from left to right):

* the file name (such as COMMAND)
* the type of file (such as COM)
* the primary storage space that it occupies—in bytes (such as 4959)
* the date that the file was stored on the disk
* the time of day that it was stored

Perhaps your DOS diskette contains so many files that their names will not all fit on the screen at one time. The names at the top disappear from the screen as the ones at the bottom are listed. This is called **scrolling**. You can stop scrolling while in DOS by pressing the Ctrl and Numeric Lock (Num Lock) key. Scrolling can be resumed by pressing any key.

The Logged Drive

When you boot the system you get the A> prompt. This means that any file commands you issue (such as dir) will apply to the file in the a: drive. The a: drive is the **logged drive**, which means that the PC will begin a new file or look for an existing file on the diskette in that drive. If you have two drives, you can change the logged drive to b: by simply typing **b:** after the A> prompt; and pressing Enter. You must include the colon after the b. You now get the B> prompt; any file commands relate to the diskette in the b: drive. If your PC only has a single drive you use the b: identifier to tell the PC that the function to be performed is on a disk other than the one in the logged drive. We will say more about that later.

File Names

When DOS displays its directory, it lists the name of the file (COMMAND) and the type of file (COM). The COM is called the **file name extension**. The extension is a part of the file name, and is added by DOS. The name of the file is COMMAND.COM. Some people say "COMMAND dot COM" (rhymes with Tom).

In addition to the name and the extension, there can also be a **file name prefix**. You use a prefix when you want to refer to a file that is not in the logged drive. For example, if you have a dual-drive PC, and you want to erase a file from the diskette that is not in the logged drive, you type erase b:payroll.bas. This command says, in effect, "Erase the BASIC program file named payroll from the diskette in the b: drive."

DOS Files

The most important file on the DOS diskette is the COMMAND file. It accepts the commands that you enter and causes them to be carried out. In addition to the COMMAND file, there are several others that perform important functions.

These files are:

- FORMAT   Prepares a new diskette to receive data
- CHKDSK   Analyzes a diskette and determines how much unused space is available
- DISKCOPY   Makes a duplicate copy of an entire diskette
- DISKCOMP   Compares two entire diskettes to determine if they are identical
- BASIC   Enables you to code and run programs written in the BASIC language
- BASICA   An "advanced" version of BASIC

In addition, there are COM files such as MODE, EDLIN, and DEBUG that you will not use until you become more familar with the computer. And, there are some demonstration programs written in BASIC (with a .BAS extension) such as DONKEY and ART. If your instructor is providing you with a DOS diskette, these programs may have been removed to make space available for other programs.

If you are going to code and execute programs written in BASIC, you need the BASIC or BASICA programs on your DOS diskette. If you are only going to execute dBASE II, VisiCalc, or WordStar, you only need the COMMAND file. If you are going to be making duplicate copies of diskettes, you need the DISKCOPY and (perhaps) the DISKCOMP files. If you will be preparing a new diskette on which to store data files, you need the FORMAT file. The CHKDSK file can come in handy when you want to know how much space you have available on a diskette before you start a VisiCalc, dBASE II, or WordStar data file.

We will explain how these files are used in the sections that follow. As we describe each operation, we will first describe when and why it is used. Then, we will describe how it is done with a dual-drive PC and a single-drive PC. You can skip over the explanation that does not apply to your PC.

Formatting a Diskette

When you buy a diskette, it is completely blank. It can be used on a variety of computers—the PC, TRS-80, Apple, Commodore, and so on. You must prepare it for your particular system, and this is called **formatting**.

When DOS formats a new diskette it checks every track sector to ensure that the diskette contains no defects that will impair proper recording. If DOS finds a bad track sector, it allocates it to a file called BADTRACK. The BADTRACK file does not appear in the directory—it is "invisible," but performs an important function. It keeps the defective sector separate from the good area where you record data files and programs. When this occurs, you will be advised with a "BAD TRACK" message on the screen.

Sometimes you will want to format a diskette so it includes DOS programs. This will enable you to execute programs on that diskette without using a separate DOS diskette. You do not need a separate DOS diskette to boot the system. When you format a disk with DOS you get the COMMAND file, plus two others that are invisible—they do not appear in the directory. The two invisible files are IBMBIO.COM, which transfers data between primary storage and the input/output units, and IBMDOS.COM, which manages the files used by any program operating under DOS, such as BASIC, dBASE II, VisiCalc, or WordStar.

After you format a diskette with DOS, you can ask for a display of the diskette's directory by typing dir in response to the A> or B> prompt (depending on which drive contains the newly formatted diskette). You should see only the COMMAND file displayed in the directory.

You cannot record data on a diskette unless it has been formatted. And, if you format the diskette to include DOS, you will not need a separate DOS diskette to execute programs on the formatted diskette. Finally, in order to perform the formatting operation, the FORMAT.COM file must be on your DOS diskette.

Formatting a Diskette Using a Dual-Drive PC

Insert your DOS diskette in drive a: and respond to the A> prompt with:

format b:

If you want to include DOS, type:

format b:/s

Press the Enter key and follow the instructions on the screen. You will be instructed to put your blank diskette in drive b: and press any key when ready. Displays on the screen will keep you informed of the computer's activity, and after completing the formatting will ask if you wish to format another diskette. If so, type Y, put a new diskette in the b: drive, and press any key. When you have no more diskettes to format, respond to the "FORMAT ANOTHER?" question with N.

Formatting a Diskette Using a Single-Drive PC

Insert your DOS diskette in drive a: and respond to the A> prompt with:

format a:

If you want to include DOS, type:

format a:/s

Press the Enter key and follow the instructions on the screen. You will be instructed to put your blank diskette in drive a: and press any key when ready. Displays on the screen will keep you informed of the computer's activity, and after completing the formatting will ask if you wish to format another diskette. If so, type Y, put a new diskette in the a: drive, and press any key. When you have no more diskettes to format, respond to the "FORMAT ANOTHER?" question with N.

Copying a Diskette

The cardinal rule in computing has always been to save backup copies of everything—programs and data files. Applied to microcomputers, it means that you should make duplicate copies of all of your diskettes. At least, make backup copies of all that you can. Some proprietary software (VisiCalc for example) has a "lock" designed in the coding that prevents it from being copied. In such situations, you must buy backup copies from the vendors for an extra cost per diskette. But for most software (including dBASE II and WordStar) you can make one (or more) backup copies. This topic of diskette copying is a sensitive one in the computing field. Be certain that you will not violate any copyright laws by backing up diskettes by first checking the vendor's literature or checking with your instructor.

There are three important points to remember about diskette copying.

1. You can copy onto a new, blank diskette, or erase and re-record on one that contains previously recorded files. If the diskette you are copying *to* contains previously stored files, *they will be erased by the copying operation.*

2. A new diskette does not have to be formatted before it can have files copied onto it. The copying operation formats as well as copies.

3. If you are copying a diskette that will include DOS, the COMMAND file as well as the two other invisible files will automatically be copied onto the new diskette.

In order to perform this operation, your DOS diskette must contain the DISKCOPY.COM file.

**Copying a Diskette
Using a Dual-Drive PC**

Insert your DOS diskette in drive a: and respond to the A> prompt with:

diskcopy a: b:

Press the Enter key and follow the instructions on the screen. You will be instructed to remove the DOS diskette from drive a: and replace it with the diskette to be copied (the **source diskette**). Insert the new diskette to be copied onto (the **target diskette**) in drive b: and press any key.

You will be asked if you want to copy another. Respond with Y or N.

**Copying a Diskette
Using a Single-Drive PC**

Insert your DOS diskette in drive a: and respond to the A> prompt with:

diskcopy

Press the Enter key and follow the instructions on the screen. You will be instructed to remove the DOS diskette and insert your diskette to be copied (the **source diskette**). Press any key.

Then, you will be instructed to replace the source diskette with the new diskette to be copied onto (the **target diskette**). Replace the diskette and press any key.

DOS will copy part of the diskette, and then ask you to reinsert the source diskette so that more can be read from it. Then you will be asked to replace the source diskette with the target diskette so that more can be recorded on it. You will continue to swap the diskettes until you see the "COPY ANOTHER?" question. Respond with a Y or N.

To avoid getting confused when DOS asks for the source diskette, remember that it is the original one (the one you want to make an extra of). It should contain some markings such as a distinctive label to distinguish it from the target diskette and should be write protected.

**Taking Care
of Your Diskettes**

It is estimated that the life of a diskette is 40 hours of read/write time. That is the time that the red light is on, and that is a lot of reading and writing. That is probably the maximum life, assuming proper handling. You can ruin a diskette in a second if you are careless.

The first thing that you should do is label your diskette. When you purchase it you should receive one or more gummed labels and one or more write protect stickers. If you are a student, put your name on the label. This will help you keep track of your property in a crowded micro lab. You may also want to add your course and section number.

If you are not a student, or if you plan on having several diskettes, you can identify them by their contents—DOS Version 2.0, dBASE II Data File, VisiCalc Files, and so on.

If you put the information on the label before it is attached to the diskette, you can use ballpoint, felt tip pen, and the like. But, if you wait until you have attached the label, use only a soft felt tip pen. You should not exert any pressure on the diskette.

You may also want to put some information on the removable diskette envelope, but don't rely solely on that. It is probably better not to identify the diskette contents (such as DOS) on the envelope. That saves you the trouble of always getting the diskette back into its own envelope.

Following are some DO's and DO NOT's that should enable you to achieve a long life for your diskette. Treat it with care—a small particle of dust, a tiny scratch, or even a thumbprint can make the entire diskette unserviceable. Observe the following guidelines:

- Keep the diskette in its envelope whenever it is not in use.
- Keep the diskette away from magnetic fields—TV, stereo, telephones, and the top of the PC screen.
- Handle only the jacket; do not touch the plastic surface.
- Do not expose the diskette to sunlight or excessive heat, such as the trunk of your car on a hot day, or on the shelf inside the rear window.
- Do not fold or bend the diskette (nor staple, paper clip, or mutilate it).
- Never try to insert or remove your diskette when the red light is on.
- Always check the diskette drives as you complete each session so that you don't forget to take your diskette(s) with you.

Comparing Two Diskettes

After you copy a diskette, you may want to have the PC compare the two to ensure that the source diskette was copied properly. In order to perform this operation, your DOS diskette must contain the DISKCOMP.COM program.

Comparing Two Diskettes Using a Dual-Drive PC

Insert your DOS diskette in drive a: and respond to the A> prompt with:

diskcomp a: b:

Press Enter and follow the instructions. You will be instructed to put one diskette to be compared in drive a: and the other in the b: drive. Press any key and await the results. If the diskettes compare perfectly, you get an "OK" message. If they don't, you will be advised which tracks contain different coding. If the list of error tracks gets too long, hold down the Ctrl key and press the Break key (labeled Break on the front and Scroll Lock on the top). This will bring back the DOS prompt.

Comparing Two Diskettes Using a Single-Drive PC

Insert your DOS diskette in drive a: and respond to the A> prompt with:

diskcomp

Press Enter and follow the instructions. You will be instructed to insert one of the two diskettes to be compared and then press any key. Then you will be instructed to remove the first diskette, insert the second, and press any key.

You will have to repeat this procedure until all tracks of both diskettes have been compared. When completed, you will be advised either that everything is "OK" or which tracks contain coding that doesn't match. If the list of error tracks gets too long, hold down the Ctrl key and press the Break key (labeled Break on the front and Scroll Lock on the top). This will bring back the DOS prompt.

Checking Available Diskette Space

Sometimes you will be using a program and will try to store a file on your diskette. You get a "DISK FULL" message, and you can't believe it. You can ask for a directory and see which files are on the diskette, but that will not tell you how much space you have used, and how much is available. The CHKDSK command will give you that information. To use it, you must have the CHKDSK.COM program on your DOS diskette.

Checking Diskette Space Using a Dual-Drive PC

Insert your DOS diskette in drive a: and the diskette to be checked in drive b:. Respond to the A> prompt with:

chkdsk b:

Press Enter and await the results. You will be advised of the capacity of the diskette (in bytes), and the number of bytes remaining available.

You can also perform this check on the DOS diskette by responding to the A> prompt with:

chkdsk

Press Enter and await the results.

Checking Diskette Space Using a Single-Drive PC

If you want to check the space left on the DOS diskette, respond to the A> prompt with:

chkdsk

Press Enter and await the results. You will be advised the capacity of the diskette (in bytes), and the number of bytes remaining available.

If you want to check the space left on a diskette other than the one containing DOS, respond to the A> prompt with:

chkdsk b:

Press Enter, change diskettes, and wait for the results.

Copying a File

You may only want to copy a single file from one diskette to another—not the entire diskette. This operation can be useful when assembling files from several diskettes onto one.

Copying a File Using a Dual-Drive PC

Your DOS diskette does not have to be inserted. Respond to the A> prompt with:

copy file name b:

In place of "file name" type the name of the file to be copied.

If everything goes properly, you will be advised "1 FILE COPIED;" if not, "0 FILES COPIED." Usually, you get the "0 FILES COPIED" message when you have forgotten to close one of the diskette drive doors, or when you have not spelled the file name correctly.

Copying a File Using a Single-Drive PC

Your DOS diskette does not have to be inserted. Respond to the A> prompt with:

copy file name b:

In place of "file name" type the name of the file to be copied. Then, await instructions for exchanging diskettes.

If everything goes properly, you will be advised "1 FILE COPIED;" if not, "0 FILES COPIED." Usually, you get the "0 FILES COPIED" message when you have forgotten to close the diskette drive door, or when you have not spelled the file name correctly.

Erasing a File

The DOS diskette does not have to be inserted to erase, or delete, a file. In response to the A> prompt type:

erase file name

In place of "file name," type the name of the file to be deleted. You must include the extension. Press Enter.

If you do not key in the file name properly, you will get the message "FILE NOT FOUND." If the deleting goes properly you get only the A> prompt. Ask for a directory display to verify that the file has been deleted.

This command works the same for a dual- and a single-drive PC. However, if you have a dual-drive unit and the file to be deleted is not on the diskette in the logged drive, include the drive prefix to the file name. For example, to the A> prompt, respond with:

erase b:payroll.bas

You use this command to remove files from your diskette when they are no longer of any value. Your diskette is likely to get crowded during the term as you continually add files. You will reach a point when you have to "clean house." Use the chkdsk command frequently to see how much space you have left. Then, when you approach the diskette's capacity, delete any unneeded files.

**Internal and
External Commands**

We have seen that some commands require that a particular file be on the DOS diskette. These are commands such as format, diskcopy, diskcomp, and chkdsk. These are **external commands** in that they are not a part of the COMMAND.COM file.

Other commands, such as dir, copy, and erase require only that the COMMAND.COM file is on the DOS diskette when you boot up. These are **internal commands**. All you need is the A> or B> prompt to perform them.

Summary

The computer is like a system of boxes. DOS is the outer box. Sometimes you only "pass through" DOS on your way to an inner box. For example, if you want to code a program in BASIC, you boot the system, get the A> prompt, and type the word basic. You then are no longer in the DOS mode, you are in the BASIC mode.

But as we have seen, you can perform a variety of important functions while in DOS. Diskette copying is one. As you continue with your use of the PC you will use this command many times.

To summarize, while in DOS you can:

- Obtain a directory of a diskette's files (dir)
- Format a diskette with or without DOS (format)
- Copy, or duplicate, an entire diskette (diskcopy)
- Compare the contents of two diskettes (diskcomp)
- Check a diskette for available space (chkdsk)
- Copy a single file from one diskette to another (copy)
- Erase, or delete, a file (erase)

In terms of its ability to perform these operations, DOS is the "workhorse" of the PC. These are operations that are necessary, whether you are programming in BASIC or using proprietary software such as dBASE II, VisiCalc, and WordStar. These DOS commands enhance the utility of the PC to function as a decision support system.

If you have previously used an operating system for a mainframe computer, you recognize the DOS tasks that we have described as rather fundamental. You know that operating systems for larger computers perform other, more encompassing tasks such as verifying that a user is authorized to have access to the system, determining which, of many, users use the system next; and allowing several programs to run concurrently.

The objective of this chapter has been to help you gain a familiarity with the main DOS commands for the IBM PC. Understanding DOS is fundamental to being able to use the many application programs that have been written for the PC. This combination of systems and applications software enables the PC to function as a decision support system.

Key Terms

Application program	Toggle key
System program	Directory
Operating system (OS)	Scrolling
Disk operating system (DOS)	Logged drive
MS-DOS, PC-DOS	File name extension
Timesharing	File name prefix
DOS diskette	Formatting
a: drive	Source diskette
b: drive	Target diskette
Booting the system	External commands
Prompt	Internal commands
DOS prompt	

(Do not fill in blanks in the book. Write answers on a separate piece of paper.)

1. The two general classes of software are _____ and _____.

2. To boot the system, you press three keys: _____, _____, and _____.

3. The first thing that DOS asks you to enter is the _____.

4. The DOS prompt looks like _____.

5. The Caps Lock key is an example of a _____ that is used to cause the PC to switch back and forth between two modes of operation.

6. When you want to see a directory of your files on the logged drive, enter _____ in response to the DOS prompt.

7. When the screen is full and one line is lost at the top as one is added at the bottom the screen is said to be _____.

8. A file name can include a(n) _____ that identifies the logged drive, and a(n) _____ that identifies the type of file.

9. Before a diskette can be used, it must be _____.

10. When you format a diskette with DOS you get the _____ file plus two others that are _____.

11. When you are copying a diskette with a dual-drive PC, the diskette that you are copying from is the _____ diskette, and the diskette that you are copying to is the _____ diskette.

12. If you take good care of your diskette, you can expect it to last for up to _____ hours of "red light time."

13. After you duplicate all of the files on a diskette, you can make certain that the source diskette is identical to the object diskette by using the _____ command.

14. To find out how much space you have used on your diskette, you use the _____ command.

15. You make duplicate copies of single files with the _____ command.

16. The _____ command is used to clean up your diskette by removing all of the files stored on it.

17. The commands that are executed from L files on the DOS diskette are called _____ commands.

18. The commands that are not executed from L files on the DOS diskette are called _____ commands.

19. Three examples of internal commands are _____, _____, and _____.

20. Four examples of external commands are _____, _____, _____, and _____.

Module 2
Decision Support System Concepts

3 Introduction to Decision Support Systems (DSS)

We are concerned with how a manager uses a computer in decision making—specifically, the IBM Personal Computer. There are several fundamental concepts that are key to understanding this particular computer application, and these concepts apply to any type of computer—large or small. In fact, the concepts have been developed primarily with mainframe systems and are now being applied in the small-scale systems area. In this chapter we describe the more important of these concepts.

Physical and Conceptual Systems

We often think of the manager as a person who manages only people. It is easy for us to overlook the other resources—such as materials, machines, and money—that the manager also manages. But, the manager is most likely aware that he or she is responsible for all of these resources. Most managers are given an annual budget that measures how well they can keep the costs of these resources within boundaries.

These resources—the personnel, materials, and machines—are all physical in nature. They exist physically. They comprise the **physical system of the firm**. It is the manager's job to assemble the needed resources and mold them into a smoothly functioning system.

A **system** is an integration of parts that work together to achieve some particular objective. In business systems, the manager builds the physical system of resources and directs it toward the achievement of business objectives—profit, service, and so on.

You must keep in mind that when we use the term manager, we are talking about managers on all levels of the firm—from the president to departmental supervisor. They all have the same *type* of responsibilities, but the responsibilities relate to different *scopes* of the firm's operations. The president is responsible for all of the people in the company, whereas a departmental supervisor is only responsible for those people within her or his department.

If the scope of the manager's responsibilities is small (a supervisor or a president of a very small company), the resources are managed primarily through *observation*. The manager observes what is going on and takes action when something should be changed or improved.

But, operations can become too large for this complete reliance on observation. The physical system becomes so big or decentralized that the manager cannot be everywhere at once. In these cases, the manager must rely on a **conceptual system** to provide information about the physical system. The conceptual system doesn't exist physically; rather, it *represents* the physical system. Perhaps the conceptual system consists of a series of printed reports that the manager receives each day. The information on the reports keeps the manager informed about the activities of the physical system. A report might reflect the level of the inventory, for example. In that case, the facts and figures on the report reflect the condition of the physical inventory of the firm. If the conceptual system is accurate and up-to-date, the manager doesn't have to be present to observe what is going on within the different areas. The conceptual system reports that information.

33

It is in this area of conceptual information systems that the computer has been applied. The first application was on an organization-wide basis as firms built, or attempted to build, the corporate management information systems (MIS). Some of these systems were successful, whereas some failed due to their large size. More recently, the application of the computer as a conceptual information system has been on a smaller scale—intended to support individual managers rather than the firm as a whole. These conceptual systems are called decision support systems (DSS). Over the course of years, a manager might construct or help construct dozens of such systems. The IBM PC can furnish the computational power and speed to make these decision support systems more effective.

Managerial Functions

We have recognized that all managers have the same type of responsibilities. A French management theorist, Henri Fayol, came to this conclusion in the early 1900s. Fayol, recognized as one of the fathers of classical management theory, contended that all managers:

- *Plan* what they want to accomplish
- *Organize* the resources necessary to accomplish the plan
- *Staff* the organization by obtaining the people and other resources necessary to accomplish the plan
- *Direct* the resources toward plan accomplishment
- *Control* the resources by comparing actual performance to the plan

These are the **managerial functions**. All managers perform them. Some managers place more emphasis on planning, some place more emphasis on directing, and so on. But, all managers perform each of the functions to some degree.

If the computer is to serve as part of a DSS, then it should support the manager in all of these functions. What has happened, however, is that the computer has supplied excellent support in planning and controlling, and not so much support in the other functions. This means that, as the manager goes about organizing, staffing, and directing, he or she looks more toward noncomputer sources for information.

Problem Solving and Decision Making

Managers are paid to solve problems. Something unforseen happens, and the manager must react and take corrective action. Certainly, no manager spends all of her or his time solving problems. There are other activities such as planning, resource allocation, improvement projects, and so forth. But the basis of good company performance is a managerial team that is adept at solving problems as they arise.

Managers make decisions in the process of solving problems. One problem solution will require several decisions. For example, the manager may have to decide:

- What is causing the problem?
- What are the possible solutions?
- Which solution is best?
- How should the solution be implemented?
- Is the solution working?

The people who build computer-based decision support systems (the managers and computer specialists) focus on the problem-solving and decision-making aspects of management. The idea is to identify the problems that a manager solves, identify the decisions that must be made to solve those problems, and identify the information needed to make those decisions. Then, one or more decision support systems is built to provide all or part of that information.

Problem Structure

Some of the problems that managers solve are more structured than others. By problem structure, we are really talking about how well a problem is understood. Do we know all, or most, of the elements that go into the solution? Can those elements be measured?

Some problems are so well structured that formulas have been devised for their solution. Once a formula exists, the manager no longer has to make the decision. A lower-level employee, or even a computer, can make it.

A good example of a **structured problem** is the determination of how much of an item, such as a raw material, to reorder from a supplier. If you order too much, the costs of maintaining the excess inventory in your warehouse will be too great. If you don't order enough, you will quickly run out of stock and lose valuable sales. The formula that balances these two costs is the economic order quantity (EOQ) formula:

$$EOQ = \sqrt{\frac{2AS}{UR}}$$

where: A is the acquisition (purchasing) cost
S is the annual sales
U is the unit cost
R is the retention (carrying) cost

Other problems are not so well structured. The decision of where to locate a new plant is one. Some of the elements, such as real estate costs, taxes, and shipping costs, can be measured quite exactly. Other elements, such as community attitudes and quality of life, are more difficult to measure. The plant location decision is an example of a **semistructured problem.**

Figure 3.1 illustrates that the semistructured problems area is where the DSS concept is applied. The DSS supports the manager by shedding light on the structured aspects of the problem. The manager must rely on other information sources to shed light on the unstructured aspects. As an example, the computer can provide cost figures for real estate, taxes, and shipping charges as the manager considers alternate plant sites. But the manager will interview community leaders in order to gauge attitudes and will meet with citizens groups to discuss quality of life issues. As the figure indicates, if the problem is completely structured like the order quantity one, the computer can do it. If the problem has no structure at all, the computer is of no help. Actually, there are very few, if any, problems with no structure at all.

Figure 3.1   Degrees of Problem Structure

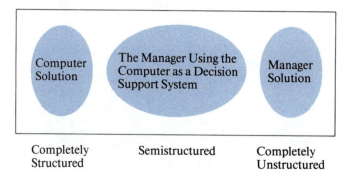

Completely   Semistructured   Completely
Structured   Unstructured

**Formal and
Informal Information**

The computer-based decision support systems are **formal systems**. A great deal of thought and planning goes into their design. They are documented in writing, and the users are trained in their operation. These systems are a part of the official control mechanism of the firm. The output of these formal systems is called **formal information**.

Managers get much information from these formal systems. But, these systems do not supply all of the information that a manager needs. Much comes from informal sources. An **informal system** is one that does not follow a prescribed pattern. It is not documented in the company's procedure manual. It functions as the need dictates. These informal information systems are comprised of a number of **informal information sources**. Some examples are unscheduled meetings, business lunches, periodicals, telephone calls, letters, memos, and the like. Several studies have found that many managers prefer these informal sources over those of a more formal nature. The output of the informal systems is called **informal information**.

**Putting the Computer
in Perspective**

So, where has this discussion taken us? We have seen that managers do more than make decisions and solve problems. Of the problems, we have seen that some are more structured than others, and that the computer is best suited to help solve the structured variety. And, we have seen that the manager obtains information from both formal systems, such as the computer, and informal systems, such as word-of-mouth communication.

The result is that the computer only supports a portion of the manager's activity—that portion dealing with solving problems that have some structure. And the more structure, the better.

Figure 3.2   A Model of an MIS

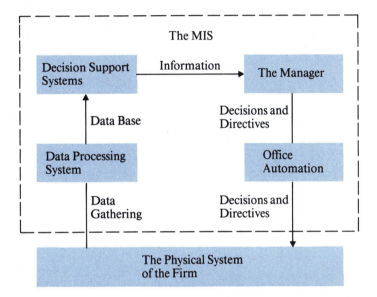

This situation is likely to change over time, perhaps very rapidly. The manager certainly relies more on the computer today than 10 years ago. And, with the boom in the small-computer area, the trend toward easy-to-use computers of all sizes, and the increasing computer knowledge among managers, we should see the computer increase in value as a decision support tool.

**Component
Parts of the MIS**

The term *MIS* was originally coined to distinguish the use of a computer from traditional processing of accounting data. The new use focused on information for management.

Over the years, however, the term MIS has become synonymous with business computing. Many firms use the name MIS department in describing their total computing operation. In this context, which is a very practical one, MIS includes all computer-related activity in the firm. Figure 3.2 illustrates that MIS is the overall network, with four major components—data processing, decision support systems, the manager, and office automation. The data processing system gathers data from the physical system of the firm and enters this data into a data base, where it is held until needed by the decision support system. The decision support system transforms the data into information for decision making. The manager uses the office automation system to help communicate the decisions and directives to the firm. Office automation includes technologies such as word processing, electronic mail, document storage and retrieval, and teleconferencing.

**The Manager/
DSS Interface**

The MIS model in Figure 3.2 shows how the DSS supplies the manager with information. There are three methods the manager uses to trigger this information flow. The methods are (1) periodic reports, (2) special reports, and (3) mathematical modeling.

Periodic Reports

The oldest and most popular of the three methods is periodic reports. **Periodic reports** are those prepared according to some time schedule, such as at the end of each month. The traditional accounting reports such as the income statement and balance sheet are examples. The computer is programmed to prepare these reports, using data from the data base.

Much computer time is spent preparing these reports, and managers use the information in performing their functions. Most of the reports support the control activity by comparing actual and planned performance.

There are two aspects of periodic reports, however, that decrease their value. First, the reports tend to describe what has already happened. It might be too late to act to solve a problem or seize an opportunity. Second, very often the reports are designed by computer specialists with little or no input from the managers. The reports represent the information that the specialists "think" the manager needs.

Special Reports

Special reports are those prepared when something out of the ordinary happens. Perhaps a report describes an accident or answers a manager's specific questions.

These reports tend to be more timely, since they respond to a current event; special reports receive more of the manager's attention because of that fact. In addition, if the manager has asked for particular information, she or he is more likely to use it.

The manager's request for information is called a **query**. The manager queries the data base for certain information. A common method for initiating the query and receiving the response is through use of a terminal connected to the firm's central computer. The manager can also have a small computer, such as the IBM PC, and query his or her own private data base or the corporate data base. It is possible to connect the PC to the central computer through the use of telecommunication lines.

The reports received in response to queries have the same appearance as periodic reports—they can be a few lines, or they can be several pages in length. The only point distinguishing the special reports from the periodic ones is the method of initiation. The manager must ask for the special reports, but receives the periodic ones automatically.

Mathematical Models

Any mathematical formula is a **model**—it represents something. For example, the EOQ formula represents the interaction of inventory purchasing and carrying costs.

The model is like a black box. You enter data describing the situation into one end, and get results out of the other. The situational data is called the **scenario**. In the EOQ example the scenario describes the costs and sales levels. The output is the optimum order quantity.

The model is attractive to the manager because it provides a means to look into the future. The model enables the manager to play the **"what-if" game**. The manager says, in effect, "What if I make this decision? What will likely be the result?" In the case of the EOQ model, the manager can say "What if sales increase from 10,000 units to 12,500 units (variable S in the model), what will be the effect on the order quantity?"

The EOQ model is an example of an **optimizing model**—it identifies the best solution. This is a rare modeling characteristic. Most models are **nonoptimizing**. They simply say "If you make this decision, this is the likely result." They do not say "This is the best decision." The manager must try out several decisions and then decide which is best.

Models can also be static or dynamic. A **static model** is like a snapshot—it applies to only a specific point in time. The EOQ model is a static model—it recommends a solution based on conditions existing right now. **Dynamic models** are more like a motion picture. They consider activity over a period of time, such as a year. For example, we could build a model that represents, or simulates, the cash flowing into and out of a firm, month-by-month, for a year. The activity of the model is called **simulation**. The model simulates some phenomenon. If a computer is used, it is called the **simulator**.

The mathematical model has been around almost as long as the computer, but it has never enjoyed widespread use. The main reason is the demand for good mathematical skills on the part of the model builder. In the past, managers have generally lacked these skills. That situation is now changing significantly as schools and colleges are turning out more quantitatively skilled graduates. Recently, several colleges have announced that all students will be issued a computer. In early 1984, Harvard decided that students entering its graduate school of business would be issued an IBM PC.[1]

In addition to the increasing modeling skills, the model-building process is becoming easier through new software systems. The combination of improved skills coupled with user-friendly modeling techniques should make this method of receiving information from the DSS more popular in the future.

Differences in Management Style

In describing how the manager uses the MIS or the DSS it is easy to talk in generalities. For example, it is easy to say "Upper level managers make greater use of environmental information than do managers on the lower level." Or, "The information used by lower level managers is more detailed than that used on the upper level." But, we must keep in mind that all managers are different. And, the differences also appear in how they solve problems.

One management scientist, Andrew Szilagyi, characterizes managers as either problem seekers, problem solvers, or problem avoiders.[2] The **problem seeker** looks

---

1. "IBM Extends Lines of Office Computers with Desktop Model," *The Wall Street Journal* (February 22, 1984): 16.
2. Andrew D. Szilagyi, Jr., *Management and Performance* (Santa Monica: Goodyear Publishing Co., 1981), pp. 220-225.

for problems to solve. This person would like to have a terminal or a small computer and use it to generate special reports. He or she scans these special reports for problem signals and then reacts.

The **problem solver** will not back away from a problem once it is identified, but he or she does not actively seek out problems to solve. This manager would use periodic reports as the means of identifying problems. Once identified, the problem solver might use a terminal or a small computer to learn more about the problem and to evaluate alternate solution strategies.

The **problem avoider** hates problems. She or he will ignore them and hope that they go away. This particular manager makes very little use of the computer.

It is important to recognize these differences in how managers react to problems. You can clearly see the necessity to tailor the DSS to fit the particular manager's needs. We can conclude that the closer the DSS conforms to the manager's problem-solving style, the better use he or she will make of it.

Summary

This chapter explored the major concepts that relate to the MIS or DSS. The concepts that we have covered should provide you with the background that you need as we proceed to study the IBM PC as a DSS—as element in an MIS.

MIS and the DSS are strictly concepts. They represent ways to think about the computer as a problem-solving tool. The concepts provide general guidelines in designing information systems but they do not represent hard and fast rules. Much depends on the individual characteristics of the manager, the manager's level within the firm, the type of firm, and the position of the firm in its industry. All of these variables must be taken into account in the design of an MIS or a DSS.

The idea of a conceptual system is central to the study of MIS or DSS. When you recognize that an upper-level manager or a manager of a large, widespread organization can be isolated from the physical systems for which she or he is responsible, you can appreciate the value of the MIS and DSS.

Another important point to remember is that a manager will use all of the means possible to stay up-to-date on happenings within the organization. The computer is only one of these means, but it is an important one. Today's manager, through use of computer-generated information, can react more quickly and effectively to problem signals than the manager of a decade ago. And this increasing reliance on the computer is likely to continue.

Think of the MIS as the total organizational computing resource. Within MIS we find data processing, decision support, and office automation. We also include the manager as an integral part of the MIS. The MIS provides a feedback loop of information that is used to keep the physical system of the firm on course. The data processing system collects the data. The decision support systems convert the data into information. The manager converts the information into decisions, and the office automation system is one of the vehicles for communicating the decision and directives back to the physical system.

The manager obtains information from a DSS by means of periodic and special reports and the output of mathematical models. In the chapters that follow, we will see how BASIC, dBASE II, VisiCalc, and WordStar play important roles in facilitating the managerial flow of information.

Key Terms

Physical system of the firm	Query
System	Model
Conceptual system	Scenario
Managerial functions	What-if game
Structured problem	Optimizing model
Semistructured problem	Nonoptimizing model
Formal system	Static model
Formal information	Dynamic model
Informal system	Simulation
Informal information source	Simulator
Informal information	Problem seeker
Periodic report	Problem solver
Special report	Problem avoider

(Do not fill in blanks in the book. Write answers on a separate piece of paper.)

1. Resources of a firm that can be seen and touched together comprise a _____ system.

2. A system can be defined as an integration of _____ that work together to accomplish some _____.

3. When the manager has responsibility for a very small system such as a shop or an office, he or she can keep informed about the activity within the system through _____.

4. The system that represents the physical system is called the _____ system.

5. The first conceptual systems were intended to represent the entire organization and were called _____; more recently the term _____ has been used to describe conceptual systems that represent only a part of the organization.

6. Henri Fayol said that all managers _____, _____, _____, _____, and _____.

7. The computer has provided its strongest support for the managerial functions of _____ and _____.

8. A manager will make multiple _____ in the process of solving a single _____.

9. If all of the elements that are involved in the solution of a problem are known, the problem is said to be _____.

10. If all of the elements that are involved in the solution of a problem are not known, the problem is said to be _____.

11. A good example of a _____ problem is the one of determining the quantity of replenishment merchandise to order.

12. The DSS concept has been applied to the area of _____ problems.

13. The computer is a good example of a _____ system that has been planned to perform in a prescribed way.

14. The manager gets much information from informal sources such as _____, _____, _____, and _____.

15. The four major components of the MIS are _____, _____, _____, and _____.

16. The manager gets information from the DSS in three different ways: _____, _____, and _____.

17. A name used for a manager's request for information from the computer is _____.

18. The situation that sets the stage for a modeling operation is called the _____.

19. When the manager "tries out" different decisions using modeling, he is said to be playing the _____ game.

20. If you were selling computers to be used as decision support systems, you would probably prefer to call on managers who were problem _____.

Module 3
Procedural
Programming
Languages

4 The Role of Programming in the DSS

During the early years of computing, the user did not have the opportunity to make the "make-or-buy" decision. There was no software to buy; you had to make it yourself. The situation is much different today with "off-the-shelf" software rapidly becoming the most popular option. In this chapter we examine the effect that this trend is having on custom programming activity.

We first identify which types of programs are usually purchased off-the-shelf and which types are usually programmed. We then describe the evolution of programming languages, and we conclude with a description of the step-by-step process that a firm follows in developing its own programs.

The Make-or-Buy Decision

The general rule is "If you can buy it, buy it." This is good business practice because you invariably can buy packaged software for less than it costs to prepare it yourself. Program development is very costly. The problem is that you can't always buy the software that you need. Most companies have unique practices and procedures, and the packaged software might not exactly fit. So, some compromise might be in order. Some firms alter their practices to fit the software.

In this book, we use the terms **prewritten software**, **packaged software**, and **off-the-shelf software** interchangeably. Someone has produced some type of application software to solve a problem that is faced by a number of firms. We are not including systems software, even though it is produced for sale. The focus of the system software is much more narrow and well defined than that of applications software. Application software ranges from a very simple report-generating program to a complete file management system for an insurance company.

The most widely used packaged software is general in nature. The best examples are the three packaged systems described in this book—dBASE II, VisiCalc, and WordStar. They perform general data base, electronic spreadsheet, and word processing tasks demanded by a wide variety of firms. For example, the same dBASE II off-the-shelf software can manage the data base of a hardware store, a small hospital, a charity organization, a church, an independent insurance agency, and so on. VisiCalc can be used to prepare a cash flow statement for these same organizations. And, all the groups can use WordStar to prepare letters, reports, and memos. All three packages address typical business problems or tasks.

Other software is more specific. For example, you can obtain software for particular industries such as real estate, medicine, and retailing. But, even though this software is tailored to an industry, it might not fit a particular firm. A furniture store, for example, might not be able to use a retailing inventory package because it does not allow for multiple storage locations.

There is more packaged software available today than ever before, and there is no doubt that the trend is in that direction. But, there are certain situations where it is still best to do the programming yourself.

Figure 4.1   Make or Buy Opportunities

	Make	**Buy**
Periodic Reports	Most programming activity is directed here—at customized reports.	Packaged software systems provide some "bread and butter" reports, such as balance sheets and income statements.
Special Reports	Custom programming is usually too slow to provide special information quickly.	Data base management systems, such as dBASE II, are good for preparing special reports.
Mathematical Models	All types of models can be prepared with custom programming.	Electronic spreadsheet systems, such as VisiCalc, permit easy modeling of a certain class of situations.

In Chapter 3, we examined how the manager obtains information from the DSS in three forms—periodic reports, special reports, and the output of mathematical models. Figure 4.1 summarizes the make-or-buy situation in terms of these three output methods.

Periodic Reports

If a computer user wants a full range of periodic reports, it will be necessary to program most or all of them. It is difficult for software houses to anticipate each and every type of report that a firm might require. This is the area where most custom programming is directed.

Many firms using small-scale systems have no inhouse programming expertise. They rely solely on packaged software. As they realize the potential for getting additional information from their data base, the next logical step is to supplement the packaged software with custom programming. The firms will either hire one or more programmers, or have an outside consulting organization do the programming for a flat fee or on a "time and materials" basis. Establishment of the firm's own programming staff is a step toward independence in use of the computer. Contracting for outside programming talent perpetuates the dependence of the firm on others for its computer expertise.

Special Reports

Custom programming is usually too slow to be of much help in preparing special reports. This is where the data base management systems such as dBASE II have so much to offer. The manager can query the data base without writing a program. It is only necessary to input some parameters (maybe two sentences of instructions) and the special report is produced. The only problem is that you are usually limited in (1) the format of the report, and (2) the amount of processing that can be performed on the data prior to the report being printed.

Mathematical Models

Just a few years ago, the small-scale system user had no selection of modeling software from which to choose. The situation is different now, and a variety of packages are available, such as standard statistical routines (regression, analysis of variance, and so on) and electronic spreadsheets. The first, and most popular, electronic spreadsheet was VisiCalc, followed by variations such as SuperCalc, Multiplan, and CalcStar. Today, there are 40 or more spreadsheets from which to choose.[1]

These spreadsheets are excellent for a certain class of problems—those that involve rows and columns of data. The financial area of the firm is rich with opportunities to apply these models in a "what-if" manner. In other parts of the firm, however, the needs are different. Situations to be modeled in marketing and manufacturing often require characteristics that the electronic spreadsheets cannot fulfill.

If the firm has a programming capability, that capability can be aimed at this area. Using a language such as BASIC, you can prepare very effective mathematical models. The process can be time-consuming and expensive, but you can prepare exactly what you need.

This is one area where the small-system user is at a distinct disadvantage compared to the mainframe user. Special modeling languages are available for the large systems that make the custom programming of simulators easier. The modeling languages have been designed specifically to facilitate the modeling process. They include GPSS (General Purpose Simulator System language), DYNAMO, and SIMSCRIPT. Such modeling languages have not yet been developed for small-scale systems. Modeling must be done with standard procedural languages. You can get the job done, but the inefficiency of the process increases as the model becomes complex.

For Best Support—Make AND Buy

For a particular program, the choice may be whether to make *or* buy. Overall, however, the best strategy is to make *and* buy. Buy what you can, like dBASE II, VisiCalc, and WordStar, and make the rest, such as programs that prepare a full set of periodic reports and simulate the important operations of the firm.

The least expensive approach to achieving a computer-based MIS or DSS is to buy off-the-shelf software. But, if you are to provide broad support to managers on all levels and in all functional areas, some custom programming will be necessary. In the past, a firm would install a packaged system, outgrow it, and add their own staff of information specialists—systems analysts and programmers. Whether this will continue to be the pattern is anybody's guess. The key is the packaged software. If it can be made so flexible and user friendly as to preclude the need for help from information specialists, then a firm will be able to stick with the packaged software. While this most probably will happen eventually, it does not seem to be an immediate possibility. We are still in a mode where firms can expect to add their own computer staffs as their needs increase.

The Evolution of Programming Languages

The computer must be instructed to take each step necessary to perform a task. The list of instructions is the **program**, and the person who prepares the program is the **programmer**.

The only language that the computer can understand is **machine language**, a string of zeros and ones that appear meaningless to a human. The zeros and ones

1. For brief descriptions of these spreadsheets, see Daniel S. Bricklin, "Spreadsheets," *PC World Annual Software Review* (1983/1984): 108ff. Bricklin, along with Robert M. Frankston, invented VisiCalc.

are used in a **binary coding system** where they represent the status of electronic switches within the CPU. A zero means that a particular switch is off, and a one means that it is on.

The very first programs were coded in machine language, but that didn't last long. It was just too slow. An approach was developed to allow programmers to code programs using a language that was more meaningful to human beings.

The first efforts involved using symbolic names for the operations to be performed (such as READ, MOVE, and ADD), and the data to be handled (such as RATE and HOURS) rather than machine addresses and codes. A term used for these symbolic names is **mnemonics**. A mnemonic is a memory device, and that is the purpose that the symbolic names served. It was easier for the programmer to remember that the hourly rate was at a storage location called RATE than at location 5312. The programming language using mnemonic or symbolic names was called an **assembler.** The program that converted the mnemonics to machine language was called an **assembly program**. Each computer had its own assembler, and that practice has continued to this day. The assembler is tailored to the computer; it is a **machine-oriented language**. Figure 4.2 illustrates a portion of a program written in an assembler.

Assemblers are the most efficient way to process data. They accomplish the task more quickly and use less of the computer's resources than any other approach except machine language. But, they are tedious to use and demand excellent programming skills.

It quickly became apparent, in the early years of computing, that programming languages should more closely approximate the languages of the programmer—English and mathematics. One of the first of such languages was **FORTRAN**, which stands for **FORmula TRANslator**. FORTRAN was developed by IBM in 1957. It rapidly became the most popular language, and is still widely used today. FORTRAN is a powerful mathematical language, and appeals to scientists, engineers, mathematicians, statisticians, and the like. FORTRAN is illustrated in Figure 4.3.

Although FORTRAN has enjoyed some use in business, it never was met with the same warm reception that it received in the scientific community. Business data processing does not place as much emphasis on advanced mathematics, and data processing (not decision support) was the reigning computer application at the time of FORTRAN's entry on the market. Business data processing is fairly simple and straightforward, but the volumes of transactions are large. The business user has traditionally been more interested in the input and output capabilities of a language than its mathematical ability. For example, there is a need to prepare attractive customer statements and financial reports. Whereas FORTRAN does an excellent processing job, it falls short in the input and output area.

So, a special language was designed specifically for business, and it was called **COBOL—COmmon Business Oriented Language**. COBOL was not the brainchild of a single computer company. Rather, it was the product of influence by the federal government. Most of the computer manufacturers cooperated by preparing the systems software necessary to program in COBOL for their computers. COBOL came on the market in 1959 and is still popular today. In fact, it is the most popular business computer language—more business data is processed by COBOL programs than any other. See Figure 4.4 for an example of COBOL coding. This example, like the others, is for only a portion of a program.

A COBOL program is longer than one written in other languages. COBOL is very "wordy." It is this wordiness that makes it a **self-documenting language**—you

Chapter 4
The Role of Programming
in the DSS

49

Figure 4.2   A Portion of a Program Written in Assembler

```
*
*
*--------> PROGRAM 12 SUBPROGRAM PROGRAM
*
*
        PRINT NOGEN                 SUPRESS MACROS
MAIN    START 0
BEGIN   SAVE  (14,12)
        BALR  3,0
        USING *,3                   BASE REGISTER NUMBER 3
        ST    13,SAVE+4
        LA    13,SAVE
        OPEN  (CARDIN,INPUT,PRTOUT,OUTPUT)  OPEN FILES
*
*--------> READ INPUT RECORDS AND PROCESS
*
READCARD GET   CARDIN,DIMAGE          READ RECORD
        MVC   NAMEOUT,NAMEIN          MOVE NAE TO PRINT
        MVC   STRTOUT,STRTIN          MOVE STREET TO PRINT
        MVC   CITYOUT,CITYIN          MOVE CITY TO PRINT
        L     15,ACONVST              LOAD ENTRY POINT
        LA    5,STATEIN               LOAD STATE ADDRESS INTO REG
        LA    10,STATEOUT             LOAD ADD OF STATEOUT INTO 10
        BALR  14,15                   BRANCH TO SUBROUTINE
        MVC   ZIPOUT,ZIPIN            MOVE ZIP CODE TO PRINT
        PUT   PRTOUT,PRTDELT          PRINT LINE
        B     READCARD                BRANCH TO READCARD .
EOF     CLOSE (CARDIN,,PRTOUT)         CLOSE FILES
        L     13,SAVE+4              RESTORE REG 13
        RETURN (14,12)               RETURN TO OS        ,
*
*--------> INPUT FILE DEFINITION
*
CARDIN  DCB   DSORG=PS,RECFM=F,MACRF=GM,BLKSIZE=80,LRECL=80,      X
              DDNAME=CRDIN,EODAD=EOF
*
*--------> OUTPUT FILE DEFINITION
*
PRTOUT  DCB   DSORG=PS,RECFM=FA,MACRF=PM,BLKSIZE=132,LRECL=132,   X
              DDNAME=ECHOUT
*
*--------> INPUT DEFINITIONS
*
SAVE    DS    18F
DIMAGE  DS    0CL80
NAMEIN  DS    CL20
STRTIN  DS    CL20
CITYIN  DS    CL20
STATEIN DS    CL2
ZIPIN   DS    CL5
        DS    CL13
*
*--------> OUTPUT LINE
*
PRTDELT DS    0CL132
```

can read a COBOL program and easily understand what it does.

COBOL and FORTRAN are examples of a **problem-oriented language**. They are designed for particular problems rather than for particular machines. Assembler is the only machine-oriented language; the rest are problem-oriented.

Both FORTRAN and COBOL were expected to have long lives, and they did. Both are over 25 years old. But another language from the early years of the com-

Figure 4.3   A Program Written in FORTRAN

```
        PROGRAM LAGUERR(INPUT,OUTPUT)
C
C     THIS PROGRAM DEMONSTRATES NUMERICAL INSTABILITY
C   IN THE FORM OF CANCELLATION ERROR FOR THE COMPUTATION
C   OF LAGUERRE POLYNOMIALS (RECURSIVELY).
C
C     THE PURE RECCURENCE RELATION USED IS:
C
C           LN(X)=(1/N)((2N-1-X)LN-1(X)-(N-1)LN-2(X))
C
C             INITIALLY:  LN-2=1    AND      LN-1=1-X
C
C     THE USER ENTERS X AND THE MAXIMUM ORDER OF THE POLYNOMIALS.
C      X IS ASSUMED GOOD TO AS MANY DIGITS AS ENTERED.
C
C     VALUES PRODUCING CANCELLATION ARE X=4.5366202969 AND ORDER=4.
C     VALUES THAT ARE STABLE ARE X=10 AND ORDER=10.
C
        IMPLICIT XOTHER(X)
    10 PRINT *,"MAXIMUM ORDER OF COMPUTED POLYNOMIALS=",
        READ *,NMAX
        PRINT *,"X=",
        CALL READX(5LINPUT,X,1,IOS)
        PRINT 92,XWRITE(X)
C
C     INITIALIZE
C
        XLNM2=1.D0
        XLNM1=1.D0-X
        N=2
C
C     COMPUTE LAGUERRE POLYNOMIAL
C
    20 XLN=(1.D0/N)*(((2*N-1)-X)*XLNM1-(N-1)*XLNM2)
C
        PRINT 91,N,XWRITE(XLN)
        IF(N .GE. NMAX) GO TO 10
            XLNM2=XLNM1
            XLNM1=XLN
            N=N+1
            GO TO 20
    90 FORMAT(2A10)
    91 FORMAT("LAGUERRE POLYNOMIAL ORDER",I4," = ",2A10)
    92 FORMAT("GOOD TO THE NUMBER OF DIGITS ENTERED, X=",2A10)
        END
```

puter has surprised everyone by remaining popular longer than intended. **Report Program Generator (RPG)** was designed to ease the conversion from punched card machines to the computer. Some people say that it really isn't a programming language, since you simply fill out a set of forms rather than code instructions. But RPG is easy to use, and many companies continued using it long after their conversion to computers was completed. It is still popular today on larger computers, but a version is not yet available for the PC.

By the mid-1960s, all of the mainframe manufacturers offered varieties of FORTRAN and COBOL, as well as their own assembler languages. These three languages plus RPG accounted for practically all of the programming. Then, in 1964 in an effort to achieve a competitive edge in the software area, IBM announced a

Figure 4.4   A Portion of a Program Written in COBOL

```
PROCEDURE DIVISION.
000 DRIVER-MOD.
    OPEN INPUT IN-FILE
         OUTPUT OUT-FILE.
    PERFORM 800-READ-MOD.
    PERFORM 100-INIT-MOD 10 TIMES.
    PERFORM 200-PROC-MOD UNTIL FLAG EQUAL "Y".
    CLOSE IN-FILE
          OUT-FILE.
    STOP RUN.

100-INIT-MOD.
    MOVE IN-REC TO TABLE-REC.
    MOVE T-ITEM-NO TO TABLE-ARG (SUB).
    MOVE T-DESCRIP TO T-DESC (SUB).
    MOVE T-PRICE TO T-PR (SUB).
    MOVE T-LOCATION TO T-LOC (SUB).
    ADD 1 TO SUB.
    PERFORM 800-READ-MOD.

200-PROC-MOD.
    MOVE IN-REC TO ORDER-REC.
    MOVE 1 TO SUB.
    PERFORM 210-LOOK-UP UNTIL SUB EQUAL 11.
    PERFORM 800-READ-MOD.

210-LOOK-UP.
    IF ITEM-NO EQUAL TABLE-ARG (SUB)
        PERFORM 220-MOVE-MOD
        MOVE 11 TO SUB
        ELSE ADD 1 TO SUB.

220-MOVE-MOD.
    MOVE ITEM-NO TO ITEM-NO-OUT.
    MOVE CUSTOMER-NO TO CUSTOMER-NO-OUT.
    MOVE QTY TO QTY-OUT.
    MOVE CUST-ORDER-NO TO CUST-ORD-NO-OUT.
    MOVE T-DESC (SUB) TO ITEM-DESC-OUT.
    MOVE T-PR (SUB) TO PRICE-OUT.
    MOVE T-LOC (SUB) TO LOC-OUT.
    MOVE DETAIL-REC TO OUT-REC.
    PERFORM 890-WRITE-MOD.

800-READ-MOD.
    READ IN-FILE AT END MOVE "Y" TO FLAG.

890-WRITE-MOD.
    WRITE OUT-REC.
```

FORTRAN/COBOL hybrid, **PL/I (Programming Language I)**. Within a few years, other computer vendors had their own PL/I languages. PL/I continues to be used in many of the larger installations. It handles business data processing tasks well and lends itself to **structured programming** (to be explained later in the chapter). The PL/I language is illustrated in Figure 4.5.

In 1962, Professors John G. Kemeny and Thomas E. Kurtz at Dartmouth College produced a language called **BASIC—Beginner's All-purpose Symbolic Instruction Code**. The name BASIC was appropriate. It was conceived as an easy-to-learn language. It didn't offer all of the bells and whistles of FORTRAN and COBOL, but it offered a quick and easy way to perform fundamental computing tasks.

Figure 4.5   A Portion of a Program Written in PL/I

```
DO I=1 TO 6;
    GET FILE (SATDATA83) EDIT (VERB_MEAN(I))(COL(1),F(3));
    PUT FILE (REPORT) EDIT (VERB_MEAN(I))(COL(15),F(3));
    END;
PUT FILE (REPORT)  EDIT('MATH MEANS')(COL(10),A);
DO I=1 TO 6;
    GET FILE (SATDATA83) EDIT (MATH_MEAN(I))(COL(1),F(3));
    PUT FILE (REPORT) EDIT (MATH_MEAN(I))(COL(15),F(3));
    END;
PUT FILE (REPORT)  EDIT ('RATIO 2')(COL(10),A);
DO I=1 TO 32;
    GET FILE (SATDATA83) EDIT (RATIO2(I))(COL(1),F(5,3));
    PUT FILE (REPORT)  EDIT (RATIO2(I))(COL(15),F(5,3));
    VERB_SCORE(I)=0;
    MATH_SCORE(I)=0;
    END;
ILOOP: DO I=1 TO 32;
    SUM=0;
    DO J=1 TO 6;
        IF J <= 2
            THEN DO;
                INTERCEPT(J)=(PERCENT(J)-(.1*RATIO2(32)))/(1-RATIO2(32));
                SLOPE(J)=(INTERCEPT(J)-0.1)/-1;
                END;
            ELSE DO;
                INTERCEPT(J)=(PERCENT(J)-(.2*RATIO2(32)))/(1-RATIO2(32));
                SLOPE(J)=(INTERCEPT(J)-0.2)/-1;
                END;
        REP(J)=INTERCEPT(J)+SLOPE(J)*RATIO2(I);
        IF REP(J)<0
            THEN REP(J)=0;
        SUM=SUM+REP(J);
        END;
    IF SUM > 1.00
        THEN DO;
            NORMAL=1/SUM;
            DO J=1 TO 6;
                REP(J)=REP(J)*NORMAL;
                END;
            END;
    DO J=1 TO 6;
        TEMPV=VERB_MEAN(J)*REP(J);
        VERB_SCORE(I)=VERB_SCORE(I)+TEMPV;
        TEMPM=MATH_MEAN(J)*REP(J);
        MATH_SCORE(I)=MATH_SCORE(I)+TEMPM;
        END;
END ILOOP;
```

In addition to its simplicity, BASIC was unique in that it was designed for use from a terminal. The older languages were intended to process data punched in cards. BASIC was first used by Dartmouth students, entering data into the central computer from remote terminals—a timesharing arrangement.

The simplicity of BASIC, and its orientation toward terminal keyboard use, made it a natural for the small-scale systems that hit the market in the 1970s. In 1975, William Gates and Paul Allen, the co-founders of Microsoft, developed the first microcomputer version of BASIC. The popularity of BASIC has gradually picked up steam, and it is the most popular language used with the small computers. Refer to Figure 4.6 for a sample of the BASIC language.

Figure 4.6   A Portion of a Program Written in BASIC

```
5360 REM THIS ROUTINE COMPUTES INTEREST EARNINGS AND CHARGES FOR
5370 REM MONTH 1.  THIS SPECIAL ROUTINE IS NECESSARY IN ORDER TO
5380 REM AVOID HAVING  NEGATIVE SUBSCRIPTS.  THE ROUTINE FOR MONTHS
5390 REM 2 THROUGH 18 APPEARS BELOW.
5400 REM COMPUTE INTEREST EARNED AND PAID
5410 IF CU(I) >= DC THEN 5500
5420 LET TL(I) = (CU(I) - DC) * (-1)
5450 LET I4(I) = (I1 / 100) * (TL(I) + X1(I)) / 12
5490 GOTO 5520
5500 LET TC(I) = CU(I) - DC
5510 LET I3(I) = (I2 / 100) * TC(I) / 12
5520 REM COMPUTE TOTAL INTEREST EARNED AND PAID
5530 LET I5(I) = I3(I)
5540 LET I6(I) = I4(I)
5550 FOR I = 2 TO 18
5560 REM
5570 REM COMPUTE CASH AT BEGINNING OF MONTH (NO BORROWING)
5580 LET CB(I) = CU(I-1)
5590 REM
5600 REM COMPUTE THE CUMULATIVE CASH QUANTITY
5610 LET CU(I) = CB(I) + CC(I)
5620 REM
5630 REM COMPUTE THE TOTAL LOANS OUTSTANDING OR THE CASH
5640 REM INVESTED.
5650 REM
5660 REM IF CUMULATIVE CASH IS LESS THAN DESIRED CASH, THEN WE
5670 REM MUST BORROW CASH TO MEET OUR NEEDS.
5680 REM OTHERWISE, WE MUST BORROW ENOUGH CASH TO FULFILL OUR
5690 REM CASH NEEDS.
5700 IF CU(I) >= DC THEN 5740
5710 LET TL(I) = (CU(I) - DC) * (-1)
5720 LET I4(I) = (I1 / 100) * (TL(I) + X1(I)) / 12
5730 GOTO 5760
5740 LET TC(I) = CU(I) - DC
5750 LET I3(I) = (I2 / 100) * TC(I) /12
5760 LET I5(I) = I5(I-1) + I3(I)
5770 LET I6(I) = I6(I-1) + I4(I)
5780 NEXT I
5790 REM COMPUTE NET INTEREST PAID OR EARNED
5800 REM
5810 REM PERFORM PRINT ROUTINE
5820 GOSUB 5860
5830 REM
5840 RETURN
```

BASIC is a problem-oriented language, but usually a compiler is not used to create the machine language. Rather, an **interpreter** transforms and executes each instruction—one instruction at a time. No object program is created.

Today, there are two distinct programming areas in business—mainframe systems and small-scale systems. In the large systems area, the data processing is generally accomplished with COBOL, PL/I, and assembler, and the quantitative analyses are performed with FORTRAN. In the small-scale systems area, BASIC is being used for both data processing and quantitative work. These five languages have been the most widely accepted in business.

There are three other languages that are also vying for recognition. **APL (A Programming Language)** was invented by Kenneth E. Iverson at Harvard in 1962. APL is a very succinct mathematical language that makes use of many special

Figure 4.7   A Program Written in APL

```
      ∇ ACC←INT ACCDIV DIV;A
[1]   ⍝ THE FUNCTION 'ACCDIV' CALCULATES A VECTOR OF ACCUMULATED DIVIDENDS
[2]   ⍝ 'INT' IS A GIVEN RATE OF INTEREST (6.5% IS STATED AS 6.5)
[3]   ⍝ 'DIV' IS A VECTOR OF DECLARED DIVIDENDS (0 3.10 5.66 8.99...)
[4]   ⍝ 'ACC' IS A VECTOR OF ACCUMULATED DIVIDENDS PLUS INTEREST
[5]   ⍝ ACC←6.5 ACCDIV 0 3.10 5.66 8.99
[6]   ⍝     PRODUCES 'ACC' WITH VALUES OF 0 3.10 8.96 18.53
[7]   A←⍳(ρDIV)
[8]   ACC←0.01×⌊0.5+100×((A∘.≥A)×(1+0.01×INT)*(A∘.-A))+.×DIV
      ∇
```

symbols. Much can be accomplished in a few lines of code, but the coding appears practically meaningless to anyone but the original programmer. APL has enjoyed support in the areas of business where one-time mathematical analyses must be performed. In these areas it has replaced FORTRAN to a certain extent. APL is illustrated in Figure 4.7.

Another currently popular language is **Pascal**, developed in the early 1970s by Swiss professor Niklaus Wirth as an educational tool. The language was named after Blaise Pascal, a 17th century French mathematician, who built the first adding machine. The programming language Pascal was designed to facilitate structured programming, and for that reason it has been widely used. It has not, however, received as much praise in the business world as in the scientific world, since the language comes up short on file-handling capabilities. It cannot directly access data in a data base; the access must be accomplished by a time-consuming

Figure 4.8   A Program Written in Pascal

```
PROGRAM COMM(SALEDATA,COMMOUT);
CONST    COM10 = 0.10;
         COM15 = 0.15;
         LIMIT = 1000.00;
VAR      AGENT: INTEGER;
         SALEAMT,COMMISSION,TOTALSALE,TOTALCOMM: REAL;
         SALEDATA, COMMOUT: TEXT;
BEGIN
    TOTALSALE := 0; TOTALCOMM := 0;
    REWRITE(COMMOUT);
    WRITELN(COMMOUT,'AGENT':15,'SALE AMOUNT':15,'COMMISSION':15);
    WRITELN(COMMOUT);
    RESET(SALEDATA);
    WHILE NOT EOF(SALEDATA) DO
        BEGIN
            READLN(SALEDATA,AGENT,SALEAMT);
            IF SALEAMT <= LIMIT THEN
                COMMISSION := SALEAMT * COM10
            ELSE COMMISSION := LIMIT * COM10 +
                (SALEAMT - LIMIT) * COM15;
    WRITELN(COMMOUT,AGENT:15,SALEAMT:12:2,COMMISSION:15:2);
            TOTALSALE := TOTALSALE + SALEAMT;
            TOTALCOMM := TOTALCOMM + COMMISSION
        END;
    WRITELN(COMMOUT);
    WRITELN(COMMOUT,'TOTALS':15,TOTALSALE:12:2,TOTALCOMM:15:2)
END.
```

Figure 4.9   A Portion of a Program Written in C

```
bf = block;
count = 0;
do {
        bufp = thrbuf;
        while (c != STX)
                c = getchr();
        lrcc = STX;
        for(i=0; i<129;i++) {
                c = getchr();
                lrcc =^c;
                *bufp++ = c;
        }
        if(c != ETX) {
                if (plscnt++ == 72) {
                        printf ("\n1");
                        plscnt = 0;
                        }
                else putchar('1');
                 putchr(NAK); putchr(1); error(); continue;
        }
        c=getchr();
        if ((lrcc=^c) != '\000') {
                if (plscnt++ == 72) {
                        printf("\n0");
                        plscnt = 0;
                        }
                else putchar('0');
                putchr(NAK); putchr(0); error(); continue;
        }
        if (plscnt++ == 72) {
                printf("\n+");
                plscnt = 0;
                }
        else putchar('+');
        putchr(ACK); putchr(0); errfls = 0;
        bufp = thrbuf;
        for(i=0;i<128;i++) {
            if (*bufp != CR) {
                *bf++ = *bufp++;
                count++;
                if (count == BLKSIZ) {
                    if ((nogood=write(newfile,block,BLKSIZ)) < BLKSIZ) {
                        printf("\007\n\nWrite error\n");
                        reset();
                    }
                    else {
                        count = 0;
                        bf = block;
```

sequential search. This limitation has discouraged Pascal's widespread use in business, both in data processing and in DSS. A sample of Pascal is presented in Figure 4.8.

A third language that is very popular with software firms is the C language, developed in 1972 by Dennis Ritchie at Bell Laboratories. C was used to reprogram the very popular UNIX operating system so that it would be usable on several different mini and micro systems. Portability is one of C's biggest assets, and because of this fact, it is very popular with software houses. Microsoft and Digital Research, for example, reprogrammed much of their software using C to take advantage of its portability. The C language is illustrated in Figure 4.9.

Figure 4.10   The Program Development and Maintenance Process

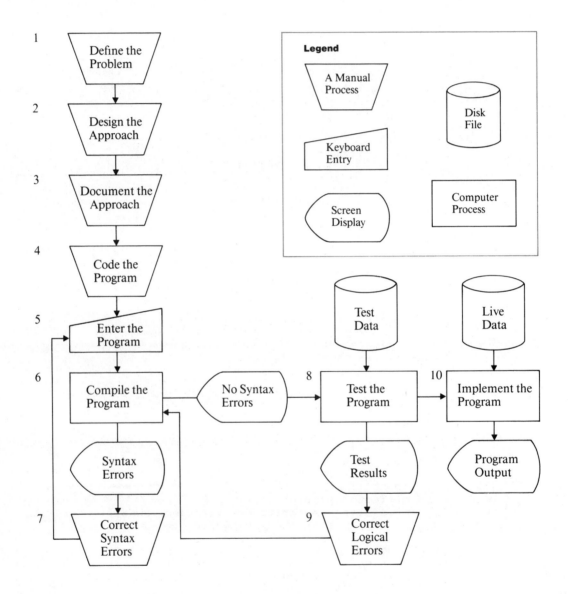

The problem with C is that it, like APL, is so succinct that it is not self-documenting. The same arguments applying to APL also fit C. For that reason, it is unlikely that C will seriously rival any of the well-entrenched business languages such as COBOL, PL/I, Assembler, and BASIC. It is difficult to see any of these languages being replaced to any great degree during the next few years. For one reason, business firms are slow to change. They have huge investments in programmers skilled in the use of the older languages. No doubt, all of this will change, but it will be an evolutionary, not revolutionary, process.

**The Programming
Process**

When a company decides to make its own software, there are a series of steps that must be taken. This is the **programming process**, and it involves both the user and information specialists. These steps are diagrammed in Figure 4.10, and described in the following sections. The wedge-shaped symbols, such as those in steps 1, 2, and 3, are used to illustrate manual processes—steps performed by a person.

1. **Define the Problem** There is some problem to be solved on the computer. Perhaps the firm is losing sales revenue when too many customers prove to be poor credit risks. A new credit approval system is needed. A manager, perhaps the president or the controller, decides to put the application on the computer. In this case, the manager is the user, and he or she must communicate the problem to an information specialist.

   The information specialist who has the responsibility of working with users in defining computer solutions to problems is the **systems analyst**. The systems analyst knows both computing and business systems. The user and the systems analyst discuss the problem until the analyst understands it thoroughly.

2. **Design the Computer Approach** The systems analyst determines the best way for the computer to handle the new application. For example, will order data be entered from remote terminals throughout the company, or from a terminal in the computer department? Should the customer credit file be stored on magnetic tape or magnetic disk? The systems analyst considers the pros and cons of the various alternatives and identifies the one that looks the best.

   The analyst reports the findings and recommendations to the user, and the user approves or disapproves the approach. In this situation, the systems analyst advises, and the user decides.

3. **Document the Approach** The systems analyst prepares written documentation to give to the programmer, describing the task that the computer is to perform. The documentation can take several forms. The most straightforward is a narrative description. This narrative can be supplemented by a **system flowchart** that presents the major parts of the system in a graphical form. Figure 4.11 is an example of a system flowchart. (Figure 4.10 is also a system flowchart.)

   The flowchart is the big picture. It must be made more detailed, and a good way to accomplish this is with a **structure chart**, also called a **hierarchy diagram**. The structure chart has the same general appearance as an organization chart, as illustrated in Figure 4.12. The overall process, or system, is represented by the box at the top, and it is successively subdivided into component parts on lower and lower levels.

   The structure chart is a blueprint for the program that organizes its parts in a series of hierarchical levels and modules. The programmer follows these rules when coding each module:

   • Each module performs only a single, basic operation, such as read a record, write a line, compute an amount, and so forth.

   • There is only a single entry and a single exit point for each module.

   • A program can be written using only three basic structures—sequence, selection, and iteration.

Figure 4.11   A System Flowchart

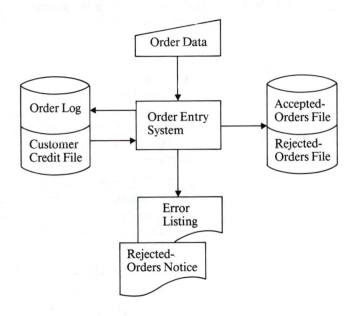

From McLeod, *MIS*, Second Edition, SRA, 1983, p. 565, Figure 17-12.

Flowcharts in Figure 4.13 are used to illustrate the three structures. The rectangle represents processing and the diamond represents a decision point where the computer can decide between two alternate paths. A program is a collection of these structures, each occurring many times.

These rules produce a program that is easier to code, debug (correct the errors), and update than if the structured approach is not followed. The value of the structured approach increases with the size and complexity of the program.

The systems analyst gives all of the documentation to the programmer, who has the task of converting the design into code that the computer can understand.

4. **Code the Program**   If the system is a simple one, the programmer may code the program directly from the documentation provided by the analyst. Most likely, however, the programmer will have to prepare some intermediate documentation that is more specific than that obtained from the analyst, yet less specific than the coding.

One example of such documentation is the **program flowchart** illustrated in Figure 4.14. The program flowchart is more detailed than a system flowchart. The program flowchart illustrates each major step that the computer must take in performing the processing. The process of drawing the flowchart helps the programmer understand the task to be performed by the computer.

Another documentation technique is rivaling the program flowchart in popularity. It is called **pseudocode**, and an example of it appears in Figure 4.15. Pseudocode looks like computer language, but it is not. It is a rather free-form way to express the detailed logic, compared to the strict techniques of flowcharting. The programmer uses pseudocode as a way to "rough out" the logic that is then transferred to the appropriate language, such as BASIC.

Figure 4.12   A Structure Chart

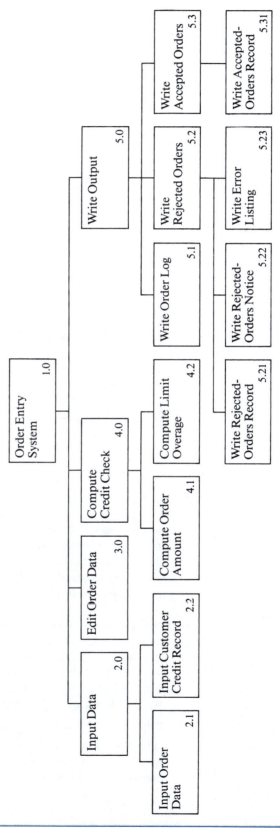

From McLeod, *MIS*, Second Edition, SRA, 1983, p. 571, Figure 17-17.

Figure 4.13   Three Program Structures

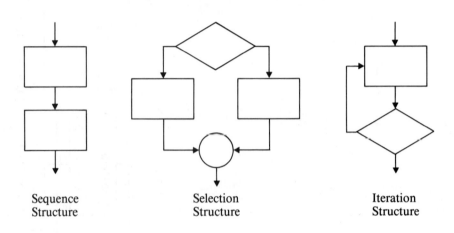

Sequence
Structure

Selection
Structure

Iteration
Structure

This is the manner in which the logic of a computer program evolves. You begin with a rather general description of what the system will do, and then the description becomes more specific at each step. The term **top-down design** has been used to describe this manner of starting with the overall system and then designing the subsystems to integrate properly so that the system goals may be met.

5. **Enter the Program**   The program instructions are now keyed into the computer—through either a terminal connected to a mainframe or a small computer.

6. **Compile the Program**   Programs written in BASIC, FORTRAN, PL/I, and so on, are in the language of the programmer. The program still must be converted into the language of the computer—machine language. This conversion process is called **compiling**. After the program written by the programmer (the **source program**) is entered into the computer, the computer uses a special type of system software, called a **compiler**, to convert the source program into machine language.[2] The output is an **object program** that can then be used to process the data.

7. **Correct Syntax Errors**   There are two kinds of errors that you can make in coding a program—syntax and logical. A **syntax error** is a violation of the language's rules. As an example, you leave out a comma or put in a space where it doesn't belong. A **logical error** occurs if you code a command properly, but it is the wrong command; for example, you want to subtract a sales discount but you add it instead.

During the compile process, any syntax errors are noted and displayed on the screen. These are corrected, and the computer is instructed to compile again. This process is repeated until a program with no syntax errors (a **clean compile**) is obtained.

---

2. Most programs that translate a BASIC source program into machine language are not called compilers but interpreters. That distinction will be explained in a later chapter.

Figure 4.14   A Program Flowchart

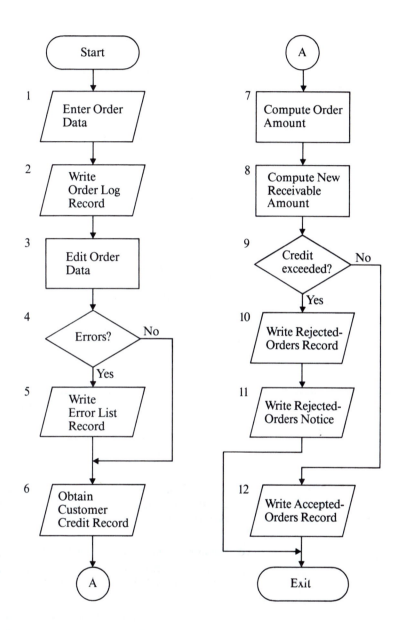

8. **Test the Program**   When a clean compile is achieved, the program can be executed with test data. The programmer creates a set of test data that checks each logical path and arithmetic operation in the program. For example, if you code a payroll program that computes overtime earnings for all employees working more than 40 hours, you should test the program with records containing fewer hours than 40, more than 40, and equal to 40. For each of the

Figure 4.15   Pseudocode

Start
Enter order data
Write order log record
Edit order data*
IF order contains errors THEN
    write error list record
(ELSE)
ENDIF
Read customer credit record
DOWHILE this order
   Multiply order quantity times unit price
      giving price extension
   Add price extension to invoice amount
ENDDO
Add invoice amount to accounts receivable
    giving new accounts receivable credit
    limit THEN
   Write rejected orders record
   Write rejected orders notice
ELSE
   Write accepted orders record
ENDIF
Exit

*The detail of the editing process is not shown.

From McLeod, *MIS*, Second Edition, SRA, 1983, p. 574, Figure 17-20.

three groups, the calculations for regular and overtime earnings should be performed with a desk calculator and compared with the computer output.

9. **Correct Logical Errors**   The programmer examines the test results and makes any corrections that are necessary. Then it is necessary to recompile and repeat steps 6 through 9 in the flowchart.

10. **Implement the Program**   When the logical errors have been corrected, the program is implemented, and the user monitors its performance to ensure that it is doing what was intended.

11. **Maintain the Program**   Once implemented, a system may be used for years. Over time, situations change. Perhaps the government changes a tax law, the firm adds a new product line, or a supplier changes the way it computes trade discounts. These changes must be reflected in the computer programs. The activity designed to keep the system current is called **program maintenance**. A significant portion of a firm's programming activity, perhaps half, is devoted to such maintenance.

    This step is not included in Figure 4.10 because all of the steps (1 through 10) must be repeated. The program modifications originate with the user, are communicated first to the systems analyst, and then communicated to the programmer, who makes the changes to the program. It is quite common, in large installations, for this maintenance activity to be carried out by analysts and programmers different from the ones who initially developed the program.

This requirement of maintaining a program is one of the major differences between business and scientific computing. Scientific computing typically involves development of a computer solution, and then the program is never used again. That is not the case in business, where some programs in use today were initially written twenty years ago.

This difference in the program life cycle helps explain the difference in popularity of certain programming languages. Languages such as COBOL and PL/I lend themselves to maintenance because they are self-documenting. This feature makes it easier for a second programmer to maintain the program and because of this, these languages are preferred in business. Other languages, such as APL and C may be more powerful, but they are more difficult to maintain.[3]

3. Many textbooks are available to explain the details of FORTRAN, COBOL, PL/I, BASIC, and Pascal programming. There is much less literature on APL and C. For a readable summary of APL, see Jacques Bensimon, "STC APL*PLUS and IBM PC APL," *Byte* 9 (March 1984): 250, 252, 253. A good description of C can be found in James Joyce, "A C Language Primer: Part 1," *Byte* 8 (August 1983): 64ff, and same author, "A C Language Primer: Part 2," *Byte* 8 (September 1983): 289ff.

Summary

There is no doubt that the trend is away from programming your own software, and toward purchasing packaged software. Most of the packaged software, however, is designed to perform data processing tasks, rather than provide management information. At the present time, if a firm is to provide its managers with a complete set of periodic reports and an ability to simulate a wide variety of operations, programming is a must. And, this situation is not likely to change dramatically within the next few years. The computer is a tool. And, just like any tool, if you understand how to get it to work for you, then you are its master—rather than vice versa.

There are many programming languages from which to choose. Each is designed to solve a particular type of problem. FORTRAN and APL are especially suited to solving mathematical problems. COBOL, assembler, and PL/I are intended for processing large volumes of business data. Of the newer languages, BASIC is used to perform both mathematical and data processing tasks. Designed for terminal use, BASIC has become the most popular language for small computers. Other languages, such as Pascal and C, are less often used by computer users to code their own applications software. C, however, is popular with software houses because of its portability.

The programming process involves a number of steps. In the beginning, the user and the systems analyst agree on an approach, then the analyst documents that approach and passes this information on to the programmer who codes, debugs, and tests the program. Once implemented, the program is monitored by the user and maintained so that it conforms to changing needs.

In the small-systems area, BASIC is the language most often used. It is easy to learn, and many enhancements have been added over the years so that it offers file handling and output capabilities that make it very attractive for business use. In the next two chapters, we will learn how to code introductory programs in BASIC and gain an appreciation for its potential as a DSS tool.

Key Terms

Prewritten, packaged, and off-the-shelf software
Programmer
Binary coding system
Mnemonics
Assembly program, assembler
Machine-oriented language
FORTRAN (FORmula TRANslator)
COBOL (COmmon Business Oriented Language)
Self-documenting language
Problem-oriented language
RPG (Report Program Generator)
PL/I (Programming Language I)
Structured programming
BASIC
   (Beginner's All-purpose Symbolic Instruction Code)
Interpreter
APL (A Programming Language)

Pascal
C
Programming process
Systems analyst
System flowchart
Structure chart
Heirarchy diagram
Program flowchart
Pseudocode
Top-down design
Compiling
Source program
Compiler
Object program
Syntax error
Logical error
Clean compile
Program maintenance

Questions   (Do not fill in blanks in the book. Write answers on a separate piece of paper.)

1. Custom programming is usually too slow to be used in preparing _____ reports.

2. Thus far, special _____ languages such as DYNAMO and SIMSCRIPT have not been developed for the PC.

3. Overall, the best programming strategy is to make _____ buy.

4. The only language that the computer can understand is _____ language.

5. A _____ name is one that helps the programmer remember what data is stored at a certain location.

6. A(n) _____ program is one using symbolic names to represent the data.

7. One of the first scientific languages was _____, announced by IBM in 1957.

8. The first special language designed specifically for business was _____.

9. A COBOL program is said to be _____ because of its ability to describe data and processes using English-like structures.

10. COBOL and FORTRAN are both examples of a _____ language.

11. _____ was intended to ease the conversion of business systems from punched card machines to computers.

12. IBM developed a hybrid of COBOL and FORTRAN called _____.

13. The most popular language used on small computers is _____.

14. Three languages that are currently vying for recognition as major languages are _____, _____, and _____.

15. The first step in writing a program is to _____.

16. The programmer usually does not work directly with the user; that responsibility belongs to the _____.

17. To blueprint a program's structure into hierarchical levels, a _____, also called a _____, is made; it has the same general appearance as an organizational chart.

18. The currently popular approach for developing a computer-based system where you begin with the overall system and then develop subsystems is known as _____ design.

19. When you compile a program, the _____ program is transformed into the _____ program.

20. The computer points out the _____ errors to you, but you must find the _____ errors through a well-planned testing program.

5 Introduction to BASIC Programming

BASIC is the most popular language used with microcomputers. It is easy to learn, yet capable of producing sophisticated analyses. In this chapter, you will be introduced to the basics of BASIC. As you study this and the other software chapters, keep in mind that this material is intended to be supplemented by classroom demonstration and explanation. First observe how the software is used. Then read the chapters and work the exercises using the PC. The chapters provide you with the rules. The more time you spend on the PC applying the rules, the better you will understand the software.

Overview

The BASIC of today is a far cry from the first version developed at Dartmouth in 1962. The original intent was to keep it simple so that it would be easy to use. As BASIC gained popularity, the various firms supplying the BASIC interpreters and compilers made changes and additions. The result is a multitude of variations—some of which have grown to be quite sizable. The IBM PC BASIC manual lists some 78 different instructions that can be used. Many of these have special uses, such as the preparation of graphics and use of the color monitor. You can code respectable programs using a much smaller subset of the whole. In this and the following chapter, we explain 14 of the instructions. This may seem like a small number (and it is), but with these 14 instructions you can code programs that prepare periodic reports and perform simulations of the firm's activity.

Whereas some languages have become standardized on a national or international scale (FORTRAN and COBOL are good examples), BASIC has not. This means that BASIC programs are not completely **portable**. A program is portable if it can be executed on various computers. The seriousness of this problem depends on the hardware involved. Many computers use Microsoft BASIC, so a program is fairly portable from one of these computers to the next. However, the BASIC languages of some computers are so unique that they pose a problem. The Apple IIe is a good example. Its method of printing is quite unlike computers such as the Radio Shack TRS-80 and the PC.

The closer that you stick to the original BASIC design, the more portable the program becomes. The method here is to use only the fundamental options. The BASIC will be "plain vanilla." Although we could enhance the language, with certain bells and whistles, we will not do that. For example, the PC version permits you to use rather descriptive names for the variable—names such as EMPLOYEE-NUMBER, GROSS-PAY, and so on. But, the original BASIC specified that names would contain only one letter, or a letter and a number, or a letter and a dollar sign. We will follow the original guideline, since all versions of BASIC will accept that scheme.

A Procedural Language

Many software packages on the market today are receiving widespread acceptance—VisiCalc, dBASE II, and WordStar are examples. These packages are not programming languages, as such. They are special-purpose software systems that are designed to solve particular types of problems. The user of these packages is therefore constrained in certain respects.

A programming language, however, consists of a set of instructions that perform many different tasks. It is left to the programmer to assemble these instructions in the proper sequence for processing. The programming language, coupled with the PC hardware, represent a powerful tool for the programmer to use. Much is left to the programmer, however, in determining how to use the tool.

The term **procedural language** describes bona fide programming languages such as BASIC. The term stresses the ability of the language to follow a step-by-step procedure in solving a problem. A big problem may require several hundred steps. Just a handful of BASIC instruction types, arranged in various sequences by the programmer, provide an almost infinite mix of procedures that can be followed to solve many different types of problems. This is the real value of BASIC compared with the more specialized software.

Loading BASIC

When you are ready to (1) code a new program in BASIC, or (2) execute a BASIC program stored on a diskette, you must first go through the DOS "box" that we described in Chapter 2. If you are unclear as to what DOS is and what it does, refer to Chapter 2 before proceeding with BASIC.

Put your DOS diskette in drive a: and boot the system. This diskette should also contain either the disk BASIC (BASIC) or advanced BASIC (BASICA) program. If you have BASIC, respond to the A> prompt by entering

BASIC

If you have BASICA, respond with

BASICA

For our purposes, the BASIC program is adequate. We will not make use of the advanced features, such as graphics, that are included in BASICA.

When you enter BASIC or BASICA (from this point on we will simply use the word BASIC), that language processor is read into primary storage from the logged diskette, and you get the **BASIC prompt**—the word OK with a flashing underline mark below it.

Keyboard Use

In this, and all other software chapters, the word *enter* is used when you are to press the Enter key after keying in data or an instruction. The word *type* is used when you do not have to press Enter.

The Function Keys

At the bottom of the screen, you will see a row of labels. These labels identify the special uses of the function keys while using BASIC. We will not use all of the operations represented by the ten function keys. We will only use the first four:

F1   LIST
F2   RUN—
F3   LOAD"
F4   SAVE"

When you want to list your program press F1 and then Enter. When you want to execute your program, just press the F2 key—you do not have to press Enter. To load or save a program, use the F3 and F4 keys—they even type the beginning quote mark for you.

Use of the function keys is optional. They can save you a few keystrokes.

Shifting to Uppercase

Each time you boot the system, the keyboard is set to lowercase. It is perfectly acceptable to keep it that way throughout your BASIC session. If you want your output to be in capital letters, however, press the Caps Lock key. This is the toggle key that is turned on or off each time you press it.

Clearing Primary Storage

It is always a good idea to clear the portion of primary storage that you will be using for your BASIC program before it is keyed in or loaded from a diskette. Otherwise, the next program will be "merged" into the existing one, and you will end up with an unusable program.

You clear storage by entering the word **NEW** in response to the BASIC prompt.

Keying in Your Program

First you will learn how you key in a new program. Later, we will discuss how to load a program from the diskette. As you enter your program, there are a few things you need to know. They are briefly described here.

Using the Keyboard

You will key your program into the keyboard in practically the same manner as you type on the typewriter. The letters can be upper- or lowercase—BASIC interprets both in the same way. Just be certain that you use the numeric keys for the digits (don't use the lowercase L for a 1, or the letter O for a zero). You can use the numeric keys across the top of the keyboard or in the numeric keypad.

After you type a line, press the Enter key (↵), which is just to the left of the numeric keypad. You enter your characters into primary storage by pressing the Enter key.

Correcting an Error Before It Is Entered

If you are typing in a BASIC instruction and make a mistake, you can correct it by backspacing to the error point and rekeying. Use the Backspace key—the large key just above Enter.

Correcting an Error After It Is Entered

If an instruction is found to have an error, and it has already been entered, you must rekey the entire line—including the line number. This replaces the old line with the new one.

If you want to delete a line, just type the line number and press Enter.

The Basic Program

A BASIC program consists of several **instructions**. Some people use the term **statement** to mean instruction. Each instruction is on a separate line, and each line must be numbered. The **line numbers** determine the sequence in which the instructions will be executed. You can enter the program lines in any sequence, but they will be executed in order of their number. And each time you list your program, the instructions will be in the proper order.

In numbering the lines, it is a good idea to number by tens—10, 20, 30, and so on. This will enable you to go back and insert additional instructions in-between original program lines.

After you have completely debugged your program, you can renumber the lines (by tens) by keying in the command **RENUM** in response to the BASIC prompt. A **command** tells the PC to perform a major operation. We will identify several more commands later in the chapter.

BASIC Instructions

Each line begins with an instruction that tells the PC to do something. For example, the READ instruction causes a record to be read and its data placed in primary storage. As mentioned earlier, we will learn 14 of these instruction types.

Objects of the Instructions

Each instruction is an individual "order" for your PC to perform a task. The instruction consists of the order (like a verb in a sentence) and the object of the order (like an object in a sentence).

The BASIC object may be the name of a data item. An example is the instruction READ X. The X is the name of a data item. After the instruction is executed, that value (maybe "23") is stored at the primary storage location named X and will remain in storage until you give X another value or turn the computer off.

In this example, X is the name of a **variable**. A variable is a value that can change during the course of the processing. A 23 may be read into location X from the first record, a 48 can be read from the second record, and so on. Programs are written with variable names so that the same instructions can be used over and over to process different data. The term *looping* is used to describe the process in which a program repeats a sequence of instructions for multiple records with different values.

Each instruction can include *multiple objects*. You could instruct the PC to PRINT A, B, C. In this example, the values stored in locations A, B, and C will be displayed ("printed") on the screen from left to right. Also, the object can be a **constant**, rather than the name of a variable. As an example, the arithmetic instruction is the LET instruction. If you want to add 1000 to the value stored at location Q, enter LET Q = Q + 1000. We are saying "Take the value at Q, add 1,000 to it, and put the new value back at Q."

In addition to variables and constants, the object of an instruction can be a line number. The GOTO instruction is an example. If you wanted the PC to next execute the instruction at line 120 (rather than the one following the current instruction), you would enter GOTO 120.

All of the instructions used as examples here would have a line number preceding them if they were part of a program. For illustrative purposes, they might appear in a program as follows. (The lines represent other instructions.)

---

30 READ X

---

90 LET Q = Q + 1000
100 GOTO 120

---

160 PRINT A, B, C

Naming Variables

In your program you must give names to all of the variables; they can be named to represent values such as customer number, sales amount, and sales tax. These values change from one transaction to the next. In this text, we are assuming a variable name must be one alphabetic character, or one alphabetic character followed by a number.

Examples: C   (for customer number)
           A   (for sales amount)
           T1 (for sales tax)

These names are used for *numeric* data. If the data is alphabetic, such as customer name, the second position must be a dollar sign.

Examples: C$ (for customer name)
           E$ (for employee name)

Each variable name should identify only one variable in a program. For example, you couldn't use S to represent both sales amount and sales date. You would have to make the names unique, such as S1 for sales amount and S2 for sales date.

Data Input

The two fundamental ways to process data are (1) batch processing or (2) online processing. In **batch processing**, all of the transactions are accumulated and processed together. It is a "mass production" approach, and is the most economical way to process data in terms of the computer time and resources needed. In **online processing**, an input device is used to key in each transaction—one at a time. Very often, the transaction is entered as it occurs. Point-of-sale terminals in a department store are a good example. When you code a program in BASIC, you have the choice of which type of processing to do, and your choice determines how the data is entered.

You can create a program either to read data from an "internal" file or to have the user enter data from the keyboard into the CPU for processing. The processed data (the output information) can be either displayed on the screen or printed on a printer.

Batch Processing

You can write a program to process data in batches. Each time you want to enter data, you code:

nn READ variable name, variable name, ...

The nn is the line number.

One or more variables may be entered with one READ instruction. For example:

            10 READ X
            40 READ N, C, A

The data must be part of the program, each line identified with a DATA instruction. For example:

50 DATA 10, 20, 23, 28

When the PC executes the first READ instruction, it reads only the first data item(s). The next time the instruction is executed the next item(s) is(are) read. It doesn't make any difference how many data items are included in one line. All of the following produce identical results:

```
10  DATA  10, 20, 23, 28

            or

10  DATA  10, 20
20  DATA  23, 28

            or

10  DATA  10
20  DATA  20
30  DATA  23
40  DATA  28
```

The DATA lines can appear anywhere in the program. Programmers usually place them at the end, just before the last instruction—the END instruction.

Online Processing You can write a program so that you can enter the data through the keyboard. When the program execution reaches the point where the data is needed, a **PRINT** instruction is executed that displays the instructions for entering the data. The PRINT instruction looks like this:

nn PRINT "instructions or question"

The instructions are enclosed in quotation marks. For example,

80 PRINT "ENTER SALES AMOUNT"

The instruction ENTER SALES AMOUNT is displayed on the screen so that you, or someone else using the program, will know what to type.

Sometimes, your program asks a question. For example,

120 PRINT "DO YOU WISH TO RUN AGAIN? (Y–YES/N–NO)"

Everything within the quotation marks is displayed on the screen.

Immediately following the PRINT instruction is an **INPUT** instruction. When the execution reaches the INPUT instruction, the execution stops and waits for you to enter the data or respond.

Let's assume that you are to enter a sales amount. The interactive portion of the program is as follows:

80 PRINT "ENTER SALES AMOUNT"
90 INPUT S

The letter S is the variable name given to the quantity that you will enter from the keyboard. When execution reaches line 90, execution stops with the prompt from line 80 displayed on the screen. You key in the amount and press Enter. Execution resumes with the next instruction, and the amount that you entered is stored in primary storage at a location named S.

If the program asks a question, the PRINT and INPUT instructions have this appearance:

120 PRINT "DO YOU WISH TO RUN AGAIN? (Y–YES/N–NO)"
130 INPUT R$

The variable name for the response (Y or N) has a dollar sign in the second position, since the response letters are alphabetic.

In addition to PRINT and INPUT, a third instruction facilitates the interactive display. It is **CLS** (clear screen), which clears the screen of any material displayed on it so that the prompt will appear at the top of the screen. Just include the CLS statement prior to PRINT:

```
70 CLS
80 PRINT "ENTER SALES AMOUNT"
```

Output

The **PRINT** instruction displays the output from your program on the screen. If your system has a printer you can use **LPRINT** to prepare hardcopy output. We will always use PRINT in our explanations, but LPRINT works exactly the same way.

Print Zones

The print line (on the screen and on the printer) is divided into print zones of 14 positions each. If you code:

```
160 PRINT A, B, C
```

the value for A will print in zone 1, beginning in print position 1. The value for B will print in zone 2, beginning in position 15. The value for C will print beginning in position 29.

All data, numeric and alphabetic (discussed in the next chapter) always begins in the left-most position of the zone. When you separate the variables with commas, you tell the computer that you want each value to print in a zone.

If you include more than six variables, the value of the seventh variable prints on the second line beginning in position 5. This is called a **wrap-around**. This is the situation if you use DOS 1.1 and the disk version of BASIC. You may only be able to get five variables on a line with other operating systems and BASIC versions. You can only display or print 80 characters on a line. (Some printers with wider carriages and paper permit more.)

Line Spacing

You insert blank lines by using **empty PRINT instructions**. An empty PRINT instruction is one with only the word PRINT.

```
140 PRINT X
150 PRINT
160 PRINT Y
```

The above sequence produces double spacing. Line 150 "prints" a blank line separating the value of X and Y.

Ending Your Program

You identify the end of your program with an END instruction. For example:

```
999 END
```

Some programmers like to use a large line number for the end instruction such as 999. The largest line number that BASIC will accept is 65529.

The END instruction doesn't have to be the last line in your program, but it usually is. When it is reached, regardless of where you have coded it, program execution stops.

**Listing and Running
Your Program**

To see your program on the screen so that you can edit it and correct errors, type **LIST** in response to the BASIC prompt. You can list your program on the printer by typing **LLIST**.

When you are ready to execute the program, type **RUN** in response to the BASIC prompt.

Editing Your Program

To correct typing errors in your program, just move the cursor to the error location (using the arrow keys) and retype. The characters that you type replace those previously there.

Use the up and down arrow keys to move the cursor to the appropriate line. You can move the cursor from the left to the right one word at a time by holding down the Ctrl key while you press the right arrow key. Pressing the Ctrl key and the left arrow produce quick moves to the left.

If you want to *insert* extra characters, move the cursor to the right of the position where the characters are to be added and press the Ins (Insert) key. Then type the characters. Press Enter when you have finished.

To *delete* characters, move the cursor to the first character to be deleted, and strike the Del (Delete) key. The character is deleted, and characters to the right move to the left one position. To delete multiple characters in a string, keep pressing the Del key. Press Enter when you are finished to store the edited line.

These procedures enable you to edit your program easier and faster than simply retyping a line.

Some Program Examples

Now let's look at some examples of simple BASIC programs using the instructions that we have described thus far. Then, you can code some similar programs and execute them on the PC as exercises.

A Batch Processing Example

```
10  READ  J, K, L
20  PRINT  K, L, J
30  DATA  30, 10, 20
60  END
```

Three variables are read—J, K, and L. And, they are printed in a different order —K, L, and J. Each variable is printed in a zone. Variable K is printed starting in position 1, L is printed starting in position 15, and J is printed starting in position 29. The printing is **left-justified** (printed on the left side) in each zone.

All of the DATA values are included in one line. The sequence of the values must correspond to the sequence of the variables in the READ instruction. This is very important; it is the only way that the PC knows which value is associated with each variable.

Note that the variables are separated with a comma followed by a space. Using a comma by itself is also okay. A space by itself does not separate variables. The same rule applies to listing the values in the DATA instruction.

The data could have been entered as:

```
30  DATA  30
40  DATA  10
50  DATA  20
```

We could have designed the program so that the user could enter the data through the keyboard.

```
10 PRINT "ENTER J"
20 INPUT J
30 PRINT "ENTER K"
40 INPUT K
50 PRINT "ENTER L"
60 INPUT L
70 PRINT K, L, J
80 END
```

The output is the same as in the batch example. Only the input is different. Note that there is no DATA instruction. We could have entered all three input values at one time:

```
10 PRINT "ENTER J, K, L"
20 INPUT J, K, L
```

In this example, you would separate the values with a comma or a comma and a space as they are entered in the keyboard. As an example, you would key in 30, 10, 20 or 30,10,20.

**Exercise 1
Load BASIC**

1. Turn on the PC. If you have a color monitor, turn it on first. Then, turn on the system unit. You will not need a printer for these exercises, so if you have one, leave it turned off.

2. If the PC is already on, boot it by pressing the Ctrl + Alt + Del keys.

3. Enter the date. Bypass the time by pressing Enter.

4. Enter **BASIC** (or **BASICA**) in response to the A> prompt.

**Exercise 2
Batch Input**

1. Clear storage by entering NEW.

2. Create a program to input four variables (A, B, C, D) and print them out in reverse order. Include all values in one DATA instruction. The values are: A = 250, B = 600, C = 375, D = 125.

3. List the program by entering **LIST** in response to the BASIC prompt.

4. Execute your program by entering **RUN** in response to the BASIC prompt.

**Exercise 3
Separate DATA Lines**

1. Modify the previous exercise by using four data instructions (one for each variable) rather than one. First, delete the old data line by typing the line number and pressing Enter. Then, enter four new DATA lines in the same slot in your program. For example, if your old DATA line was 30, the new ones could be 30, 32, 34, 36. You can add the new lines below the original program.

2. List your revised program.

3. Execute your program by entering **RUN**.

Exercise 4
Online Input

1. Clear storage.

2. Enter a program that allows you to enter four variables from the keyboard. The variables are A, A1, B, B1. Print them out on two lines—A and A1 on one line and B and B1 on another. Hint: This will require two PRINT instructions. The four variables should be entered with separate INPUT instructions.

3. List the program.

4. Execute the program. Enter the following values: A = 10, A1 = 12, B = 40, B1 = 60.

Exercise 5
One INPUT Statement

1. Modify the above program so that all four data items are entered with a single input instruction.

2. Renumber the lines by entering RENUM.

3. List the program.

4. Execute the program using the same values as in Exercise 4.

Arithmetic Operations

Many arithmetic operations are performed with the **LET** instruction. For example, if you want to *add* the value named A to the value named B and let the sum equal C, you would enter:

$$160 \ \text{LET} \ C = A+B$$

Of course, you must previously have stored values at locations A and B, perhaps with READ or INPUT or other arithmetic instructions.

To *subtract*, you use the minus sign (dash):

$$170 \ \text{LET} \ D = C-A$$

To *multiply*, use an asterisk:

$$200 \ \text{LET} \ X = Y*Z$$

To *divide*, use a slash or diagonal:

$$220 \ \text{LET} \ M = N/P$$

The value N is divided by the value P, and the quotient stored in M.

Spacing within the LET instruction is not critical. Whether you use multiple spaces or no spaces between the characters, the PC understands them the same way. The following produce the same result:

$$220 \text{LETX} = Y+Z$$
$$220 \ \text{LET} \ X = Y + Z$$

You do not even need the space after the line number. This applies to all BASIC instructions.

Exponentiation and
Square Roots

You raise a number to a certain power by using a caret:

$$110 \ \text{LET} \ Y = X^2$$

In this example, the value X is squared, and the result stored at Y.

The exponent can be a variable:

110 LET Y = X^B

Here, the value at B will determine the power to which X is raised.

You can calculate a square root by including SQR before the value or equation:

60 LET V = SQR(R)
300 LET F = SQR(2 * A * B)

Multiple Arithmetic Operations

You can perform multiple arithmetic operations in a single instruction.

300 LET E = (B + (C − D)) * F

Execution always begins within the inner parenthesis and works outward. The term **nested** is used to describe operations enclosed in parentheses within parentheses. The example above includes *nested parentheses*. Here D is first subtracted from C, and the difference is added to B. The sum of this operation is multiplied by F.

The sequence in which operations are performed is important. For example, if p = 4, q = 5, r = 27, s = 3, and z = 2, and you code:

40 LET X = P * Q + R / S^Z

Exponentiation is done first—(S^Z). That portion of the expression is given a value of 9.

Next, multiplication and division are performed moving from left to right—(P×Q) and (R / S^Z). The values in the expression are now 20 + (27/9), or 20 + 3.

Finally, any addition and subtraction are performed, moving from left to right (PQ + R/S^Z). The value 23 is stored at location X.

Some Arithmetic Examples

In a payroll program, you multiply rate (R) times hours (H) to get gross pay (G).

10 READ R, H
20 LET G = R * H
30 PRINT R, H, G
40 END

If employees receive time-and-a-half for all hours worked over 40, you code:

10 READ R, H
20 LET G = 40 * R + (H − 40) * R * 1.5

In this example, we assume that all employees work more than 40 hours. This is not a realistic assumption, but is necessary at this point. (Later, when we learn how to make logical decisions, we will use an IF instruction to handle the situation properly.)

This example includes one set of parentheses. Its contents (H − 40) will be computed first. Then, multiplication and division are performed from left to right.

First   40 * R
Second   (H − 40) * R
Third   (H − 40) * R * 1.5

Finally, any addition and subtraction are performed from left to right:

$$40 * R + (H - 40) * R * 1.5$$

Another example is the EOQ formula discussed in Chapter 3.

$$EOQ = \sqrt{\frac{2AS}{UR}}$$

In BASIC, this formula could appear as:

nn LET E = (2 * A * S / (U * R))^.5

We can compute the square root by raising the parenthetical expressions to the one-half power. Or, we can use the built-in square root **function** that BASIC offers.

nn LET E = SQR (2 * A * S / (U * R))

A function is a series of instructions that can be triggered with a single abbreviation, such as SQR for square root. When you want the PC to compute a square root, you simply code SQR.

SQR is the only one of the several BASIC functions that we will introduce in this book. See the IBM BASIC manual for a description of the others.

Notice that in both EOQ instructions we enclosed U * R in parentheses. Had we not, the PC would have continued multiplying and dividing one variable at a time from left to right. The results would have been a BASIC instruction that computed:

$$EOQ = \sqrt{\frac{2AS}{UR}}$$

It doesn't hurt to use too many parentheses (as long as they do not change the sequence of computation). But, too few does affect how the PC performs calculations. As an example, these extra parentheses do not affect the sequence:

nn LET E = SQR((2 * A * S)/(U * R))

When you use several pairs of parentheses, *always* count the number of left ones and the number of right ones. They should be equal.

Exercise 6
Multiplication

1. Use READ/DATA instructions to read two variables—P (unit price) and Q (quantity). P = 12.50; Q = 8

2. Multiply P times Q and obtain T (total price).

3. Print a line with P, Q, and T.

Exercise 7
Two-step Computation

1. Use PRINT/INPUT instructions to enter two variables—E (employee number) and G (gross pay). E = 1220; G = 1,750.

2. Compute I (income tax) equal to 23 per cent of the gross. Hint: You will have to include a constant in the instruction, like the 2 in the EOQ instruction. Then subtract I from G to get N (net pay).

3. Print a line with E, G, I, and N.

Using the Printer

If your PC includes a printer, you can easily get hardcopy output by simply using **LLIST** instead of LIST and **LPRINT** instead of PRINT. Then, the output goes to the printer in addition to the screen.

The most popular printers used on the PC are the IBM Graphics Printer and the Epson MX and FX Series. A brief description is included in Chapter 1 (under the section entitled The Printer) of the procedure to follow in aligning the paper in one of these units.

It is possible to attach several varieties of printers to the PC. Your instructor will tell you how to turn the printer on and use the control keys if it is not one of the IBM or Epson models.

Storing Your Program

With your program only in primary storage, it will be deleted if you turn off the computer or load another program. To prevent this, you can store it on a diskette with the SAVE command. Just enter **SAVE** in response to the BASIC prompt, and follow it with a quote mark (") and a file name. For example:

SAVE"PAYROLL

You do not need to type an ending quote mark. The file name must not exceed 8 characters. Although it is possible to include several special characters such as $, %, and so on, it is a good practice to use just letters and digits. When you press Enter, the program will be stored on the diskette in the logged drive. The diskette must not be write protected.

If the logged drive is a: and you want to store the program on a diskette in the b: drive, add the drive identification as a prefix to the file name:

SAVE"B:PAYROLL

You always use the prefix to address a file on a diskette in a drive other than the logged drive.

Retrieving Your Program

To call up a program once you've stored it on a diskette, enter NEW to clear storage, and then enter

LOAD"file name

NEW and LOAD are both commands.

If you can't remember the name used to save the file, type FILES in response to the BASIC prompt to get a directory. (Remember that when you are in DOS you use another command, DIR.) But, FILES works only for the logged drive. If you want a directory of the diskette in the nonlogged drive you have to go back to DOS.

Returning to DOS

When you are in BASIC, and want to return to DOS, type **SYSTEM** in response to the BASIC prompt. SYSTEM is also a command. You get the DOS A> prompt. By pressing Ctrl + Alt + Del you also get back to DOS, but you have to reenter date and time.

Processing Multiple Transactions

So far, you have learned to handle only single transactions: reading a record, processing it, and outputting it.

The PC can handle multiple transactions, but you have to build a **loop** into the program so that the processing is repeated for each transaction. Use the **GOTO** instruction to set up the loop.

Let's go back to our first example of a batch program:

```
10 READ  J, K, L
20 PRINT  K, L, J
30 DATA  30, 10, 20
60 END
```

We can modify it so that it goes through a processing loop for each transaction read.

```
10 READ  J, K, L
20 PRINT  K, L, J
25 GOTO  10
30 DATA  30, 10, 20
40 DATA  10, 40, 5
50 DATA  300, 18, 70
60 END
```

The GOTO instruction at line 25 causes the execution to revert to line 10 and read another record. Notice also that we added two more data transactions at lines 40 and 50.

While this program might look good at first glance, we have a problem. You must tell the computer when to stop, and this program doesn't do that. Program execution will never reach line 60 since the GOTO at line 25 is always executed.

We can solve the problem by putting a special record at the end of the input file, such as one containing all zeros. This record is a **dummy end-of-file record.** Each time we read a record we can test to see if it is the dummy end-of-file record. If so, program execution can be directed to line 60. If not, execution continues with the PRINT instruction at line 20. In the next section you will see how this is accomplished.

Logical Operations

Logical operations are performed with the IF instruction. An IF instruction has the following forms:

```
nn IF expression GOTO line number
nn IF expression THEN line number
```

or

```
nn IF expression-1 THEN expression-2
```

The Line Number Form

In the **line number** form, if the expression is true, the next instruction executed is the one specified after the GOTO. Otherwise, the instruction immediately following the IF instruction is executed. An example is:

```
110
120 IF  A=B  GOTO  160
130
```

If the value of A is equal to the value at B, the next instruction is 160. Otherwise, it is 130. The instruction 120 IF A=B THEN 160 produces the same result.

This is the form of IF instruction that can solve the end-of-file problem. By inserting an IF/GOTO instruction at line 15 and a dummy end-of-file record at 55, the PC can determine when the end is reached. Line 55 is not a data record. It contains three fields, just like the data records, but the first field (J) contains a trailer value (0) that serves as an end-of-data marker.

```
10  READ  J, K, L
15  IF  J = 0  GOTO  60
20  PRINT  K, L, J
25  GOTO  10
30  DATA  30, 10, 20
40  DATA  10, 40, 5
50  DATA  300, 18, 70
55  DATA  0, 0, 0
60  END
```

The Expression-2 Form

In the **expression-2** form, some operation or operations (expression-2) is(are) performed only if expression-1 is true. For example:

$$180 \text{ IF } X > Y \text{ THEN LET } X = X + 1$$

The value at X is incremented by 1 only when X has a value greater than that of Y. Otherwise, expression-2 is not performed.

It is important to note that the line number form can change the sequence in which program instructions are executed; the expression-2 form cannot. Regardless of whether expression-1 is true or false, the next instruction is always the one immediately following the IF instruction.

Expression-2 can contain several BASIC operations, but it is better coding practice to include only a single one. If several are required, it is best to branch to another location, using the GOTO form, and perform those operations there.

Relational Operators

In an expression two values are compared with the following relational operators:

=	the two values are *equal*
<> or ><	the two values are *unequal*
>	the first value is *greater than* the second
<	the first value is *less than* the second
=> or >=	the first value is *equal to or greater than* the second
=< or <=	the first value is *equal to or less than* the second

The second value can be a variable or constant. For example:

```
60  IF  A > B  GOTO  140
90  IF  A = 8  THEN PRINT "ERROR"
```

IF/THEN/ELSE

The expression-2 form can be expanded so that you execute one expression (expression-2) when expression-1 is true, and another expression (expression-3) when expression-1 is false. The IF/THEN/ELSE statement takes this form:

nn IF expression-1 THEN expression-2 ELSE expression-3

We can use the IF/THEN/ELSE to solve the problem encountered earlier of some employees working over 40 hours and getting overtime, and others not. The following instruction includes the arithmetic in expression-2 that is executed for employees working over 40 hours, and the arithmetic in expression-3 that is executed for employees not working over 40 hours. Program execution for both groups resumes with the next instruction.

20 IF H > 40 THEN G = 40 * R + (H − 40) * R * 1.5 ELSE G = R * H.

Selecting from More than Two Alternatives

An IF instruction can be used to select between two alternatives. If there are more than two, multiple IF instructions are required. For an illustration, assume that there are four product classes—1, 2, 3, and 4. If we have just read an input record containing the class code (C), we can determine which code it is with four IF instructions:

```
60 IF C = 1 GOTO 100
70 IF C = 2 GOTO 200
80 IF C = 3 GOTO 300
90 IF C = 4 GOTO 400
100 GOTO 500
```

The routine for processing class code 1 records is at line 100, for code 2 records it is at line 200, and so on. Line 500 contains an **error routine**, since it is executed when a code is not in the 1–4 range. Perhaps the error routine prints out an error message and aborts (stops) the run. It would be a mistake to omit line 100 and replace line 90 with GOTO 400. Then, anything other than 1–3 would cause a branch to 400; it would not necessarily take a code 4 to cause the branch.

Exercise 8
Print, Save, Logic

1. Use READ/DATA instructions to enter three variables—B (balance on hand), R (reorder point), and Q (reorder quantity).

2. The data records are:

B	R	Q
100	90	150
225	250	350
16	16	50
0	32	60
300	210	500

3. If the balance on hand is *below* the reorder point, print a line on the printer with B in zone 1, R in zone 2, and Q in zone 3.

4. Save the program on your diskette as INVEN1.

5. Display the directory of the diskette containing INVEN1.

6. Return to DOS.

7. Display the directory of the INVEN1 diskette.

Exercise 9
Load and Modify a Saved Program

1. Clear storage and load INVEN1 from your diskette.

2. Modify the logic so that you print a line when the balance is *equal to or less than* the reorder point.

3. Execute the program and save it on your diskette as INVEN2.

4. Obtain a directory of the INVEN2 diskette while you are using BASIC. Do the same while in DOS.

Summary

A procedural programming language enables you to tailor the computer to the unique characteristics of your problem. The most popular procedural language for personal computers is BASIC. With only a few BASIC instructions you can prepare a wide variety of programs.

Each BASIC program is a list of instructions, with each instruction identified by a line number. Each instruction consists of an order to do something and an object. The object can be a variable, constant, or line number. The only order that does not have an object is END.

If you want to process your data in batches, you use READ and DATA instructions. If you want to enter your data online, you use PRINT and INPUT instructions.

Output can be displayed on the screen or printed on the printer. The data is positioned in print zones.

All arithmetic is performed by the LET instruction. You can add, subtract, multiply, divide, and raise numbers to certain powers. Parentheses are used to control the sequence of the calculation, which normally proceeds from left to right and from inner parentheses to outer parentheses.

The SAVE command stores programs on the diskette; the LOAD command retrieves them. Always type NEW before loading a program from the diskette or keying in a new program.

You process multiple transactions by building a loop into your program with the GOTO instruction. A dummy end-of-file record tells the computer when the last data record has been read.

Logical operations are performed by the IF instruction. If an expression is true, you can branch to another location in the program or perform an operation. The IF/THEN/ELSE form enables the program to perform one action when an expression is true, and another when the expression is false.

If your program must select between more than two alternatives, you need more than one IF instruction. Always include an error routine that handles unacceptable codes when the user enters improper data.

In this chapter you have learned all of the instructions necessary to prepare simple programs in BASIC. We have used the following instructions:

READ
DATA
PRINT, LPRINT
INPUT
CLS
END
LET
GOTO
IF

In addition, we used the following commands used in conjunction with BASIC:

> NEW
> RENUM
> LIST, LLIST
> RUN
> SAVE
> LOAD
> SYSTEM

In the next chapter, you will learn how to use some BASIC enhancements and how to solve more complex problems.

Key Terms

Portable
Procedural language
BASIC prompt
Instruction
Line number
Command
Variable
Constant
Batch processing
Online processing
Wrap-around
Empty PRINT instruction
Left-justified
Nested parentheses
Function
Loop
Dummy end-of-file record
Error routine

Questions   (Do not fill in blanks in the book. Write answers on a separate piece of paper.)

1. When a program can be processed on several different types of computers, it is said to be _____.

2. A _____ language is one containing a rather large set of instructions that enables the computer to perform a wide variety of operations.

3. Before you can code or execute a program written in BASIC you must type the words _____ or _____ in response to the DOS prompt.

4. The BASIC prompt is the word _____ with a flashing underline mark beneath it.

5. You clear storage of any previous program by entering _____ in response to the BASIC prompt.

6. Each instruction in a BASIC program must be preceded by a _____.

7. After you finish debugging your program you can cause the lines to be renumbered by tens by entering _____.

8. When naming alphabetic data you must include a _____ in the second position.

9. _____ processing accumulates and processes all transactions as a group, and _____ processing processes each transaction as it occurs.

10. When you are processing data in batches, a data record is made available for processing with the _____ instruction.

11. If your program includes READ instructions, it must also include _____ instructions.

12. The dialog between the user and the PC during online processing is accomplished with a combination of _____ and _____ instructions.

13. You display output on the screen with a(n) _____ instruction and on the printer with a(n) _____ instruction.

14. You can clear the screen by incorporating the _____ instruction in your program.

15. You "print" blank lines on the screen or printer by using _____ PRINT instructions.

16. The last instruction executed in your program is the _____ instruction.

17. Many arithmetic operations are performed with the _____ instruction.

18. Sets of parentheses included within outer sets are said to be _____.

19. If you wanted to compute an EOQ, you might use the square root _____.

20. In an IF statement the word THEN is followed either by a(n) _____ or a(n) _____.

1. READ sales records containing 4 variables—N (customer number), C (customer class), P (price), and Q (quantity).

2. READ the following DATA statements:

N	C	P	Q
123	1	10.00	6
150	2	7.50	8
168	2	9.95	3
291	2	0.98	12
406	1	4.49	14
551	2	29.29	4

3. Use a dummy end-of-file record.

4. Print a line on the printer for each record except the dummy end-of-file record.

5. Each line will contain (from left to right)—N, C, P, Q, and T (total price).

6. Total price for class 1 customers is computed by multiplying P times Q. Total price for class 2 customers is computed by multiplying P times Q, and then reducing the total price by 10 percent—a 10 percent price discount. There are only two classes of customers (1 and 2), but code your program so that you branch to the END statement if another digit is encountered.

7. Execute the program and save it as SALES1.

8. Obtain a hardcopy listing of the program.

1. Modify SALES1 to accept the input data through the keyboard, one variable at a time. Key question: How will you handle the end-of-file logic?

2. Execute the program and save it as SALES2.

3. Obtain a hardcopy listing of the program.

6 BASIC Programming Part 2

In Chapter 5 you learned the basics of BASIC. In this chapter you will learn some additional techniques that greatly increase the value of BASIC as a means of building decision support systems.

Processing Alphanumeric Data

Very often, you will need to include alphabetic data, such as customer name, in the data record. Also, you may need to include special characters, such as dollar signs, commas, and so on. The term **alphanumeric** describes alphabetic, numeric, and special character data. The alphanumeric field in the data record can contain any character in the PC character set—letter, digit, or a special character (including a blank). The rule for naming an alphanumeric variable is to include a dollar sign in the second position.

Exercise 1 Alphanumeric Data

1. Enter the following program:

```
10 READ C$, N, A
20 PRINT C$, N, A
30 DATA A&S RENTAL CO., 123, 10.00
40 END
```

2. Execute the program. Does it run correctly?

Exercise 2 Alphanumeric Data Names

1. Modify the program in Exercise 1 by removing the dollar sign from the alphanumeric data names.

2. Execute the program. Does it work?

Adding Comment Lines

You can add comments throughout your program with the **REM** (remark) instruction. These instructions are only for the benefit of someone who needs your program code; REM lines are not executed. For example, you may document the beginning of your program:

```
10 REM  INVENTORY PROGRAM
20 REM  WRITTEN BY SYLVIA SARDINAS
30 REM  DATE WRITTEN: JUNE 1, 1985
```

You can include REM instructions anywhere in the program—they are especially useful to separate major parts.

```
150 GOTO 20
160 REM  ********************
170 REM  END OF JOB ROUTINE
180 PRINT "FINAL TOTAL"; A
190 END
```

REM instructions are also a good way to incorporate a **data dictionary**, or a description of the data names, in your program. As an example, at the beginning of your program you can list all of the variables in the following format:

```
40  REM  DATA DICTIONARY
50  REM
60  REM  NAME  DESCRIPTION
70  REM  C    CUSTOMER NUMBER
80  REM  C$   CUSTOMER NAME
```

Expanding the Printing Capability

One aspect of a programming language that contributes to its complexity is its printing routines. The designers of the original BASIC solved this problem with the print zones. The zones are simple, but they offer limited capability. We can enhance the appearance of BASIC printed output by bypassing the zones, using "tab stops," chaining several print instructions together, and using a new PRINT instruction—PRINT USING.

Bypassing the Zones

If you separate variables with semicolons rather than commas, the variables will be printed closer together. Each numeric value will be followed by a space; each positive value will be preceded by a space; each negative value will be preceded by a minus sign.

If you code:

```
140  PRINT A; B; C; D; E
```

And D has a negative value, the print line will appear as:

```
_14_ _250_ _16_-420_ _312
```

(The underline marks are used to show where the spaces will be on the line; they do not print.)

The TAB Function

You can set "tab stops" on a print line, just as you can using a typewriter. Simply precede the variable with the word **TAB** followed by the print position in parentheses. Do not leave a space between the word TAB and the first parenthesis.

```
160  PRINT TAB(40) X
```

In the above example, the value for X will print beginning in position 40.

If you want to print several variables on the line, separate the variables with spaces or semicolons. *Do not use commas.* Both of the following produce identical results.

```
180  PRINT X  TAB(10) Y  TAB(20) Z
180  PRINT X; TAB(10) Y; TAB(20) Z
```

In these examples, X will print starting in position 1 since it has no TAB function, Y will print starting in position 10, and Z will print starting in position 20.

The variables are printed or displayed from left to right; therefore a tab stop cannot be to the left of a print position already used.

```
160  PRINT TAB(30) X TAB(20) Y
```

This example will cause Y to be printed on the next line beginning in position 20.

**Chaining Multiple
PRINT Instructions**

Several PRINT instructions can produce a single line by "chaining" them together with semicolons.

```
200 PRINT X;
210 PRINT Y;
220 PRINT Z
```

The instructions will print all three variables on the same line. The semicolon says, in effect, "Continue on the same line with the next PRINT instruction." Note that the last instruction is not followed by a semicolon.

**Exercise 3
Bypassing the
Print Zones**

1. Enter and execute the following program:

```
10 READ A, B, C, D
20 PRINT A, B, C, D
30 DATA 1, 2, 3, 4
40 END
```

2. Modify the program by replacing the commas in line 20 with semicolons. What happens when you execute the program?

3. Modify the program again by deleting the semicolons and adding TAB functions so that B prints in position 8, C in position 20, and D in position 50. Execute the program.

**Exercise 4
Chained Print
Statements**

1. Enter and execute the following program:

```
10 READ A, B, C, D
20 PRINT A;
30 PRINT B;
40 PRINT C;
50 PRINT D
60 DATA 1.234, 923.7, 10.50, 0.923654
70 END
```

2. Modify the program by deleting the semicolons in lines 20, 30, and 40. Execute the program. What happens?

**The PRINT USING
Instruction**

One of the reasons COBOL is so popular is its ability to add special characters to output data, and the way it aligns that data in an attractive format. The early versions of BASIC did not offer such a capability. A special PRINT instruction, **PRINT USING**, has been added to BASIC that gives it almost as much output excellence as COBOL.

If you code:

```
140 PRINT USING "$##,###.##"; Y
```

assuming that Y has a value of 12345.26, it will be printed as $12,345.26. Each pound sign designates where a digit can be printed, the number is aligned on its decimal point, and a comma is inserted for thousands of dollars. The space separating the semicolon and the variable name is optional.

With the previous PRINT USING instruction, the following values are printed as:

Value	Printed As:	Comment
01000.00	$1,000.00	1
100.00	$ 100.00	2
.25	$ 0.25	3
2.555	$ 2.56	4

Comment 1   Leading (leftmost zeros are eliminated)

Comment 2   If there are no thousands of dollars, the comma is not printed.

Comment 3   If there are no dollars, a zero is printed to the left of the decimal.

Comment 4   Rounding occurs on truncation. **Truncation** is the "chopping off" of characters when there is no space to print them. If the digit to be truncated is 5 or greater, the digit to the left is increased by 1.

An important consideration in using the PRINT USING instruction is how many pound signs to use. The pound signs serve as a **mask**. If the mask is too small for the data, you will get a condition called overflow. **Overflow** is the deletion of leftmost characters when there is no space to print them. In this case, you will be notified by a percent sign printed to the left of the number.

If R has a value of 123, and you code:

80 PRINT USING "##"; R

You will get:

%123

There is a difference between truncation and overflow: Truncation can occur either on the left or the right end of the number, and overflow always occurs on the left. You get no signal when truncation occurs; you get a percent sign signal on an overflow.

The real value of PRINT USING is in printing dollar and cents amounts. When such amounts are printed in the zones, with semicolons, or with the TAB function, they are left-justified. This means that the printout would appear as:

10.25
1.50
250.50
1234.75

As you can see, this appearance leaves something to be desired. With PRINT USING, the amounts print as:

10.25
1.50
250.50
1234.75

Another problem that is solved with PRINT USING is truncation of unwanted positions so that only two decimal positions will print—as "cents." If there are more than two decimal positions (such as 12.782), there is no way to get rid of the unwanted positions if you use the print zones, semicolons, or TAB function. Also, if there is only one decimal position (such as 12.7), there is no way to add a rightmost zero. PRINT USING handles both of these conditions:

Value	Printed As:
123.50	$123.50
123.501	$123.50
123.5	$123.50

In addition to aligning dollar and cents fields on the demical point, PRINT USING can also be used to right-justify integer fields. Otherwise, all numeric fields are left-justified. For example, the instruction PRINT USING "####"; X can produce:

$$123$$
$$6$$
$$42$$
$$6102$$

With PRINT USING, it is also possible to print an alphabetic "message" and a variable on the same line. You might want to print:

FINAL TOTAL $12,345.60

The proper term for the alphabetic message is **string constant**. The term *string* is used to describe an alphanumeric data field. You can obtain the desired results by chaining together two print commands:

180 PRINT "FINAL TOTAL" TAB(20);
190 PRINT USING "$##,###.##"; T

The line would appear as follows, with the string constant starting in position 1 and the total amount in position 20.

FINAL TOTAL $56,280.75

Whenever you want to print several variables on the same line, you can enter:

180 PRINT USING "## ## ##"; X, Y, Z

If X = 13, Y = 22, and Z = 16, the computer will print

13 22 16

The blank spaces within the quote marks provide the desired spacing.

You can obtain the same results by chaining multiple PRINT USING instructions with semicolons.

180 PRINT USING "## "; X;
190 PRINT USING " ## "; Y;
200 PRINT USING " ##"; Z

Notice the blank positions within each mask. They provide the desired spacing.

1. Use PRINT/INPUT instructions to enter the following data:

Employee No. (N)	Employee Name (N$)	Units Produced (U)
1004	SMITH, FRED	403
1110	ADAMS, ANNE	1287
1276	ROZEK, ADRIENNE	621
1342	JONES, AL	173
1379	PENNINGTON, WILFRED	1101
1401	DE LA ROSA, WILLIAM	844

2. Compute a "production bonus" by multiplying the number of units produced over 500 by $1.75. Employees not producing over 500 units get no bonus.

3. Print a line for each employee receiving a bonus. The line contains (from left to right) employee number, name, units produced, and bonus. Use the TAB function to properly align the numbers. Use the following tab stops:

Employee No.	10
Employee Name	20
Units Produced	45
Bonus	60

4. Use PRINT USING on the units produced column to achieve right-justification.

5. Use PRINT USING on the bonus column to print dollars and cents.

6. Execute the program and get a hardcopy output if your system includes a printer.

7. Save the program as BONUS on your diskette.

Printing Headings

You can print report headings such as report name, date, and column headings with string constants. As an illustration, you can print the report name with:

nn PRINT "   PAYROLL REPORT"

Notice that blanks spaces are included at the beginning of the constant so that the report name will be centered over the data columns. Blank spaces do not have to be included after the last character to print on the line.

If you are using the print zones to print the report data, you can print column headings using commas to separate each one.

nn PRINT "DATE","CUSTOMER NO.","AMOUNT"

Notice that each column heading is a string constant bounded by quote marks, and that the comma follows the quote mark.

The column heading and the data will both be left-justified in the zone:

ZONE

CUSTOMER NO.
123
4529
62

You notice that the string constant prints in the first position of the zone, but the numeric values do not. A space always precedes a positive numeric value.

The headings can also be aligned using the TAB function. That is a good way to get precise alignment.

nn PRINT "DATE" TAB(9) "CUSTOMER NO." TAB(22) "AMOUNT"

**Exercise 6
Headings**

1. Load your BONUS program and modify it to include a report named PRO-DUCTION BONUS REPORT, and a date line immediately below with the date PERIOD ENDING SEPTEMBER 30, 1985. Then, insert a blank line and print the column headings on two lines:

EMPLOYEE	EMPLOYEE	UNITS	
NUMBER	NAME	PRODUCED	BONUS

   Then, insert a blank line before listing the data.

2. Center the report name and date headings over the four data columns. Center each column heading over its data column.

3. After you execute the program, save it as BONUS2.

Printing Totals

In all of our examples thus far, we have been printing detail lines with no total lines at the bottom. In order to print the totals, they must be accumulated as the detailed data is processed (as transaction records are read).

As an example, let's read transaction records containing only sales amounts, print out the amounts as they are read, accumulate a total of all of the amounts, and print out the total at the end of the job. This is the first example of an **end-of-job routine**—something done at the end of the record processing. This type of processing is also called an **end-of-file routine**—something done when you reach the end of the input data file.

```
10 LET  T = 0
20 READ  A
30 IF  A = 0  THEN  70
40 LET  T = T + A
50 PRINT  A
60 GO TO  20
70 PRINT
80 PRINT  T
90 END
```

At line 10 the total field (T) is set to zero. This is called **initialization**. It is always a good idea to set fields to zero before they are used to accumulate totals. There might be data in those positions that were entered from a previous program, in which case you would add your amounts to that data, and your totals would be wrong.

The instruction that accumulates the amounts is at line 40. The empty PRINT statement at line 70 inserts a blank line between the listing of detail amounts and the total, which is printed at line 80. Lines 70 and 80 represent the end of job routine.

Figure 6.1   A Program Flowchart

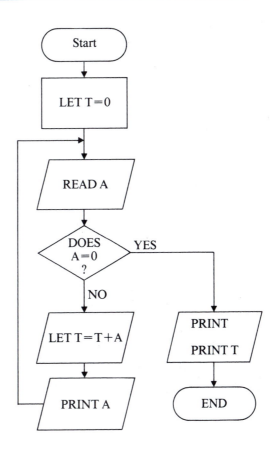

Figure 6.1 is a *program flowchart* of the program.[1] The oval symbols labeled
"Start" and "End" are **terminal symbols**—they identify the beginning and the
end of the process. The rectangle is the **processing symbol**, and is used to illustrate
an arithmetic operation that the computer performs, such as one within a LET
instruction. The parallelogram is the **input-output symbol**, and is used for the
READ, INPUT, and PRINT instructions. The diamond is the **logic symbol**, and
is used for the IF instruction. You can clearly see the loop in the program, as well
as the end-of-job routine.

Exercise 7
Totals

1. Modify your BONUS2 program so that both the units produced and the bonus
amount are accumulated.

2. At the end of the file, insert a blank line and print out the total units produced
and the total bonus so that they appear directly below their respective data
columns.

3. At the left of the totals, on the same line, print TOTALS.

4. Save the file as BONUS3.

1. The flowchart in Figure 6.1 is presented to illustrate program flow. Additional flowcharts will be used later in the
chapter for the same purpose. For a complete discussion of flowcharting, see any book devoted to the subject,
such as Marilyn Bohl, *Flowcharting Techniques* (Chicago: Science Research Associates, 1971).

Looping

You have learned that the GOTO instruction enables you to build a loop into your program. The loop allows you to repeat the processing for each data record. However, there are some instances when you want to go through the loop a certain number of times. Perhaps you have made a 24-month installment loan and you want to print out the remaining balance (B) for each month after each payment (P) is made. You would use a **FOR/NEXT loop** to control program execution so that the procedure is performed 24 times.

```
 80  FOR  X = 1 to 24
 90  LET  B = B − P
100  PRINT  B
110  NEXT  X
```

The **FOR** instruction marks the beginning of the loop, and the **NEXT** instruction marks its end. The loop's contents (lines 90 and 100) are performed the number of times specified in the FOR instruction. Both the FOR and the NEXT contain the variable X. Any variable name can be used, but it must be the same in both instructions—that is what "ties them together." The variable is called the **index variable**.

In the example, the 1 in the FOR instruction is called the **initial value**. The FOR causes the computer to count the number of times the loop is executed, and the initial value specifies where counting is to begin. The 24 is called the **terminal value**, and it sets the limit on the number of times the FOR/NEXT loop is executed. Here, we are saying "Starting at 1, keep a count of the number of times the loop is executed, and continue to execute it until you have done it 24 times."

The initial and terminal values can also be variables:

```
80  FOR  Q = 1 TO N
80  FOR  Z = X TO 4
80  FOR  P = R TO S
```

The FOR/NEXT loop is illustrated by the program flowchart segment in Figure 6.2. The hexagon is a **preparation symbol**; it is used to show how the loop is prepared by the FOR instruction for execution 24 times. The terminal symbol is used for the NEXT instruction. The two paths coming from the terminal symbol illustrate the sequence of program execution, depending on the value of X. After the FOR/NEXT loop has been executed the specified number of times, the instruction following the NEXT instruction is executed.

There is no standard way to flowchart the FOR/NEXT loop. The symbols used in Figure 6.2 are only one approach.

**Exercise 8
FOR/NEXT Loop**

1. Design a form that can be used for inventory clerks to complete when they take a physical inventory of warehouse merchandise at the end of the year. The form consists of 20 lines on a page, each containing the following:

   ITEM NO. _ _ _ _ _ NAME _ _ _ _ _ _ _ _ _ _ _ _ _ _ _ QUANTITY _ _ _ _ _

   There are 5 underline marks after the item number, 15 after the name, and 5 after the quantity.

2. Develop a BASIC program to print the page, using a FOR/NEXT loop. Double space the lines on the form.

3. Save the program as COUNT.

Figure 6.2   Flowchart of a FOR/NEXT Loop

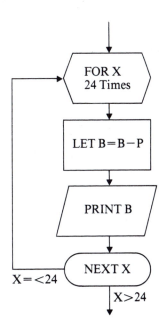

Exercise 9
Sales Simulator

1. Create a program to simulate 20 days of sales for a department store. Use a FOR/NEXT loop so that the program will be executed 20 times.

2. For each execution, read the number of units sold for that day, and multiply that number times the unit price of $19.95 to obtain sales revenue.

3. For each execution, print (from left to right) the day number, number of units sold, and sales revenue.

4. Print appropriate report and column headings.

5. Accumulate totals on units and sales revenue.

6. The daily sales units are 18, 20, 21, 24, 17, 12, 26, 29, 25, 25, 13, 14, 19, 21, 22, 18, 23, 28, 31, 40. Use READ/DATA instructions to enter the data. You do not need an end-of-file test after the READ since you know exactly how many data items to read.

7. Execute the program and save it as SALES.

Figure 6.3   Lists and Matrices

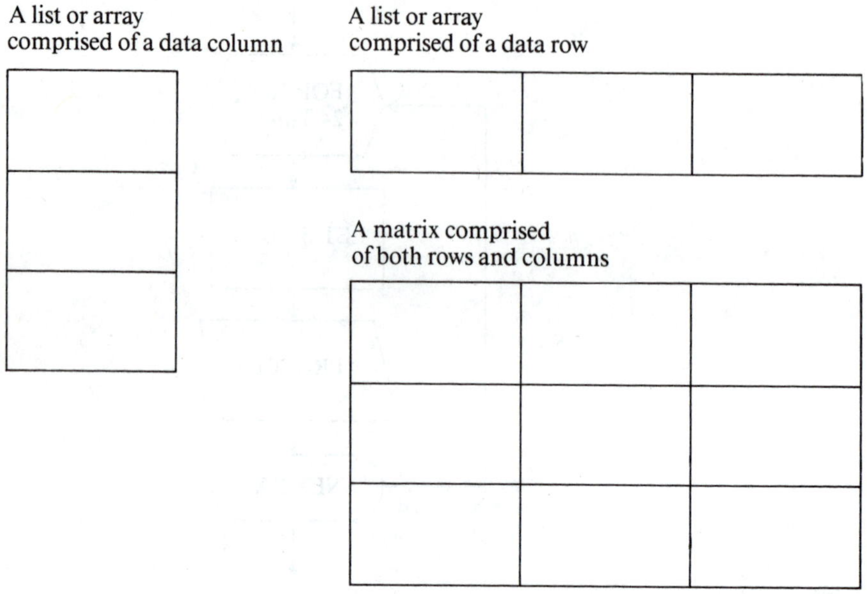

A list or array
comprised of a data column

A list or array
comprised of a data row

A matrix comprised
of both rows and columns

Lists and Matrices

All of the data that you have processed up until now has been single items. Very often, you will have to process data in lists or matrices. A **list**, or **array**, is a one-dimensional table. A **matrix** is a table of two or more dimensions. You can think of a list as a vertical column or a horizontal row of data. See Figure 6.3. The column or row provides the single dimension. A matrix has both rows and columns, as illustrated in the figure. The rows and columns provide the two dimensions.

Giving the List Dimension

You must first specify how many entries, called **cells**, are in the list. This is done with a **DIM** (dimension) instruction.

$$40 \ \text{DIM} \ X(10)$$

Here we are saying, "Set up a list of 10 cells, and call it X."

Initializing the List

You then usually initialize the list cells, giving them certain values. If you wanted to set each cell to a value of 0, you would code:

```
120 FOR L = 1 TO 10
130 LET X(L) = 0
140 NEXT L
```

You will notice that each cell in list X is referred to with a subscript (L). Hence, X is a **subscripted variable**. In this example, we are using the index variable in the FOR/NEXT loop as the subscript. Each time the loop is executed, a different cell in X will be initialized to 5, starting with cell 1 and ending with cell 10.

Printing the List

If you wanted to print the list, you would code:

```
200 FOR  P  =  1  TO  10
210 PRINT  X(P)
220 NEXT  P
```

Exercise 10
Dimension and
Initialize a List

1. Dimension a list called L with 15 cells.

2. Initialize each cell to zero. Use a FOR/NEXT loop containing a LET instruction.

3. Save the program as TABLE1.

Loading the List

To load the list with data, you set up a FOR/NEXT loop containing a READ instruction, as follows:

```
60 FOR  L  =  1  TO  10
70 READ  X(L)
80 NEXT  L
90 DATA  6, 2, 1, 3, 4, 0, 8, 9, 5, 7
```

The list name (X) is the same one used in the DIM instruction. You can use the same index variable name (L, for example) over and over in the same program if you like. Once you exit a FOR/NEXT loop, you can use the same index variable name again.

Exercise 11
Load and Print
a List

1. Read the program TABLE1 from your diskette into primary storage.

2. Add another FOR/NEXT loop that loads the list with the values 1 through 15. (Cell 1 will contain a 1, cell 2 will contain a 2, and so on.) Each time you execute the loop, store the value of the index variable in the cell, using a LET instruction.

3. Add another loop that prints the list.

4. Save the program as TABLE2.

Matrices

Assume that you need to build a two-dimensional table, or matrix, showing:

Sales Region	Product Class		
	1	2	3
1			
2			

The DIM instruction specifies the number of rows (2), followed by the number of columns (3).

```
60 DIM  Y(2, 3)
```

Figure 6.4   Nested FOR/NEXT Loops

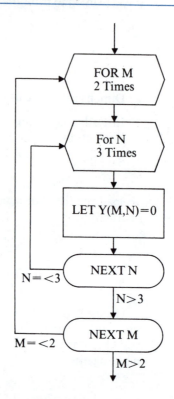

Since the table has two dimensions, **nested FOR/NEXT loops** must be used to initialize the table contents to zero. Figure 6.4 illustrates the two loops that are coded below:

```
 70 FOR  M  =  1  TO  2
 80 FOR  N  =  1  TO  3
 90 LET  Y(M,  N)  =  0
100 NEXT  N
110 NEXT  M
120
```

The variable M specifies the row number, and N specifies the column. Any variable name can be used, except for the name used for the table.

First, lines 70 and 80 are executed, setting M and N to 1. Then line 90 is executed, setting the cell at row 1 and column 1 to zero. Next line 100 is executed, incrementing N by 1 and comparing it to the terminal value. The computer checks to see if the inner loop has been executed the proper number of times. If not (N = or < 3), then program execution is resumed at line 80 and the cell at column 2 on row 1 is initialized. When the inner loop has been satisfied (N > 3), line 110 is executed and a test is made to determine if the outer loop has been satisfied (M > 2). If not (M = or < 2), then execution is resumed at line 70, and row 2 will be addressed. When the outer loop has been satisfied (M > 2), line 120 is executed.

The cells in table Y are initialized in the following order:

Iteration	Index Variables	Row	Column
1	(M = 1; N = 1)	1	1
2	(M = 1; N = 2)	1	2
3	(M = 1; N = 3)	1	3
4	(M = 2; N = 1)	2	1
5	(M = 2; N = 2)	2	2
6	(M = 2; N = 3)	2	3

Each time a cell in a two-dimensional table is addressed, you must use two subscripts. As an example, assume that region 2 has just sold $10,000 of product class 3. If you entered the transaction with a READ and DATA instruction:

```
200 READ M, N, T
300 DATA 2, 3, 10000
```

You can add the transaction to the table with:

```
210 LET Y(M, N) = Y(M, N) + T
```

You do not have to use M and N in the READ, you can use any variable names:

```
200 READ P, Q, T
210 LET Y(P, Q) = Y(P, Q) + T
```

Line 210 says, "Take the contents of the cell at row P (which is 2) and column Q (which is 3), add the transaction amount to it, and put the updated total back where it came from."

You can print out a two-dimensional matrix with only one FOR/NEXT loop. You do not need nested loops unless you are going to print the table one cell at a time. The following procedure prints the matrix, row-by-row, with each row printing as a separate line.

```
110 FOR Z = 1 TO 2
120 PRINT Y(Z, 1), Y(Z, 2), Y(Z, 3)
130 NEXT Z
```

Notice that the first subscript is a variable (Z). It is incremented each time the loop is executed. The second subscript is a constant. We always want to print out column 1 of the matrix in zone 1, column 2 in zone 2, and column 3 in zone 3.

Exercise 12
Two-Dimensional Matrix

1. Dimension a matrix with 8 rows and 4 columns.

2. Initialize the matrix cells to zero.

3. Read the following data records and add them to the appropriate matrix cells. Note that you can have multiple transactions per cell.

Row (R)	Column (C)	Amount (A)
1	4	8.50
2	3	12.75
3	1	6.60
6	1	19.95
2	3	29.90
4	4	0.98
8	4	6.50

5

4. Print the matrix, using zones. Print each row on a separate line.

5. Save the program as MATRIX.

**Exercise 13
Print a Matrix
Using the TAB Function**

1. Load MATRIX and modify the PRINT instruction so that column 1 is printed starting in position 10, column 2 in position 20, column 3 in position 30, and column 4 in position 40. Use the TAB function for column spacing. Use a PRINT USING mask to print dollars and cents.

2. Execute the program and save it as MATTAB.

Multiple-Page Reports

The FOR/NEXT loop provides an efficient way to print headings at the top of each page when your report is longer than one page.

Most computer paper is 11 inches long, and the printer prints 6 lines per inch. So, you can get 66 lines on a page. If you subtract an inch at the top and an inch at the bottom for margins, you have 54 lines for data.

Let's assume that you want to print a 1-line heading at the top of each page, skip a line, and then print 52 data lines. The coding, flowcharted in Figure 6.5, would appear as:

```
10    PRINT "      REPORT NAME"
20    PRINT
30    FOR L = 1 TO 52
40    READ  A, B, C
50    IF  A = 0 THEN 999
60    PRINT  A, B, C
70    NEXT  L
(12 empty PRINT statements, lines 80 through 190)
200   GOTO  10
210   DATA  16, 42, 18

        ↓       ↓       ↓

350   DATA  8, 16, 36
360   DATA  0, 0, 0
999   END
```

You will notice that there are two loops—an inner and an outer loop. The inner, FOR/NEXT loop causes the READ instruction to be executed 52 times. Each of the 52 records is printed on a line, filling the page. When the end of file is reached, the program ends.

When a page is filled, execution "falls out" of the FOR/NEXT loop and the empty PRINT instructions at lines 80 through 190 cause the printer to space to the next page. After the printer has been positioned on the next page, the report heading is printed. This is the second, outer loop.

Figure 6.5   Printing Multiple-Page Reports

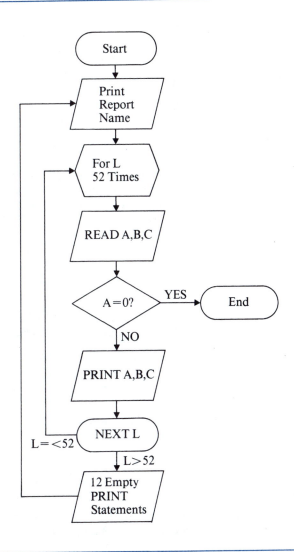

Exercise 14
Multipage Printing

1. Retrieve your COUNT file from the diskette. (You saved it in Exercise 8.)

2. Modify it so that it prints 27 lines per page, double-spaced. Allow for a 1-inch margin at the top and the bottom. Use a FOR/NEXT loop to cause the 27 lines to be printed.

3. Also modify the program to print 3 pages. Use a second, outer FOR/NEXT loop to cause the page printing and skipping to be repeated 3 times.

4. Execute and save the program as COUNT2.

Summary

In this chapter you learned how to handle alphanumeric data. An alphanumeric field can contain any character in the IBM PC character set, and the name of the field has a dollar sign in the second position.

You can use the REM instruction to add comment lines throughout the program. The lines can identify the program, programmer, date coded, and major modules within the program.

Much of our attention was devoted to the subject of expanding the printing capability of BASIC. By using semicolons instead of commas, you bypass the print zones, and the data prints closer together. By using the TAB function, we cause a data field to print at any location on the print line. A single PRINT instruction can include several data fields, each positioned with a TAB function. In certain situations, you may wish to chain several PRINT instructions together. Chaining is especially useful in combining a PRINT instruction that prints a string constant with a PRINT USING instruction that prints an amount. The PRINT USING instruction is especially powerful—providing for the insertion of dollar signs and commas and printing two decimal positions for cents. PRINT USING can also be used to right-justify numeric integer fields.

You can print totals at the bottom of your report by accumulating the totals as the transactions are processed and printing the totals at the end of the job (or file). Before a data field can be used to accumulate a total, you must initialize the field to zero. Otherwise, preexisting data can be added to the total.

With the FOR/NEXT loop, a routine can be repeated a given number of times. This is useful when you print multipage reports and when your program must handle lists or matrices.

When you process data in lists or matrices, the DIM instruction reserves the space, and then FOR/NEXT loops initialize the list or matrix, read data into it, and print it. Matrices require nested FOR/NEXT loops for the initialization and loading, but not for the printing.

In this chapter we added to the list of BASIC instructions from Chapter 5 by describing:

REM
PRINT USING
FOR
NEXT
DIM

We also studied the TAB function.

Key Terms

Alphanumeric	Initialization	Preparation symbol
Data dictionary	Terminal symbol	List, array
Truncation	Processing symbol	Matrix
Mask	Input-output symbol	Cell
Overflow	Logic symbol	Subscripted variable
String constant	Index variable	FOR/NEXT loop
End-of-job routine	Initial value	Nested FOR/NEXT loop
End-of-file routine	Terminal value	

Questions

(Do not fill in blanks in the book. Write answers on a separate piece of paper.)

1. Data that can be numeric, alphabetic, or special characters is said to be _____.

2. You can add comments throughout your program with _____ instructions.

3. Variable names should be defined at the beginning of your program in a _____.

4. If you want variables to print very close together on a line with only one or two spaces between them, you separate the variables in the PRINT instruction with a _____.

5. You can cause a variable to print at any point on the line by specifying the leftmost position with a _____ function.

6. Multiple PRINT instructions can be "chained" together by putting a _____ at the end of all the instructions except the last.

7. The form of the PRINT instruction that provides the most flexibility in terms of printing dollar signs and eliminating unwanted decimal positions is the _____ instruction.

8. Lost characters on the right-hand part of the number are an example of _____, and lost characters on the left-hand part are an example of _____.

9. An alphabetic message such as FINAL TOTAL is called a _____ constant.

10. If you wanted to print a final total after all detail records have been processed, you would use an end-of-_____ routine, also known as an end-of-_____ routine.

11. The process of cleaning up storage areas by setting them to zeros or other desired values is called _____.

12. The ovals in a program flowchart are _____ symbols.

13. Input and output operations are indicated in a program flowchart with _____.

14. The diamond signifies a _____ operation

15. When you incorporate a loop in your program that is to be executed a certain number of times, it begins with a _____ instruction and ends with a _____ instruction.

16. In the FOR instruction FOR X = 1 to 24, the X is called the _____, the 1 is the _____, and the 24 is the _____.

17. You tell the PC the size of a matrix with the _____ instruction.

18. You identify a particular cell in a matrix by adding a _____ to the data name.

19. If your matrix has two dimensions, the DIM instruction would contain _____ values and you would use _____ subscripts when referring to a cell.

20. If you were printing out the contents of a two-dimensional matrix, the first subscript would be a _____ and the second would be a _____.

Assignment 1
Sales Report

1. Use a READ instruction to enter the following data:

Customer Number	Customer Name	Customer Class	Order Date	Order Amount
42	ACME CO.	1	09-30-85	$ 216.32
617	AJAX, INC.	4	10-01-85	4189.16
32	ABC CO.	3	09-27-85	250.94
1014	WIDGET, LTD.	2	10-11-85	19.90
283	XYZ, INC.	1	10-04-85	782.50
2456	MEXICO CO.	4	10-05-85	33.46
62	FOMBY & SONS	4	09-17-85	0.12
314	ETONIC	1	10-16-85	7.01
4271	HI-CLASS CO.	2	10-16-85	33.90
198	DELRAY LABS	3	09-29-85	419.80
87	SUNCO	2	10-01-85	665.65
913	WORLD OIL	1	10-04-85	29.29

2. Print a report titled SALES REPORT with appropriate column headings.

3. Accumulate the order amounts and print out a total, labeled MONTHLY TOTAL.

4. Get a printout if your system has a printer; save the program as SALEREP1.

Assignment 2
Summary Report

1. Modify the SALEREP1 program to accumulate order amounts for each customer class in a list named L. There are 4 customer classes. Accumulate the amounts as the transaction records are processed.

2. Do not print the transactions as they are read; print the MONTHLY TOTAL.

3. Then, print out the list with each cell identified (Example: CUSTOMER CLASS 1).

4. Save the program as SALESREP2.

Assignment 3
Multipage Report

1. Your instructor will give you a file named PASTDUE. You can copy it onto your BASIC diskette using the COPY command. This is an accounts receivable file with 90 data records coded as lines 500–589. Each record represents money owed to the company.

2. Load the PASTDUE file into primary storage and display it on the screen to verify that you have loaded the multiple records properly. The records have the following format:

500 DATA 1234, ACME AUTOMOTIVE, 60, 1234.00

The line number is followed by the word DATA, the customer number, customer name, number of days that the accounts receivable amount is past due, and the receivable amount.

3. Using lines 1–499, create a program that will read the receivables records and print them, double-spaced. Do *not* clear storage before keying in your program, or you will lose the data records. You want to "merge" your BASIC instructions with the data to produce a single program. After you enter the first instruction, enter LIST to verify that your program contains both the instruction and the data. Then, continue to enter your program.

4. Leave a one-inch margin at the top and bottom of each page. Print a report heading and column headings on each page. Print all of the fields in the data record. Print them in the same order, from left to right, as they appear in the data record.

5. Accumulate the total receivable amount and print it at the end of the listing.

6. Execute the program and save it, using the original name PASTDUE. This will replace the data file with the file containing both the data and the instructions.

Module 4
Data Base
Management
Systems

7 The Role of the Data Base Management System in the DSS

Data is transformed into *information* by an information processor, such as a computer. The data is the raw material of information. A firm's data base, or its reservoir of data, is perhaps its most valuable resource. The data can be used to understand what has happened in the past and what is happening presently, and to project what might happen in the future. A special class of software has been developed to manage a firm's data base. This is the data base management system (DBMS). In this chapter, we first explain the role of the data base in the DSS, and then the role of the DBMS.

The Organization of Data

Firms have traditionally organized their data into files. You visit any business office and you see file cabinets, file drawers, file boxes, and file folders. A **file** is a collection of data records relating to a particular subject. For example, a payroll file contains data relating to the firm's payroll system. If a file is a collection of records, then what is a record? A **record** is a collection of data relating to a subunit within the file. For example, in a payroll file you find records relating to the individual employees. Each employee has a payroll record. The employee record is the subunit within the payroll system.

Each record is subdivided into pieces of data called **data items** or **data elements**. A data item is the smallest unit of data—it cannot be further subdivided. In a payroll record, you would expect to find data items such as name, employee number, hourly rate of pay, number of dependents, and so on.

This, then, is the hierarchy of data:

* Files
  * Records
    * Data items

A file consists of multiple records, and each record consists of multiple data items. The data item is the lowest level in this hierarchy, and the file is the highest.

In using a DBMS you have to define the structure, or format, of the data. For example, in using dBASE II you must identify each data item within the record and, for each, specify the name of the item, whether it is numeric or alphanumeric, the number of positions, and the number of decimal positions in a numeric field.

File Media

A file can be recorded on various types of media. In early, manual accounting systems, the files were represented by line entries on ledger sheets. Each line was a record. Perhaps you have worked with such ledger files in an accounting course. The ledger sheets were replaced by punched card files during the period prior to the computer era when punched card machines were popular. A punched card file was a tray or box of cards, each card being a record.

The computer era introduced magnetic recording media. The first computers used reels of **magnetic tape**. Tape storage is still popular today, especially in mainframe installations. Records are recorded on the tape, one after the other. The records must be processed the same way—the first one, the second one, the third one, and so on. This is called **sequential processing**.

Sequential processing is the most efficient way to use the computer, but it has a serious drawback. It doesn't enable the computer to locate a record in a file directly, without sequentially searching for it. This sequential searching is impractical if you want to process data online.

In 1957, IBM invented a computer that stored data on **magnetic disks**. The computer was the RAMAC 305 pictured in Figure 1.1. RAMAC was an acronym for Random Access Method of Accounting and Control. Random access was something new; the computer could access a record for processing without having to sequentially search for it. Eventually, the term random access gave way to **direct access**. And, the secondary storage devices facilitating direct access became known as **direct access storage devices**, or **DASDs**.

The first DASDs were stacks of rotating metal disks, permanently mounted in a cabinet. A **disk stack** could store millions of bytes and provide access to any record in a fraction of a second. Over the years, both the capacity and access speed of the units have greatly increased.

For a few years, during the late 1960s and early 1970s, removable disk stacks called **disk packs** were popular. You could remove one disk pack, containing your payroll master file for example, and replace it with another file, such as your inventory master file. But, as the storage capacities increased, the disk packs became less popular. Users wished to keep all of their files online at one time.

Today, the secondary storage of large mainframe systems is predominantly in the form of permanently mounted stacks of metal disks. These disks are known as **hard disks**. Also, the term **Winchester disk** is a name given to a type of hard disk that was invented by IBM during the 1970s. The disks and the read/write heads are sealed inside a contamination-free unit so that dust particles, cigarette ashes, and so forth will not interfere with the recording. This type of disk has been a popular addition to small computer systems to increase their storage capacity and speed. The IBM PC XT has such a unit as a standard feature. A number of manufacturers provide a hard disk that can be added to the PC. However, most PC configurations include floppy diskette drives.

The most common secondary storage device for a personal computer is the diskette, or floppy disk, discussed in Chapter 1. This type of disk was also invented by IBM, almost 20 years ago, for its mainframe computers. Originally, it came in an 8-inch size. Later, it was reduced to 5¼ inches, and this size is the most commonly used.

Before we leave the topic of file media, you must understand that files can be recorded on paper media. A batch of source documents, such as sales orders waiting to be processed, is a file. Each sales order is a record. And, a report is a file. Each line on the report is a record. Any collection of records is a file, regardless of the medium.

**Chapter 7
The Role of the
Data Base
Management
Systems in the DSS**

111

Figure 7.1   A File Maintenance Operation

A. Magnetic Tape

B. Magnetic Disk

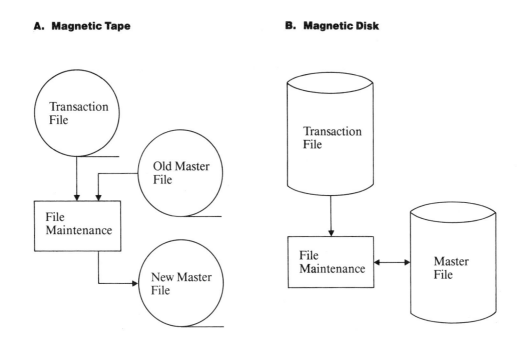

Types of Files

There are different types of files, and many are created by the firm's accounting system. The most important type is the **master file**, which contains relatively permanent information. Examples are the inventory master file, the customer master file, and the personnel master file. These master files are the conceptual representation of the firm's physical system, and the firm attempts to maintain them in a current and accurate condition.

It is a good idea to keep duplicate copies of all master files as a safeguard against accidental or intentional destruction. These duplicate files are called **backup files**. If something happens to the original file, the backup file is used.

The activities of the firm, such as sales, purchase orders, and employee hours, are recorded in **transaction files**. These transaction files are processed against the master files to keep the master files current. The process is called **file maintenance**; it is illustrated with two system flowcharts in Figure 7.1. The top flowchart (7.1a) illustrates file maintenance using magnetic tape for both the transaction file and the master files. The circle with a tail is the system flowchart symbol for magnetic tape. The rectangle is the system flowchart symbol for computer processing; it usually represents a single program. You will notice that there are two master files—an old one and a new one. The old one reflects the condition of the data before the transactions are processed, and the new one reflects the condition after. This situation of two files (old and new) is a characteristic of magnetic tape.

In the lower flowchart in the figure, the files are recorded on magnetic disks. The upright cylinder is the system flowchart symbol for magnetic disk storage. There is only one master file. The old data is replaced with the new data. The existence of only a single file is a characteristic of magnetic disk storage.

In any file maintenance operation, whether on tape or disk, you must be able to:

• *add* new records to the file

• *delete* records from the file

• *change* (or update) data items within a record

These operations keep the file current, so that it accurately reflects the status of the physical system of the firm.

The Pre-Data Base Approach

During the early years of the computer, firms treated their data in the same manner as they did with punched card and manual systems. The data was organized into files, and there were many, many files. If a person decided to start collecting some data, a new file was created. There was no master plan that coordinated data used by several groups. The result was much duplication, or redundancy, in the firm's data. And the files did not always match. One file would say that 250 widgets were on hand, and another file would say 225.

The only visible effect that the computer had on a firm's files was the storage medium. The firms converted their data from punched cards and ledger sheets to magnetic tape and magnetic disks. One major problem that these firms encountered was data errors. When the firms tried to convert from their previous systems they found missing data, erroneous data, data in different formats, and so forth. The computer would not accept this hodgepodge of data, so the data had to be standardized and verified before it could be recorded on the computer medium. This data conversion problem was especially difficult for firms with large files, such as banks and insurance companies.

The conversion from manual and punched card filing systems to computer storage was a major accomplishment for the firms implementing mainframe computer systems. The new files enabled them to process more data faster and more accurately. And, this was one of the major reasons that the computers were implemented. But, the new files did not improve management information very much. It was still very difficult for a manager to get information from the computer.

As an example, assume that a sales manager wanted to know which customers had been buying a certain new product. The sales manager wanted to survey the sales representatives calling on those firms to learn their secrets of success. The manager needed a report showing each salesperson's customers that had bought the product. Perhaps all of the data was in the computer, but it was in separate files. Figure 7.2 illustrates this situation. (The symbol at the end of the sequence is used for printed documents.)

In this system, the manager wanted to select the data from each file that was needed to prepare the report. The process is analogous to selecting food items for a cafeteria tray. In the first step, the file containing a description of product sales by customer was screened to select those records for the subject product. Since the product sales file was maintained in product number sequence, the selected records had to be resequenced in step 2 so that they would be in customer number order. In step 3, data was selected from the customer master file, in customer number sequence, identifying the sales representatives assigned to the customers. In step 4, the selected records had to be sorted into sales representative number sequence, since that was the sequence of the sales representative master file. In step 5, information was selected from the sales representative master file, and the desired

Chapter 7
The Role of the
Data Base
Management
Systems in the DSS

113

Figure 7.2   Obtaining Information From Separate Files

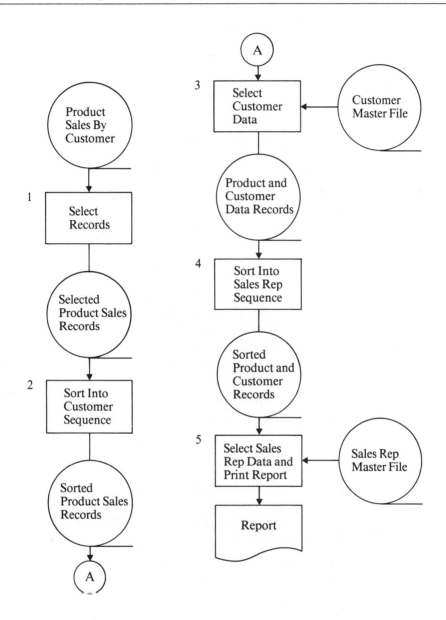

report printed. Many steps were required since the information was in different files, and the files were arranged in different sequences.

This is the way that special requests for information were handled during the pre-data base period. It was time-consuming and expensive. Perhaps special computer programs had to be written to handle the request. Oftentimes, it was weeks before the manager received a response.

Figure 7.3   Obtaining Information From a Data Base

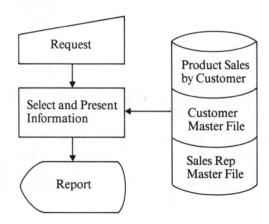

The Data Base Concept

In the early 1960s, General Electric developed a software system called Integrated Data Store (IDS), that arranged data from several files so that the data could be retrieved without special programming. IBM and North American Aviation jointly developed a similar system called Data Language I, or DL/I. In the late 1960s and early 1970s, other companies developed the same type of software.

These software systems are called **data base management systems (DBMS)**, and they are so complex that few firms consider developing their own. Most systems in use today are the products of hardware or software firms. The systems are designed so that any type of firm can use them.

The DBMS helps the firm manage its data base. The **data base** is the total collection of computer data in a firm, organized and stored in a manner that facilitates easy retrieval. The firm's files still exist, but they are linked in certain ways so that they form an integrated unit—the data base. In such firms, the hierarchy of data becomes:

* Data base
  * Files
    * Records
      * Data items

Let's see how the request for product sales information would be handled in a firm with a computerized data base and a DBMS. The retrieval process is illustrated in Figure 7.3.

First, notice that different symbols are used. The rectangle still represents processing, but there is only one step required. The symbol at the top represents an online keying process. As shown here, the manager enters the request into a terminal or the keyboard of a small computer. The request is processed by the DBMS and the data is retrieved from the files. Even though there are still three files, maintained in different sequences, the DBMS can extract from each the data that is needed. That is the real beauty of a DBMS. Once retrieved, the report data is made available to the manager. The report symbol represents a display on a screen such as that found on the PC.

Chapter 7
The Role of the
Data Base
Management
Systems in the DSS

115

Figure 7.3 differs from Figure 7.2 in two respects. First, the hardware is changed. Newer, lower-priced small computers, terminals, and diskette storage units make the data base approach feasible for a wider range of companies. No longer are only the giant firms able to afford the necessary hardware. The second difference relates to how the hardware is used. The DBMS software and the way that the data is arranged on the diskette file makes the rapid retrieval possible.

Before we leave this comparison of the data base approach with the pre-data base approach, a word of explanation is in order. The pre-data base approach is still followed by many firms that have not implemented a DBMS. Many mainframe users have not invested the time and money to convert to the data base approach—a large undertaking. Many small computer users have not developed their applications to a point where it is obvious that a DBMS is needed.

The Data Base Management System

A DBMS performs three basic functions. It enables you to *store* data in the data base, it enables you to *retrieve* data from the data base, and it *controls* the data base. There are many DBMS products on the market. Those for mainframe systems have a purchase price of about $100,000. Those for microcomputers can be purchased for a few hundred dollars. The price is largely determined by how well they perform the three functions.

Storage

The systems vary in the configuration of the data that is stored. The more expensive mainframe systems store many files, each file containing many records, each record containing many data items, and the data items containing many characters. The systems for microcomputers offer more constrained capacities because of limited primary and secondary storage space.

Retrieval

The feature of the DBMS that is most visible to the user is retrieval. The larger systems offer much more flexibility in terms of how the information is displayed. With a larger DBMS, a user can specify certain processing of the data and can customize the output in terms of headings and spacing. The user of a small-scale system DBMS does not usually have such flexibility.

Control

Much of the control activity of the DBMS can be invisible to the user. He or she asks for some information and receives it without knowing the processes that the DBMS has performed. The DBMS can be designed to screen each request for information and determine that (1) the person making the request is an authorized user, (2) the person has access to the requested file, and (3) the person has access to the requested data items in the file. In order to pass these screens, the user must give the operating system the proper identification and password. And the user must be listed in the various directories maintained by the DBMS that authorize particular uses of the data. A mainframe DBMS might perform all of the control functions very well. The micro DBMS might perform none. This is the area of greatest difference between the various DBMS products on the market.

Figure 7.4   The DBMS as a Gatekeeper

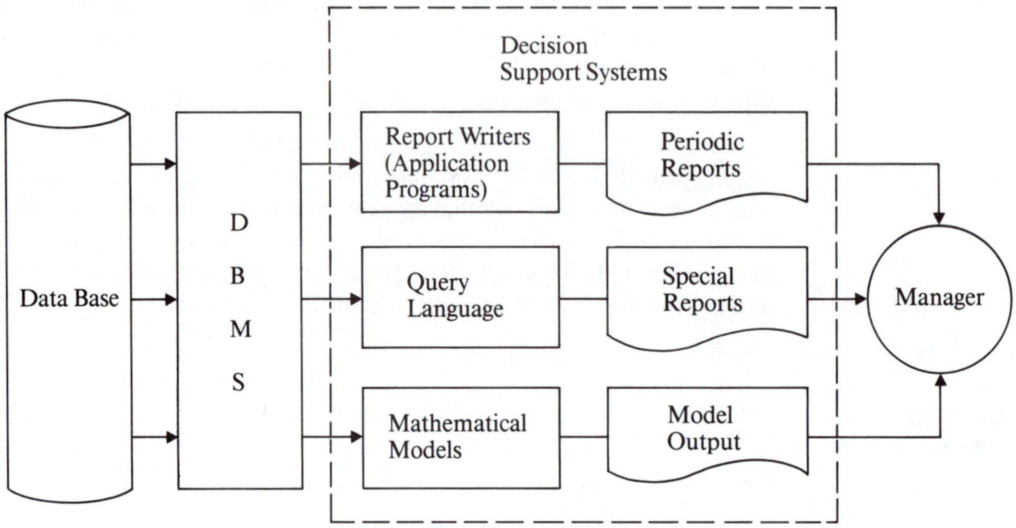

The DBMS in the MIS

Chapter 3 explained that the manager obtains information from the MIS in the form of periodic reports, special reports, and the output of mathematical models. In all three of these instances, the DBMS serves as a gatekeeper and makes the data available. This situation is illustrated in Figure 7.4. The periodic reports are prepared by application programs. These programs make requests to the DBMS for the data needed from the data base.

Sometimes special reports can be prepared without coding additional programs. The DBMS might offer a **query language** that can be used by the user. The user enters a few instructions, and this is all that is needed to trigger preparation of the report.

Mathematical models also must obtain their data from the data base, and the data is provided by the DBMS. So, regardless of how the manager receives the information, it is the DBMS that provides the raw data for the processing.

Each application program, query request, and mathematical model represents a DSS. Each is used to support the manager in some way as decisions are made and problems are solved. The DBMS provides the all-important link between the decision support systems and the data base.

Firms Without a DBMS

Many firms, even ones with good computer systems, do not use a DBMS. Does this mean that these firms cannot have a good MIS or network of decision support systems? No. Just as a firm can have an MIS without a computer, it can also have an MIS without a DBMS. And, it can have a good MIS.

In Chapter 3 we saw that an MIS is composed of a data processing system, an office automation system, decision support systems, and the firm's management. Of these subsystems, the management is the most important. A good management team can overcome both hardware and software constraints and get the information needed. It might take a day or more to obtain the information, but

Chapter 7
The Role of the
Data Base
Management
Systems in the DSS

117

it can be done. And, managers may not act immediately on the information they receive. So, perhaps the need for immediate access is not as great as the information specialists and hardware and software vendors lead us to believe. It is difficult to conceive, however, of a good management team remaining blind to the key role that a DBMS can play in the MIS and DSS.

Future Trends

More and more firms will implement a DBMS as the costs continue to decrease and the performance improves. This trend toward use of a DBMS will be most apparent at the small-computer level where new and better software is the name of the game. Just a few years ago, the small-system user had no DBMS software from which to select. Today, there are at least 115 such systems available for the IBM PC alone.[1] All of these systems do not offer the same capabilities, but there are a variety of good systems and the quality is increasing.

One area where improvement is needed is user friendliness. Although it is easier to use a DBMS to obtain needed information than to code a program, some of the data base software is overly complex. If managers are going to use the DBMS, they must be able to do so with very little effort and very little training.

Since the majority of firms implementing a DBMS on microcomputers will be small organizations installing their first computer, a key point should not be overlooked. That point is the fact that the smaller firms will be following the same paths that the larger firms followed in implementing mainframe systems. The smaller firms will undergo the same difficulties in converting their files, and so on. With this in mind, it will pay the small firm to take advantage of the insights from larger firms that solved their problems through trial and error. These insights are available from knowledgeable persons such as consultants, hardware and software vendors, and from the literature.

1. George Tate, "Data Management," *PC World Annual Software Review* (1983/1984): pp. 164ff.

Summary

Data is organized into a hierarchy of files, records, and data items. The file media can consist of ledger sheets, punched cards, magnetic tape, magnetic disks, and paper media such as source documents and reports. The magnetic disks can be hard disks and floppies—diskettes. A Winchester disk is a sealed unit containing both the disks and the access mechanism.

Transaction files are used to update master files. Often backup file copies are made of master files as insurance against loss of data if master file diskettes are damaged or lost. The process of updating a master file with transaction data is called file maintenance. A different file maintenance process is followed depending on whether magnetic tapes or magentic disks are used as the master file medium.

Before the data base era, extraction of data from multiple files was a time-consuming process. The DBMS has streamlined all of that. Although the files in a data base remain separated physically, the DBMS can extract the needed data very quickly. This rapid access is of real value in a DSS.

The DBMS enables data storage, retrieval when needed, and control of the contents to prevent unauthorized access. There are a variety of DBMS products on the market today, and they vary greatly in the efficiency with which these three functions are performed.

Regardless of how the manager receives information from the DSS (periodic report, special report, or mathematical model), the DBMS can serve as the interface between the data base and the DSS. Although it is not absolutely necessary to have a DBMS in order to have a DSS, the trend is in that direction. DBMS products are becoming more powerful, yet easier to use. And the prices keep coming down. Smaller firms implementing a computer system and a DBMS for the first time would well observe the lessons larger firms have learned making the transition as smooth as possible.

Key Terms

Data item, data element
Magnetic tape
Sequential processing
Magnetic disk
Direct access
Direct access storage device
  (DASD)
Disk stack
Disk pack
Hard disk

Winchester disk
Master file
Backup file
Transaction file
File maintenance
Pre-data base approach
Data base concept
Data base management system
  (DBMS)
Data base
Query language

Chapter 7
The Role of the
Data Base
Management
Systems in the DSS

119

(Do not fill in blanks in the book. Write answers on a separate piece of paper.)

1. A file contains multiple _____.

2. A record is a collection of _____ or _____.

3. _____ is the processing of records in the same order as they appear in the file.

4. The term DASD is used to describe magnetic disks, and it stands for _____.

5. The term _____ refers to metal disks permanently mounted in a cabinet, whereas the term _____ describes removable disks.

6. A hard disk that is contained within a contamination-free cover is known as a(n) _____ disk.

7. With the advent of floppy disks, the ones made of metal are now called _____ disks.

8. A file that contains relatively permanent data is a _____ file.

9. A second file to use in case anything happens to the first one is called a _____.

10. A file containing the records to be used in updating the master file is the _____ file.

11. When you perform a file maintenance process on a master file stored on _____ you end up with two files—an old one and a new one.

12. When you perform a file maintenance process on a master file stored on _____ you end up with only a single file

13. When you perform a file maintenance operation, you must be able to _____, _____, and _____ records.

14. During the pre-data base era it was especially difficult to obtain reports, because the data often had to be assembled from multiple _____.

15. The software system that takes care of the data in a data base for you is called the _____.

16. The total collection of computer data in a firm is the _____.

17. The three basic functions that a DBMS performs are _____, _____, and _____.

18. Of the three basic DBMS functions, the one usually performed in the least effective manner by a microcomputer DBMS is _____.

19. A DBMS might offer a _____ language that enables a manager to retrieve information quickly and easily.

20. If you had to choose between a good management team and a DBMS as the key ingredient in a DSS, you should choose the _____.

8 Introduction to dBASE II

One of the most popular data base management systems for microcomputers is dBASE II, a product of Ashton-Tate. dBASE II can play an important role in a DSS for microcomputers. The manager can use dBASE II to build a data base and keep it current by adding, deleting, and modifying records. And, the manager can retrieve all or selected parts of the data base and produce summary reports on the screen, or print summary or detailed reports on the printer. In this chapter, you will learn how to build and maintain a data base on the IBM PC using dBASE II. This discussion is based on dBASE II/86 Version 2.4.

dBASE II Overview

In the previous chapter, we saw that the DBMS serves as a gatekeeper, connecting the various decision support systems to the data base. Figure 8.1 illustrates how dBASE II plays this role. We have also previously seen that the manager obtains information by periodic reports, special reports, and mathematical model output. In the figure, we see that dBASE II supports all three retrieval methods. The LIST and DISPLAY commands (which we will study in this chapter) can be used to produce special reports. The REPORT command (which we will study in the next chapter) can be used to prepare both special and periodic reports. The dBASE II command files not discussed in this text can be used to function as mathematical models.

In Chapter 7, you learned that a data base management system (DBMS) performs three basic functions—storage, retrieval, and control. dBASE II does the first two very well, but is not designed to contribute significantly to the overall control of IBM PC operations. In this respect, it is typical of data base management systems for small computers.

Figure 8.1   The Role of dBASE II In a DSS

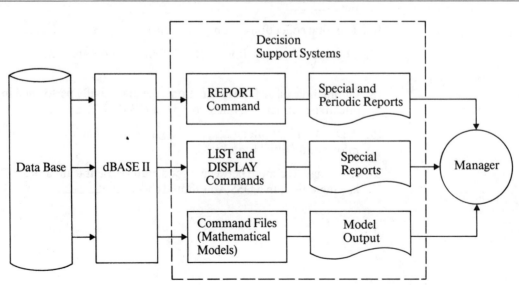

It is unfair to compare dBASE II with a mainframe DBMS such as IMS, System 2000, or ADABAS. The mainframe packages are much more powerful, but they are also much more expensive. In truth, dBASE II probably doesn't qualify as a DBMS. Rather, it is an extremely powerful file manager that uses some sophisticated techniques for logically organizing data. But, even with its limitations, it is one of the best data-handling systems at the small-computer level.

Control

Lack of a control capability might be considered a shortcoming, since control of computer hardware, software, and the data base is an important consideration. The fact that only single users normally use the PC at one time greatly simplifies the control task. This means that the PC hardware can be kept secure by installing it in an area with restricted access. Also, the software and data base, in floppy disk form, can be kept under lock and key. Thus, the potential control problem that dBASE II is to solve is much less severe than that of a large, multiuser system. And, control can be achieved through procedures external to dBASE II, rather than rely on its built-in features.

Storage

You create files by keying the data, a data item at a time, into each record. Each file within the dBASE II data base must fit within the following constraints:

Number of records per file	65,535
Number of characters per record	1,000
Number of fields per record	32
Number of characters per field	254

It should not be difficult for a firm, especially a smaller one, to live within these constraints, since they apply to individual files and not the entire data base. A data base usually includes multiple files.

Once the records have been created, they can be edited to correct errors or to update items so that they reflect the current situation. For example, customers may change their addresses or telephone numbers. Also, additional records can be added, and selected records deleted. With these commands, you can maintain each file in the data base in an up-to-date condition. The files, in diskette storage, are the conceptual representation of the physical system of the firm, or a part of that system.

Retrieval

The manager can query the data base to retrieve records that meet certain selection criteria. As an example, a credit manager may want to know which customers are more than 90 days past due in their payments. Or, a plant superintendent may want a list of employees with overtime earnings last month.

Records can be sorted before they are displayed on the screen or printed on the printer. Therefore, a variety of reports can be prepared from the same data. For example, a sales statistics file can be used to prepare a report in customer number sequence, showing sales totals by customer. The same file can be sorted in sales-person sequence to prepare a report of sales by salesperson. And, the same file data can be presented in item number sequence showing sales by inventory item.

The information can be displayed on the screen or printed on the printer. The information can be simply listed without headings, or it can be formatted in a report form with page and column headings, date, and page numbers.

**dBASE II Use
in Small Firms**

In a small firm, the IBM PC can be the firm's only computing resource, performing all of the data processing and DSS tasks. dBASE II can be used to create accounting files, such as the payroll, inventory, and accounts receivable files. These files provide the data for the accounting applications and also for selected decision support systems. As an example, the accounts receivable file can be used to print customer statements and also to prepare the report of delinquent customers requested by the credit manager.

In this situation, dBASE II performs the file management function. The data processing function is performed by programs written in a procedural language such as COBOL and BASIC.

**dBASE II Use
in Large Firms**

In a large firm, a mainframe or super minicomputer usually is used as the central computing resource. The mainframe will perform the bulk of the processing—all data processing and the larger DSS tasks.

Scattered throughout the firm there may also be microcomputers in the managers' offices. The managers can use micros such as the IBM PC as information processors in their own decision support systems. Each DSS can function in a standalone manner, using its own data base, or it can be connected to other computers and their data bases. When PC's are connected in this manner, they are said to form a **network.** Networking enables users to share both computing power and data bases.

Networked systems introduce control problems not present in standalone systems. The networked systems represent a more sophisticated computer use and require considerable inhouse computing expertise.

Because networking is outside the scope of this text, we will not describe this use of the PC. Rather, we will describe how a manager in a large or small firm can use the IBM PC as a standalone DSS. In this manner, dBASE II serves as the file manager and may also provide some of the computational power.

**A Preliminary Note
on Keyboard Use**

In this, and all other software chapters, the word *enter* is used when you are to press the Enter key after keying in data or an instruction. The word *type* is used when you do not have to press Enter.

Loading dBASE II

You will need to insert your DOS diskette in drive a: to boot the system. The COMMAND.COM file is the only file that must be on the diskette.

When DOS asks for the date, do not bypass it by pressing Enter. Key in the current date, since it will be used by dBASE II to keep a record of the date the files are created and to print on any reports that you prepare. It is not necessary, however, to enter time of day. You can bypass that by pressing Enter.

When you get the A> prompt, replace the DOS diskette with the dBASE II diskette. The dBASE II diskette must contain three files—DBASE.COM, DBASEOVR.COM, and DBASEMSG.TXT. This diskette should not be write protected since dBASE II will store nondata files on it as you proceed with your session. We will discuss those nondata files later.

It is possible that you have both DOS and dBASE II on the same diskette. In that case, simply leave the diskette in the drive when you get the A> prompt.

If your PC has two diskette drives, you can insert a formatted disk in drive b: for use in storing your data files. Otherwise, your data files will be stored on the diskette in the a: drive. But even if you use a diskette in drive b: for your data files, you must keep the dBASE II diskette in drive a: unprotected.

When you get the A> prompt, enter **dbase**. You will get a copyright notice, version number, date, and the **dBASE II prompt**—a dot (.) followed by a flashing underline mark. You may now enter dBASE II commands.

Correcting Errors in Entering Commands

If you catch an error in a command *before* you press Enter, simply backspace and rekey. If you enter a command that has misspelled, missing, or extra words, dBASE II will give you an opportunity to correct the error. You will be asked if you want to correct it and retry. If so, type Y and then specify the portion of the command that is in error. Then specify what the corrected portion should be. For example, you specify to change CREITE to CREATE.

The advantage of this correction technique is that you do not have to rekey the entire command, only the error portion. In most cases, especially for the novice, it is easier to simply press Enter, get the dot prompt, and rekey the entire command. This is often less time-consuming than trying to figure out exactly how to correct the error portion of the command. So, when you get the message "***UNKNOWN COMMAND   CORRECT AND RETRY (Y/N)?" either type N or press Enter, then rekey.

Specifying the Structure of a Data Base Record

The first step in creating a data base file is to specify its structure. You must name the file and then describe the fields within each record. Once this structure has been specified, you will be able to enter data.

Recall from Chapter 7 that a data base is composed of files, each file contains records, and each record contains data items or elements. When you specify the structure of a dBASE II file, you are describing the format of the records contained within the file. All records are assumed to have the same format. You describe the format in much the same way that you describe the data records in a procedural language such as BASIC—list the data elements in sequence, and identify for each element its name, type of data, number of positions, and number of decimal positions if it is a numeric item.

To specify the structure for a dBASE II file:

♦ Press the Caps Lock key so that the data you enter will be in uppercase.

♦ In response to the dBASE II prompt (.), type **CREATE**.

♦ dBASE II responds with ENTER FILENAME:

♦ Enter a file name—up to 8 characters (letters or numbers), no blanks or the following special characters / < > . , ; : = ? * [ ]
For example, type **SALES** or **PAY-FILE**.

If you have a dual-drive PC, and you want to use the diskette in the b: drive for the data, include the b: prefix to the file name. For example, type **B:SALES**. All subsequent references to the file must include the prefix.

♦ dBASE II establishes a file called SALES.DBF. The DBF extension stands for "data base file."

♦ dBASE II then asks for the structure of the file—that is, the name of each field, the type of data in each field (character, numeric, or logical), the size of each field, and whether the field contains decimal places. The following is displayed:

ENTER RECORD STRUCTURE AS FOLLOWS:
  FIELD   NAME, TYPE, WIDTH, DECIMAL PLACES
  001

♦ Now for each field, enter a line such as the following that describes a 20-character customer name field (with no decimal places). Do not enter a space after the comma.

FIELD
001   NAME,C,20

You use the letter C for character (alphanumeric) data.

Since the field contains no decimal places, that specification (following field width) is omitted.

Press Enter after you type each field specification.

♦ Describe the remainder of the record format as follows:

002   NUMBER,C,5
003   TERRITORY,C,2
004   DATE,C,6
005   ORDERNUM,C,5
006   AMOUNT,N,7,2

The field name can be up to 10 characters. It must start with a letter and include no spaces. It can contain digits and colons.

Code a numeric field with a C if it contains data that will not be accumulated. This is the reason that number, territory, date, and ordernum are coded C in the example. The amount field is coded N since we might want to accumulate a total of the sales amounts. We will not be using "logical" data in the text.

You will notice that the amount field contains 2 decimal positions. It is a dollars and cents field that contains an amount as large as $9,999.99. When field size is specified as 7, and number of decimal places as 2, we indicate that there will be 4 dollar positions, one decimal point position, and 2 cent positions.

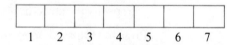

There are two critical times as you use dBASE II for error recovery, and this is one of them. If, while keying in the specifications, you realize that you have made an error *before* you press Enter, simply backspace and rekey. If you have already pressed Enter you will have to reboot the system by pressing Ctrl + Alt + Del and repeating the previous steps.

You can modify the structure of an existing file with the MODIFY STRUCTURE command. This is a fairly common occurrence in an installation as you need to add fields to a file to accommodate changing demands. In our introductory coverage of dBASE II, however, we will not describe the use of the MODIFY STRUCTURE command.

When you have keyed in the last data field for the last record, press Enter twice—one time to enter the field, and one time to signal the end of the file.

The SALES file that you have specified is one that can be used to record in-formation describing orders that your firm's customers place for your products. One order record is entered for each order.

Entering Data into the Data Base

After you specify the structure of the record and press Enter twice, dBASE II saves the structure and then asks if you want to enter data by displaying:

INPUT DATA NOW?

If you key in anything but a Y or an N, you get a question mark. dBASE II is waiting for a Y or an N. If you key in an N, you get the dot prompt. Normally, you begin the create process when you are ready to enter data, so you type **Y** in response to the enter data question.

♦ A "mask" reflecting the structure of the first record (00001) is displayed. The size of each field is indicated with colons. The cursor is positioned at the first position of the first field. The structure of the SALES file is as follows:

```
RECORD #00001
NAME         :_____:
NUMBER       :_____:
TERRITORY    :__:
DATE         :_____:
ORDERNUM     :_____:
AMOUNT       :_____:
```

The underline marks are not displayed. They are included here so that you can see the field sizes.

♦ Type in the data for the first record. When you fill the field (for fixed-length data such as customer number) or press Enter (for variable-length data such as customer name), the cursor will be positioned at the next field. When the last field of a record is filled, the structure for the next record is displayed.

When you enter the amount, you will only need to key in the digits and the dec-imal point. dBASE II handles the decimal alignment automatically. For example,

If you enter:	dBASE II will store:					
123.45	1	2	3	.	4	5
40		4	0	.	0	0
62.457		6	2	.	4	5

As you key in the amount, it will not appear onscreen as though decimal alignment is taking place. But when you press Enter (or fill the field), the amount is stored properly.

It is not necessary to key in rightmost zeros. For example:

If the number is:	Key in:
400.00	400
7.50	7.5

Each time you fill the space allotted to a field, you will hear an audible beep. There is no beep when you press Enter after you key in the contents of a variable-length field, such as name and amount. This audible response assures you that you are keying in the proper number of characters for each fixed-length field. You do not have to watch the screen; you quickly learn when to anticipate the beep as you enter the data. When you do not hear the beep at the proper time, you know that you have made a mistake.

If you make a mistake before you press Enter or fill the field space, you may backspace and rekey. Simply backspacing over characters does not erase them. New data must be rekeyed in those positions.

As you key in the data, you can move the cursor up and down (from one line to another) and left and right (from one character to another) with the arrow keys on the numeric keypad at the right of the keyboard. This enables you to go back to previous fields in the record and make corrections.

If, for some reason, you happen to accidentally get back to the dBASE II prompt (.), enter **USE SALES** and then enter **APPEND**. Then, continue entering the data.

After you have entered all of the data, you may leave the data entry mode in two ways:

1. If the cursor is at the first position of the next record, just press Enter.

2. If you have already typed some data, or the cursor is at a position inside the record, press Ctrl + Q. (Hold down the Ctrl key and press the Q key.) When you press Ctrl + Q, the data record on the screen is not written into the file.

When you leave the data entry mode, the dot prompt will appear. Enter **QUIT**. *This causes your file to be written onto the diskette. Unless you enter QUIT, your file remains in primary storage and can be lost.* QUIT causes you to exit dBASE II and get the DOS prompt. To get back into dBASE II, simply enter DBASE.

It is extremely important that you remember to enter QUIT to record the data on the diskette. It is very disheartening to spend a lot of time keying in data and then realize that you ended your session without entering QUIT. You usually make this mistake only once. QUIT must be entered each time you end a dBASE II session.

Editing Your Data Base

After you key in the data, you normally will want to **edit** it, or correct any errors. You have exited dBASE II, and have the DOS prompt on the screen. It is not necessary to reinsert the DOS diskette. With your dBASE II diskette in drive a: type **DBASE**. You will get the dBASE II prompt.

Enter the word **USE** followed by the name of the file to be edited, such as USE SALES. If your data file is on the diskette in the b: drive, enter USE B:SALES.

You will get the dBASE II prompt and respond by typing EDIT 1. The 1 identifies the first record. If for some reason you do not want to start editing at the beginning of the file, you can type any other record number, for example EDIT 23. dBASE II will then display the record that you wish to edit.

You can edit multiple fields in a record by moving the cursor and keying in new data. Use the following keys to position the cursor:

Ctrl+X or the **down arrow** moves the cursor to the next field

Ctrl+E or the **up arrow** moves the cursor to the previous field

Ctrl+D or the **right arrow** moves the cursor to the next character

Ctrl+S or the **left arrow** moves the cursor to the previous character

Do *not* use the spacebar to position the cursor, as this blanks out the characters that are spaced over. After you have positioned the cursor to the location to be edited, type in the new data. This erases the old data.

It is quicker to use the arrow keys to move the cursor than to use the Control keys plus another. You might want to practice using the Control key combinations, however, since WordStar uses them to move the cursor quickly more than one position at a time. In either software system, experiment with both approaches and then select the method that suits you best.

After you have created a file, you will usually want to verify that you keyed in the data correctly. To do this, you display each record on the screen and compare the data with the source document. When you spot an error, correct it. This is called **sight verification**. To do this, start at the beginning of the file by typing EDIT 1 in response to the dot prompt. Then verify the accuracy of the data displayed for record 1. If the data is correct, press Ctrl+C, and dBASE II will advance to the next record. When you spot an error, move the cursor to the error field and retype. The new data will replace the old. When you have completed correcting all of the error fields in the record, press Ctrl+C. This makes the changes to the record in primary storage and advances to the next record. This is how you can step through your file, correcting errors.

If you need to go back to the previous record, press Ctrl+R. This records any changes that you have made to the record on the screen.

When you want to exit the edit mode, press Ctrl+W. This records any changes that are on the screen and returns you to the dot prompt.

If you want to exit the edit mode and not make changes that are on the screen, press Ctrl+Q.

When you get the dot prompt after pressing Ctrl+W, type **QUIT**. This copies the changes from primary storage to the diskette. Remember to always type QUIT when you have completed creating, editing, or adding records to a file.

At this point you have created a file for your data base. You have named the file, specified the format, entered the data, and edited it to ensure its accuracy. If the data that you entered is current, then you can expect the file to be an up-to-date conceptual representation of some aspect of your firm's operations.

Create a File

1. Boot the system and enter today's date.

2. Load the dBASE II program by typing **dbase** in response to the DOS prompt.

3. If your PC has two diskette drives, put a formatted diskette in the b: drive.

4. Press Caps Lock so that the data you enter will be in uppercase.

5. Enter **CREATE** in response to the dBASE II prompt.

6. Enter the file name—SALES or B:SALES.

7. Enter the following file structure:

Field	Specifications
001	NAME,C,20
002	NUMBER,C,5
003	TERRITORY,C,2
004	DATE,C,6
005	ORDERNUM,C,5
006	AMOUNT,N,7,2

If you catch a mistake before pressing Enter, backspace and correct it. If you have already pressed Enter, reboot the system and start over.

8. After entering the last specification, press Enter twice to get the question "INPUT DATA NOW?" Respond with **Y** and enter the data in the list that follows. Do not be concerned about making errors, as you can correct them later when you edit the file. If you see that you have typed the wrong character, you must backspace and retype. You can move to the previous field with the up arrow or to the next field with the down arrow, if necessary.

Customer Name	Customer Number	Terr.	Date	Order Number	Amount
ACE RENTAL	60209	23	102384	12340	7000.00
DOLLAR FURNITURE	58890	12	102484	12346	400.00
CITY HARDWARE	44469	16	102284	12347	350.00
DOLLAR FURNITURE	58890	12	102684	12348	500.00
ACE RENTAL	60209	23	102284	12350	2500.00
HANDY MAN	11160	01	102384	12361	3000.00
82 LUMBER	01123	12	102684	12362	50.00
CITY HARDWARE	44469	16	102484	12366	499.95
82 LUMBER	01123	12	102284	12370	250.00
ACE RENTAL	60209	23	102384	12371	229.95
ACE RENTAL	60209	23	102684	12372	350.00
CITY HARDWARE	44469	16	102484	12373	3000.00
DOLLAR FURNITURE	58890	12	102484	12389	2999.95
82 LUMBER	01123	12	102484	12401	450.00
ACE RENTAL	60209	23	101684	12411	410.00
HANDY MAN	11160	01	102284	12412	379.95
DOLLAR FURNITURE	58890	12	102284	12414	29.95
ACE RENTAL	60209	23	102684	12420	6325.00
ACE RENTAL	60209	23	102384	12421	119.95
CITY HARDWARE	44469	16	102484	12422	10.00

9. Follow the procedure outlined in "Editing Your Data Base" to correct any keying errors that you made.

10. Now, assume that someone discovered that an error was made in assigning a customer number to Ace Rental. The number should be 60290 instead of 60209. Repeat the editing process, correcting all occurrences of the Ace Rental customer number error. (There are seven of them.) Use Ctrl + C to go from one record to another, and the arrow keys to move the cursor. Don't forget to enter QUIT when you are finished.

Obtaining Printed Output

There are several different ways to obtain printed output from dBASE II. In the following exercises you will be asked to use the printer if your PC system includes one. You will be using two printing techniques. First, you can print what is displayed on the screen by holding down a Shift key and pressing the Prt Sc key. When you use this technique, it is always a good idea to first clear the screen by entering ERASE. Then enter LIST, followed by Shift + Prt Sc. We will call this the **Prt Sc technique**.

The second technique enables you to print a long listing as it is displayed on the screen. If you press the Ctrl + P keys you will "toggle on" the printer, and it will print the displayed output. You press Ctrl + P to "toggle off" the printer when you are finished. We will call this the **print switch toggle technique**.

Exercise 2
Print Screen Technique

1. Align the paper in the printer so that it will start printing at the top of the page. Follow the instructions in Chapter 1.

2. Load dBASE II and enter **USE SALES**.

3. Enter **ERASE**.

4. Enter **LIST**.

5. Hold down the Shift key and press the Prt Sc key.

6. Switch the printer offline and feed to a new sheet with the Form Feed key. Then switch the printer online for the next exercise. This way, the printout for each exercise will be on a separate sheet. Follow this procedure for all exercises.

Exercise 3
Print Switch
Toggle Technique

1. Press Ctrl + P to turn the printer on.

2. Enter **LIST**. Note that you do not have to repeat the USE SALES command. Once you select a file with USE, it stays selected. The SALES FILE is still "in use" from Exercise 2.

3. Press Ctrl + P to turn the printer off.

4. Use Form Feed to feed the paper in the printer.

Adding Records
to Your Data Base

You can add records to your data base with the APPEND command. In the case of the SALES file you might want to add new sales order records each day, as new sales are made. In response the dot prompt, type **USE SALES** and then press Enter. Then, type **APPEND** and press Enter.

dBASE II uses the APPEND command to determine how many records are in the file (for example, 20), and then displays the structure of the next record to be added (e.g., record 21). In this manner you can continue to add records to a file without having to keep track of how many records are in the file, and where to add the next one. dBASE II does this for you.

After you have added the new records to the file, press Enter when the cursor is at the first position of the next blank record to exit the APPEND mode. Type QUIT to write the expanded file to your diskette. If the cursor is not at the first position, press Ctrl + Q. This will let you quit but will not record changes that are on the screen. Then type QUIT.

Deleting Records from Your Data Base

You can delete records from your data base with the DELETE command. This is not the Del key; you must enter the word DELETE. In the case of the SALES file you might want to delete records when customers return merchandise that they previously purchased. Then, the SALES file represents net sales—gross sales less returns.

Marking Records for Possible Deletion

You must specify the records that you want deleted by dBASE II record number. If you do not remember the numbers, get a listing that shows the numbers for each record by entering LIST. Then, in response to the dBASE II prompt, type **DELETE RECORD n**, with n being the record number. For example, you could type DELETE RECORD 8.

When you instruct dBASE II to delete a record, the record is not removed immediately from the file. The reason is that you might later want to add it back into the file. So dBASE II just "marks" the record with an asterisk. You see the asterisk when you list the records in your file. Even though the asterisked record remains in the file, it is not included in any dBASE II processing.

Recalling Marked Records

If you later decide to add a "deleted" record back into the file, enter **RECALL RECORD n**. For example, RECALL RECORD 10. Perhaps you have marked several records for deletion, but the only one that will be recalled is the one specified in the recall command. If you decide that you want to recall all of the records, enter **RECALL ALL**.

Removing Marked Records

When you decide that the records marked for deletion should be physically removed from the file, enter **PACK** in response to the dot (.) prompt. The PACK command deletes the records and tells you how many records remain. The remaining records are renumbered so that there are no gaps where deleted records were located.

Exercise 4
Adding Records to a File

1. If you are starting a new session, instruct dBASE II which file is to be used by entering **USE SALES**.

2. Enter **APPEND**.

3. Add the following records. They will be records 21 through 24.

Customer Name	Customer Number	Terr.	Date	Order Number	Amount
CITY HARDWARE	44469	16	102784	12428	250.00
DOLLAR FURNITURE	58890	12	102784	12430	49.50
HANDY MAN	11160	01	102784	12436	100.00
SCHULTZ APPLIANCE	99987	01	102784	12439	2995.00

4. Use the print switch toggle technique to obtain a printed copy of the appended file.

Exercise 5
Deleting Records from a File

1. Assume that two customers who bought merchandise have returned it. They are:

City Hardware, order number 12347
82 Lumber, order number 12362

2. Enter **LIST** to identify the record numbers.

3. To mark each record for deletion, enter **DELETE RECORD**, followed by the record number.

4. Use the Prt Sc technique to obtain a printed copy of the file with the two records marked for deletion.

Exercise 6
Recalling a
Marked Record

1. Assume that a mistake was made in marking one of the records for deletion. It should have been order number 12428 for City Hardware, not order number 12347.

2. Recall the 12347 order number record by entering **RECALL RECORD**, followed by the record number.

3. Mark the 12428 record for deletion.

4. Obtain a hard copy of the file as it now exists by using the Prt Sc technique.

Exercise 7
Deleting a
Marked Record

1. The receiving department has just confirmed that the merchandise identified by the two records marked for deletion has been returned. Enter **PACK** to delete the records.

2. Obtain a printed copy with the Prt Sc technique.

Displaying Your
Data Base

It is very easy to display your file on the screen. Just enter **LIST** in response to the dBASE II prompt.

If there are too many records to fit on the screen, you can stop the scrolling on the screen by pressing Ctrl + S. Scrolling can be resumed by pressing the same keys.

Removing
Record Numbers

If you do not want the record numbers to be included in the display, enter **LIST OFF**.

Selecting Records

You can use the LIST command to list single records onscreen when you know the record number. The format of the command is

LIST RECORD n

where n is the record number. For example, you could enter LIST RECORD 126.

You can also select certain records for the display by entering **LIST** (or **LIST OFF**) **FOR** expression. The expression includes the following **relational operators**:

<	less than
>	greater than
=	equal to
<=	less than or equal to
>=	greater than or equal to
<>	not equal to

For example, to select all of the records in the SALES file from territory 16, you would enter LIST FOR TERRITORY = '16.' The **search argument** (the 16) should be bounded with quote marks (either single or double). This applies to both numeric codes (like the 16) and alphanumeric names (like Ace Rental). Quotes should *not* be used on numeric amount fields. If you wanted to list all of the Ace Rental records, you would enter LIST FOR NAME = "ACE RENTAL".

You can also include **logical operators** with the relational operators. The logical operators are .AND., .OR., and .NOT. For example, you may want to retrieve those records for customer sales in territory 16 where the amount is greater than $400. You would enter LIST FOR TERRITORY = '16' .AND. AMOUNT > 400. These conditions, incorporating relational and logical operators, give the manager a powerful data base querying ability.

**Other Uses of the
LIST Command**

The LIST command can also be used to display the structure and file names of your data base. To display the structure type **LIST STRUCTURE**. To display the names of the files, type **LIST FILES ON A: LIKE *.*** or **LIST FILES ON B: LIKE *.***. The asterisks are **global descriptors**. They say, in effect, "List files with any name, and with any extension." If you only want to list the data files, enter **LIST FILES ON A: LIKE *.DBF**.

You will make frequent use of the LIST FILES command. As you add files to your diskette it quickly becomes filled, and dBase II will display "DISK FULL." You must make space for new files by deleting old ones that are no longer useful. The LIST FILES command enables you to review the file directory so that you can identify the files to be deleted. You will learn how to delete files in the next chapter.

The DISPLAY Command

In addition to LIST, there is an output command named DISPLAY. DISPLAY works just like LIST, except that records are displayed in groups of 15. To initiate the process, enter **DISPLAY ALL**. To cause the next set of 15 records to be displayed, press any key.

With the DISPLAY command, you can also display selected records. If you want to display only a single record, enter **DISPLAY RECORD n**. You can also use the "off" option with the DISPLAY command, as well as incorporate an expression. For example, if you want to display all records with a territory code of 16, enter DISPLAY FOR TERRITORY = "16".

**Exercise 8
Listing without
Record Numbers**

1. Obtain a listing of the SALES file by entering **LIST OFF**.

2. Obtain a printed copy of the list using the print switch toggle technique.

**Exercise 9
Selected Listing**

1. Obtain a listing of all orders in the SALES file with amounts greater than $300 by entering **LIST FOR AMOUNT > 300**.

2. Print a copy of the list using either technique.

**Exercise 10
Listing with
Logical Operators**

1. Obtain a listing of all orders in the SALES file from territory 23 with amounts of $3000 or more; enter **LIST FOR AMOUNT > 2999.99 .AND. TERRITORY = "23"**.

2. Print the list.

Exercise 11
Displaying Groups
of Records

1. Display the SALES file in groups of 15 records. Enter **DISPLAY ALL**.

2. Print the display.

3. Press any key to cause the next group of records to be displayed.

4. Print the display.

Exercise 12
Selected Display

1. Repeat exercise 9, using the DISPLAY command.

2. Obtain a printed copy.

Exercise 13
Display with
Logical Operators

1. Repeat exercise 10, using the DISPLAY command.

2. Obtain a printed copy.

Other Display Methods

In addition to the LIST and DISPLAY commands, you can select records to be displayed with the GO and GOTO commands. If you want to display the first record in the file, enter:

> USE file name
> GO TOP
> DISPLAY

If you want to display the last record, enter:

> GO BOTTOM
> DISPLAY

If you want to display record number 18, enter:

> GOTO 18
> DISPLAY

This might appear to be less efficient than simply entering DISPLAY 18. That is true if only record 18 is involved, but if you have several records to display, you can enter:

> GOTO 18
> DISPLAY
> 23
> DISPLAY
> 46
> DISPLAY
> 62

Perhaps you want to check certain records to verify that they contain particular data. For example, you may want to check to make certain that someone else made some changes to some records. If you know the record numbers, you can call the records up on the screen with the GOTO command.

1. Clear the screen.

2. Display the first record of the SALES file by entering:

**GO TOP
DISPLAY**

3. Display the last record by entering:

**GO BOTTOM
DISPLAY**

4. Display records 6, 15, and 21 by entering:

**GOTO 6
DISPLAY
15
DISPLAY
21
DISPLAY**

5. Obtain a printed copy of the entire display.

Modifying Data Rapidly

In certain instances, you will want to make the same modification to a field in all records of a file. As an example, assume that your inventory file has a field named PRICE. Because of inflation, your firm has decided to increase all prices by 15 percent. You could edit each record in the file, computing the new price and keying it in. A more rapid approach would be to use the REPLACE command. You would enter a command with the format

REPLACE ALL field name WITH expression

For example:	USE INV-FILE
REPLACE ALL PRICE WITH PRICE*1.15

The word ALL specifies that the replacement is to apply to all records in the file. The field to be modified, PRICE, is specified, as well as the new contents—PRICE*1.15. dBASE II will make the replacement to each record in the file and then display a message on the screen advising you of the number of replacements made.

This is a powerful file maintenance command and can be expanded even further by adding a condition for the replacement. For example, assume that your firm only wanted to increase the price of items with a price of less than $100.00. You would enter:

USE INV-FILE
REPLACE ALL PRICE WITH PRICE*1.15 FOR PRICE < 100

It is also possible to replace field contents with alphanumeric data. You might, for example, want to enter a customer's name (ACE WRECKING) in the name field of all records with a customer number of 12386 (Ace's number). You would enter

REPLACE ALL NAME WITH 'ACE WRECKING' FOR
CUSTOMER = "12386"

You can use either single or double quote marks.

The ability to incorporate both an arithmetic and a logical expression into a data replacement command offers practically unlimited opportunities. For example, you can increase the sales commission for all sales representatives with over $10,000 in sales, or you can decrease the sales discount for all customers over 90 days past due in their payments.

Exercise 15
Replace Field Contents
with Computed Values

1. Create a file named PAYROLL.

2. Enter the following structure:

Field	Specifications
001	NUMBER,C,4
002	NAME,C,20
003	RATE,N,5,2
004	HOURS,N,4,1
005	EARNINGS,N,9,2

3. Type in the following data:

Number	Name	Rate	Hours	Earnings
2333	ADAMS	12.50	40.0	(zero)
2460	BROWN	20.00	39.0	(zero)
2525	CHAVEZ	6.75	47.5	(zero)
2602	DILLON	5.00	40.0	(zero)
2717	EVANS	2.00	46.2	(zero)
2800	FOLTZ	55.00	30.0	(zero)

Use the Enter key to enter zeros in the earnings field.

4. Edit the file and correct any errors.

5. Use the REPLACE command to give all employees a 10 percent raise. Enter:

USE PAYROLL
REPLACE ALL RATE WTIH RATE*1.1

6. Obtain a printed listing.

7. Use the REPLACE command to give all employees with a rate below 50.00 an additional 5 percent raise. Enter:

REPLACE ALL RATE WITII RATE*1.05 FOR RATE < 50

8. Obtain a printed listing.

9. Use the REPLACE command to compute the earnings amount by entering:

REPLACE ALL EARNINGS WITH RATE*HOURS

10. Obtain a printed listing.

The last computation illustrates the arithmetic ability of dBASE II. When defining the structure of the file, it is important that the field to receive the results of the computation be large enough. If not, an overflow will occur, and the field will be filled with zeros.

Summary

The DBMS maintains the data base in an up-to-date condition so that its contents can be used to produce information. This file maintenance involves adding new records to a file, deleting unwanted records, and making changes to records. In dBASE II, you maintain files with the CREATE, EDIT, APPEND, DELETE, RECALL, PACK, and REPLACE commands. This is how dBASE II performs its **storage** function.

In addition to keeping the data current, the DBMS can perform a control function to a certain degree by restricting access to only those who are authorized, and by detecting errors as data is entered. dBASE II provides very little support in this area. There is no control over access simply because the PC is a single-user system. The user can secure the hardware by locking the door to the room when the system is not in use, and by keeping software and data diskettes in a secure place. Duplicate copies of diskettes are the best precaution against loss or damage. The manner in which data is entered into a record structure helps to reduce errors. The audible beep is the signal that the proper number of characters have been keyed into a fixed-length field. One of the major types of input errors is too many or too few characters in a field, causing all following fields to be out of registration. The display of the entire record for editing, and the easy movement of the cursor also make error correction easy and ultimately increase the accuracy of the data.

The third function that a DBMS performs is **retrieval**. This is how the manager obtains data from the data base to transform it into information. The retrieval function is the one of real value to a decision support system. If the manager cannot retrieve the contents of a data base, then the up-to-date and accurate condition of the data is immaterial. dBASE II enables retrieval through use of the LIST and DISPLAY commands. The ability to add a "FOR expression" clause greatly increases the power of the commands for decision support. The manager does not have to look at all of the records in the file, but can select certain records. The GO and GOTO commands are also useful in retrieving selected records.

All of the processes introduced in this first chapter might seem very elementary. They are. But to appreciate what dBASE II is contributing to the firm's data resource, one must understand how the same processes are done without a DBMS. All of these processes would have to be coded in a procedural language, and that task would be so slow and expensive that most firms would not attempt it. The result would be lessened DSS capabilities.

If we were to review the breakthroughs that have occurred during the past 20 years that have contributed to our modern MIS and DSS, we could identify quite a few. Telecommunications, direct access storage devices, user-friendly languages, and graphics are a few. There is no doubt, however, that the DBMS would be high on the list. As you read in the beginning of the chapter, the DBMS is the gatekeeper to the firm's data resource.

Key Terms

Network	Relational operators
Edit	Search argument
Sight verification	Logical operators
Prt Sc technique	Global descriptor
Print switch toggle technique	

Questions (Do not fill in blanks in the book. Write answers on a separate piece of paper.)

1. dBASE II restricts you to _____ records per file, _____ characters per record, _____ fields per record, and _____ characters per field.

2. A PC is said to be _____ when it is connected to a mainframe computer by communications lines.

3. You call up dBASE II from DOS by entering _____ in response to the DOS prompt.

4. To build a data base the first thing to do is specify the _____.

5. As you key data into the data base structure you get an audible signal when _____.

6. Before you can perform any type of operation on a file, you must specify the correct file to use by entering _____ in response to the dot prompt.

7. You cause the new file data to be recorded on the diskette by entering _____.

8. When editing your data do not use the _____ to move the cursor, because this blanks out the data.

9. When editing your data you advance to the next record by pressing Ctrl + _____.

10. You can print data base contents displayed on the screen by holding down the _____ key and pressing the _____ key.

11. If you want the printer to print the output that is displayed on the screen you can "toggle on" the printer by typing _____.

12. You add records to your data base with the _____ command.

13. To mark for deletion the eighth record in the file, you would enter _____ in response to the dot prompt.

14. If you change your mind and decide not to delete the eighth record in the file that has been marked for deletion, you would enter _____.

15. Records are physically removed from the file by entering _____.

16. If you wanted to list all of the records in a file with the code 23 in a field named REGION you would enter _____.

17. To get a directory of all files with a DBF extension on the a: drive you would enter _____.

18. The DISPLAY command lists the records in groups of _____.

19. If you wanted to calculate and store a 20 percent increase in monthly salary for all employees in your data base (the field name is SALARY) you would enter _____.

20. If you wanted to increase the PRICE of all inventory items in your data base by 35 percent when the PRICE is less than $50 you would enter _____.

Assignment 1
Create a
Data Base File

1. Create a structure for an accounts receivable file. Name the file ACCREC. Define the record structure as:

Data Item	Data Type	Field Size	Decimal Positions
Customer number	C	4	–
Customer name	C	20	–
Customer class	C	1	–
Order number	C	5	–
Days past due	C	3	0
Order amount	N	7	2

2. Enter the following data in your data base file:

Customer No.	Customer Name	Cust. Class	Order No.	Past Due	Order Amount
1087	PITKIN MOTORS	1	10629	0	42.00
2365	A&A AUTO SUPPLY	1	40382	0	100.00
5827	BIG E AUTO SUPPLY	2	71114	30	99.95
4001	TRIUMPH FACTORY	1	60987	120	1250.00
6972	ROSS MOTORS	2	31482	30	295.00
4692	FRED BROWN MOTORS	2	29107	60	7.50
3013	PLAINS AUTO PARTS	1	70771	90	12.94
5594	SOONER HARDWARE	2	20912	0	429.50
7610	WEST MOTORS	2	20913	120	500.00
6661	BIG A MOTORS	2	41290	90	1250.00
9028	ALPINE CAR CO.	1	56820	90	17.95
0312	WILLIAMSON MOTORS	1	31042	30	425.00
5169	REGAL AUTOS, LTD.	2	99989	60	500.00
6382	EUROPEAN IMPORTS	2	21036	30	7.95
0008	SIMPSON PAINT SHOP	1	41920	0	12.50
0124	RED RIVER AUTO SUPPLY	1	41919	120	426.95
2389	CUSHING CAR CO.	1	72083	90	1190.30
3636	DEUTCHLAND MOTORS	1	61734	60	500.00
3824	THE CAR SHOP	2	20912	30	10.00
3623	ARBUCKLE MOTORS	1	88614	0	127.50

3. Obtain a printed copy of the file.

Assignment 2
Record Addition
and Deletion

1. Add the following records to the file:

0006	FRIENDLY MOTORS	2	33131	0	55.75
0012	TRIUMPH SPARES	1	70296	30	175.00

2. Obtain a printed copy.

3. Remove the records from the file for Ross Motors, Alpine Car Co., and The Car Shop.

4. Obtain a printed copy.

1. Turn the printer on with the print switch toggle.

2. List the records in the ACCREC file that are 120 days past due.

3. List the records that are over 30 days past due.

4. List the customer class 1 records that are less than 60 days past due.

1. Create a file named INVEN with the following structure:

Data Item	Data Type	Field Size	Decimal Positions
Item number	C	4	–
Item name	C	18	–
Balance on hand	N	3	–
Reorder point	N	3	–
Order quantity	N	4	–
Monthly usage rate	N	3	–

2. Enter the following data:

Item Number	Item Name	Balance on Hand	Reorder Point	Order Quantity	Usage Rate
5100	Lens	20	15	(skip)	12
5252	Rim	18	20	(skip)	8
5400	Bracket	59	60	(skip)	36
5550	Lever	104	200	(skip)	14
5980	Handle	223	150	(skip)	212
6000	Bulb	0	60	(skip)	408
6200	Reflector	82	82	(skip)	64
6515	Plate	516	660	(skip)	330
7000	Hinge	35	50	(skip)	19

3. Compute an order quantity of 2.5 times the monthly usage rate for all items with a balance on hand that is less than the reorder point.

4. Clear the screen and list the file.

5. List only those items with a computed (greater than zero) order quantity.

6. List those items with a zero order quantity.

7. Print the display.

9 dBASE II Part 2

In the previous chapter, you learned how to create data files using dBASE II and how to display or print all or part of the files. These processes are fundamental to creating a DSS. Especially useful is the ability to selectively retrieve records that meet a particular criteria. This ability provides one of the three basic avenues to the DSS—preparation of special reports.

In this chapter you will expand the uses for dBASE II in a DSS by learning how to obtain backup copies of your files. As with any backups, these serve as a safeguard against data loss. You also will learn to arrange records in various sequences and to prepare reports with headings, subtotals, and final totals. The sequencing and report preparation commands greatly enhance the ability of dBASE II to produce special reports and can be used to produce periodic reports.

The combination of the computing power of the IBM PC, a current and accurate data base, and a DBMS such as dBASE II can keep the manager apprised of the status of the physical system of the firm by reporting what has happened in the past and, to a certain extent, what is happening now.

Backup Files

It is very easy to make a backup copy of a dBASE II data file. And it is a good practice. It is one way to compensate for the lack of built-in internal control features of dBASE II by providing your own external controls.

Copying with a Dual-Drive System

You can make a copy of a file on the same diskette by first entering

USE file name

and then entering

COPY TO new file name

For example:

USE SALES
COPY TO BACKUP1

Here, we are preparing a duplicate copy of the SALES file, named BACKUP1.

To make a copy on a diskette in the other drive, just add the appropriate prefix to the name of the new file. For example, to copy the SALES file on a diskette in drive a: to a file named SALES2 on a diskette in drive b: you enter:

USE SALES
COPY TO B:SALES 2

Copying with a Single-Drive System

You can make a copy of a file on the same diskette by following the procedure outlined above for the dual-drive system. If you want to make a copy onto another diskette, you should exit dBASE II and follow the DISKCOPY procedure described in Chapter 2.

Verifying the Copying Operation

You can verify that the copying operation was performed properly by listing the copied file. Enter:

USE name of backup file
LIST STRUCTURE
LIST

When you copy a file, you also copy its structure. The structure can be verified with the LIST STRUCTURE command.

If the copied file is too large to edit visually, you can use the DISKCOMP command explained in Chapter 2.

Exercise 1
Backup File on the Same Diskette

1. Enter **USE SALES** to identify the file to be copied.

2. Enter **COPY TO SALES2**.

3. Enter **USE SALES2** to identify the file to be listed.

4. Enter **ERASE** to clear the screen.

5. Enter **LIST STRUCTURE** to obtain a display of the structure, and obtain a printed copy with the Prt Sc technique if your system includes a printer.

6. Enter **ERASE** to clear the screen.

7. Enter **LIST** to display the backup file; use Prt Sc to obtain a printed copy.

Exercise 2
Backup File on a Different Diskette (Dual-Drive System)

1. Enter **USE SALES**.

2. Enter **COPY TO B:SALES**. Note that you can use the same name SALES. The prefix distinguishes the drive a: file from the drive b: file.

3. Enter **USE B:SALES**.

4. Enter **LIST STRUCTURE,** and obtain a printout with Prt Sc.

5. Enter **LIST** to display the records in the backup file. Use PRT Sc to obtain a printed copy.

Exercise 3
Backup on a Different Diskette (Single-Drive System)

With a single-drive system, the data file must be on the same diskette as the dBASE II programs. So, rather than make a backup copy of a single file, you use DOS to perform a DISKCOPY for the entire diskette.

1. Insert your DOS diskette (containing the DISKCOPY file) into the a: drive.

2. Boot the system and get the A> prompt.

3. Enter **DISKCOPY.**

4. Follow instructions on the screen for changing diskettes.

5. When the diskette has been copied, insert your backup in the a: drive and enter **DBASE** in response to the A> prompt.

6. Enter **USE SALES**.

7. Enter **LIST STRUCTURE**. Use Prt Sc to obtain a hard-copy output.

8. Enter **LIST** to display the file records on the screen. Use Prt Sc to obtain a printed copy.

Sorting

Your reports would not be very informative if you couldn't rearrange the data. Sorting has long been a fundamental data processing task. Various characteristics of the data can be revealed simply by presenting the data in alternate sequences.

You can arrange records in either descending or ascending sequence based on a particular data field that serves as the **sort key**. For example, you could sort inventory records in ascending order using part number as the sort key. The format of the SORT command is

SORT ON key TO file name (DESCENDING)

You must specify the field that is to serve as the sort key, as well as the name of the file that is to contain the sorted records. The word DESCENDING in parentheses is an option. If you include the word, the records are arranged in descending sequence (10, 9, 8, etc.) according to the sort key. If DESCENDING is not specified, dBASE II assumes ASCENDING (8, 9, 10), which is the default option. In computer terminology, a **default option** is something that the computer does when you do not give it special instructions.

To perform the inventory item number sort, you would enter:

SORT ON ITEMNO TO TEMP

ITEMNO is the sort key, and TEMP is a temporary file that will hold the sorted records until they can be copied back to the original file. You never sort a file to itself in dBASE II. In addition to the SORT command, you must also tell dBASE II which file to use, and after the sort you must initiate the copying process. The complete command sequence is:

> USE INVEN
> SORT ON ITEMNO TO TEMP
> USE TEMP
> COPY TO INVEN

An example of a descending sequence sort is a report where the manager's attention is to be called to the first items in the list. An inventory activity report might list the items in a descending sequence according to units sold. The fast-moving items are listed first. Another example is a listing of employees in sequence based on the number of years of education. Reports such as these are called **exception reports;** they enable the manager to spot trends and important characteristics of the data primarily due to the way the data is arranged. The commands needed to sort the personnel records based on education are as follows:

> USE EMPFILE
> SORT ON EDYEARS TO TEMP DESCENDING
> USE TEMP
> COPY TO EMPFILE

**Exercise 4
Sort Records into
Ascending Sequence**

1. Sort your SALES file from the previous chapter into ascending sequence, using the customer number as the sort key. Tell dBASE II which file to use by entering **USE SALES.**

2. Execute the sort by entering:

SORT ON NAME TO TEMP1

Figure 9.1   Major and Minor Sort Keys

Date	Order Number
7/03	012376
7/03	109247
7/03	318492
7/03	440921
7/04	378924
7/04	779763
7/05	001002
7/05	529684
7/05	631632

Major Sort Key   Minor Sort Key

3. Obtain a printed copy of the sorted records by entering:

USE TEMP1
LIST (do not press Enter)

Then, toggle the printer on and press Enter.

4. Copy the temporary file back to the original file with:

COPY TO SALES

Exercise 5
Sort Records into
Descending Sequence

As the new sales manager for your firm, you want to know who your best customers are. Sort the SALES file into descending sequence based on sales amount. This will produce an exception report. The customers with large purchases will appear at the beginning of the report so that they can receive your full attention.

1. Enter **USE SALES.**

2. Execute the sort by entering:

SORT ON AMOUNT TO TEMP2 DESCENDING

3. Obtain a listing and copy the temporary file back to the original file as in Exercise 4.

In both of the above exercises, we used only a single sort key. Very often you will wish to sort records on multiple keys. A good example is the customer order number within date. We want all of the dates listed in order, and for each day we want the customer orders listed in sequence according to the order numbers. An example of such a listing appears in Figure 9.1. Order number is the **minor sort key**—it is within the larger grouping (date). Date is the **major sort key**—it is the most important key.

Figure 9.2   Three Levels of Sort Keys

State	Sales District	Salesperson
14	102	3765
14	102	4109
14	102	5172
14	417	1092
14	417	4163
14	417	4987
14	417	5001
21	088	1092
21	088	3142
21	109	0004
21	109	7192
21	109	9929

Major Key   Intermediate Key   Minor Key

It is possible to have more than two keys—three is common. In that case, the middle key is called the **intermediate sort key.** An example appears in Figure 9.2, sales records are arranged by salesperson (minor) within sales district (intermediate) within state (major). It is a rare instance in business reporting to have more than three keys. Sometimes you will have three keys plus a final, overall total. A greater number of keys makes the report difficult to comprehend.

To sort on multiple fields you perform a series of sorts, starting with the minor key and ending with the major key. If you wanted to sort a sales statistics file in the above sequence, you would enter:

```
USE SALESTAT
SORT ON SALEREP TO TEMP
USE TEMP
COPY TO SALESTAT
USE SALESTAT
SORT ON DIST TO TEMP
USE TEMP
COPY TO SALESTAT
USE SALESTAT
SORT ON STATE TO TEMP
USE TEMP
COPY TO SALESTAT
USE SALESTAT
ERASE
LIST
```

As you can see, sorting on multiple keys requires many steps.

1. Create a SALESTAT file. When you specify the size of the bonus field, make it as large as the sales amount field. When you enter the data, skip over the salesperson name and bonus fields using the Enter key.

State Code	Sales District	Salesperson Number	Salesperson Name	Sales Amount	Bonus
10	2	100		50.00	
12	3	300		100.00	
10	2	100		80.00	
14	2	200		75.00	
12	3	300		125.00	
16	1	200		250.00	
14	2	100		279.95	
10	1	100		29.95	
10	1	200		49.95	
10	2	300		129.45	
12	3	300		70.00	
12	3	200		110.00	
14	2	100		225.00	
14	1	100		10.00	
16	2	100		5.00	
10	2	300		72.50	
12	1	200		500.00	
16	2	300		37.50	
16	2	100		42.00	
10	3	100		41.50	
16	3	100		79.00	
14	1	300		110.00	
10	2	200		125.00	
12	3	200		29.95	

2. List the file to verify that the proper fields contain data, and that the name and bonus fields do not.

3. Sort the file into salesperson number within sales district within state sequence following the procedure outlined previously.

4. Use the print switch toggle technique to list the sorted file.

The SORT command is not always the best way to rearrange the data sequence for report preparation. The SORT command physically rearranges the records, and this movement takes time. As the size of the file increases, the time becomes prohibitive.

Rather than specifying SORT, you can get the same results by using the INDEX command. The INDEX command does not physically rearrange records. Instead, it prepares an **index,** much like an index of key terms in a book, that is used to retrieve the records in the proper order as they are needed for report preparation.

The index process is illustrated in Figure 9.3. Records are arranged in secondary storage in a random sequence with regard to customer number. An index is created in primary storage that lists the customer numbers (the index key) in ascending

Figure 9.3   Rearranging Record Sequence with the INDEX Command

Primary Storage

Secondary Storage

Index

Customer No.	Address
4	250
6	310
10	410
13	370
18	210

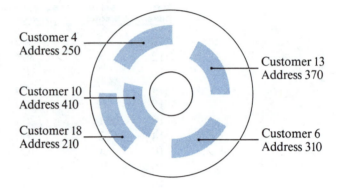

Customer 4
Address 250

Customer 10
Address 410

Customer 18
Address 210

Customer 13
Address 370

Customer 6
Address 310

sequence. Associated with each key field is the secondary storage address where that record is located. When the records are printed, the index specifies the order in which the records are selected and their location.

dBASE II creates a special **index file** on the logged diskette when you use the INDEX command. For this reason, you have to keep your dBASE II diskette unprotected. You give the index file a name such as NAMEIND and maintain it on the diskette as long as it is needed. The file will appear in your directory as NAMEIND.NDX. When it is no longer needed you can delete it. You will learn about file deletion later in the chapter.

The beauty of the index file, aside from its value in achieving record rearrangement, is the fact that it is updated automatically by dBASE II each time you add or delete records. This means that you do not have to recreate the index each time you want to use it. If you use the SORT, on the other hand, the entire file must be resorted when records are added or deleted.

Creating the Index

To create the index, first specify the name of the file to be indexed. For example, enter **USE SALES**. Then identify the index key(s) and the name of the index. The format of the command is

INDEX ON key(s) TO index name

To create an index of the SALES file in customer number sequence, and name the index file NUM-IND, you would enter:

USE SALES
INDEX ON NUMBER TO NUM-IND

Only data fields identified as character fields can be used for the keys. You cannot use fields identified as numeric or logical. If you try, you will get a syntax error message.

Using the Index

You can obtain a listing of the file in the order specified by the index by entering a command with the format

USE file name INDEX index name

and then entering **LIST**. An example would be:

USE SALES INDEX NUM-IND
LIST

Multiple Index Keys

As with the SORT command, it is possible to have more than one level of key, such as order number within date. To accomplish this two-level sequencing, you would enter:

USE SALES
INDEX ON DATE + ORDERNUM TO TERR-FILE

This creates a new index incorporating both date and order number. Then you would enter:

USE SALES INDEX TERR-FILE
LIST

Whenever there are multiple keys, the keys are listed in sequence with the major key first and the minor key last. The keys are separated by a plus sign. For example, to arrange the records in salesrep within district within state sequence, you would enter:

INDEX ON STATE + DIST + SALESREP TO INDEX1

Exercise 7
Index on One
Numeric Key

You are to index the SALES file on the date field.

1. Enter **USE SALES**. Then, enter **INDEX ON DATE TO DATE-IND**.
2. Enter **USE SALES INDEX DATE-IND**.
3. Erase the screen.
4. Enter **LIST**.
5. Obtain a printed copy of the resequenced file.

Exercise 8
Index on One
Alphabetic Key

This exercise illustrates that records can be sequenced using alphabetic keys as well as numeric.

1. Follow the procedure listed in exercise 7, changing the name of the index key from DATE to NAME.
2. Specify the name of the index file as NAME-IND.

Exercise 9
Index on Two Keys

You are to index the SALES file records on NUMBER within TERRITORY.

1. Enter **USE SALES**. Then, enter **INDEX ON TERRITORY + NUMBER TO TERRNUM**
2. Enter **USE SALES INDEX TERRNUM**. Enter **LIST**.
3. Obtain a printed copy of the listing.

The FIND Command

You have learned two basic ways to obtain a record from the data base. First, if you know the record number, you can enter:

LIST RECORD n
DISPLAY RECORD n

Or, you can enter:

GOTO n
DISPLAY

If you don't know the record number, you can select records that satisfy some condition. Perhaps you want to select the record for customer number 12876. You enter:

LIST FOR condition
DISPLAY FOR condition

You would enter

LIST FOR NUMBER = "12876" or DISPLAY FOR NUMBER = "12876"

There may be instances when you want to find all of the records in a file that contain some particular characteristic. As an example, you might have purchased a mailing list, on diskette, complete with zip codes. You only want to send letters to people in the Chicago area (zip code 60XXX), so you would find those records by using the FIND command. This command requires that the file first be indexed on the search argument—the data item for which you are searching. In this case, the search argument is zip code, so the file must first be indexed by zip code. In order to do this you would enter:

USE MAILLIST
INDEX ON ZIP TO ZIPINDEX
USE MAILLIST INDEX ZIPINDEX
FIND 60
DISPLAY

The FIND 60 command says, in effect, "Search through the index, and tell me the record numbers of those records where the zip code begins with 60."

The FIND process stops when the first record is found that matches the search argument. If you want to continue the search, enter DISPLAY NEXT n. You could instruct DISPLAY NEXT 6 or DISPLAY NEXT 20.

Another example of a FIND application would be to search an inventory file to find all items of a particular type. A furniture store, for example, might want to put all lamps on sale, and the item number does not identify the type of item. However, the item name field always specifies LAMP first, such as:

LAMP, BED
LAMP, DESK
LAMP, STUDY
etc.

The sales manager could enter:

USE INVENTOR
INDEX ON NAME TO NAMEDEX
USE INVENTOR INDEX NAMEDEX
FIND LAMP
DISPLAY

You should understand that the FIND command can select records where *part* of a data field meets a search criterion. The LIST FOR condition and DISPLAY FOR condition commands only work with the *entire* contents of a data field, such as a LIST FOR PRICE > 10.00.

The LOCATE Command

Another command can be used to search a file that is not indexed on the field you wish to scan. This is the LOCATE command. You might want to display the personnel records of all employees with the name "Smith." You would enter:

> USE PERSONNEL
> LOCATE FOR NAME = 'SMITH'
> DISPLAY

The search argument should be enclosed in single or double quotes.

One problem with this example is that you will get all names that begin with the letters "SMITH" such as SMITHSON, SMITHEY, and so on.

When the first record is found, dBASE II advises you with RECORD n. Then, you can display it with DISPLAY RECORD n. If you want to continue the search, enter CONTINUE.

More than one condition can be included. You might want a list of all Smiths in zip code area 60606. You woud enter:

> USE PERSONNEL
> LOCATE FOR NAME = 'SMITH' .AND. ZIP = '60606'
> DISPLAY

Exercise 10
Finding Records

1. Create a customer file named CUSTFILE containing the following data. All fields are character fields except the sales field. It is numeric.

Customer Number	Customer Name	Customer Class	Credit Rating	Cumulative Sales (000)	Zip Code
223	BECKER FEEDS	1	A	21230	80303
240	BEECH TOOL CO.	2	A	7421	81213
259	BELLFAST AERO.	1	B	63294	81303
260	BELOIT STOVE	2	A	52914	80302
266	BERKELEY LABS	3	C	67015	81303
268	BIG Y AUTO PARTS	1	B	2012	81303
280	BOSTWICK CANDY CO.	3	A	17	80302
282	BOWEN FURNITURE	2	C	3132	81213
291	BROCKTON GLOVE MFG.	1	B	335	80202
294	BROWN MFG. CO.	1	B	56043	80114
301	BURTON ELECTRIC	2	A	19712	80304
302	BUTLER PHOTO EQUIP.	3	C	7134	80303
303	CBN INDUSTRIES	1	C	12015	80114
304	CABOT IRON CO.	2	A	8	80301
309	CALLON MILLS	1	A	78656	80302
310	CAMERON LUMBER	3	C	91213	81303
311	CAN WIRE & CABLE	1	B	4203	80202
312	CANTON AUTO CO.	2	A	8816	81213
314	CAPITOL CONSTRUCTION	1	B	512	80304

2. Index the file on zip code.

3. Find all records with zip codes beginning with 81.

4. Display all records until you reach the end of the file.

5. Print the displayed records.

**Exercise 11
Locating Records that
Satisfy One Condition**

1. Use the LOCATE command to display the records of all customers with names beginning with "CA."

2. As each record is located, display it on the screen and enter **CONTINUE** to continue the search.

3. When the end of the file has been reached, print the display.

**Exercise 12
Locating Records
Satisfying Two Conditions**

1. Use LOCATE to display the records of all customers with a credit rating of A and cumulative sales in excess of $50,000.

2. Print the display.

**Preparing a Report of
Data Base Contents**

Up until this point, we have supplied the manager with various types of output—displays and printouts of individual records and listings. While the information content of all this output can be quite high, it hardly qualifies as reports. For example, we have not incorporated headings or accumulated totals.

The REPORT command is designed to present the output from dBASE II in a format similar to that produced by a procedural language. We can use the REPORT command to produce periodic and special reports.

The first time that you enter REPORT in response to the dot prompt, you will be asked to specify the format of the report. dBASE II will build a format file on the diskette in the logged drive. Then, the next time you want to print the report, you merely have to identify the format file.

When you enter REPORT the first time, you will receive the following prompts:

1. "ENTER REPORT FORM NAME"   This name will be assigned to the report specifications. For example, you can name your format file SALE-FORM. The file will appear in your directory as SALEFORM.FRM.

2. "ENTER OPTIONS, M = LEFT MARGIN, L = LINES/PAGE, W = PAGE WIDTH"   Unless you specify otherwise, dBASE II will set the left margin at position 8, print 56 lines per page, and print 80 characters on a line. If you want to use these dimensions, simply press Enter. These default options are excellent for the IBM Graphics Printer. There is no reason not to use them for standard reports.

3. "PAGE HEADING? (Y/N)"   The heading will be centered at the top of each page.

4. "ENTER PAGE HEADING"   Type the heading, such as SALES BY CUSTOMER.

5. "DOUBLE SPACE REPORT? (Y/N)"   If you respond with N, the report will be single-spaced.

6. "ARE TOTALS REQUIRED? (Y/N)"   These are final totals on any field(s) that you have specified as numeric. If you have multiple numeric fields in a record, you will later be asked which ones are to be totaled.

7. "SUBTOTALS IN REPORT? (Y/N)"   These are totals at the end of the minor control group of records, such as the records for each customer.

8. "ENTER SUBTOTALS FIELD"   If you indicate that you want subtotals, enter the name of the field that identifies the subtotal group. The subtotal field is *not* the amount field to be totaled. Rather, it is the control field for the group of records to be totaled. For example, if you want subtotals of amount by customer, the subtotal field is customer.

9. "SUMMARY REPORT ONLY? (Y/N)"   Respond Y if you want only a heading line and a total line for each summary total group. If you want all of the records listed, respond with N.

10. "EJECT PAGE AFTER SUBTOTALS? (Y/N)"   If you respond with a Y, each subtotal group will print on a separate page.

11. "ENTER SUBTOTAL HEADING"   If you responded Y to the subtotals question (number 7 above), you will be asked to enter the subtotal heading. This heading will print at the beginning of each subtotal group. For example, if subtotals are to be printed for each customer's records (subtotal on NUMBER), an appropriate heading would be SALES FOR CUSTOMER. dBASE II will automatically add the control field contents after the heading that you specify. For example, the report heading will be printed as SALES FOR CUSTOMER 20 at the beginning of the records for customer 20.

12. "COL WIDTH, CONTENTS"   You will be asked to specify each data column in the report by identifying its width and the data field to be used. The width is *not* the size of the data field, but the number of spaces in which the data field and its column heading will be printed. Usually the heading is wider than the data. For example, customer number may be only 5 positions. But if you want to print CUSTOMER as the column heading, you would specify the width as 10. CUSTOMER would require 8 spaces, plus an extra space on each side. The extra spaces ensure that the headings do not run together.

13. "ENTER HEADING"   Type the heading, such as CUSTOMER. Do not include the extra spaces.

14. "ARE TOTALS REQUIRED? (Y/N)"   If you have indicated that you want totals, you must specify the *numeric* fields to be totaled by responding with a Y. You get this message on each numeric field.

After you have specified the final column in the report, press Enter twice. This will cause the report to be displayed on the screen so that you can verify its format. The display on the screen will scroll rapidly. Press the Esc key to stop the scrolling and get the dot prompt. If you want to take another look at the format, respond to the dot prompt with

REPORT FORM format file name

For example, if you named your report format file SALEFORM in response to question 1 above, you would enter REPORT FORM SALEFORM.

Since dBASE II will print the report automatically when you have entered all of the specifications, you should enter USE file name before entering the REPORT command. Otherwise an attempt will be made to print the report without data.

Verify the Printed Output

After the report is printed, visually scan it to verify that the data printed correctly. This is especially necessary for a detailed report that uses multiple keys. dBASE II only is concerned with the minor key as a subtotal field. This means that you might have a condition where the major key changes but the minor one does not, and dBASE II does not recognize the end of the control group. As an example, all of the following records would print as two groups, when they actually represent five groups.

Major Key	Minor Key
10	3
12	3
14	3
14	4
16	4

This is a serious weakness in the dBASE II REPORT command. If you prepare a detailed report, always scan the major control column to verify that all entries for a group have the same key value.

With a summary report, you have no way of knowing whether the records were grouped correctly or not.

Correcting Report Specification Errors

In the previous chapter, we stated that there are two critical error points in dBASE II in terms of data entry. One is when you specify the format of the data record. The other is when you specify the format of the report. If you make an error in defining a file specification you can use a MODIFY STRUCTURE command. This book does not describe that command in order to keep the discussion on an introductory level. The same situation applies with the report format. There is a MODIFY REPORT FORM command that can be used to correct errors in the specification. Using the same reasoning as before, that command will also not be described in this text.

If you realize you have made an error in entering the report specifications (a common error is to use the width of the data items for the column width), the easiest solution is just to create a new format file. Press Esc to stop printing and respond to the dot prompt with an instruction to delete the erroneous format file. (The procedure for deleting files is described at the end of the chapter.) Then, repeat the entire file-specification process. If you have deleted the erroneous format file, you can use the same name again.

Documenting the Report Specifications

It is a good technique to obtain a hard-copy printout of your report specifications before you initiate the report preparation. To do this, use the print switch toggle to print the specifications as they are displayed on the screen. This printout can be retained as part of the documentation for the report.

Exercise 13
Report Specifications for a Detailed Report

Create a report specification for a report entitled SALES BY CUSTOMER WITHIN TERRITORY. The data will come from the SALES file.

1. Index the SALES file on NUMBER WITHIN TERRITORY. Name the index file TERRNUM.

2. Enter **USE SALES INDEX TERRNUM**.

3. Enter **ERASE** to clear the screen. Toggle the printer on so that you can get a printed copy of the specification.

4. Create a report format file named CUSSTER.

5. Use the default options for page margins and lines per page.

6. The report is to be a detailed listing, double-spaced.

7. Accumulate both subtotals and a final total of the amounts. The subtotal field is TERRITORY, since you want subtotals of the amounts for each TERRITORY group. Do not eject the page after each subtotal group.

8. The subtotal heading is TRANSACTIONS FOR TERRITORY.

9. You are to print the following data columns, from left to right. Determine the column width and column headings. Remember, the width of the columns is more likely to be influenced by the column heading than the data.

> TERRITORY
> NUMBER
> NAME
> DATE
> ORDERNUM
> AMOUNT

10. When you have specified the last column, toggle the printer off.

11. Press Enter the second time to trigger the display of the report on the screen. Press the Esc key to stop the display from scrolling. Verify from the screen display that the format is the way you want it. If the format is not correct, delete the format file and create a new one. Repeat the process until you are satisfied with the format.

Printing the Report

If the report format is what you want, you obtain a printed copy by entering

USE data file name INDEX index file name

followed by

REPORT FORM format file name TO PRINT

The TO PRINT phrase designates that the printer, in addition to the screen, is to receive the output. For example, if you wanted to print the SALES file in customer number sequence, you would enter:

> USE SALES INDEX NUM-IND
> REPORT FORM SALEFORM TO PRINT

You also use these commands if you want to prepare the same report at a later date. You do not have to create a format file each time.

The Report Format

A page number is printed in the upper left-hand corner of each page of the report. Immediately below the page number is the date that you entered when you loaded DOS.

The name of the report is centered in the middle of the line width that you specify. If you use the default width of 80 characters, the center of the report name will be 40 character positions from the left margin.

Immediately below the report name are the column headings, positioned in order from the left margin using the column widths that you specified.

If you specified subtotals, the subtotal headings are printed at the beginning of each subtotal group, aligned on the left margin and preceded by an asterisk. If the report is a detailed report, the records for the subtotal group will be listed below the heading. The subtotals will be printed at the end of each group, identified with **SUBTOTAL** at the left margin. The subtotals will print below the columns containing the numeric data being totaled.

If the report is a summary report, the records will not be listed. A summary total group will include only the heading line and the subtotal line. Actually, the subtotals occupy two lines—the label **SUBTOTAL** is on one line, and the totals are on the next line.

Final totals, when specified, will be printed at the bottom of the report. The totals will be identified with **TOTAL** at the left margin, and the totals will appear below the columns of data being totaled.

A detailed report, using data from the SALES file, is illustrated in Figure 9.4. A summary report, using the same data, appears in Figure 9.5.

Exercise 14
Print Detailed Report

Use the index file that you created in Exercise 9 (TERRNUM) and the format file created in Exercise 13 (CUSTTER) to print a Sales by Customer Within Territory report using data contained in the SALES file.

1. Enter **USE SALES INDEX TERRNUM**.

2. Enter **REPORT FORM CUSTTER TO PRINT**.

Exercise 15
**Report Specifications
for a Summary Report**

Create a report specification for a report titled SALES SUMMARY BY TERRITORY.

1. Enter **ERASE** to clear the screen. Toggle the printer on.

2. The name of the format file is TERRSUM.

3. Use the default options for page size.

4. The report is to be a summary report, single-spaced.

5. Accumulate a final total of the sales amounts, plus subtotals of the sales amounts for each territory. Do not eject the page after each subtotal group.

6. The subtotal heading is SALES TOTAL FOR TERRITORY.

7. Specify that only the AMOUNT column should print. Determine the column width and column heading.

8. Toggle the printer off.

9. Press Enter to initiate report preparation. Press Esc to stop scrolling. Verify the report format from the screen display. Create a new format file if necessary.

Exercise 16
Print Summary Report

Use the index file TERRNUM and the format file TERRSUM to print the Sales Summary by Territory report.

Figure 9.4   A Detailed Sales Report

```
   NUMBER       CUSTOMER NAME      TERRITORY     DATE    ORDER NUM.    AMOUNT

 * TOTAL SALES FOR CUSTOMER NUMBER 01123
   01123    82 LUMBER              12          102484     12401        450.00
   01123    82 LUMBER              12          102284     12370        250.00
 ** SUBTOTAL **
                                                                       700.00


 * TOTAL SALES FOR CUSTOMER NUMBER 11160
   11160    HANDY MAN              01          102384     12361       3000.00
   11160    HANDY MAN              01          102284     12412        379.95
   11160    HANDY MAN              01          102784     12436        100.00
 ** SUBTOTAL **
                                                                      3479.95


 * TOTAL SALES FOR CUSTOMER NUMBER 44469
   44469    CITY HARDWARE          16          102484     12373       3000.00
   44469    CITY HARDWARE          16          102484     12366        499.95
   44469    CITY HARDWARE          16          102284     12347        350.00
   44469    CITY HARDWARE          16          102484     12422         10.00
 ** SUBTOTAL **
                                                                      3859.95


 * TOTAL SALES FOR CUSTOMER NUMBER 58890
   58890    DOLLAR FURNITURE       12          102484     12389       2999.95
   58890    DOLLAR FURNITURE       12          102684     12348        500.00
   58890    DOLLAR FURNITURE       12          102484     12346        400.00
   58890    DOLLAR FURNITURE       12          102784     12430         49.50
   58890    DOLLAR FURNITURE       12          102284     12414         29.95
 ** SUBTOTAL **
                                                                      3979.40


 * TOTAL SALES FOR CUSTOMER NUMBER 60290
   60290    ACE RENTAL             23          102384     12340       7000.00
   60290    ACE RENTAL             23          102684     12420       6325.00
   60290    ACE RENTAL             23          102284     12350       2500.00
   60290    ACE RENTAL             23          101684     12411        410.00
   60290    ACE RENTAL             23          102684     12372        350.00
   60290    ACE RENTAL             23          102384     12371        229.95
   60290    ACE RENTAL             23          102384     12421        119.95
 ** SUBTOTAL **
                                                                     16934.90


 * TOTAL SALES FOR CUSTOMER NUMBER 99987
   99987    SCHULTZ APPLIANCE      01          102784     12439       2995.00
 ** SUBTOTAL **
                                                                      2995.00


 ** TOTAL **
                                                                     31949.20
```

Reporting Selected Records

The utility of the REPORT command can be increased substantially by incorporating one or more conditions as you did with the LIST FOR and DISPLAY FOR commands. The format of a conditional REPORT command is

REPORT FORM format file name FOR condition(s) TO PRINT

This command enables you to retrieve the same data as with the LIST FOR and DISPLAY FOR commands, plus present the output in an attractive report format.

Figure 9.5   A Summary Sales Report

```
NUMBER   AMOUNT

* TOTAL SALES FOR CUSTOMER NUMBER 01123


** SUBTOTAL **
        700.00


* TOTAL SALES FOR CUSTOMER NUMBER 11160


** SUBTOTAL **
        3479.95


* TOTAL SALES FOR CUSTOMER NUMBER 44469


** SUBTOTAL **
        3859.95


* TOTAL SALES FOR CUSTOMER NUMBER 58890


** SUBTOTAL **
        3979.40


* TOTAL SALES FOR CUSTOMER NUMBER 60290


** SUBTOTAL **
        16934.90


* TOTAL SALES FOR CUSTOMER NUMBER 99987

** SUBTOTAL **
        2995.00

** TOTAL **
        31949.20
```

For an example of how the conditional REPORT command works, use the customer file from Exercise 10 to print a detailed report showing the cumulative sales by zip code for all customers with credit rating A.

To prepare this report you first arrange the records in sequence by zip code within credit rating. Since this is a multiple-key sequencing, the INDEX command can accomplish the sequence with one instruction. Enter:

Figure 9.6   A Report of Selected Records

Sales for Customers with Credit Rating = A

Number	Name	Class	Credit	Sales
304	CABOT IRON CO.	2	A	8
260	BELOIT STOVE	2	A	52914
280	BOSTWICK CANDY CO.	3	A	17
309	CALLON MILLS	1	A	78656
223	BECKER FEEDS	1	A	21230
301	BURTON ELECTRIC	2	A	19712
240	BEECH TOOL CO	2	A	7421
312	CANTON AUTO CO.	2	A	8816
			Total	188774

USE CUSTFILE
INDEX ON CREDIT + ZIP TO ZIPCRED

Now, assuming that you have a format file named ZIPCRED you can print the report by instructing:

USE CUSTFILE INDEX ZIPCRED
REPORT FORM ZIPCREDI FOR CREDIT = "A" TO PRINT

You will obtain the report illustrated in Figure 9.6.

You can use more than one condition, as you have previously with other commands. For example, to include only zip code 81303 customers with cumulative sales over $10,000, you would enter:

REPORT FORM ZIPCRED1 FOR ZIP = "81303" .AND. SALES >
10000 TO PRINT

The conditional REPORT command makes it possible for the manager to prepare reports from only a portion of a file. Such reports are exception reports—the manager asks for reports of exceptional situations and is not concerned with the rest of the data.

Exercise 17
Conditional Selection
of Report Records

1. Use the customer file from Exercise 10, indexed on customer name within credit rating.

2. Create a format file named CREDIT.

3. Print both a final and subtotals on the amount field. Subtotals are printed for each credit class.

4. Print a detail listing, double-spaced, and do not eject to a new page for each control group. Use the default page-size options.

5. The report heading should read SALES BY CREDIT RATING.

6. The subtotal heading should read SALES FOR CREDIT RATING—.

7. Print the following data columns, from left to right

>   Customer name
>   Credit rating
>   Cumulative sales amount

The REPORT Command in Perspective

The REPORT command provides an easy-to-use method of obtaining reports with headings, subtotals, and totals. The command can be used to prepare both periodic and special reports. dBASE II is excellent for generating special reports. They can be prepared much more quickly than with a procedural language; dBASE II can be used to prepare periodic reports as well. However, if there are persons in the firm who can code in a procedural language, such as BASIC, then it should be used for the periodic reports. If the report is to be prepared over and over it would justify the extra effort and cost. Although the dBASE II report format is good, you can do a much better job using BASIC. This is especially true of the summary report format, where the dBASE II arrangement leaves much to be desired.

Obtaining a Directory of Your Files

As you created a data base, indexed it, and prepared reports, several files were written on your logged diskette. It is a good idea to periodically obtain a status of these files. To obtain a directory of all of the files (dBASE II files plus files you have created) enter

LIST FILES ON drive name LIKE *.*

For example, if you want a directory of files on the diskette in the b: drive, you would enter LIST FILES ON B: LIKE *.*.

Your diskette contains six types of files, each identified by its three-character extension. The six types are:

- COM   dBASE II file—do not delete
- PRG   dBASE II file—do not delete
- TXT   dBASE II file—do not delete
- DBF   a data file that you have created
- NDX   an index file that you have created
- FRM   a format file that you have created

dBASE II saves the NDX and FRM files on the diskette in the logged drive. The DBF files are saved on the diskette in either drive. If you specify a prefix, the diskette in that drive is used. If you do not specify a prefix, the diskette in the logged drive is used.

If you have a dual-drive system, a good arrangement is to use the drives as follows:

a: Drive	b: Drive
DOS	DBF files
dBASE II files	
NDX files	
FRM files	

Keep the a: drive as the logged drive and always include the b: prefix when referring to a data file. This arrangement "dedicates" one drive to the data file and enables you to use the entire diskette for data.

Now that you know what kinds of files you can have, you can selectively list only a certain type in your directory. For example, if you want to list only the index files, enter LIST FILES ON A: LIKE *.NDX.

Deleting Files

To delete a file simply enter

DELETE FILE file name + extension

For example, you could enter DELETE FILE SALEFORM.FRM to mark the SALESFORM file for deletion. You must include the word FILE, and you must include the extension.

After entering your file deletion command, obtain another directory to verify that the file has been deleted. At this point it is appropriate to use the CHKDSK command (see Chapter 2) to determine how much space you have available on the diskette.

It is important to delete files when they are of no further value. They only occupy space on the diskette, and the diskette will quickly become full.

Summary

One way to enhance the control of your data base is to make backup copies. The dBASE II COPY command can be used to create a duplicate copy on the same or another diskette. It is best to copy the files to a separate diskette as a safeguard against loss. Do not store both diskettes together. Keep one locked in a file cabinet in your office, and another somewhere else—perhaps at home.

You can arrange records in various sequences either with the SORT or the INDEX command. The INDEX command has several advantages:

♦ The index is automatically updated as records are appended and deleted.

♦ No temporary file is needed.

♦ Multiple keys can be handled with a single instruction.

♦ Indexing is accomplished faster, since records are not physically rearranged.

Sorting has one advantage in that it can arrange records in either ascending or descending sequence. Indexing only produces lists of records in ascending sequence. Both commands can handle either alphanumeric or numeric keys.

Records can be selected from the data base for display with the FIND and the LOCATE commands. Both commands retrieve single records at a time, but can be instructed to continue the search through the entire file. The FIND command requires that you index the file on the search argument file. And, only a single search argument can be used. LOCATE, on the other hand, can retrieve records using keys other than the ones indexed. And LOCATE enables more than a single condition to be employed in the search.

While FIND and LOCATE are useful, they do not match the REPORT command in terms of DSS support. You create a format file for each report that causes headings to be printed, special spacing of the data columns across the page, totals to be printed, and so on. Either detailed or summary reports can be printed, although the format of the summary reports is decidedly inferior to that produced by a procedural language.

The ability to incorporate conditions into the REPORT command makes it a powerful query language. The manager can quickly retrieve selected records, arranged in an attractive format, with accumulated subtotals and totals.

As you use dBASE II, you create a number of files—data base files (DBF), index files (NDX), and report format files (FRM). You should use the DELETE FILE command periodically to remove unwanted files from your diskette.

Key Terms

Sort key	Major sort key
Default option	Intermediate sort key
Exception report	Index
Minor sort key	Index file

Questions   (Do not fill in blanks in the book. Write answers on a separate piece of paper.)

1. To review the structure of a data base you would first specify the file with the _____ command, and then you would enter _____.

2. You arrange records in sequence based on a particular field called the _____.

3. If you don't specify ascending or descending sequence when sorting, dBASE II assumes _____.

4. To sort an inventory file (INVEN) in ascending sequence based on the ITEM-NO field and to store the sorted records in a temporary file named TEMP you would have to enter two commands: _____ _____.

5. To write the temporary file back to the inventory file you would enter two commands: _____ _____.

6. In a sort sequence that uses a hierarchy of sort keys, the most important one is the _____, and the least important one is the _____.

7. To resequence records quicker and easier than with SORT, you would use the _____ command.

8. Assume that you have specified the file (PAY-FILE) to be indexed. To create an index file named IND-FILE using employee number (EMP-NO) as the key, you would enter _____.

9. To list the indexed PAY-FILE in the order of the index, you would enter _____.

10. When you have multiple keys in an INDEX command, they are separated by a _____, and the major key is listed _____.

11. You have specified the file to use and now must search for all records with a NAME of Jones and number of years of education (YRS-ED) in excess of 12. You would enter _____.

12. When you enter REPORT FORM SALES, the SALES specifies a _____ file with a(n) _____ extension.

13. When you use the REPORT command you can print _____ level(s) of subtotals.

14. When you specify the format of a report you must specify if totals will be required for all _____ fields.

15. When you use the REPORT command you can have multiple levels of sort keys but dBASE II will recognize only the _____ one.

16. You have created a format file named REGION and have specified the file to use. To print the records with SALES greater than $10,000, you would enter _____.

17. The REPORT command does a better job of printing a _____ report than a _____ report.

18. Do not delete the files on your diskette with the extensions _____, _____, and _____.

19. To obtain a directory of all the files on the diskette in the a: drive you would enter _____.

20. To delete an unwanted format file named STATE you would enter _____.

<table>
<tr><td></td><td>1. Use the SORT command to sort the SALES file from Chapter 8 into customer number sequence.

2. Print the sequenced file.</td></tr>
</table>

Assignment 1
Numeric Sorting

1. Use the SORT command to sort the SALES file from Chapter 8 into customer number sequence.

2. Print the sequenced file.

Assignment 2
Alphanumeric Sorting

1. Use the SORT command to sort the SALES file into customer name sequence.

2. Print the sequenced file.

Assignment 3
Multiple Sort Keys

1. Use the SORT command to arrange the SALES file into descending amount sequence within ascending territory sequence. Remember, you must sort on the minor key first, then the major key.

2. Print the output.

Assignment 4
Numeric Indexing

1. Use the INDEX command to index the ACCREC file (from Chapter 8) into customer number sequence.

2. Obtain a printed listing.

Assignment 5
Alphabetic Indexing

1. Use the INDEX command to arrange the ACCREC file into sequence using the customer name field.

2. Obtain a printed listing.

Assignment 6
Multiple Index Keys

1. Index the ACCREC file by customer name within customer class.

2. Obtain a printed listing.

Assignment 7
Detailed Report

1. Using the indexed ACCREC file from Assignment 6, enter the REPORT command to prepare a detailed listing of all records. Use the default options for page size.

2. The name of the report is ANALYSIS OF RECEIVABLES.

3. Double-space the report and eject to a new page for each subtotal group.

4. Print a subtotal heading RECEIVABLES BY CUSTOMER CLASS =.

5. Print subtotals on the order amount field. The subtotal control field is customer class.

6. Print the following data columns, from left to right, with column headings:

>   Customer number
>   Customer name
>   Order number
>   Order amount

7. Print a final total on the order amount field.

Module 5
Electronic
Spreadsheets

10 The Role of Electronic Spreadsheets in the DSS

The most widely adopted software package in the history of computing is VisiCalc. In addition, it is the first major piece of DSS software designed specifically for small-scale computers. The success of VisiCalc spawned a multitude of similar packages such as SuperCalc, Multiplan, and CalcStar. These packages are called electronic spreadsheets since they all deal with data and formulas arranged in rows and columns. The spreadsheets are mathematical models that enable the user to project the firm's performance into the future. In this chapter we first look at modeling as a means of obtaining management information. Then you will learn how the electronic spreadsheet serves as a modeling tool.

Introduction to Modeling

A **model** is an abstraction of something; it represents something. The thing that the model represents is the **entity**. If a model represents a firm, then the firm is the entity. If the model represents a firm's inventory, then the inventory is the entity. During the early years of the MIS—in the late 1960s—managers attempted to construct very large models, often representing one or more firms. In many cases those models proved to be too cumbersome and inaccurate. The models were hard to use and didn't represent their entities well. Managers and management scientists reacted to this disappointing performance by reducing the scope of the models. Entities became parts of the firm's operation, rather than the entire firm. This approach of focusing on parts rather than the whole has been an underlying principle of the DSS concept.

Any mathematical formula is a model. The most basic business model is the **profit model**, $P = R - C$. In the profit model, P stands for profit, R for revenue, and C for cost. The letters P, R, and C all represent something—some aspect of the firm's operation. P, R, and C are **variables** in that they can assume different values. In this example, the variables do not represent physical entities, such as inventory units or personnel. Instead, they represent monetary values. In business, especially in the accounting or financial area, this use of monetary values as the modeling ingredient is very common. In other areas, such as manufacturing and marketing, it is common to use quantities, such as hours worked or units sold, as the ingredient.

Some popular business models are not much more complicated than the profit model. The EOQ model that you saw in Chapters 3 and 5 is a good example. It includes only four variables. But, other models are much more complex, even when the goal is to keep their scope within manageable limits. Some models end up with hundreds of formulas, such as the EOQ one, all linked together in some manner.

Types of Models

In Chapter 3, you were first introduced to models of several types. You learned a distinction between a static and a dynamic model. Recall that a *static model* does not include time as a variable. It deals with a situation at a particular point in time, like a snapshot does. A good business example is the balance sheet, illustrated in

Figure 10.1   A Balance Sheet—A Static Model

```
            CONSOLIDATED BALANCE SHEET

            Longhorn Plastics Industries
              As of December 31, 1985
Assets

Current assets:
      Cash and time deposits                    $    63,400
      Short-term investments                         59,500
      Receivables from customers, less allowances   717,500
      Other receivables                             55,300
      Inventories                                  695,600
      Prepaid expenses and other assets            42,700

      Total current assets                     $1,634,000

Investments                                       764,600
Other assets and deferred charges                 102,200
Properties, plants and equipment                2,687,300

      Total assets                             $5,188,100

Liabilities

Current liabilities
      Accounts payable                         $   331,900
      Accrued payroll and other compensation       134,400
      Taxes, including taxes on income             160,000
      Other current liabilities                    156,600
      Long-term debt due within one year            31,100

      Total current liabilities                    814,000

Long-term debt, less amount due in one year     1,017,500
Noncurrent liabilities and deferred credits       118,800
Future taxes on income                            304,000

      Commitments and contingent liabilities   2,254,300

Stockholders' equity

Capital stock:
      Serial preferred stock                        66,000
      Common stock                                  73,100
Additional capital                                 190,000
Retained earnings                               2,604,700

      Total stockholders' equity               2,933,800

      Total liabilities and stockholders' equity  $5,188,100
```

Figure 10.1. The balance sheet presents the financial condition of the firm in terms of its assets and liabilities on a certain date, such as December 31, 1985.

When a model includes time as one of its variables it is a *dynamic model*. The model represents the behavior of the entity over time. It is like a motion picture. The income statement, pictured in Figure 10.2, is an example. The figures on the income statement, the revenues, costs, and profits, are based on operations covering a period of time, such as January 1 through December 31, 1985.

Figure 10.2   An Income Statement—A Dynamic Model

```
                      INCOME STATEMENT

                Great Lakes Boat and Marine

    For the Period January 1, 1985 through December 31, 1985


Gross sales                                        $54,000
        Less: Returns and allowances                 4,000

Net sales                                          $50,000

Cost of goods sold
     Beginning inventory at cost          $ 8,000
     Purchases at billed cost     $31,000
       Less: Purchase discounts     4,000
     Purchases at net cost        $27,000
     Plus freight-in                2,000
       Net cost of delivered purchases     29,000
     Cost of goods available for sale      37,000
       Less: ending inventory at cost       7,000
     Cost of goods sold                            30,000

Gross margin (gross profit)                        $20,000

Expenses

     Selling expenses
        Sales commissions          $  6,000
        Advertising expense           2,000
        Delivery expense              2,000
           Total selling expense            $10,000

     Administrative expenses
        Office salaries            $  3,000
        Office supplies               1,000
        Misc. admin. expense            500
           Total administrative expense      4,500

     General expenses
        Rent                       $  1,000
        Misc. general expense           500
           Total general expense             1,500

        Total expenses                             16,000

Net profit                                      $   4,000
```

Also in Chapter 3, you learned to distinguish between models that select the best solution and those that only describe a single solution that is not necessarily the best. An *optimizing model* is one that selects the best solution among the alternatives. For a model to be able to do this, the problem must be very well structured. You must know what ingredients (variables) make up the problem and how they interrelate. The best example of an optimizing model is **linear programming (LP)**. LP models handle two kinds of problems—mix and routing. LP can be used to determine the best mix of ingredients for a new sausage, or it can determine the best route for city buses to follow. In making these mix and routing decisions, LP has the objective of maximizing something (such as profit) or minimizing something (such as expenses).

Since most business problems are not well structured (the manager doesn't know all of the ingredients and how they interrelate), most models are not the optimizing type. Most are nonoptimizing. A *nonoptimizing model* permits a manager to describe a particular situation, or scenario, and the model will project what the outcome of that situation might be. For example, a scenario might include the factors influencing the level of sales—price, advertising budget, number of salespersons, and so on. Then, the manager will assign values to the scenario items and use the model to project the sales level. The model does just that, but does not tell the manager which combination of scenario values will produce the highest sales level. The manager must find that out independently. The manager plays the what-if game. The manager says, "What if I increase price by $10? What will likely be the effect?" The manager uses the model again with the higher price and compares the results to those achieved earlier. In this manner, the manager can try out different decisions to identify the best one, or at least the one that appears to be the best.

In this example, we introduced the term scenario in the context of a non-optimizing model. You should understand that an optimizing model also has a scenario. As an example, assume that you are using LP to determine the mix of items to stock in a furniture store. The profit and floor space figures for each item represent the scenario. The scenario is the setting in which models, *all* models, function.

A third way to classify models is based on whether the formulas include probabilities. A **probability** is simply the chance that something will happen. Probabilities range from 0.00 (for something with no chance) to 1.00 (for something that is a sure thing). Probabilities are often presented as percentages. A weather forecaster, for example, will say "There's a 30 percent chance of rain." A mathematician would say "The probability of rain is 0.30."

A model that includes probabilities is called a **probabilistic model**. One that does not is a **deterministic model**. Probabilistic models would appear to do the best job of fitting business problems, since very little in the dynamic world of business is a certainty. But, probabilistic models are harder to work with than deterministic ones. For that reason, probabilistic models are not as popular as deterministic models.

Simulation

When a model is used to represent some entity with its mathematical expression, the model is said to *simulate* the entity. The model is the tool, and the process of using the tool is simulation.

Some modeling experts use the term *simulation* in a restricted manner, to describe the use of a dynamic model. To these experts, simulation is the behavior of the model over time. Other persons use the term simulation to mean the use of any kind of model; to them, simulation is synonymous with modeling.

Whether simulation is used to describe only dynamic models, or all models, you should understand that you do not "simulate the model." The model does the simulating.

The Scenario

Let's take a simple example about the scenario. Assume that we want to model the behavior of a firm's inventory. This will be a dynamic model. We will simulate the behavior of an inventory item over a period of ten days.

Figure 10.3   Output From a Simple Inventory Model

Day	Beginning Balance (B)	Usage Rate (R)	Ending Balance (E)
1	200	10	190
2	190	10	180
3	180	10	170
4	170	10	160
5	160	10	150
6	150	10	140
7	140	10	130
8	130	10	120
9	120	10	110
10	110	10	100

One of the scenario items that the manager would have to supply is the beginning balance—how many units we have on hand at the beginning. Another scenario item is the usage rate—how many we use each day. The model will take the beginning balance and subtract the usage rate from it to arrive at the ending balance. The formula is:

$$E = B - U$$

Where: E is the ending balance
B is the beginning balance
U is the usage rate

If the manager inputs a beginning balance of 200 and a usage rate of 10, the output of the model would appear as the listing in Figure 10.3. This is a dynamic model, like a motion picture. Each day is a frame of the film.

Notice that two of the ingredients in the formula change values during the simulation—B and E. The name **state variable** is used to identify a scenario item that takes on varying values. These items reflect the state of the entity during the simulation.

Usage rate (U) remains constant during the simulation. The name for this type of scenario item is **parameter**. A parameter does not change values during the simulation.

We have been using the term *scenario item*. Actually, a better term is **attribute value**. A model consists of several attributes, and each has a value. Our inventory model has three attribute values. Two (beginning balance and ending balance) change values during the simulation and are state variables. One (usage rate) does not change value and is a parameter.

Modeling in Perspective   Models can play an important role in the firm's MIS. Of the three ways to get information from the MIS (periodic reports, special reports, and model output), only modeling takes a look into the future. And, that is where the manager wants to focus her or his attention. A periodic report tells what has already happened, and a special report can tell what is happening now. But this information has relevance only in that it provides the manager with a basis for predicting the future. The manager must do the predicting, and some managers can do this with a high degree of skill. The model, on the other hand, does the predicting for the manager. The manager only has to evaluate the model's output, deciding how realistic it is. This, in itself, is no small task. But the model does the number crunching for the manager.

You would think that the ability of the model to predict would make it a widely used management tool. The fact is that most managers have failed to adopt modeling, with the main reason undoubtedly being the mathematics involved. Many, perhaps most, managers don't have the mathematical background to create the models. And, those with the background don't have the time. So, managers have generally turned over the modeling chore to management scientists—people with the mathematical skills. The only problem with this approach has been the lack of managerial background of many of the management scientists—they know the math but not the management.

There have been problems caused by the different capabilities and interests of the managers and the management scientists. But, these problems have by no means been universal. There are many firms where these two groups have worked together effectively to build good models. And, the problems that have existed are likely to be less prevalent in the future as the modeling tools become easier to use, more user-friendly.

Rather than mathematical ability, the key to effective model use is knowing how to evaluate the output. No model is perfect. Business phenomena are too complex to model with complete accuracy. For this reason, the manager never uses the model output without injecting his or her experience and intuition. This is the DSS concept—the model addresses the structured part of the problem, and the manager is responsible for the unstructured part. Together, the model and the manager form a problem-solving team.

The Electronic Spreadsheet

If you have taken an accounting course, you know that an accountant or a bookkeeper posts figures to a form with rows and columns, called a **spreadsheet**. You have, no doubt, seen such forms in an office supply store and perhaps have used them yourself. The spreadsheet provides a convenient space in which the accountant can manipulate many figures. It is a type of worksheet.

An **electronic spreadsheet** is simply a spreadsheet represented electronically in a computer's storage. The term only became popular after Daniel S. Bricklin and Robert M. Frankston at the Personal Software firm invented VisiCalc. The name VisiCalc became so popular that the name of the firm was changed to VisiCorp. Before long, other similar packages appeared on the market, and the term *electronic spreadsheet* was coined to describe this new class of DSS software. Today, there are more than 50 electronic spreadsheet products on the market.[1]

The electronic spreadsheet is a modeling tool. It enables the manager to describe a scenario and simulate a part of the firm's operation. The availability of a spreadsheet for a small-scale computer makes it possible for that computer to function as more than a data processing system. The spreadsheet opens up new opportunities for the micro to function as a DSS.

1. For a brief description of the most popular electronic spreadsheets, see Daniel S. Bricklin, "Spreadsheets," *PC World Annual Software Review* (1983/1984): pp. 108ff.

Figure 10.4   Rows and Columns of the Spreadsheet

	YEAR			
	1	2	3	4
SALES REVENUE				
EXPENSES				
MARKETING				
MATERIALS				
LABOR				
ADMINISTRATION				
TOTAL				
GROSS PROFIT				
INCOME TAX				
NET PROFIT				

A spreadsheet can be a static or a dynamic model. When used to produce a balance sheet (as in Figure 10.1), the spreadsheet is a static model. When used to produce an income statement (Figure 10.2), the spreadsheet is a dynamic model. The spreadsheet format of rows and columns lends itself especially to a dynamic use. As illustrated in Figure 10.4, the various revenue and expense items can be listed down the rows, and the time periods can be arranged across the columns. This is a very natural arrangement of the data. You can look across the columns and see how the condition of the entity changes over time.

Some spreadsheets can be used as both optimizing and nonoptimizing models. But, these tend to be the more expensive software packages. A good example is **IFPS (Interactive Financial Planning System)**. IFPS was originally designed for use on a mainframe computer, but has been rewritten to fit on a microcomputer with large primary storage. Most of the electronic spreadsheets, such as VisiCalc, operate strictly as nonoptimizing models.

The same situation exists in terms of probabilities. IFPS can easily be used as both a probabilistic and a deterministic model. Most spreadsheets, including VisiCalc, are most often used in a deterministic manner.

So, depending on the spreadsheet, you might be restricted as to the types of problems handled. If you have IFPS, you can use it without much restraint. If you have a more modest package, however, it might be more difficult to use it in a probabilistic, optimizing manner.

Figure 10.5   Functional Application Areas

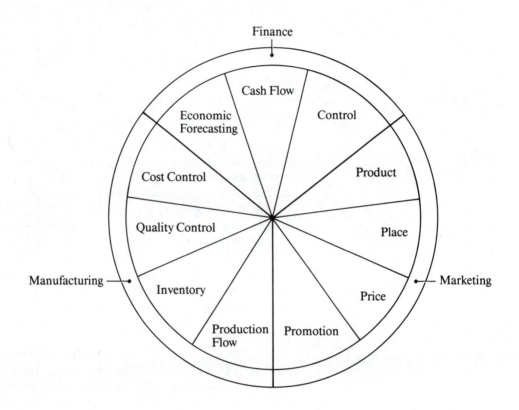

Application Scope

Spreadsheets certainly fit the accounting format. But, what about other areas of business? Can we expect spreadsheets to be used by managers in all areas of the firm? We will conclude this chapter by looking at the three main functional areas of a firm—finance, marketing, and manufacturing—and identifying the types of problems solved by managers in those areas. And, we will evaluate the electronic spreadsheet as a DSS tool for solving those problems. Figure 10.5 is a diagram showing the three functional areas of the firm, subdivided into the eleven application areas that we will discuss.

Finance

The financial area of the firm is concerned with money—obtaining it (from loans and stock offerings), controlling it (by means of operating budgets), and using it (by investing it). The accounting department is a part of the financial function, and it gathers much of the data used in making financial decisions. Other data comes from the environment, such as data describing the national economy.

Financial managers solve problems relating to three areas: long-range economic forecasting, cash flow, and control.

Economic Forecasting   The financial function prepares long-range forecasts to project the performance of the firm in its environment. The forecasts use various economic indicators to project the state of the economy, industry growth, and activity of the firm. This type of forecasting is best performed using sophisticated models developed with a procedural language such as FORTRAN. Spreadsheets might be useful making some of the projections—those not requiring complex formulas or an extensive data base of economic data. Spreadsheet potential: Poor.

Cash Flow   One problem facing the financial manager is how to obtain the needed finances for the firm. Another problem is how to use those finances most profitably. Neither area is one where the spreadsheet has been applied with much success. The decisions are generally unstructured and use routines programmed in a procedural language. For example, computer programs in BASIC or FORTRAN can help the manager decide between borrowing money or selling stock. Similar computer support is used in making the investments decision. Computer programs, using data bases of corporate financial data, help the manager decide where to invest surplus funds.

Having made the acquisition and investment decisions, the firm can simulate the cash flowing in and the cash flowing out each month for the next year or so. This is an area where the spreadsheet has been used effectively. You can develop a **cash flow model** much more quickly with an electronic spreadsheet than with a procedural language. Spreadsheet potential: Good.

Control   Practically every firm has an **operating budget** that is established for a fiscal (financial) year. Each department is given a certain amount of funds for its operations, and then the actual expenses are compared to the budget—usually on a month-to-month basis. This is the type of problem for which a spreadsheet is well-suited. This is likely the area where the spreadsheets have been applied most often and with the most success. Spreadsheet potential: Excellent.

Marketing   The marketing manager makes decisions that shape the mix of products and services offered to customers. Marketers have coined the term "4 P's" to describe the ingredients of the marketing offering: product, place, price, and promotion. We will use those four ingredients as the four areas of marketing decision making.

Product   Product decisions usually relate to which new products should be added to the line and which existing products should be deleted. Since this is an area where uncertainty prevails, probabilistic models are best-suited. The more expensive spreadsheets, such as IFPS, could be used here, along with models coded with a procedural language. The more limited spreadsheets, however, would not fit this type of problem. Spreadsheet potential: Fair.

Place   Place decisions relate to the channel of distribution for the firm's products —wholesalers and retailers. The place area has been a good one for modeling, with the decisions relating to (1) selection of the best distribution networks, and (2) control of those networks. In the selection area, a spreadsheet would not be of much use unless it could optimize the solution. IFPS has this capability, which enables it to function like an LP model. The selection decision lends itself more to LP than to most electronic spreadsheets.

In the control area, spreadsheets can be used in a number of ways. If the firm owns and operates its own wholesaling and retailing outlets, each could be analyzed financially, using a spreadsheet. For example, income statements and balance sheets could be prepared for each outlet, and the results of particular decisions (like an increase in shipping charges) simulated. Another control application is **inventory management**. A dynamic model of inventory behavior could be used to make decisions of how much stock to carry and when to reorder. The uncertainty relating to daily usage rates and time required by vendors to replenish stock calls for a probabilistic model. Spreadsheet potential: Good.

Price   The decision here is what price to charge. A spreadsheet is excellent for reflecting, in the form of an income statement, the results of raising or lowering the price. The **pricing model** could be dynamic—showing the year-by-year effects of the price change in terms of profit. If the equation for determining demand gets too complex, however, a procedural language would be best. Spreadsheet potential: Excellent.

Promotion   This is an area where no modeling technique has been effective. The area is concerned with the firm's advertising strategy and its sales force. Marketers have experimented with models that select the best mix of ad media (radio, TV, and so on), and with models that assign salespersons to territories, but none have been very successful. It is unlikely that a spreadsheet would fare any better. Spreadsheet potential: Poor.

Manufacturing   The manufacturing manager attempts to use the production facilities (the plant, its equipment, and its employees) in the most effective manner. These facilities are used to convert raw materials into finished products. The problems faced by the manufacturing manager fall into four categories: production flow, inventory, quality control, and cost control.

Production Flow   The computer has been applied successfully to schedule production and to manage the purchase of raw materials. But, the models have been specially programmed using either a procedural language such as FORTRAN or a special modeling language. Quite possibly, a spreadsheet could be used to map out, day-by-day and month-by-month, the firm's production schedule and raw material level. But, such a projection would appear to be best suited to a probabilistic model. Spreadsheet potential: Poor.

Inventory   The manufacturer faces the same problems in managing the inventory of materials as does the marketer in managing the inventory of products. So, the same demands for a probabilistic model, apply here. Spreadsheet potential: Good.

Quality Control   A spreadsheet could be used to report on the financial condition of a supplier or potential supplier. Very often, that condition is taken into account. The idea is to select those suppliers who will stay in business and represent long-term, reliable sources. Perhaps the what-if game could be played with this supplier data to gauge the effect of price changes, changes in quantities purchased, and so forth.

As the manager attempts to control the quality of the production process, standard statistical software and reports prepared by procedural languages or DBMS software give the manager the needed quality information. Spreadsheet potential: Fair.

Cost Control   This area is actually a subset of the firm's operating budget (prepared by the finance function). Since so many of the manufacturing resources (materials,

Figure 10.6   Summary of Electronic Spreadsheet Potential

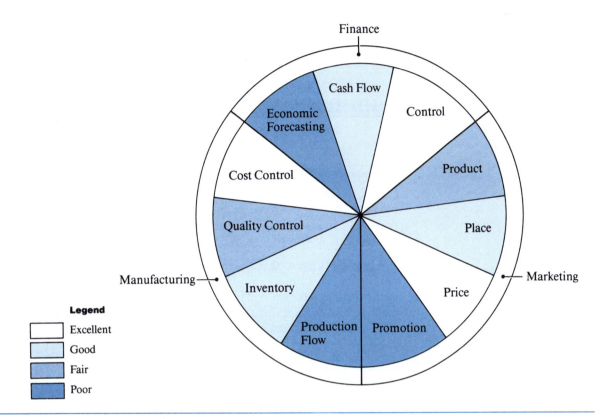

machines, and personnel) can be measured accurately and converted to costs, the manufacturing manager receives many cost reports. This is an excellent area for spreadsheet application. The effect of changes in costs can be simulated, period-by-period. Spreadsheet potential: Excellent.

Summary of Potential Applications

You must understand that this description of possible spreadsheet application areas is very general. It is intended to give you some flavor for the type of problems that managers face, and the fact that no single DSS technique, such as the spreadsheet, can solve them all. Each problem is unique and calls for a special type of DSS.

Each firm is also unique, and what works well as a DSS in one firm might not work well in another. Our discussion assumed a manufacturing operation. Other industries such as banking, health care, and insurance have special applications that would have to be evaluated individually.

Figure 10.6 graphically summarizes our discussion of application areas and the evaluation of electronic spreadsheets as possible decision support systems. Three application areas have excellent electronic spreadsheet potential—financial control, pricing, and production cost. In the case of pricing, the rating of "excellent" assumes that probabilities can be handled. Otherwise, the rating is "good."

Three other areas have good potential—cash flow, place, and inventory. The "good" ratings for place and inventory assume an ability to handle probabilities. Otherwise, the support would be "fair."

The remaining five areas receiving a "fair" or "poor" rating would likely lend themselves to other DSS approaches—customized programs written in a procedural language or a special modeling language and statistics software.

Summary

A mathematical model can be built to represent some part of a firm's operations. Computers can be used to perform the calculations quickly and accurately. A model can be static or dynamic. It is static if time is not a variable; otherwise, it is dynamic. A model can be optimizing if it points out the best alternative; otherwise it is nonoptimizing. Models can also be probabilistic if they can handle probabilities.

The phenomenon that the model represents is the entity, and the process of representation is simulation. The manager provides the setting for the simulation in the form of a scenario. The various items comprising the scenario are called attribute values, and these can be parameters or state variables. State variables change during the simulation, whereas parameters do not.

The main advantage of modeling is its ability to project the future, although not with perfect accuracy. The main disadvantage is the requirement for good mathematical skills. This requirement has resulted in specialists developing many of the models to be used by managers, often with poor results. The availability of easy-to-use modeling tools is likely to increase the use of models and improve their performance.

The electronic spreadsheet is perhaps the most user-friendly of the new breed of modeling tools. That, in part, explains its popularity. But the spreadsheet cannot help solve all kinds of business problems. It lends itself to those situations where the data can be presented in rows and columns. It can handle static or dynamic situations, but only the more expensive software is designed to incorporate probabilities and identify the optimal solution. Generally speaking, the best applications are financial control, pricing, and manufacturing cost control. More application areas will be added in the future as managers continue to experiment with this relatively new modeling tool.

Key Terms

Model	Parameter
Entity	Attribute value
Profit model	Spreadsheet
Linear programming (LP)	Electronic spreadsheet
Probability	IFPS (Interactive Financial Planning System)
Probabilistic model	Cash flow model
Deterministic model	Operating budget
State variable	Inventory management
	Pricing model

(Do not fill in blanks in the book. Write answers on a separate piece of paper.)

1. The phenomenon that a model represents is called the _____.

2. A(n) _____ model is like a snapshot and a(n) _____ model is like a motion picture.

3. A(n) _____ model produces the best answer.

4. The attributes of a model that change value during the course of the simulation are _____.

5. The attributes that do not change value during the simulation are _____.

6. Of the three basic ways that the manager can receive information from the DSS, _____ is the only one with an ability to predict the future.

7. The reason that modeling has not been more widely accepted is the lack of sophisticated _____ skills by many of the managers.

8. A large sheet with many rows and columns is known as a _____.

9. The best financial application for electronic spreadsheets is _____.

10. The best marketing application for electronic spreadsheets is _____.

11. The best manufacturing application for electronic spreadsheets is _____.

12. If an application area does not lend itself to electronic spreadsheets, then a model can be created using a _____ language or a _____ language.

13. An example of a very elaborate electronic spreadsheet is IFPS, which stands for _____.

14. When a spreadsheet is used to reflect a balance sheet, it is being used as a _____ model.

15. When a spreadsheet is used to reflect an income statement, it is being used as a _____ model.

16. The first electronic spreadsheet to gain widespread acceptance was _____.

17. Applying modeling to the DSS concept, the model handles the _____ part of the problem and the manager handles the _____ part.

18. The key to effective use of a model is _____.

19. State variables and parameters are both examples of _____.

20. The process of using a model is called _____.

11 Introduction to VisiCalc

VisiCalc was introduced in 1979, and by early 1982 more than 200,000 copies had been sold. Other software firms were quick to recognize the success of VisiCalc, and they introduced similar products. Today, there are in excess of 50 such packages on the market, and more than one million copies have been sold. In late 1982, VisiCorp started delivery on an advanced version of VisiCalc, and by mid-1983 10,000 copies had been shipped. Our discussion in this and the next chapter is aimed at the advanced version, Version 1.2.

VisiCalc is a general-purpose software system that can be used for solving problems involving data arranged in a matrix of rows and columns. The matrix, called an electronic spreadsheet, lends itself to answering what-if questions. If you make a change to any value in the spreadsheet, all formulas using that value are recalculated. You can see the results of the change quickly and easily.

In this chapter you will become acquainted with the VisiCalc screen display; moving the cursor around the screen; entering labels, formulas, and values; and most of the VisiCalc commands. After completing the chapter, you will be able to build static VisiCalc models that can be applied to a variety of problems throughout your firm. In the next chapter, the techniques of building dynamic VisiCalc models will be presented.

The VisiCalc Spreadsheet

The VisiCalc spreadsheet includes 254 rows (numbered 1 through 254) and 63 columns (identified with the letters A–Z, then AA–AZ, and finally BA–BK).

The intersection of each row and column is a **cell**, or an **entry**. As an example, the entry in the upper left corner of the spreadsheet is column A and row 1. The column and row identifications of a particular entry are the **coordinates**. The entry in the lower right corner is BK254. The coordinate identifies the column, followed by the row. Each entry is a separate, addressable storage position that can contain a label (such as PROFITS), numeric value (such as 5,000) or formula (such as +B1–B2). The labels and values appear on the screen; the formulas do not. The products of the formulas appear on the screen.

Loading VisiCalc

Your diskette must contain the DOS COMMAND.COM file, the VisiCalc file VC80.COM, and a file named AUTOEXEC.BAT that enables you to bypass the DOS date and time prompts. When you put your diskette in the a: drive and boot the system, the VisiCalc spreadsheet appears on the screen, ready to use.

Remove your diskette from the drive, and replace it with a blank, formatted diskette. You will have no more use for the VisiCalc diskette during this session. You will use the blank diskette to store your spreadsheet for future use. Since you only need one diskette drive to use VisiCalc, there is no difference between the procedure followed for single-drive and dual-drive systems.

Figure 11.1 illustrates the VisiCalc screen display after you boot the system. There are three rows at the upper left of the screen that provide information to you as you use VisiCalc. The first row contains the location of the cursor (entry A1), the

Figure 11.1   The VisiCalc Screen

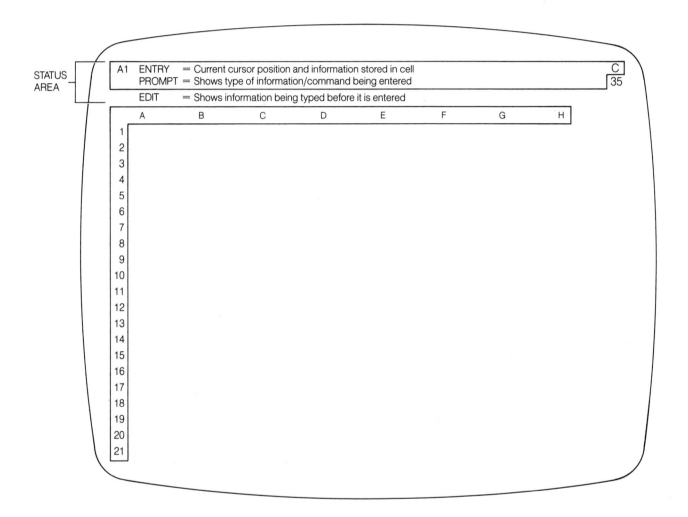

second row contains a copyright notice, and the third row identifies the serial number of your VisiCalc diskette. The second and third lines clear when you press any key.

Most of the screen is devoted to the spreadsheet area. The columns are identified in the horizontal band, and the rows are identified down the left side. The portion of the spreadsheet appearing on the screen includes rows 1 through 21 and columns A–H. The entire sheet is too large to fit on the screen at one time. You can move the spreadsheet so that different parts appear on the screen in the same manner that you move a microfiche in a viewer.

Moving the Cursor

As you begin your session, the cursor is located in coordinate A1. The cursor is rectangle shaped, filling the coordinate. One of the secrets to successful use of VisiCalc is being able to move the cursor quickly and accurately. Each time you press an arrow key the cursor moves one cell in that direction. When you hold the arrow key down, the cursor moves in that direction very rapidly—one cell after another. You stop the movement by releasing the key.

When the cursor reaches the edge of the spreadsheet you are warned with an audible beep. You cannot continue to move the cursor in that direction.

You can move the cursor directly to a coordinate by holding down the Shift key and pressing the key with the greater than (>) sign on it, and then entering the coordinate address, such as A50. The greater than key is called the **GO TO key**. Use the GO TO key to move the cursor more than a few spaces.

Another key can also move the cursor a great distance very quickly. It is the Home key. Each time you strike the Home key, the cursor moves to coordinate A1.

Exercise 1
Moving the Cursor

1. Put your VisiCalc diskette in the a: drive and boot the system. When the VisiCalc spreadsheet appears on the screen, replace the VisiCalc diskette with a blank, formatted diskette.

2. Press the right arrow key. Notice that the cursor moves from A1 to B1. Press the down arrow key. The cursor moves from B1 to B2.

3. Hold the right arrow key down and notice the cursor move across the screen. When the cursor gets to column H, the sheet begins to scroll to the right— column I appears on the right and column A disappears on the left. Hold the right arrow key down until the last column (BK) is reached. You get an audible beep when you reach the edge.

4. Hold the down arrow key down until the bottom row (254) is reached. Again, you get a beep.

5. Use the GO TO key to move the cursor to coordinate A200. Then use it to move to coordinate Z30.

6. Press the Home key to return to coordinate A1.

A Preliminary Note on Keyboard Use

In this, and all other software chapters, the word *enter* is used when you are to press the Enter key after keying in data or an instruction. The word *type* is used when you do not have to press Enter.

Entering Labels and Values

As you enter contents into a cell, information is displayed in the three rows at the upper left of the screen. The upper row is the entry contents line, the second one is the prompt line, and the third is the edit line.

Everything that you type appears on the **edit line**. If you violate some VisiCalc rule in entering the material, you will get an audible beep and the entry will be canceled. If you make a mistake before you press Enter, simply backspace and retype. If you have already pressed Enter, retype the entire cell contents and reenter.

Figure 11.2   Screen Response on Data Entry

After you type the first letter P of PROFIT:

A1	Entry Contents Line
Label	Prompt Line
P	Edit Line

After you type the entire label:

A1	Entry Contents Line
Label	Prompt Line
PROFIT	Edit Line

After you press Enter:

A1 (L) PROFIT	Entry Contents Line
	Prompt Line
	Edit Line

VisiCalc responds to the first character that you type in a cell by displaying either an L or a V on the **prompt line**. L stands for label and V for value. If you type a digit, a plus or minus sign, or a decimal point, VisiCalc assumes that you are entering a value and displays the V. If you type anything else, VisiCalc assumes that you are entering a label and displays the L.

After you type the cell contents and press Enter, the **entry contents line** displays three items of information—the coordinate, whether the contents are a label or a value, and the actual contents. For example, if you enter the label PROFIT in cell F1, the entry contents line will display F1 (L) PROFIT.

Figure 11.2 illustrates how the contents of the three lines at the top of the screen change as you type and enter information.

Cell Contents

Each cell or entry can contain a label, a value, or a formula. The **labels** identify the spreadsheet that you build and its columns and rows. **Values** are constants that remain unchanged during a calculation. Only you can change a value. **Formulas** contain both constant values and variable names. The variable names refer to cells, and the values in those cells are used by the formulas. When the values of any of the variables in a formula change, the formula is automatically recalculated and the results are displayed on the screen.

Values

Values include the digits 0–9, the plus and minus sign, and the decimal point. You cannot include dollar signs and commas. When you type an acceptable numeric character, the prompt line reads Value.

As you key in numeric values, both leading and trailing zeros are ignored. You can store as many as 13 digits at an entry. The leftmost position in the entry always remains blank so that displayed values do not "run together." Numeric data is right-justified in the entry.

Labels

Labels usually begin with a letter. When you type the first letter, the word *Label* appears on the prompt line. Sometimes, a label will begin with a number, such as 1ST QUARTER. To enter this as a label rather than a value, begin with a quotation mark—"1ST QUARTER. An ending quotation mark is not needed. The quotation mark does not become a part of the label; it only serves as an identifier.

A label cannot begin with a space. If you want to include one or more leading spaces, begin with a quote mark and follow it with the spaces (" LABEL). Label data is left-justified in the entry.

Formulas

Formulas express relationships between constants (that is, values such as 5,000) and variables (that is, coordinate references such as A3). You can use the following **arithmetic operators** to express the relationships:

+   Add
−   Subtract
*   Multiply
/   Divide
^   Exponentiation

Like most programming languages, the order of computation is from left to right, and contents of parentheses are computed first. You can use as many as nine levels of parentheses. Unlike most languages, multiplication and division are not done before addition and subtraction. There is no hierarchy for the operations. You specify the operations to be done first by enclosing them in parentheses.

You cannot enter a formula that begins with a letter, since VisiCalc will think it is a label. So, intead of typing B1+B2, you can key in (B1+B2) or +B1+B2. Also, you should not insert any spaces in a formula (for example, VisiCalc will not accept B1 + B2).

If your formula produces an answer that is too large to display in the cell on the screen, you get an overflow condition. The overflow is signaled by displaying a series of greater than signs ($>>>>$) in the cell. The simple solution to this problem is to increase the size of the cell. You will learn how to do this later in the chapter.

Recalculation

The characteristic of VisiCalc that probably has been most responsible for its popularity is its recalculation feature. Any time that you change a value, all formulas using that value are automatically recalculated. This facilitates what-if modeling. If you have a VisiCalc model that simulates the effect of a price change on profit, for example, you position the cursor on the cell containing price and enter various amounts—one after the other. Each time you enter a new price, the spreadsheet is recalculated. You can look at the cell containing profit and see the effect of the price change.

VisiCalc can recalculate the values in your sheet in either a rowwise or a columnwise manner. In a **rowwise recalculation**, the cells on one row are recalculated before moving to the next row. Row 1 is recalculated, then row 2, and so on. In a **columnwise recalculation**, the cells in one column are recalculated before moving to the next column. Column A is recalculated, then column B, and so on.

If your model is a simple one, such as an income statement for a single time period, it doesn't matter whether recalculation is accomplished rowwise or columnwise. However, if your model were an income statement such as the one illustrated in Figure 11.3, and several years' data were displayed in columns, you would want a columnwise recalculation. The sales revenue for each year is obtained by multiplying the quantity sold by the unit price. You can specify the quantity for one year is, say 10 percent more than that of the previous year. Each year (column) is therefore dependent on the previous year (column) for its quantity figure. In this case, you would want columnwise recalculation.

If your model were an inventory simulation such as that illustrated in Figure 11.4, you would want rowwise recalculation. Here, each row represents a day's inventory activity. The ending balance for one day is used as the beginning balance for the next. Hence, each day (row) is dependent on the previous day (row) for its beginning balance. In this case, you would want rowwise recalculation.

If you don't specify which direction you wish for recalculation, VisiCalc assumes columnwise. Refer to Figure 11.1 and look in the upper right-hand corner of the screen. You will see the **Order Indicator**—C for columnwise. Later, you will learn how to change from columnwise to rowwise (R), and then back to columnwise.

While you are looking at the figure, look just below the order indicator. You see a number. This is the **available primary storage space**, in kilobytes. As you fill in your sheet, this space shrinks.

Exercise 2
Entering Labels and Values

1. With the cursor at A1, type **REVENUE** (press the Caps Lock key to get uppercase). Press the Enter key to record your input at the entry location.

   Notice the top line at the left of the screen. This is the entry contents line. You should see:

   A1 (L) REVENUE

   A1 is the coordinate where the cursor is located. (L) identifies the data as a label, followed by the data itself (REVENUE).

   The entry contents line indicates what is actually stored at the cursor location.

2. Now, press the right arrow key to move the cursor to B1. Enter the value **5000**. The entry contents line should read:

   B1 (V) 5000

Figure 11.3   An Income Statement Requiring Columnwise Recalculation

```
              CURRENT PERIOD DECISIONS
PRICE                                  $40
PLANT INVESTMENT                        $0
MARKETING                         $550,000
RESEARCH & DEVELOPMENT                  $0


-----------------------------------------------------------------
              OPERATING STATEMENT

MARKET POTENTIAL                  216109
SALES VOLUME                      201000
PRODUCTION, THIS QUARTER          200000
INVENTORY, FINISHED GOODS              0
PLANT CAPACITY, THIS QUARTER      504643


-----------------------------------------------------------------


                  INCOME STATEMENT

RECEIPTS, SALES REVENUE                              $8,040,000
EXPENSES, MARKETING                     $550,000
      RESEARCH AND DEVELOPMENT                $0
      ADMINISTRATION                    $275,000
      MAINTENANCE                       $150,000
      LABOR                           $1,236,000
      MATERIALS                       $1,250,000
      REDUCTION, FINISHED GOODS          $12,000
      DEPRECIATION                      $883,125
      FINISHED GOODS CARRYING COSTS           $0
      RAW MATERIALS CARRYING COSTS       $62,500
      ORDERING COSTS                     $50,000
      PLANT INVESTMENT EXPENSES               $0
      FINANCE CHARGES AND PENALTIES           $0
      SUNDRIES                         $373,342
TOTAL EXPENSES                                       $4,841,967
PROFIT BEFORE INCOME TAX                             $3,198,033
INCOME TAX                                           $1,531,681

NET PROFIT AFTER INCOME TAX                          $1,666,352


-----------------------------------------------------------------
-----------------------------------------------------------------
```

3. Move the cursor to A2 and press the letter **C**. Look at the second line from the top on the left. This is the prompt line. It prompts you what to do next. It should dislay the word *label*. Continue to enter the label by typing **OSTS** and pressing Enter.

4. Move the cursor to B2 and enter **3000**.

5. Move the cursor to A3 and enter **PROFIT**.

Figure 11.4   An Inventory Model Requiring Rowwise Recalculation

```
ORDER QUANTITY........ 150

REORDER POINT......... 175
```

DAY	BEG BAL	REC	USG NUM	USG	END BAL	BO QTY	LD NUM	LD TM	REC DUE
1	200		62	30	170		19	8	9
2	170		63	30	140				
3	140		73	30	110				
4	110		2	15	95				
5	95		16	20	75				
6	75		69	30	45				
7	45		83	35	10				
8	10		10	20	0	10			
9	0	150	88	35	105		13	7	16
10	105		65	30	75				
11	75		27	25	50				
12	50		95	40	10				
13	10		55	30	0	20			
14	0		25	25	0	25			
15	0		0	15	0	15			
16	0	150	12	20	70		87	9	25
17	70		93	40	30				
18	30		43	25	5				
19	5		25	25	0	20			
20	0		52	30	0	30			
21	0		31	25	0	25			
22	0		72	30	0	30			
23	0		98	40	0	40			
24	0		97	40	0	40			
25	0	150	98	40	0	40	95	10	35

```
AVERAGE INVENTORY LEVEL      40


SERVICE LEVEL
    QUANTITY ORDERED        725
    QUANTITY BACKORDERED    295
    SERVICE PERCENT          59 %

COST ANALYSIS
    CARRYING COSTS      $  1485
    SERVICE COSTS       $ 61500
    TOTAL  COSTS        $ 62985
```

6. Move the cursor to B3 and enter the formula **(B1-B2)**, including the parentheses. There are no spaces in a formula. Before you press Enter look at the third line from the top at the left of the screen. This is the edit line. It displays the formula.

7. Press Enter and notice that the formula moves from the Edit line to the Entry Contents Line. Also notice that entry B3 contains the product of the calculation—2000.

Exercise 3
Recalculation

1. Using the model that you entered in Exercise 2, move the cursor to B1 and key in **6000**. Do not press Enter yet.

2. Look at the revenue amount at B3.

3. Press Enter.

4. See the effect of the recalculation as the revenue amount at B3 changes.

Commands

VisiCalc is not a procedural programming language such as BASIC. So, instead of writing a program that causes a series of operations to be performed, you use commands. You must enter each command when you want that operation performed. You initiate the process by typing a slash, or diagonal (/). Each time you do this the prompt line reads:

Command: BCDEFGIMPRSTVW-

The letters are abbreviations for the commands. VisiCalc is prompting you with your choices of commands.

Your first reaction to the string of letters in the command prompt might be one of confusion. The letters look confusing, but they really aren't. It only takes a little practice to become familiar with the abbreviations. And, you can gain this familiarity as you learn the commands—one command at a time. In the sections that follow, and in the next chapter, we will describe each VisiCalc command.

The FORMAT Command

You have some control over how data is displayed on the screen. Normally, numeric values are right-justified in the cell, and labels are left-justified. If you want to change or expand on this format, you type the letter **F** in response to the prompt line menu of command choices. You do not have to press Enter. As you type F, you will see the prompt line change to:

Format: DGILR$*

This is another menu. VisiCalc is referred to as being **menu-driven**. It assists you in selecting the commands by displaying menus. The next character you type specifies the format for the cell where the cursor is positioned.

I   Display the value as an integer. This rounds the value to the nearest whole number.

L   Left-justify the item.

R   Right-justify the item.

$ Display the value with a decimal point and two positions to the right. This does not include the dollar sign or commas. Rounding occurs.

*   If you want to prepare a bar graph and print a string of asterisks in the entry rather than a value, this command will cause one asterisk to be printed for each integer value. For example, if there is a 5 in the entry, ***** will be displayed.

G   If you do not want this entry to be formatted differently from the general format, type **G**. The **general format** specified right-justification for values and left-justification for labels.

D   If you want to erase the existing format, type **D**. This returns the cell to the global format (discussed below).

There are two things that you should understand about the FORMAT command:

1. You are only formatting the cell where the cursor is located.

2. You are only affecting how data is displayed—not how it is stored. For example, if you specify integer for numeric data, VisiCalc retains in storage any digits to the right of the decimal point.

The GLOBAL Command

The term **global**, when applied to computer software, means that a function or operation is universally applied. In other words, it applies throughout—to everything. You recall from dBASE II that we asked for a file directory by using *.* for the file name. The asterisks were global descriptors—they, in effect, said "Display all file names with all extensions." In VisiCalc, the term global means that something applies to all cells of the spreadsheet unless you have specified otherwise for individual cells.

If you type /G, the prompt line will read:

Global: CORF

The CORF tells you that you have four options that may be applied globally.

The C represents *column width*, or the number of positions that are displayed for each cell. If you do not specify otherwise, VisiCalc assumes a column width of 9 positions. The default option is 9. If you want to change that, type C in response to the prompt line cue. The prompt line then reads:

Column Width

Now enter in the width you desire—from 3 to 77.

Two important points concerning column width are:

1. This command changes the width of the display; it does not change how the data is stored.

2. Consider the size of both your labels and your values when you select the column width. Most likely, the labels (such as the row identifiers in the first column) are wider than the values.

When you type **O** in response to the CORF prompt, you can change the order of recalculation from columnwise to rowwise. The prompt line reads:

Reeval Order: R C

Type **R** to specify rowwise; type **C** to return to columnwise. You do not have to press Enter.

Recalculation can be automatically performed when a value changes, or it can be initiated by pressing the ! key. Recalculation can be either columnwise or rowwise. This is the **recalculation mode**, and it is specified by typing R in response to CORF. The prompt line reads:

Recalc: A M

For automatic recalculation, type **A**; for manual recalculation (using the ! key), type **M**. Again, you do not have to press Enter. If you do not specify a manual recalculation mode VisiCalc assumes automatic. The recalculation can be time-consuming on large sheets, so you might want to trigger it only at specific times. That is when you specify manual. When recalculation is taking place, an ! appears in the upper right-hand corner of the screen.

By typing **F** in response to CORF, you affect the format of *all* entries that do not have their own individual format. With the FORMAT command, you affect *individual* entries. With the GLOBAL command, you affect all entries not formatted individually. So, in this case, the term global does not mean "without exception." An exception is made for individually formatted entries. In using the global format, follow the letter F with the same letters used for the FORMAT command—$, I, and so on. They work exactly the same way. You do not have to press Enter.

To return to the general format that was in effect when you began your VisiCalc session, type **/GFG**. The second G specifies general.

The BLANK Command

If you want to blank out the cell where the cursor is you type **/B** and press Enter. The sequence for initiating a command is always the same—a slash (/), followed by the command letter. For some commands, such as FORMAT, you do not have to press Enter. For others, like BLANK, you do.

When you blank out an entry, you erase the data stored at that position, but the format remains in effect. If you want to blank out the format, type **/FD**.

The CLEAR Command

This command clears the entire spreadsheet. Type **/C** and the prompt line reads:

Clear: Type Y to confirm

Since the action is nonrecoverable, VisiCalc wants you to be sure you wish to destroy all row and column entries. If you want to clear, type **Y**. If you change your mind, press any other key.

It is good practice to always use this command before creating a spreadsheet or loading a sheet from the diskette. This practice prevents VisiCalc from merging two sheets when one sheet is loaded from the diskette on top of another sheet already in primary storage.

Some VisiCalc users get into the habit of rapidly typing /CY to clear the sheet, without thinking about the Y. This is a bad habit, since it bypasses the confirmation step.

Exercise 4
A What-If Model

1. If your PC configuration includes a printer, make certain that it is turned on.

2. If your screen still contains a display from Exercise 2, clear the screen by typing **/CY**. The cursor should return to A1.

3. Type the label **SALES REVENUE**. Enter it by pressing the down arrow key. This also moves the cursor to the cell below, saving you a keystroke. This is good technique for entering data.

4. You notice that the default column width of 9 is not wide enough to display all of the label in A1. Change to a column width of 18 by typing **/GC18**. Now you see all of the label displayed.

5. With the cursor on A2, type **EXPENSES**. Enter the label with the down arrow key.

6. Continue with this technique, entering the following labels. The leading quote mark and the three blank spaces (represented by the underline marks) give you an indention.

    A3 "_ _ _ MANUFACTURING
    A4 "_ _ _ MARKETING
    A5 "_ _ _ ADMINISTRATION
    A6 TOTAL EXPENSES
    A7 PROFIT
    A8 DECISIONS:
    A9 "_ _ _ UNIT PRICE
    A10 "_ _ _ VOLUME

7. You have entered all of the labels you will need at the present time. Next, to enter formulas in column B, press the **Home** key to move the cursor to A1. Now press the right arrow key.

8. With the cursor at B1, you will enter the formula for computing sales revenue. We want to multiply price (a value to be entered later in B9) times quantity, or volume (a value to be entered later in B10). Enter the formula **+B9*B10** with the down arrow key. You could have entered (B9*B10). Notice a zero in B1; this is because you haven't yet specified values for B9 and B10.

    (We should comment at this point that this example uses a technique that should be avoided—a forward reference. A **forward reference** is one made to a cell below or to the right. The references in B1 to values at B9 and B10 are forward references. Since VisiCalc computes values in a left-to-right and a top-to-bottom fashion, it is easier for it to "look back" than to "look ahead" to obtain values. It is always best to design a spreadsheet with only **backward references**—above and/or to the left. You will eliminate our example's forward references in a later exercise.)

9. Press the down arrow key again to move the cursor to B3. Enter the formula **(B10*12.50)**. Manufacturing costs are $12.50 per unit produced.

10. At B4, enter the formula **+B10*8.75**. Marketing costs are $8.75 per unit.

11. At B5, enter **50000+(B10*2.25)**. Administrative costs are a fixed cost of $50,000 plus a variable cost of $2.25 per unit. Parentheses are necessary so that the multiplication is done first. Otherwise, VisiCalc would add the contents of B10 to 50000, and then multiply by 2.25. When you enter the formula, you notice that B5 displays 50000. This is the constant in the formula; the variables are still blank.

12. At B6, enter **(B3+B4+B5**. The right parenthesis is not necessary.

13. At B7, enter **+B1−B6**.

14. You have now built a what-if model. Move the cursor to B10 with the GO TO key. Enter the volume 60000 with the up arrow key.

15. With the cursor at B9, you will play the what-if game by varying price and seeing the results. Enter a price of 25.00. Use the Enter key so that the cursor will stay at B9. In this manner, you can easily enter varying prices.

16. You can see the results of a $25.00 price—a profit of $40,000. Continue to enter price figures until you get a profit of $100,000. Now, what price generates a profit of $200,00? This is how the manager plays the what-if game.

17. If your PC has a printer, use the print screen or the print switch toggle technique to obtain a hard copy of your spreadsheet. (See Chapter 8 for an explanation of these two techniques.)

18. Do not clear the screen, since you will save your spreadsheet in the next exercise.

The STORAGE Command

The STORAGE command is used to save your VisiCalc spreadsheet on a diskette or on the printer, and to retrieve a stored spreadsheet from the diskette. When you type /S, the prompt line reads:

Storage: L S D Q #

We will not discuss the pound sign (#) in this text. It is used when you want to store or load data in a format that facilitates exchange between two programs. For example, you can produce data using VisiCalc that can later be processed by a BASIC program.[1]

Respond to the STORAGE prompt with S when you want to *save* your spreadsheet. Make certain that you have a formatted diskette that is not write protected in the logged drive. You will then be prompted to enter the "File for Saving." The rules for naming a VisiCalc file are:

♦ Use no more than 8 characters.

♦ The first position must be a letter.

♦ No special characters such as * are allowed.

You can specify the nonlogged drive by adding an A: or B: prefix. VisiCalc, when it saves the file on the diskette, will add a .VC extension.

When saving a file name that is already on the diskette, you must confirm your intention with a Y. This is a built-in check to ensure that you do not accidentally erase an earlier version of the file that you want to save. When you save a spreadsheet, you save the labels, values, formulas, global characteristics, and even the cursor location.

It is possible to save the file on the printer, although that is not the way to print a spreadsheet. When you save a file on the printer, you use **LPT1:** for the file name. You must include the colon. The spreadsheet entries are printed one at a time, in reverse order. The coordinates containing formulas print the formulas themselves, not the values that they produce. Your output is not a spreadsheet with data, however this is an excellent way to document the arithmetic formulas that are built into a spreadsheet.

When you want to *load* a saved file from the diskette into primary storage, first clear the screen with **/CY** and then type **/SL.** You will be prompted for the file name. If you can't remember what it is, press the right arrow key and watch the prompt line. Keep pressing the arrow key until the file name appears. Then press Enter. If the word "ERROR" appears while the file is loading, disregard it. If you have your VisiCalc spreadsheets stored on the diskette in the b: drive, you must enter B: before pressing the right arrow key.

1. The data interchange format (DIF) is explained in the VisiCalc manual. Also, you can obtain information from the DIF Clearinghouse, P.O. Box 526, Cambridge, MA 02139. DIF is a trademark of Software Arts, Inc.

To *delete* a file, respond to the STORAGE prompt with a **D** and the file name. You must then confirm your intentions by typing **Y** in response to the prompt line cue.

Although it may at first seem strange, the STORAGE command is used to *quit* VisiCalc. Type **/SQ**. This must be confirmed with a Y or canceled by pressing any other key. Actually, there is a sound logic to locating the QUIT command within the storage category. Each time you want to quit, you are prompted to store. The prompt is intended to prevent you from accidentally terminating a session without storing your spreadsheet for future use.

Exercise 5
Saving Your
Spreadsheet

1. Save the what-if model that you built in Exercise 4 by typing **/SS**.

2. Respond to the "File for Saving" prompt with **WHATIF1**. Press Enter. When the red light on the logged drive goes off, the file has been saved.

Exercise 6
Loading Your
Spreadsheet

1. Type **/CY** to clear the spreadsheet.

2. Enter **/SL** to specify a file loading operation.

3. Press the right arrow key until the name of your file appears on the edit line. The name should appear as A:WHATIF1.VC.

4. Press Enter to load your sheet.

The INSERT Command

To insert a row or column, move the cursor to the row below the point where the inserted row will be added, or to the column to the right of the point where the inserted column will be added. Type **/I**; the prompt line reads:

Insert: R C

If you want to insert a row, type **R**. If you want to insert a column, type **C**. You do not have to press Enter.

If any formulas on the spreadsheet contain references to coordinates on the rows or columns that were moved to make room for the insertion, those coordinates are automatically updated. For example, if a formula refers to D12, and the insertion caused column D to become column E, the referenced formula will be changed to E12.

Exercise 7
Inserting Rows

Your WHATIF1 model does a good job of computing profit. Let's add a line that computes income tax and another one that subtracts the tax from the (gross) profit, giving net profit.

1. Move the cursor to any coordinate on row 8 and type **/IR**. This inserts a blank line at row 8.

2. With the cursor at A8, enter **INCOME TAX**.

3. With the cursor at B8, enter the formula **(B7*.48)**. We will use a simplified formula of 48 percent.

4. With the cursor on row 9, type **/IR**. This inserts another blank line at row 9.

5. Move the cursor to A9 and enter **NET PROFIT**.

6. With the cursor at B9 enter the formula **(B7−B8)**.

7. Move the cursor to A7 and enter **GROSS PROFIT**.

8. Move the cursor to B11 and enter a new price—**$37.50**.

9. If your PC has a printer, use the STORAGE command to obtain a hard-copy record of your spreadsheet formulas. Type **/SS**, and then specify **LPT1:** as the file name.

10. Now, save your income tax model on your diskette. But do not erase the original version (WHATIF1) that we built in Exercise 4. Type **/SS**, and get the "File for Saving" prompt.

Press the right arrow key until the name A:WHATIF1.VC appears on the edit line. Use the Backspace key to position the cursor on the 1. Now, type **2** and press Enter. Your income tax model will be saved as WHATIF2.VC. The earlier model, WHATIF1.VC, is still on the diskette. To verify that both models are on your diskette, type **/SS** and then press the right arrow key to view the file names. Cancel the save operation by pressing the Break key. This is a good way to save versions or "generations" of a model.

The MOVE Command

You can move (not copy) a row or column to a new location by typing /M. The prompt line reads:

Move: From ... To

You are being prompted to identify the location of the row or column to be moved (FROM) and the location to which it should be moved (TO). You do not have to specify whether it is a row or column to be moved—VisiCalc can determine that. If the same row is identified in both addresses, for example "FROM B1 to C1," VisiCalc knows that it is a column move. If the column letters are the same, for example, "FROM B1 to B8," VisiCalc knows that it is a row move.

The technique for moving a *row* is to first position the cursor anywhere on the row to be moved. Then, type /M. In response to the prompt, type a period. This causes the Edit Line to display the cursor location followed by an **ellipsis (...)**. For example, the edit line would display "D12 ... ." Then, type the TO coordinate. Use the same column identifier as in the FROM coordinate (D), followed by the number of the TO row (such as 6). The Edit Line line reads "D12 ... D6." Now press Enter.

Use the same technique for a *column* move. Position the cursor on the column to be moved. Type a period. The Edit Line will reveal the FROM coordinate (for example, C19 ...). Then, type the identifier of the TO column (for example, F) followed by the same row number as the FROM coordinate (19). The Edit Line reads "C19 ... F19." Now, press Enter.

If the cursor is not positioned on the FROM row or column, you must press the Backspace key once to erase the cursor location on the edit line. Then, key in the FROM coordinate and proceed as above.

Exercise 8
Moving Rows

The WHATIF2 model would look better if the decisions were above the income statement. Let's move rows 10–12 to rows 1–3.

1. Position the cursor on A10. Type **/M**.

2. Press the period key.

3. Enter **A1**. Row 10 should now be row 1. The old rows 1–9 are now rows 2–10.

4. Position the cursor on A11. Type /**M**. Press the period key and enter **A2**.

5. Move row 12 to row 3 in the same manner.

The EDIT Command

Recall that in dBASE II we edited our file after we created it. We also do editing in VisiCalc—we edit (or correct) labels, values, or formulas that are stored at entries.

Before we discuss the VisiCalc editing procedure, one point should be made clear. Unless the entry is very long and complex, such as a lengthy formula, it is quicker to simply retype the entire entry.

To edit an entry, move the cursor to the entry and type /**E**. An **edit cue**, a box, is displayed at the first character of the entry as it is displayed on the edit line. The arrow keys can be used to move the cue:

+ The right arrow moves the cue 1 position to the right.
+ The left arrow moves the cue 1 position to the left.
+ The up arrow jumps the cue to the start of the entry.
+ The down arrow jumps the cue to the end of the entry.

To *delete* one or more characters, move the cue to the right of the character(s) to be deleted. Then press the Backspace key for each character to be deleted. To *insert* one or more characters, move the cue to the right of the position where the insertion is to occur. Then type the data to be inserted. Press Enter at any position in the entry to make the changes permanent. If you decide against making the changes, press the Break key.

If you try to make a change that is against the rules, VisiCalc will beep and position the cue at the point of the violation.

The above procedure is used after you've keyed in your spreadsheet and you are checking for errors. You may, instead, prefer to correct errors as you go along. If you discover an error while entering the data, you can initiate the edit mode by keying Ctrl + E. The edit cue will be positioned at the end of the entry. Proceed as above.

Exercise 9
Editing

Let's change the income tax formula in your WHATIF2 model from 48 percent to 42 percent.

1. With the cursor at B11, type /**E**.

2. Watch the edit line. Use the right arrow key to move the edit cue to the position just to the right of the "8" in ".48".

3. Press the Backspace key to delete the 8.

4. Type **2**.

5. Press Enter.

6. Follow the same procedure to change GROSS PROFIT to PROFIT BEFORE TAX.

7. Change NET PROFIT to PROFIT AFTER TAX.

The LABEL REPEATING Command

When you type a slash (/) to initiate a command, you get the abbreviations for the commands on the prompt line. The rightmost character is a hyphen (–). You type the hyphen in response to the prompt when you want to use the LABEL REPEATING command. With this command you can type a character once and it is repeated across the entry. To use the LABEL REPEATING command:

1. Type a slash (/).
2. Type a hyphen (–).
3. Enter the character to be repeated.

For example, if you want to fill an entry with pound signs (#), you type / – # and press Enter.

The REPLICATE Command

In this chapter, we are learning how to develop a static VisiCalc model. With our WHATIF2 model, we can simulate one period's activity. In the next chapter, we will expand the WHATIF2 model so that it can simulate four quarters' activity.

Presently, the period's values appear in column B. Later, we will add values in columns C, D, and E. We are going to use the REPLICATE command now to prepare for the dynamic, four-period model.

First, let's display a row of diagonals (/) across the sheet on row 13 to serve as a bottom border. We want the diagonals to extend from column A through column E. To do this we position the cursor at entry A13 and fill it with diagonals using the LABEL REPEATING command. Now you are ready to use the REPLICATE command that repeats, or duplicates, the contents of one or more entries. When you type **/R** the prompt line reads:

Replicate: Source range or ENTER

Since you want to replicate the contents of the cursor location (entry A13), press Enter.

Then, type the range of the receiving area: **B13.E13**. Then, you press Enter to complete the replication. A step-by-step illustration appears in Figure 11.5.

The REPLICATE command replicates values and labels and their format. We will learn more about the REPLICATE command in the next chapter.

Exercise 10 Replication

1. Follow the procedure outlined above to replicate the row of underline marks from A13 (which you must first enter) to B13 through E13. The underline mark is located on the same key as the minus sign or dash. Hold the Shift key down to enter the underline mark. Use the LABEL REPEATING command to enter the underline marks in A13.

2. Replicate a row of hyphens to separate the decisions portion of your spreadsheet (the first 3 rows) from the rest. You must first insert a blank line. The hyphens should extend through column E.

The DELETE Command

To delete a row or column, move the cursor to any position on the row or column and type **/D**. The prompt line reads:

Delete: R C

VisiCalc does not ask you to confirm a deletion. When you press R or C, the deletion is made. You do not even have to press Enter.

Figure 11.5   Replicating a Single Entry

1. Position the cursor at A13.
2. Fill the entry with diagonals.
3. Press Enter.
4. Type /R.
5. The prompt line reads: Replicate: Source range or ENTER
6. Press Enter.
7. The edit line reads: A13...A13:
8. Row 13 appears as:

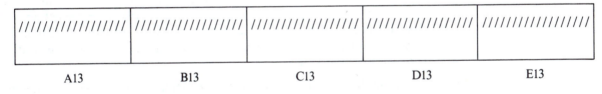

////////////////				
A13	B13	C13	D13	E13

9. Type B13.E13
10. The edit line reads: A13...A13:B:13.E13
    This says, in effect, "Replicate the contents of entry A13 through entry A13 (a single entry) in entry B13 through entry E13."
11. Press Enter.
12. Row 13 appears as:

////////////////	////////////////	////////////////	////////////////	////////////////
A13	B13	C13	D13	E13

When you type **R** (for row) or **C** (for column), the row or column is deleted, and VisiCalc reviews the entire spreadsheet, checking to see if the deleted row or column changes any formula references. If so, they are automatically updated. There is no indication that this "rippling" effect is occurring and it may take a few seconds, so be patient. If the deleted row or column contains coordinates referred to in other locations, those locations are changed to read ERROR.

Exercise 11
Deletion

The line of diagonals at the bottom of the spreadsheet looks a little gaudy. Let's delete it.

1. Move the cursor to any point on row 14.

2. Type /**DR**.

The TITLES Command

You can use labels across the top of the spreadsheet to identify the columns. You simply position the cursor at an entry and type in the label. You perform the same operation down the left margin to label the rows.

These titles are fine as long as you are working near the top and left margins. However, when you move to the lower right-hand part of the spreadsheet, the titles scroll off of the screen. It is possible to "freeze" the titles along the margins so that they do not scroll with the data entries. This is accomplished with the TITLES command.

Figure 11.6   Freezing Row and Column Titles at the Same Time

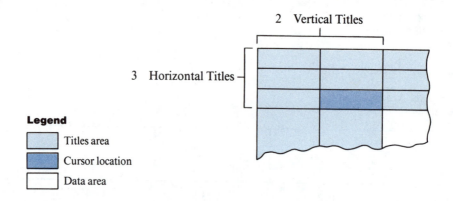

Legend

☐ Titles area

■ Cursor location

☐ Data area

When you type **/T**, the prompt line reads:

Titles: H V B N

If you want to freeze *horizontal* titles (such as those at the top of columns), you type **H**. If you want to freeze *vertical* titles (such as those down the left side of the spreadsheet), you type **V**. You can freeze *both horizontal and vertical* titles at the same time by typing **B**. If you have previously frozen titles, and you want to unfreeze them, type **N** for no titles.

You tell VisiCalc which columns or rows to freeze by first positioning the cursor on the appropriate row or column and then responding to the prompt with H, V, or B.

If you want to freeze titles on multiple rows, such as the first three rows, position the cursor on the lower row (3). Type **H**, and all three rows are frozen. If you want to freeze titles on multiple columns, such as the leftmost two, position the cursor on the rightmost column (B). Type **V**.

If you want to freeze both horizontal and vertical titles, position the cursor at the intersection. For example, if you want to freeze titles on columns A and B, and rows 1, 2, and 3, position the cursor on B3. Then type **B**. Figure 11.6 illustrates the cursor location when both titles are frozen at the same time.

If you have a long title that is too big for a single entry, you split it and put different parts in separate entries. Let's assume that column width is 9, and you want to print the title MONTHLY CASH FLOW ANALYSIS (26 characters) at the top of the report in entries C3, C4, and C5. Move the cursor to C3 and type " MONTHLY. Press the right arrow key to move the cursor to C4, and type CASHFLOW. Move the cursor to C5 and type **REPORT**.

Once you have frozen titles, they become the margins of your sheet. If you try to move the cursor into the titles area with an arrow key, VisiCalc will beep. You can use the GO TO key (>) to enter the titles area.

Exercise 12
Titles

We already have titles down column A of the WHATIF2 model. Let's add some at the top.

1. Insert 5 blank lines at the top of the spreadsheet.

2. To align the report title at the left margin on the first line, with the cursor in A1, enter **PRO FORMA INCOME S**. (The period is not a part of the label.)

3. With the cursor at B1, enter **TATEMENT**.

4. With the cursor at B3, enter **QUARTER**.

5. With the cursor at B4, enter **1**.

6. Notice that the QUARTER and the 1 do not line up properly. We need to right-justify QUARTER. With the cursor in B3, type **/FR**.

7. Freeze the titles by positioning the cursor on entry A4 and typing **/TB**. Use the arrow keys and try to scroll the titles off of the screen to verify that they are frozen.

8. Save your model as WHATIF3. You now have three generations of your model stored on the diskette.

The PRINT Command

The PRINT command is used to write either to a printer or to a diskette. To initiate the process, first position the cursor at the upper left-hand corner of the "rectangle" to be written. For the WHATIF2 model, the rectangle extends from coordinate A1 to coordinate B14. Position the cursor at A1. Then type **/P**. The prompt line reads:

Print: File, Printer

You can respond by typing an F for a diskette write or a P for a printer write. This is not the diskette write command that is used to create a backup copy of your spreadsheet, so we will not pursue diskette writing here. Type a **P**.

The prompt line next displays:

Print: Lower right, "Setup, – , &

Type in the coordinate of the lower right-hand corner of the rectangle to be written **(B14)**. On most popular printers, such as the IBM Graphics Printer, Epson MX-100, and Epson FX-80, this is enough. Press Enter to start printing. The remainder of the prompt line refers to coding necessary for certain other printers. If your printer requires special instructions, your instructor will give them to you.

If you wish to stop printing, press the Break key.

If the printer cannot print an entire row on a line, the excess data is printed on one or more subsequent lines. This is called **wrap-around**.

Exercise 13
Printing the
WHATIF3 Model

1. Print your WHATIF3 model by moving the cursor to A1 with the Home key.

2. Type **/P**.

3. Specify the lower right-hand corner of the rectangle by entering **B13**.

Exercise 14
Printing the WHATIF1
and WHATIF2 Models

1. Use the same procedure from Exercise 13 to prepare a printed copy of your WHATIF1 and WHATIF2 models.

Summary

The VisiCalc electronic spreadsheet offers many opportunities for use as a what-if model. The opportunities are limited only by the manager in formulating solutions to problems as rows and columns of data and formulas.

You move the cursor with the arrow keys, the GO TO key (>), and the Home key. The upper portion of the VisiCalc screen aids you as you build and use your model. As you type, the characters appear on the edit line. Once you enter a label, value, or formula, it appears on the entry contents line along with its coordinate and an indication of whether it is a label or a value. Most of the screen displays a portion of the spreadsheet. The screen can scroll over the spreadsheet in much the same way as a microfiche viewer can scan a microfiche.

Each time you change a value used in formulas, the formulas are recalculated. The recalculation proceeds in a columnwise or a rowwise direction, according to your specification. This automatic recalculation is the key to the value of VisiCalc and facilitates the what-if projection process.

As you use VisiCalc, you enter commands. In effect, you perform the same function as a computer's CPU as it executes programs. You determine the sequence of processes to be performed.

In this chapter, you learned how to use the following commands:

FORMAT	EDIT
GLOBAL	LABEL REPEATING
BLANK	REPLICATE
CLEAR	DELETE
STORAGE	TITLES
INSERT	PRINT
MOVE	

These are all of the commands that you need to build a static model with a single time period. In the next chapter, you will learn how to develop dynamic models involving multiple time periods.

Key Terms

Cell, entry	Columnwise recalculation
Call	Order Indicator
Coordinate	Available primary storage space
GO TO key	Menu-driven
Edit line	General format
Prompt line	Global
Entry contents line	Recalculation mode
Label	Forward reference
Value	Backward reference
Formula	Ellipsis
Arithmetic operator	Edit cue
Rowwise recalculation	Wrap-around

Questions   (Do not fill in blanks in the book. Write answers on a separate piece of paper.)

1. VisiCalc rows are identified with the numbers _____ through _____, and the columns are identified with the letters _____ through _____.

2. The row and column identifiers for a particular cell are called _____.

3. Another name for a cell is _____.

4. What happens when you try to move the cursor off the spreadsheet? _____

5. The key with the "greater than" ($>$) sign on top of it has a special use in VisiCalc; it is called the _____ key.

6. You can move the cursor to entry A1 by pressing the _____ key.

7. There are three lines at the top of the screen that display special information. Reading from the top, they are the _____, the _____, and the _____.

8. Each cell can contain a _____, _____, or _____.

9. If you wanted to insert a label 1ST QUARTER, you would type _____.

10. If you wanted to enter the formula A1 + A2 you could type _____ or _____.

11. Unless you specify otherwise, VisiCalc will recalculate in a _____ direction.

12. You initiate a command by typing a _____.

13. If you type a $ in response to the FORMAT command prompt, the amount in that cell will be displayed with _____ positions to the right of the decimal point.

14. The _____ command applies to all cells that have not been formatted separately with the FORMAT command.

15. The default option for the column width is _____, but can be reduced to _____ or increased to _____ with the GLOBAL command.

16. It is a good idea to always use the _____ command before you load a spreadsheet from the diskette.

17. As you design your spreadsheet, you should always try to avoid _____ references.

18. When you want to quit VisiCalc, you must type _____.

19. If you want to freeze three rows of titles at the top of the sheet and two columns of titles at the left, you would position the cursor on coordinate _____ and type _____.

20. VisiCalc knows that it is a row move if the row identifiers in the FROM and the TO coordinates are _____.

You are the manager of marketing planning for Optical Reading Corporation (ORC), a manufacturer of OCR equipment. One day, your boss Butch Breasley, the vice president of marketing, calls you into his office and tells you that he would like to put the division's budget performance on the computer. Up until now, it has been handled manually by your section. Butch explains that he would like to have a standard computer-based system that could be used at the division, region, and branch office levels.

At the beginning of each fiscal year, an operating budget is established for the division as a whole, and then it is subdivided into regional and then branch office budgets. As the budget is prepared for each organizational unit, amounts are allocated to each month by dividing the annual amounts by 12. Amounts are established for the following accounts; salaries $40,000; travel $12,500; entertainment $3,250; telephone $1,625; rent $9,250; furniture $2,500; supplies $1,000; miscellaneous $9,000.

Butch thought it might be a good idea to use VisiCalc for the budget.

Knowing how important it is to get the problem specifications right the first time, you ask Butch questions about the report layout. He tells you that he wants the title "Monthly Budget Report" centered at the top, with the organizational unit, such as "Sales Division," immediately below. Then, on the next line is the date, such as "For the Month of August, 1985." There are five columns of data, and each has a column heading. Starting at the left is the "Account" (salaries and so on). Next is the "Monthly Budget Amount" (the amounts listed above), followed by the "Monthly Actual Expenses." For the month of August, the following actual expenses were incurred; salaries $38,625; travel $13,450; entertainment $4,720; telephone $1,460; rent $9,250; furniture $725; supplies $1,863; miscellaneous $8,426.

The two rightmost columns show the variance of actual to budgeted expenses. The rightmost column is labeled "Variance Percent." In it, the percent is listed for the actual expense divided by the budgeted amount. For example, if the budget is $10,000, and the actual is $12,500, the variance percent is 1.25. A manager would say "I'm 125 percent of budget" or "I'm 25 percent over budget."

The second column from the right is titled "Variance Amount." In it, the budget is subtracted from the actual, and the variance (plus or minus) is printed. Butch also tells you that he wants totals in all of the quantitative columns, and he adds "Dress it up any way that you like—you know, underlines, spaces, and such."

You sketch out a rough drawing of the report format, frown, and ask "Do you want a total on the variance percent column also?" Butch replies that that wouldn't make a whole lot of sense, and asks your opinion. You think a while and say "Well, we could either average the eight variance percent figures, or we could divide total actual by total budget." Butch says that he likes the second idea the best.

You tell Butch that you will give him a printout of the August 1985 data for the Sales Division. He says "Great, I'll be looking forward to seeing it. If this works out okay, I would like to consider some more applications."

12 VisiCalc Part 2

In Chapter 11 you learned how to build a static model using VisiCalc. The model dealt with only a single time period. In this chapter you will learn how to simulate multiple time periods with a dynamic model. Additionally, you will learn some of the VisiCalc functions that increase its arithmetic and logic ability, learn how to set up windows for viewing two parts of the spreadsheet simultaneously, and identify some techniques intended to make VisiCalc modeling easier and more efficient.

Dynamic Models

The VisiCalc columns are often used to represent periods of time in a dynamic model. The columns can represent days, months, quarters, and years.

The first step in building a dynamic model is to build a static model for the first time period and then replicate this model for the subsequent time periods.

We can use the WHATIF3 model from Chapter 11 as a starting point. We can use it for quarter 1, and replicate it for quarters 2, 3, and 4. The result will be a model that simulates four quarters of activity.

The key to this transformation of our static model into a dynamic model will be the use of the REPLICATE command—specifically, how to replicate formulas.

More on Replication

The REPLICATE command works differently on constants (labels and values) than on formulas. If you want to replicate a constant—a label named YEAR or a value such as 1250, you simply type /R, the source range, the target range, and press Enter. Let's say that you have just typed the label MONTH in B5, and you want to replicate it in entries C5 through M5:

1. Position the cursor on B5.
2. Type/**R**.
3. Press Enter.
4. Type **C5**.
5. Press the period key.
6. Type **M5**.
7. Press Enter.

Exercise 1
Replicate Labels

1. Load your WHATIF3 model from your diskette into primary storage.

2. With the spreadsheet displayed on the screen, position your cursor at B3, where QUARTER is stored.

3. You will replicate QUARTER in entries C3, D3, and E3. Type /**R**.

4. Press Enter.

5. Type **C3**.

6. Press the period key.

7. Type **E3**.

8. Press Enter.

Figure 12.1 Relative Replication

Before the Replication

Entry	B5	C5	D5	E5	F5		K5	L5	M5
Value	1000	1100							
Formula	—	+B5*1.1							

After the Replication

Entry	B5	C5	D5	E5	F5		K5	L5	M5
Value	1000	1100	1210	1331	1464		2358	2594	2853
Formula	—	+B5*1.1	+C5*1.1	+D5*1.1	+E5*1.1		+J5*1.1	+K5*1.1	+L5*1.1

If you wanted to replicate a *formula,* such as +B3*1.15, you would follow this procedure, plus specify whether each coordinate is **relative** or **no-change**. Those terms demand an explanation.

Assume you want to build a dynamic model that projects operations for a 12-month period. You want to key in the number of sales units for month #1, and then increase this number by 10 percent each month thereafter. You key the initial number of units (such as 1000) into the first month's entry (such as B5). Then, in the second month's entry (C5) you enter the formula +B5*1.10. Then, you replicate the formula for the third through tenth months (entries D5 through M5).

Figure 12.1 shows the situation before the replication. You need a formula in D5 that multiplies 1.1 times the contents of the prior period's units (C5), not B5. The same requirement exists for formulas in entries E5 through M5. Unless you change the coordinate each time you replicate the formula so that it refers to the prior period, rather than to B5, all of your projected sales units will be 1100. The coordinates must be *relative* to the previous period, not continuously referring to the initial coordinate.

When you enter the REPLICATE command and press Enter, the edit cue highlights the coordinate (B5) in the formula and prompts you to enter N (for no change) or R (for relative). You respond with **R**, and the formula is replicated eight times. Each time, the coordinate in the formula is changed to refer to the previous coordinate. Figure 12.1 illustrates the results of the replication.

For an example of a replication where there is *no change* from one period to another, assume that you key 1000 into B5, and enter the formula +B5*1.10 in coordinate C5. You then replicate the formula in C5 so that it appears in coordinates

Figure 12.2 "No Change" Replication

Before the Replication

Entry	B5	C5	D5	E5	F5		K5	L5	M5
Value	1000	1100							
Formula	—	+B5*1.1							

After the Replication

Entry	B5	C5	D5	E5	F5		K5	L5	M5
Value	1000	1100	1100	1100	1100		1100	1100	1100
Formula	—	+B5*1.1	+B5*1.1	+B5*1.1	+B5*1.1		+B5*1.1	+B5*1.1	+B5*1.1

D5 through M5. But, in this instance, when the edit cue highlights the coordinate in the formula to be replicated, you respond with N, for no change. Figure 12.2 illustrates the results. The value in each replicated column is 1100.

Exercise 2
Replicate a Formula

You wish to identify each of the four quarters on your Pro Forma Income Statement (WHATIF3). Quarter 1 is identified. You could simply move the cursor to C4 and enter a 2, to D4 and enter a 3, and so on. That wouldn't be too difficult for only four quarters. But, what if you wanted to simulate 48 quarters?

An easier approach is to replicate the quarter number, increasing it by one each time.

1. Position the cursor at C4 and enter the formula **(B4+1)**.

2. With the cursor at the same location, type **/R** and press Enter.

3. Type **D4**.

4. Press the period key.

5. Type **E4**.

6. Press Enter.

7. The prompt line displays your formula (B4+1) with the coordinate B4 highlighted. You are prompted to enter R for relative or N for no change. Enter an **N**, and note what happens. Scroll the screen with the right arrow key. The quarters read: 1, 2, 2, 2. VisiCalc used the same formula (B4+1) to identify quarters 2, 3, and 4. It should have used (C4+1) for quarter 3, and (D4+1) for quarter 4.

8. Correct the error by repeating steps 2–6 above. Then, when VisiCalc asks R or N, enter an **R**. This time, the quarter numbers should be correct: 1, 2, 3, 4.

Figure 12.3   Replicating a Column or Row One Time

A. Replicating a column

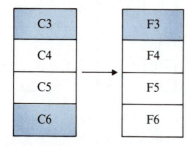

B. Replicating a row

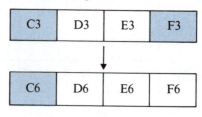

**Replicating Columns
or Rows**

To replicate a single entry as you have done up until now, you simply position the cursor on the entry and press Enter. If the cursor is on E3, the edit line reads E3…E3. The source range of the replication is one entry—E3 through E3.

If you want to replicate a range of entries (such as C3 through F3), place the cursor at C3 and type **/R**. Then with C3 showing on the edit line, press the period key, type **F3**, and press Enter. The edit lines reads C3…F3.

If you do not want the cursor location involved in the source range, type **/R** and then press the Backspace key once to erase the cursor location from the edit line. Then type in the source range.

The range of entries to be replicated can be either a column or a row. The column or row can be replicated only once, or several times. Figure 12.3 illustrates *replicating a column or row one time.* As an example, assume that you want to replicate the column C3 through C6, with the contents copied to column F3 through F6. The procedure is:

- Place the cursor on the first position of the column to be replicated (C3).
- Type **/R**.
- The edit line reads C3.
- Press the period key.
- The edit lines reads C3… .
- Type the last position of the column to be replicated (**C6**) and press Enter.
- The edit line reads C3…C6: .
- Type the first position of the column to receive the data (**F3**) and press Enter.
- The replication occurs.

If any of the entries to be replicated contain a coordinate (such as a variable in a formula), you will be asked to respond N (no change) or R (relative). After responding to each, the replication occurs.

A single replication of a *row* is accomplished in exactly the same manner. In Figure 12.3, the cursor is positioned on C3, then type **/R.F3** Enter **C6** Enter.

To accomplish a single replication, it is necessary to tell VisiCalc the beginning and ending coordinates of the "sending" row or column and the first coordinate of the "receiving" row or column. Those coordinates are shaded in Figure 12.3.

Figure 12.4 Replicating a Column or Row Several Times

A. Replicating a column

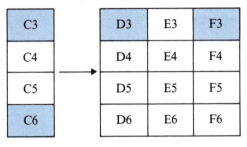

B. Replicating a row

C3	D3	E3	F3

C6	D6	E6	F6
C7	D7	E7	F7
C8	D8	E8	F8

Very frequently, in building a dynamic model you will wish to replicate a column or a row several times. Earlier we said that you start with a static model, and then repeat it several times to achieve a dynamic model. Take your WHATIF projections, for example. You can replicate the various formulas in column B so that they appear in columns C, D, and E as three additional time periods. Figure 12.4 illustrates *replicating a column or row several times.* Assume that column C3 through C6 is a static model that you have built. You want to replicate it three times as shown in the figure. The procedure is:

♦ Place the cursor on the first position of the column to be replicated (C3).

♦ Type **/R**.

♦ Press the period key.

♦ Type the last position of the column to be replicated (**C6**) and press Enter.

♦ Type the coordinate in the upper left-hand corner of the "rectangle" receiving the data (**D3**).

♦ Press the period key.

♦ Type the coordinate of the upper right-hand corner of the rectangle (**F3**) and press Enter.

When you press Enter, you will be asked to reply N or R *to each coordinate in each entry to be replicated* before that entry is replicated. As an example, assume that entry C3 in Figure 12.4 contains three coordinates in a formula. You respond N or R to each, and then entry C3 is replicated into D3, E3, and F3. Then you have to respond N or R to the coordinates in C4, and so on.

A row is replicated several times in basically the same manner. The only difference is that you identify the upper left-hand and lower left-hand corners of the rectangle to receive the replication. Note the shaded boxes in Figure 12.4b.

This ability to replicate a column or row several times is a powerful modeling tool, and no doubt contributes much to the popularity of VisiCalc.

**Exercise 3
Dynamic Model**

Let's revise the WHATIF3 model so that our price decision will apply for four quarters, and the sales volume will increase by five percent each quarter.

1. With the cursor at B7, replicate the price in entries C7 through E7.

2. With the cursor at C8, type the formula +**B8*1.05**.

3. With the cursor still at C8, replicate the formula in entries D8 and E8. The coordinate B8 in the formula should be treated as relative.

4. You can replicate all of the formulas in entries B10 through B18 with one replication. You will replicate column B several times, as illustrated in Figure 12.4. With the cursor at B10, type /**R**.

5. Press the period key, type **B18**, and press Enter. The edit line should read B10...B18: .

6. Type **C10**.

7. Press the period key.

8. Type **E10** and press Enter.

9. You will be asked to specify R or N for each coordinate to be replicated on each line. Respond with an **R** each time.

10. When column B has been replicated in columns C, D, and E, your model is complete. Move the cursor to B7, and enter a price of **$19.95**.

11. Print the Pro Forma Income Statement.

12. Save your model as WHATIF4.

Built-In Functions

VisiCalc includes approximately 30 built-in **functions** that perform certain mathematical and logical operations. Some of these functions like INT (for integer), ABS (for absolute value), and SQRT (for square root) can also be found in procedural languages such as BASIC. These functions enable you to perform operations with a minimum amount of coding. We will not describe all of the functions here, as some are rarely used in business decision making. The ones described here enable you to use VisiCalc as a DSS for problems lending themselves to spreadsheet format.

It might help you put the functions into proper perspective if you realize that the functions augment formulas that are stored at certain entries. The functions give the formulas an added computational and logical dimension. You can have multiple functions in one entry.

The format of a function is:

@FUNCTION-NAME(ARGUMENT(S))

The first character is an "at sign" (@), followed by the function abbreviation, and then the argument(s). The **function-name** is the verb that specifies the action to be taken. The **argument** is the object of the action. For example, if you wanted to compute the square root of the value stored at entry E8, you would enter @SQRT(E8).

Arguments can be values, coordinates, or other functions. Insert no spaces separating the items of the function.

The first seven functions described on the following pages expand the mathematical ability of VisiCalc in solving business problems. The eighth function lends a logical dimension.

@INT   If you want the product of a formula to be expressed as an **integer**, precede the formula with @INT. The formula is enclosed in parentheses. For example:

$$@INT(C3+C4)$$

This integer function affects the storage of the data, not just the display as does the FORMAT command /FI. Also, unlike /FI, the value is not rounded.

@ABS   If you want the **absolute value** of a number or a formula you type, for example:

$$@ABS(2*A1*A2)$$

The resulting value will always be stored as positive, even though it may be negative when computed or entered.

For example: @ABS(1) = 1;   @ABS(−1) = 1

@AVERAGE   The **arithmetic mean** (average) of a list of values is computed. Any blank entries in the list are ignored. For example, if this function is stored at I5, the computed average of the entries in the specified range will be displayed at I5.

$$@AVERAGE(I1...I4)$$

The arguments do not have to be arrayed in a range, as shown here (I1 through I4). The arguments can be **noncontiguous entries**. In such a case, the arguments are separated by commas. An example is @AVERAGE(A6,B5,C9,F12).

@MAX and @MIN   These functions select the largest and smallest numbers in a list. The list can contain either a range of items (M10...M18), or noncontiguous entries (F3,R19,P2,C6).

$$@MAX(M10...M18)$$
$$@MIN(F3,R19,P2,C6))$$

@SUM   This function sums all of the arguments and can be expressed as:

$$@SUM(C3,C4,C5,C6,C7,C8)$$

or it can be expressed as a range:

$$@SUM(C3...C8)$$

@SQRT   If you wanted to compute an economic order quantity:

$$E = \sqrt{\frac{2AS}{UR}}$$

and the acquisition cost (A) is located at V1, the annual sales (S) is at V2, the unit cost (U) is at V3, and the retention cost (R) is at V4, the function would appear as:

$$@SQRT(2*V1*V2/(V3*V4))$$

@IF   The format of the logical IF function is:

@IF(Argument1,Argument2,Argument3)

Argument 1 is an expression that is either true or false. Argument 2 specifies what to do if the expression is true. Argument 3 specifies what to do if it is false.

For example, if you wanted to give a 10 percent raise to an employee whose salary (B10) is less than $24,000 a year, you would enter:

$$@IF(B10<24000,B10*1.1,B10)$$

Assume that this function is stored at L12, and B10 has a value of 20000. Then the screen would display a value of 22000 for entry L12. If B10 has a value of 30000, then that value would be displayed at L12.

Exercise 4
Functions   We want to print a sales report showing sales by month for 12 months, for 5 sales regions.

1. With the cursor at A1 type **SALES**. Enter the word with the down arrow key.

2. Enter **REGION** at A2. Move the cursor down column A, entering:

    EAST at A4
    MIDWEST at A5
    SOUTH at A6
    SOUTHWEST at A7
    WEST at A8

3. Right justify the label MONTH in B1. Replicate it in C1 through M1.

4. Type a **1** in B2. Enter the formula **+B2+1** in C2. With the cursor at C2, replicate the formula in D2 through M2. The coordinate is treated as relative.

5. Enter the following sales amounts:

						MONTH						
REGION	1	2	3	4	5	6	7	8	9	10	11	12
EAST	10	11	12	14	15	17	19	21	20	19	22	23
MIDWEST	8	8	7	9	10	9	11	13	12	11	14	16
SOUTH	4	5	4	6	7	6	8	7	9	9	8	10
SOUTHWEST	7	8	8	9	9	10	12	12	14	15	17	19
WEST	12	14	12	15	16	18	19	21	21	19	20	23

6. In the 4 columns to the right of the 12 months' sales figures, we want to identify the:

TOTAL	MINIMUM	MAXIMUM	AVERAGE
SALES	MONTHLY	MONTHLY	MONTHLY
VOLUME	SALES	SALES	SALES

Insert a blank line at the top of the screen and enter these column headings in rows 1–3 of columns N, O, P, and Q.

7. With the cursor at N5, enter the formula **@SUM(B5...M5)**. Type a period to get the ellipsis.

8. With the cursor at O5, enter the formula **@MIN(B5...M5)**.

9. With the cursor at P5, enter the formula **@MAX(B5...M5)**.

10. With the cursor at Q5, enter the format **/FI** and the formula **@AVERAGE (B5...M5)**.

11. Replicate the formulas in N5 through Q5 in the four rows immediately below—a rectangle bounded by columns N and Q and rows 6 and 9. After the replication is performed, examine the values in columns N through Q for the five regions. Are they correct? Correct any error(s).

12. Insert two blank lines at the top of the screen and enter the report name **MONTHLY SALES BY REGION** in entries G1, H1, and I1. There are 23 characters in the title, and the three coordinates will accept 27 characters. In G1 enter two spaces before the letters. Fill G1 and then move the cursor to H1. Fill H1 and enter the remaining characters in I1.

13. Save the model on your diskette as REGSALE.

14. Now you will print the output. The problem is that the report is too wide for a printer such as the IBM Graphics Printer that prints 80 characters on a line. In fact, the report is too wide to fit on two sheets. You will have to print three sheets and tape them together. Follow this procedure:

    ◆ Position the cursor at A1, and type **/PP**. Specify the lower right-hand corner of the rectangle to be printed as H11.

    ◆ Press Enter and get a printout of the first seven months.

    ◆ Use the Form Feed key to align the top of a new sheet of paper in the printer.

    ◆ Use the right arrow key to scroll the screen to the left so that H1 is in the upper left-hand corner. Move the cursor to H1 with the GO TO key.

    ◆ Type **/PP**, and specify the lower right coordinate as **O11**. What you see (on the screen) is what you get. Press Enter and get a printout of Month 7 through the Minimum Sales column.

    ◆ Repeat the process to get a printout of columns O, P, and Q.

    ◆ Tape the report together, overlapping columns H and O. You will have to trim some paper away at the seams.

This technique of overlapping the multisheet report at the seams is the recommended way to piece the sheets together. It ensures that the columns are being aligned properly. If your printer is aligned properly, and you use the Form Feed key as described, the result will be an attractively assembled report.

The WINDOW Command

You learned all of the basic VisiCalc commands in the previous chapter with the exception of the WINDOW command. This command enables you to view two portions of a large spreadsheet at the same time. Now you have a spreadsheet large enough to demonstrate its use: the Monthly Sales by Region sheet that you just saved in Exercise 4.

The two portions of the spreadsheet selected for viewing are called **windows**. You can have a window on the left side of the screen and another on the right. This is a *vertical* split. To accomplish this, move the cursor to the leftmost column of the sheet to be displayed at the right of the screen, and type /**W**. The prompt line reads:

Window: H V 1 S U

Type **V** for vertical.

For a *horizontal* split (one window above another), move the cursor to the top row of the window to be displayed at the bottom. Type /**WH**. The H is for horizontal.

The key to setting the windows up properly is positioning the cursor in the correct column or row before you type /W. The best approach is to display the material on the screen that you want to view in one of the windows. Using your Monthly Sales by Region sheet as an example, you would probably want to set up two vertical windows, with the right one displaying the four "totals" columns (N through Q). Then, you could scroll the left window, change the sales amounts, and see the results in the right window. To accomplish this:

♦ Scroll the sheet so that column Q is at the right of the screen.
♦ Position the cursor anywhere in column N, and type /**WV**.

You now have two windows, and you can scroll each independently of the other by moving the cursor. When you establish the windows, the cursor is always initially located in the left (vertically displayed) window or the upper (horizontally displayed) window. You can move the cursor from one window to another with the semicolon (;) key. It works as a toggle key.

If you want the two windows to scroll in a *simultaneous* fashion, type /**WS**. S is for simultaneous. If you want to release this option, type /**WU**. U is for *unsimultaneous*. If you want to revert to only the single spreadsheet, type /**W1**.

There are a few things you need to know about windows:

1. If you change a value in one window, it can change a value in the other window. This is true when a formula in one window includes a coordinate from the other window.

2. You can freeze titles separately in both windows.

3. If you have frozen titles in the spreadsheet before creating the windows, the titles will be frozen in both windows.

4. You can have separate global formats and column widths in each window.

5. When you specify the dividing lines on the screen to separate the windows, you are fixing the sizes of the windows. So, first decide how large each window should be. Do not be influenced by the data on the screen, as it can be scrolled within each window.

6. The windows have no influence on how the spreadsheet is printed with the PRINT command (/P). The PRINT command takes its data from primary storage—not from the screen.

7. If you want a hard copy of the screen display of the two windows, use the Prt Sc key.

Exercise 5
Windows

1. Load the file REGSALE from your diskette.

2. Use the right arrow key to scroll the spreadsheet to the right so that column Q is at the right of the screen. (Column J is at the left.)

3. Position the cursor at any point on column N and type **/WV**. You now have two vertical windows. The one on the right enables you to view the "totals" columns.

4. With the cursor in the left screen, scroll the spreadsheet in the left screen until column A is at the left. Notice that the right window did not scroll. You could have achieved simultaneous scrolling by typing /WS.

5. Position the cursor at A6 and freeze the titles (in the left window only) by typing **/TB**. Verify the action by moving the cursor to B7 and then trying to move back to column A and up to row 6. The PC should beep each time you try.

6. The left window contains the titles, plus three columns of data. The right window contains the four "totals" columns. You can play the what-if game by changing one or more data values in the left window and seeing the results in the right window. Position the cursor on B9, and enter a new set of data for the southwest region—**11, 13, 14, 15, 16, 18, 20, 22, 23, 23, 24, 25**. Note the changes in the "totals" columns each time you enter a new value.

7. Restore the screen to a single window by typing **/W1**.

Global Parameters

VisiCalc assumes certain conditions called **global parameters**. In the previous chapter, we saw that the term global means "universally applicable." So, these global parameters apply to the entire spreadsheet unless we change them. In effect, they are default options. As you recall, we encountered this term in dBASE II in reference to the page specifications for the REPORT command. The same situation exists with the VisiCalc default options. If we don't change them, they are in effect. The VisiCalc global parameters are:

Column width	9
Order of recalculation	Columnwise
Recalculation mode	Automatic
Format	General (not global)
Windows	1
Cursor position	A1
Fixed titles	None

When you first call up the VisiCalc spreadsheet, this is the situation with which you begin to work.

Pointing the Cursor

The VisiCalc spreadsheet is so large that it is often difficult to remember (or to see) which coordinates contain a certain value. For example, suppose you are writing a formula and want to subtract total costs. But, you don't know exactly where the total cost coordinate is. At the point in the formula where you want to specify the costs coordinate, you can use the arrow keys to move the cursor to that location. Then you press Enter. The cursor moves back to the original location of the formula, and the edit line contains the costs coordinate. You put it there without typing it—you simply pointed the cursor to its location and pressed Enter.

A good place to point the cursor is with the PRINT command. Remember that VisiCalc asks for the lower right-hand coordinate. Simply move the cursor to that location and press Enter.

Try to use this technique at every opportunity, not just for large sheets. It should save time and improve accuracy. For example, in a formula, move the cursor to the location of the first variable and then key in the arithmetic operator (such as a plus sign). This enters both the coordinate and the operator. Then follow with the next operator(s).

**Exercise 6
Pointing the Cursor**

1. Load the REGSALE file from your diskette.

2. Add a row of hyphens between the column headings and the data. Presently, a blank line (row 6) separates the two. Enter hyphens in A6. Use the LABEL REPEATING command.

3. With the cursor at A6, type **/R**.

4. Press Enter so that the source range on the edit line reads A6...A6.

5. Move the cursor to B6.

6. Press the period key. This enters the B6 coordinate. You typed it by "pointing" to it with the cursor and then entering it with the period key. The edit line reads A6...A6:B6...

7. Use the right arrow key to move the cursor to Q6. Look at the edit line; it reads A6...A6:B6...Q6. Press Enter; the hyphens are replicated. You entered all of the coordinates without typing in a single one; you pointed to them with the cursor.

8. Save the spreadsheet as REGSALE1.

**Suggested VisiCalc
Technique**

This concludes the discussion of VisiCalc mechanics. The chapter concludes with a discussion of some techniques that should make VisiCalc modeling easier and more effective. Through use, you will be able to develop your own techniques. But, as a starter, here are a few:

1. Never begin work on a spreadsheet without having at least one extra blank, formatted diskette handy. It is a good idea to have two—one for backup. Each time you save your sheet, remove the diskette and insert the backup (or switch to the alternate drive), and save again.

2. Plan the layout of your sheet before you start to create it. In this way you do not have to shift things around later to put rows in the right order, expand column widths so that labels will fit, and so on.

3. Always clear primary storage (/CY) before loading or creating a spreadsheet.

4. Use the arrow keys rather than the Enter key to enter labels and values. For example, if you are entering a column of labels, enter a label with the down arrow key. Then, the cursor is positioned so that the next label can be entered.

5. Enter a column of labels and then a column of values. This is faster than entering a label and then its value, a label and its value, and so on. Always verify, however, that the values are paired with their correct labels.

6. On large spreadsheets, use the cursor to identify coordinates. Rather than key in the coordinate, move the cursor to the location and press Enter. Coordinates in a formula can be entered with the arithmetic sign (+, −, *, /, ^) keys.

7. Always design your spreadsheets with *backward references*. In other words, if a formula includes coordinates, those coordinates are located above and/or to the left. This will facilitate recalculation, which begins in A1. Avoid *forward references* (below and/or to the right), as each one requires a manual recalculation (!) operation.

8. Avoid **circular references**. These are references that two formulas make to each other, or that a formula makes to itself. For example, entry D8 cannot contain (D8 − C8). If you save and then load a sheet containing circular or forward references, those entries will contain "ERROR." The references must be corrected.

9. Save your spreadsheet on the diskette frequently. Type /SS and then use the right arrow key to identify on the edit line the most recent file name. Use the Backspace key to position the cursor immediately to the right of the file name and add a suffix, such as 2. Then press Enter to save the file. It is always a good idea to save the file before using commands that drastically change the sheet, such as DELETE, REPLICATE, MOVE, BLANK, and INSERT.

10. Enter report titles and column headings last. Otherwise, you may decide to reduce the size of the columns and truncate part of the titles that were entered previously.

11. If a title is larger than one coordinate, center it in two or more coordinates. Determine how many characters are in the title (say 12) and subtract that from the number of positions in adjacent coordinates (say 18). Divide the difference (6) by two, and insert that many (3) blank spaces before keying in the beginning of the title in the leftmost coordinate. The report title will appear as:

Left Coordinate   Right Coordinate

12. When you print a report that is too wide for your printer, print the report in sections and then tape them together. Repeat the columns that fall at the "seams" to facilitate alignment. For example, print columns A–I, and I–M. Align on column I.

Summary

Were you only able to simulate static situations with VisiCalc, it would still be a powerful DSS tool. But its ability to easily expand a static model into a dynamic one with the REPLICATE command is a bonus. It is much easier to build a dynamic model using VisiCalc than to code a program with a procedural language. The procedural language model would require the use of tables and subscripting, increasing its complexity. VisiCalc shines by comparison.

The VisiCalc functions also add to its computational ability, but most of the functions do not seem necessary in processing business data. The SUM function is used frequently, but the other functions are used only sparingly.

The WINDOW command helps you to manipulate a large spreadsheet. As you play the what-if game by changing the scenario in one window, you can see the results in the other window.

When you load the VisiCalc program, certain global parameters go into effect. You can change these as the situation demands.

The ability to point the cursor to coordinates when issuing a command or creating a formula increases your accuracy and speed during the model-building process. Other techniques also contribute, and these will be sharpened through continued use.

Key Terms

Relative coordinate	Absolute Value
No-change coordinate	Arithmetic mean
Function	Noncontiguous entries
Function-name	Window
Argument	Global parameter
Integer	Circular reference

Questions   (Do not fill in blanks in the book. Write answers on a separate piece of paper.)

1. When VisiCalc is used as a dynamic model, the _____ of the spreadsheet usually represent the time periods.

2. If you are converting a static model to a dynamic one, you most likely will make major use of the _____ command.

3. When replicating a formula, you must specify whether it is to be regarded as _____ or _____.

4. You have to respond N or R for each _____ contained within a formula.

5. When replicating a row several times, you identify the _____ and the _____ corners of the rectangle to receive the replication.

6. VisiCalc includes some 30 _____ that perform certain mathematical and logical operations.

7. You tell VisiCalc that you want to use a function by typing a(n) _____.

8. To use one of the functions to compute the arithmetic mean of five values stored in cells J1 through J5, you would enter _____.

9. If arguments are not located next to each other in a row or a column, they are said to be _____.

10. To reduce the price of an inventory item located at cell F20 by 30 percent if the value is less than $1,000, and to reduce the price by 40 percent if the value is $1,000 or more, you would enter _____.

11. The maximum number of windows that you can have on a spreadsheet is _____.

12. The windows can be arranged either _____ or _____.

13. You move the cursor from one window to another by pressing the _____ key.

14. If you want a printed copy of the screen display of two windows, you should use the _____ key.

15. You do not always have to type in the coordinates; it is possible to achieve the same results, perhaps more accurately, by _____.

16. Before you begin a VisiCalc session, it would be a good idea to have _____ formatted diskette(s) handy.

17. When building a spreadsheet, you should use the _____ key(s) rather than the Enter key whenever you have the opportunity.

18. When you build a spreadsheet it is a good idea to enter a(n) _____ of labels and then a(n) _____ of the corresponding values.

19. A(n) _____ reference is when a formula refers to itself.

20. When building a spreadsheet, you should enter the titles and column headings _____.

Assignment 1
Resource Planning

You are sitting in your office reading *The Wall Street Journal* when the phone rings. It's Butch. He says it's urgent that you come into his office—right now.

When you walk in, you are greeted by a big smile. "That budget performance system is working like a charm," he says. "All of the offices are on it, and I just got the last of the monthly reports this morning. If a little VisiCalc is good, then some more must be great. I'm ready to talk about the next application. Sit down."

Butch begins to explain: "I have always wanted to computerize our resource planning activity. As you know, each year the marketing division projects the sales activity for the corporation for the coming fiscal year. This sales forecast is used by all of the organizational units in planning their resource needs for the year. It's ironic. We prepare the forecast that everybody else uses for their planning, but we probably do the poorest job of using it ourselves. I would like for you to put it on VisiCalc."

You respond that you think it's an excellent idea, and that you will get right on it. You ask Butch to explain more about what we wants.

"The key to everything is personnel. We have to have a certain personnel mix and level in order to meet our sales objectives. All of our budgeted expenses— salaries, travel, entertainment, and so forth—are based on the number of personnel that we have."

"What about rent?" you interrupt.

Butch answers, "In the short run rent is a fixed expense—so much per month. But, in the long run, it also varies with personnel. The more people we have, the larger our sales offices must be."

You press Butch for some guidelines that you can use in building the VisiCalc model. "Just what is the relationship between personnel and our objectives?" you ask.

"One sales team—a sales representative and two systems analysts—can sell one OCR system per month. And, after they sell it, they can install it. We can use a figure of $225,000 for the revenue derived from one sale. So, a sales team should be able to sell 12 systems at $225,000, or about $2,400,000 in annual revenue."

"$2.7 million," you reply.

Butch says, "If we want to sell $27 million, then we need 10 teams working the entire year. I figure a sales rep costs about $2000 per month in salary (not counting commission, which we're not concerned with here), and a systems analyst goes for about $2250. To determine personnel needs, we start with our sales forecast, which is in numbers of systems per month. That tells us how many sales teams we need. Then we use a cost-per-person approach in coming up with all of the budget items."

"What does our sales forecast look like for next fiscal year?" you ask. "It's April now, and our fiscal year starts in November. That gives us 7 months to get geared up."

Butch pulls out a typed forecast, which lists:

Month	Number of Systems
November	8
December	9
January	10
February	10
March	12
April	13
May	15
June	17
July	19
August	21
September	21
October	22

"If we're going to sell 8 units in November, then we have to have 8 sales teams, right?" you ask.

"For the sales rep let's use $2,125, and for the analyst let's use $2,400. These are a little high, but I would like to allow some room for raises. Now, does that do it?"

You look over your notes, knowing the importance of getting the specifications right the first time. "I think I need to know the system forecast for the first six months of fiscal year (FY) 1985 and 1986 if I am to give you a resource projection for FY 84/85. You see, we must hire sales reps and analysts during the last six months of FY 84/85 to meet the sales forecast for the next year."

"You're right," Butch concedes. "I just happen to have those figures. Here they are."

November 1985	22 systems
December 1985	23 systems
January 1986	23 systems
February 1986	24 systems
March 1986	24 systems
April 1986	25 systems

Butch asks, rather impatiently, "Now do you have everything that you need?"

You reply that you believe you do, and, as a final check, summarize your task. "I'll prepare a projection for the next 18 months of these expenses for the sales division. The first six months, May through October 1984, will get us geared up to meet the FY 84/85 sales forecast. The last 12 months, November 1984 through October 1985, will be the budget projection that you need. Do you want all 18 months, or just the last 12?"

"Give me all 18. I'd like to be able to see what we have to do during the next 6 months in order to meet next year's goals. But, let me have totals for both the 6-month period and the 12-month period. I want to be able to see the figures separately by fiscal year. Any more questions?"

"Only one," you reply. "What about format? What do you want the report to look like?"

"I'll leave that up to you. Just be sure and give me monthly totals on everything, and I would like to see totals for each budget item. Let me know when you have something." With that, Butch returns to the papers on his desk, and you check your mailbox to find today's issue of *The Wall Street Journal* with a headline "Electronic Spreadsheets Make Fiscal Planning Easy."

"Right," Butch responds. "But we can't just hire them on November 1 and expect them to start selling immediately. I estimate that a team must be on board 6 months before we can expect an order."

"So, we have to have 8 teams on board in May if we are to meet the November target. That means we better start hiring, as we have only 6 teams now."

"You've got it." Butch says.

"Let me see if I've got this straight," you say. "We take the number of forecast systems and convert that into a head count. Then we compute the salaries—"

Butch interrupts, "Exactly. Then we use some dollar amounts per person for the remainder of the expenses."

"Do you know what those are?" you ask.

"Not really. I think you had better come up with some," Butch says. "Why don't you do that and run all of this through VisiCalc?"

You dig through old expense account forms and bills and develop the following average monthly expenses per person:

Telephone	$ 42.25
Travel	563.70
Entertainment	84.65
Supplies	38.10

During an employee's first month, approximately $910 is spent on furniture—a desk, chair, wastebasket, and file cabinet. All of these expenses vary directly with the number of personnel. The rent figure does not. Rather, it remains at a level of $8,450 per month for all of the office locations within the division. The final budget item, miscellaneous, includes everything not included in the other accounts, such as education and fringe benefits. During the past year, the miscellaneous category was about $450 per person per month.

You present these figures to Butch. "These look good. You've done a good job. On these expenses that vary with the head count, let's round them off—use $50 for telephone, $600 for travel, $60 for entertainment, $40 for supplies, and $450 for miscellaneous. Let's use $8,500 per month for rent, and a one-time expense of $925 for furniture. That should just about do it, shouldn't it?"

"Are you sure about the $60 for entertainment? They've been spending $84..."

Butch interrupts, "That's too much. I'm going to clamp down on that. The $60 is fine."

You ask, "What about salaries?"

Module 6
Word Processing

13 The Role of Word Processing In the DSS

It's easy to see how data base management systems and electronic spreadsheets fit into the DDS. The data base contains the raw material of information, and the spreadsheets were developed with what-if modeling in mind. But, seeing word processing in a DSS or MIS context is not easy. This point is borne out in the lack of attention given to the subject in the literature of business. Much has been written about word processing and data processing.[1] But relatively little has been written about the role of word processing in an MIS or a DSS.[2]

In Chapter 3, we identified how the MIS is subdivided into three subsystems—data processing, DSS, and office automation. Of the three subsystems, office automation represents the greatest potential, for it is a virtually untapped resource. Office automation includes all applications of electronic equipment that help office staffs accomplish administrative and clerical tasks. The applications that have been linked to office automation include electronic mail, image storage and retrieval, document transmission, teleconferencing, and word processing. Of these applications, word processing has been developed the most fully to date. And the indications are that word processing will be the most popular office automation application for quite some time. In this chapter we first describe word processing in a general sense, and then relate it to a decision support system.

History of Word Processing

Word processing got its start in 1964 when IBM announced a new version of the Selectric typewriter. The Selectric was the first with a "ball" typing mechanism. The new version was called **MT/ST—Magnetic Tape/Selectric Typewriter**. The MT/ST was a regular Selectric with a magnetic tape unit attached. As a letter was typed, the copy was stored on the tape. The copy from the tape could be corrected and the letter typed automatically as many times as needed. Each time, the operator simply typed in the name and address of the person to receive the letter. The product was a form letter that looked as if it had been specially typed for the recipient, using a good-quality electric typewriter.

IBM coined the term word processing to distinguish its typewriter products from its computer products, which were associated with data processing. During the following years, the idea of word processing caught on, and other companies offered automatic typewriters. In the early 1970s a prospective purchaser of word processing equipment could choose from typewriters with attached tape reels, tape cartridges, and magnetic disks. These units were used largely for direct mailing, and little thought was given to integrating them into the MIS.

---

1. See, for example, Paul H. Cheney, "You Can Merge DP and WP," *Computer Decisions* 12 (October 1980): 110, 112; J. R. Hansen, "The DP Future of Word Processing," *Infosystems* 25 (May 1978): 74–76; and J. A. Murphy, "Merging Word and Data Processing: A First Step Toward Total Information Integration," *Computerworld* 15 (December 29, 1980): 49–50.
2. Raymond McLeod, Jr. and Donald H. Bender, "The Integration of Word Processing into a Management Information System," *MIS Quarterly* 6 (December 1982): 11–29.

Figure 13.1   The IBM Displaywriter

International Business Machines Corp.

The Mini-Micro Boom   When small computers began to gain popularity during the early 1970s, some manufacturers were quick to see the use of these small systems not as data processors, but as word processors. One of the pioneering firms was Wang, and the Wangwriter was intended for use as a word, not data, processor. Another example of a small system dedicated to word processing is the IBM Displaywriter, pictured in Figure 13.1.

Today many other firms manufacture dedicated word processors, including Exxon, NBI, Lanier, Micom, and Digital Equipment Corporation. These systems have many built-in features that make both training and operating much easier.

Word Processing
Software   The idea of special-purpose or dedicated word processors was fine for certain companies—those large enough to afford both word processor and data processor computers. But a small company could benefit from the versatility and lower capital investment of one computer that could do both data and word processing. There would be only one piece of hardware, and it could do both jobs by means of special software. Data processing software had been around for years; why not word processing software?

So, word processing software began to hit the market. Some, such as SCRIPSIT, was developed by the computer manufacturer for use on their product—in this case Tandy's Radio Shack TRS-80. But the most successful software efforts, in terms of packages sold, were those of software firms such as Peachtree Software (Peachtext package), MicroPro (WordStar package), and Information Unlimited Software (Easy Writer). There are many more.[3] These packages were intended for use on the popular microcomputers—the IBM PC, Apple, Commodore PET, and so forth.

While this small-system software development was occurring, word processing software was also developed for use on mainframe computers. One of the most successful was the University of Waterloo (Ontario, Canada) SCRIPT package that could fit on several mainframe systems.

3. See Camilio Wilson, "Word Processing," *PC World Annual Software Review* (1983/1984): 124ff. for a brief description of over 100 word processing packages.

Choosing Among Standalones, Micros, and Mainframes

By 1980, companies had three basic avenues to follow in implementing word processing—standalone word processors such as the Displaywriter, word processing software such as WordStar for a small computer such as the IBM PC, and word processing software such as Waterloo SCRIPT on a mainframe computer.

The choice is influenced greatly (but not completely) by the size of the firm. A small firm, unable to afford dedicated word processing hardware, usually selects a small computer and adapts it to word processing through software. A medium-size firm, one not large enough to afford a mainframe system, will select a standalone word processor to go along with the firm's micro, mini, or supermini data processor.

The mainframe user has a choice of going the software route (such as with SCRIPT) or purchasing standalone word processors. Here, company size is not the factor. Rather, it is philosophy. Adherents to the dedicated hardware approach point to the efficiency of the units intended for word processing. Supporters of the software approach stress how it makes the corporate data base available to the word processor user. This argument concerning the data base is especially strong when word processing is to be integrated into the MIS or DSS.

Users of small computers also can access the data base while using word processing software. As an example, files created in dBASE II with an .SDF extension or files created in VisiCalc with a .PRF extension can be read by WordStar. We have not addressed such integration in this text, but it represents a sophisticated way to use small-computer software. However, all packages do not have this integrating ability.

Word Processing Closes the Loop

Earlier, we distinguished between the physical system of the firm and its conceptual information system. The manager, often cut off from the physical system, uses the conceptual system to remain current on events that occur in the physical system. Figure 13.2 illustrates how the manager obtains information that has been converted from data by an information processor. The data originates primarily within the

Figure 13.2   Information Flow to the Manager

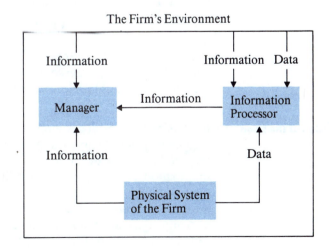

firm—this is the accounting data. Some data, such as economic statistics obtained from the government, is environmental in nature.

You will notice in Figure 13.2 that *data* does not flow directly to the manager; it is always refined into *information* by the information processor. This is the role of the information processor in an MIS or DSS.

But, the information processor is not the only source of information for the manager. Information also comes directly from the physical system. For example, a shop supervisor meets with the plant superintendent to describe a problem caused by outdated equipment. Also, information can come directly to the manager from the environment. Perhaps the vice president of finance receives a telephone call from a banker alerting her or him to an expected rise in interest rates.

The information coming from the information processor is **hard information**—it is the product of a formal procedure and it is derived from a data base. The information coming directly from the physical system and from the environment is generally **soft information**. Much is verbal, and it is a spur-of-the-moment type of thing. Something unexpected happens, and a message is sent. Often, there is no data base to support the information; much is speculation. Both of these information flows, hard and soft, are important to the manager. A manager would not have a good MIS and could not develop a good DSS if either flow were missing.

Open-Loop versus Closed-Loop Systems

Some systems have feedback loops and some do not. The heating system in your home is an example of a system with a feedback loop. You set the thermostat to a certain temperature and the heater is turned on and off to maintain the temperature. When the temperature falls below the setting, and electrical circuit from the thermostat to the heater is closed and the heater turns on. when the temperature reaches the desired level, the circuit is opened and the heater is turned off. There is a circuit, or a feedback loop, from the environment to the heater. Such a system is called a **closed-loop system**.

Other systems have no such loop. Perhaps you purchase an electric space heater with no temperature setting to plug into the wall socket to heat your bedroom. You turn the heater on and it puts out heat. If the room gets too hot, the heater doesn't automatically shut off. And if the room gets too cold it doesn't automatically turn on. This system without a feedback loop is called an **open-loop system**.

A business is much like the thermostatically controlled heater. The managers play the role of the thermostat—they act to keep the firm on course as it strives to achieve its objectives. The objectives perform the same function as the thermostat setting. The manager's decisions, instructions, policies, procedures, and so on serve the same purpose as the electrical signal sent to the heater.

Composition of the Loop

In a business, the feedback loop is composed of three different media. First, *data* is gathered from the firm and its environment. Second, the data is transformed into *information* by the information processor. Third, the manager, acting on the information, issues *directives* to the firm. Notice that there are two points on the loop where the media changes forms. These two transformation points are the information processor and the manager. The *information processor* converts the data into information, and the *manager* converts the information into directives. This is the basis for the DSS concept—the manager and the information processor (the computer) work together as a problem-solving unit. They are the two key elements in the feedback loop.

The Weak Link

The computer has played a significant role in improving the feedback loop. The computer has functioned as the information processor. As we have seen, the manager does not rely entirely on the computer for management, but it does make a contribution. The degree of the contribution is based largely on the managerial style of the firm's managers. If they place much value on computer-provided information, then the computer makes a real contribution.

On the other hand, the portion of the feedback loop from the manager to the firm—the directives—has benefited very little from the computer. In practically all cases, the directives are communicated in the form of soft information: personal conversations, telephone calls, meetings, memos, and letters. These are all very informal communications. Only when the directives are put into the form of written policies and procedures do they become formal.

Word Processing
Closes the Link

This area of directives is where word processing fits into the MIS and DSS. Some of these directives can be communicated using word processing. Memos, letters, procedures, and policies can all be prepared using any of the three types of word processing systems we have discussed.

Word processing makes it possible for the manager to react more quickly to disturbances both from within the firm and from its environment. Written directives can be roughed out, edited and corrected, retyped, and transmitted much faster with word processing than with conventional typing and retyping.

For example, assume that top management reacts to a high turnover rate among senior employees and decides to revise its personnel policies relating to retirement. With the corporate policy manual in a word processing file, the manual can be scanned electronically for all references to retirement. Then, those sections can be printed for management review. Revisions can be keyed into the word processing system and the revised portions reprinted. In this example, word processing makes two key contributions. First, it eliminates the need for someone to laboriously search through the policy manual, looking for references to retirement. This could take days in a large corporation with a voluminous policy manual. Second, the managers have all of the pertinent information before them as they make decisions. They can be confident that they have all of the facts. With word processing, administrative tasks are performed much more quickly, but also more accurately. And with word processing, the final product can be much more attractive than copy prepared on an ordinary typewriter.

Information Flow
from the Manager

Figure 13.3 illustrates the flow of information from the manager. The two arrows leading from the manager to the firm represent the directives, closing the feedback loop. The heavy arrow represents those directives communicated by word processing.

The manager also has a responsibility to communicate information to the environment. These communications include personal letters, press releases, annual and quarterly reports to stockholders, government reports, and mass mailings to customers and prospects. This outward information flow also takes two forms—that handled by word processing and that communicated by conventional means. The two arrows in the figure leading from the manager to the environment represent the outward flow of information to the environment.

If word processing is to be a DSS tool, managers should utilize word processing to the greatest extent possible in the areas illustrated in Figure 13.3.

Figure 13.3   Information Flow from the Manager

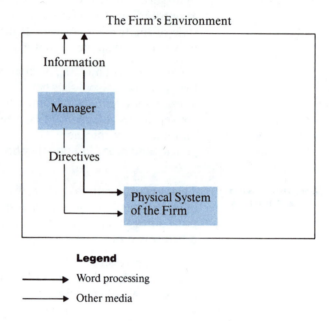

The Firm's Environment

Information

Manager

Directives

Physical System
of the Firm

Legend

→ Word processing

→ Other media

**Putting Word Processing
in Perspective**

Because many people think of word processing as "form letters," it is easy to mistake its role in the MIS or DSS. Since managers do not operate a typewriter, the assumption is that they will not personally be involved with word processing. Rather, word processing is seen as a secretarial tool.

To be honest, the same criticism could be leveled at the other software systems that we have studied. Most managers will not personally code programs, create and maintain data bases, and build spreadsheet models. It is more likely that someone else, such as a staff assistant, will perform those functions for the manager. But this does not diminish the role of the software systems in an MIS or a DSS. The programs, data bases, and spreadsheets support the manager in decision making. The same can be said for word processing. It improves the flow of information both within the firm, and between the firm and its environment. It plays an integral role in a DSS.

So, even if the word processing software and hardware is operated by the manager's secretary rather than the manager, word processing is still a DSS tool. But, we should not assume that no managers will operate the keyboard themselves. Just as there are some managers who create programs, build and maintain data bases, and develop spreadsheet models, there are some who use word processing.

The key point is not who *uses* the tool, but who *benefits* from it. A good manager will see how word processing facilitates information flow and will incorporate it into his or her MIS and DSS.

Summary

Word processing has been in existence for 20 years, but for most of this time it was thought of and managed separately from the MIS or DSS. Only recently has its role, or potential role, as a DSS tool been recognized.

A firm can implement word processing by obtaining a standalone word processing system, by using word processing software on a small computer, or by using word processing software on a mainframe computer. The latter avenue has the added advantage of making the corporate data base available to the user.

Word processing is focused on that part of the feedback loop in a firm that has been virtually neglected by the computer. This is the transmission of directives from the manager to the physical system of the firm. In addition, word processing makes it easier for the manager to communicate information to the firm's environment.

In this text you have seen how four software systems are used in a DSS. These systems are BASIC, dBASE II, VisiCalc, and WordStar. The first is a procedural language and the last three are user-friendly software packages that have wide application. Knowledge of these systems contributes to a manager's **computer literacy**, a term that means "understanding computers." We have accomplished that step in this text. And, we have gone one step farther. We have described how these systems are used in a DSS. Knowledge of this contributes to the manager's **DSS literacy**.

The tools are available to the manager. In the future, we will see more and more managers take advantage of the tools as decision support systems.

Key Terms

MT/ST, Magnetic Tape/Selectric Typewriter
Hard information
Soft information
Closed-loop system

Open-loop system
Computer literacy
DSS literacy

(Do not fill in blanks in the book. Write answers on a separate piece of paper.)

1. Of the three subsystems in the MIS, the one offering the greatest potential is _____.

2. Some applications that are included in office automation are _____, _____, _____, _____, and _____.

3. The _____ can be identified as the first word processing machine.

4. When a small computer can perform only word processing, it is said to be _____ to word processing.

5. Word processing software is available to use on both _____ and _____.

6. When a firm considers word processing, the two basic alternatives are _____ and _____.

7. Information coming to the manager from the computer is an example of _____, and information coming from telephone calls is an example of _____.

8. A system with a feedback loop is called a(n) _____ system.

9. The three different media flowing along the feedback loop are _____, _____, and _____.

10. The two points along the feedback loop where the media changes form are the _____ and the _____.

11. The weak link in the feedback loop has always been the transmission of _____ from the manager to the physical system.

12. The office automation application that helps to close the weak link is _____.

13. The manager has a responsibility to communicate information to the physical system of the firm, but he or she also has a responsibility to communicate information to the _____.

14. Many people see word processing as a tool to be used only by the _____.

15. The key point in recognizing the role of word processing in a DSS is not who operates the equipment, but who _____ from it.

16. Give four examples of directives: _____, _____, _____, and _____.

17. In the feedback loop the information processor has been most successful transforming _____ into _____.

18. An example of an open-loop system (other than one in the text) is _____. An additional example of a closed-loop system is _____.

19. The value of using word processing software on a mainframe computer is that the user has access to the firm's _____.

20. An example of a word processing software package designed specifically for one computer is _____; an example of a package designed for use on many computers is _____.

14 Introduction to WordStar

Word processing enables managers to prepare written communications to persons both inside and outside the firm faster, more accurately, and in a more attractive form than by any other means. In this chapter, you will learn the basics of WordStar, a product of MicroPro that is one of the most popular of the many word processing software packages on the market. After studying the chapter and working the exercises and assignments, you will be able to generate business letters, memos, and straightforward reports with WordStar. Our discussion in this and the next chapter is based on WordStar Version 3.30.

Loading WordStar

Your WordStar diskette contains DOS, the three WordStar files (WS.COM, the main program; WSMSGS.OVR, the menus and messages; and WSOVLY1.OVR, the overlay file), plus a document file named CUTOVER. To initiate WordStar, put your diskette in the a: drive and boot the system. When you get the A> prompt, type **ws** and press Enter.

Unless you want to use your WordStar diskette for your document files, insert a formatted diskette in the b: drive. We will assume that if your PC has two diskette drives your document diskette (the letters and reports that you type) is in the b: drive. Keep your write-protected WordStar diskette in the a: drive and your document diskette in the b: drive throughout the session. If your PC has a single drive, use it for your unprotected WordStar diskette. You will store your document files on this same diskette.

A Preliminary Note on Keyboard Use

In this, and all other software chapters, the word *enter* is used when you are to press the Enter key after keying in data or an instruction. The work *type* is used when you do not have to press Enter.

WordStar Menus

One way for a software system to achieve user friendliness is through the use of menus. The menus list the options available to the user, and prompt him or her concerning what to do next. We know from our study of VisiCalc that it uses very modest menus—abbreviations such as CORF that become meaningful as you gain familiarity with the system. WordStar has a much more elaborate set of menus that spell out in considerable detail the available options.

The menus are intended to make it easier to learn and use WordStar, and they do. But at first, the menus seem overpowering. As you use WordStar, you gradually become acquainted with the menus and they represent tools that you can use if and when you need them.

It might speed up your orientation period if you understand that the menus exist in a hierarchy, as illustrated in Figure 14.1. You will notice that there are three levels of menus in the upper portion of the figure, and one level of help messages at the bottom. The highest level menu is the Opening Menu. Next comes the Main Menu, and then come five menus on the same level—Help, Quick, Onscreen, Block, and Print.

229

Figure 14.1   The Hierarchy of WordStar Menus

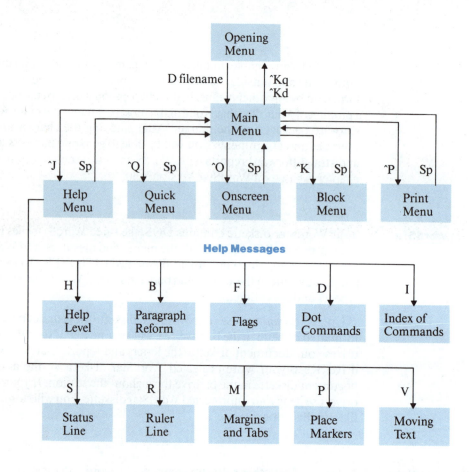

Sp = Space bar

The arrows in the figure identify how you get from one menu to another. The lettering on the arrows will be explained later. Just understand at this point that there are a lot of menus and messages, and that they are interrelated in a logical way. Refer to the figure frequently as we introduce the various menus and messages. The figure serves as a good "road map" of the menu and message structure.

The Opening Menu

When you first load WordStar, the screen displays the **Opening Menu.** See Figure 14.2. At the top are various commands that you execute by typing the appropriate letter. We will use the most common of these commands in this text. In the center of the menu is a directory of your files, and at the bottom is a band of abbreviations that define special shortcuts you can take by pressing the PC function keys as you use WordStar.

There are several actions you can take with the Opening Menu on the screen, but only two are necessary when you begin a WordStar session:

1. Change the logged drive.

2. Open a document (data) file.

Figure 14.2   The Opening Menu

```
          not editing
                 < < <  O P E N I N G   M E N U  > > >
     ---Preliminary  Commands---    ¦ ---File  Commands-- ¦ -System  Commands-
L  Change logged disk drive         ¦                     ¦ R  Run a program
F . File directory      now ON      ¦ P  PRINT a file     ¦ X  EXIT to system
H  Set help level                   ¦                     ¦
    ---Commands to open a file---   ¦ E  RENAME a file    ¦ -WordStar Options-
     D  Open a  document  file       ¦ O  COPY    a file   ¦ M  Run MailMerge
     N  Open a non-document file    ¦ Y  DELETE a file    ¦ S  Run SpellStar

directory of disk A:
  CUTOVER      COMMAND.COM  WS.COM      WSMSGS.OVR   WSOVLY1.OVR




1HELP   2INDENT 3SET LM 4SET RM 5UNDLIN 6BLDFCE 7BEGBLK 8ENDBLK 9BEGFIL 10ENDFIL
```

If you are going to use the diskette in the b: drive to store your document files (letters, reports, and so forth), you must *change the logged drive* before you start to work on those files. Otherwise, WordStar will try to record on the a: drive. You change the logged drive by responding to the menu with an **L** and then entering **b:** to identify the new logged drive.

With WordStar, as opposed to dBASE II and VisiCalc, you should not press the Caps Lock key. This is because your WordStar material will be mostly lowercase characters, just like typewriter copy. You will use the Shift keys to obtain uppercase letters when needed.

With the b: drive as the logged drive, you can *open a document file.* To do this while the Opening Menu is displayed, type **D** and then enter the file name, which can contain 1 to 8 alphabetic letters or digits. If you make a mistake while keying in the file name, simply backspace and retype.

The Main Menu   When you enter a file name, the **Main Menu** appears on the screen. See Figure 14.3. This menu lists the commands for cursor movement, scrolling, deletion, and so on. All of the commands consist of the caret (ˆ) followed by a letter. In WordStar the Control key appears as a (ˆ) on the line above the menu; you don't press the key marked (ˆ). You hold the Control key down while keying in the single letter that follows. So, to enter a command from the Main Menu, you press the Control key, then press the appropriate letter key.

Some WordStar commands require that you press the Control key and press two or three letter or number keys. An example is ˆKq. *You only hold the Control key down for the first letter*—in our example, the K. You release the Control key for any additional command letters, such as the q.

Each time you enter a command, it appears in the upper left corner of the screen. The caret represents the Control key. The letter entered with the Control key pressed is in uppercase (K), and the letter entered with the Control key released is in lowercase (q).

Figure 14.3   The Main Menu

```
      A:LETTER   PAGE 1 LINE 1 COL 01               INSERT ON
                  < < <      M A I N    M E N U    > > >
      --Cursor Movement--     ¦ -Delete- ¦   -Miscellaneous-   ¦  -Other  Menus-
  ^S char left ^D char right !^G  char  ! ^I Tab    ^B Reform ¦ (from Main only)
  ^A word left ^F word right !DEL chr lf! ^V INSERT ON/OFF     !^J Help  ^K Block
  ^E line  up  ^X line down  !^T word rt!^L Find/Replce again!^Q Quick ^P Print
        --Scrolling--        !^Y  line  !RETURN End paragraph!^O Onscreen
  ^Z line down ^W line up    !          !  ^N Insert a RETURN ¦
  ^C screen up ^R screen down!          !  ^U Stop a command  ¦
  L----!----!----!----!----!----!----!----!----!----!----!--------R

                                                                       .
                                                                       .
                                                                       .
                                                                       .
                                                                       .

  1HELP   2INDENT 3SET LM 4SET RM 5UNDLIN 6BLDFCE 7BEGBLK 8ENDBLK 9BEGFIL 10ENDFIL
```

Occasionally, you may make a mistake while entering a command, and WordStar does not recognize it as a command, for example, holding down the Shift key instead of the Control key. If you look in the upper left-hand corner of the screen you can see whether your entry was recognized as a command. If you see the caret followed by the appropriate letters, you know that the command was entered.

If you start to enter a command and then change your mind, type ^U. This is the **interrupt command.** Use ^U for all commands except Print (discussed later). In certain cases, you will have to follow the interrupt command by pressing the Esc key. A prompt on the screen will tell you when this is necessary.

Just below the Main Menu is the ruler line. We will discuss it shortly. It defines your margins and tab stops.

Returning to the Opening Menu

If you start to work on a file and realize that you need to return to the Opening Menu (for example if you logged the wrong drive), type ^Kq. The K refers to a file command, and q stands for quit. You want to abandon (quit) the file you are working on without recording it on the diskette.

Exercise 1 Opening and Main Menus

1. If your PC includes a printer, make certain that it is on, and the paper is aligned with the print head just below the perforation. See Chapter 1 for details on how to set up the printer. Follow this procedure for all WordStar exercises.

2. Insert your DOS/WordStar diskette in drive a: and boot the system.

3. Respond to the A> prompt with **ws**, then press Enter.

4. You will see the Opening Menu. Read it and use the Prt Sc key to make a printed copy.

5. If you are using a dual-drive system and are going to use a diskette in the b: drive for your document files, type **L** to switch the logged drive. Type **b:** in response to the prompt.

6. Type **D** to open a document file.

7. Name the file **Letter.** Press Enter.

8. The Main Menu is displayed. Read it and obtain a printed copy. If you want this message to be on a separate sheet, switch the printer to offline, press the Form Feed button, and switch the printer back online.

9. Type **^Kq** to return to the Opening Menu. Remember, the caret (^) is not the caret key; it is the key labeled Ctrl.

10. Remove your diskette if you wish to end the session. Otherwise, continue with the next exercise. Follow this procedure as you go from exercise to exercise.

Getting Help

WordStar includes so many commands that it is difficult to remember them all. So, you can receive help in the form of menus. When you ask for a menu, it is displayed at the top of the screen, reducing the size of the area below for your document display. The novice prefers to always have the appropriate menu on the screen. The fact that it reduces the size of the document area is a small price to pay. The expert prefers to use the entire screen for the document. WordStar lets you specify four **help levels**—expert (0), novice (3), and two (1,2) in between.

You set the help level by pressing the F1 function key (at the left of the keyboard). Many of the WordStar commands can be initiated with one function key, as opposed to using the standard WordStar commands. For example, the WordStar command to set the help level is H if you are in the Opening Menu, or ^Jh elsewhere. This chapter identifies commands by the function keys to use. But, don't be confused when you see different codes (the WordStar commands) on the screen.

When you press F1, you get the help level message and are prompted to enter the help level desired (0, 1, 2, or 3). The screen explains these levels. When you use level 3, you get all menus and messages. With a level 0, you get none. Keep the level at 3 for the time being (by pressing the space bar). Later, you may want to try a lower level.

There is a master menu of help messages—the **Help Menu** that can be displayed by typing **^J** with the Main Menu on the screen. See Figure 14.4. You are only able to get this menu at help levels 2 or 3. The Help Menu lists the various help messages that you can obtain. As an example, you can get a message that explains the ruler line by pressing the R key. You type ^J to get the Help Menu and then R to get the ruler line message. This means that if you want to see the ruler line message, you have to first obtain the Help Menu. When you enter the command ^Jr, you get both. All help messages work this way. When you have finished reading the message, you press the space bar to return to the Main Menu.

Exercise 2
Help Menus

1. With the Opening Menu on the screen, reissue the command to open a document file named Letter. The file name Letter that you opened in Exercise 1 was not recorded on the diskette when you abandoned it with the ^Kq command. You do not have to switch the logged drive again. The b: drive remains the logged drive until you switch to the a: drive or exit WordStar.

2. With the Main Menu on the screen, type **^J** to get the Help Menu. If your system has a printer, use either the print screen or the print switch toggle technique to obtain a hard copy. See Chapter 8 for an explanation of these techniques.

Figure 14.4   The Help Menu

```
^J         A:LETTER  PAGE 1 LINE 1 COL 01              INSERT ON
              < < <     H E L P   M E N U     > > >
                                     ¦                ¦  --Other   Menus--
   H   Display & set the help level  ¦ S   Status line ¦  (from Main only)
   B   Paragraph reform (CONTROL-B)  ¦ R   Ruler line   ¦  ^J  Help  ^K  Block
   F   Flags in right-most column    ¦ M   Margins & Tabs ¦ ^Q  Quick ^P  Print
   D   Dot commands, print controls  ¦ P   Place markers ¦  ^O  Onscreen
   I   Index of commands             ¦ V   Moving text   ¦  Space Bar returns
                                     ¦                ¦  you to Main Menu.
L----!----!----!----!----!----!----!----!----!----!--------R



1HELP    2INDENT 3SET LM 4SET RM 5UNDLIN 6BLDFCE 7BEGBLK 8ENDBLK 9BEGFIL 10ENDFIL
```

3. Type an **R** to obtain the ruler line message. Obtain a printed copy.

4. Press the space bar to return to the Main Menu.

5. Type **^J** and get the Help Menu again.

6. Type an **M** to get the margins message. Make a printed copy.

7. Press the space bar. You do not go back the Main Menu. Instead, you get a second "page" of the margins message—devoted to line spacing and justification. Make a printed copy.

8. Press the space bar again, and you get a third page, which explains tab stops. Make a printed copy.

9. Press the space bar again and get a fourth page, which explains how to enter a columnar table. Do not make a printed copy. Instead, type **^U** to interrupt the multipage message display. Then press the Esc key to return to the Main Menu.

Let's review what you accomplished with Exercise 2. Refer to Figure 14.1 and see the route that you followed. You started with the Opening Menu and then went to the Main Menu. Then you got the Help Menu and from there went to the ruler line message. After viewing the one-page display, you returned to the Main Menu. You got the Help Menu again and then viewed three pages of the margins and tab messages before returning to the Main Menu with the ^U command. This is the way that you maneuver up and down the hierarchy of WordStar menus and messages.

It is critical to your understanding of WordStar that you know how to use the various menus and messages. Perhaps you would like to obtain a printed copy of all the remaining menus and messages. (Do not worry about the dot command message or the place marker message as we will not be using those WordStar features in this text.)

The Ruler Line

All menus and messages, except the Opening Menu, include the ruler line. The **ruler line** defines the width of the typing line. It identifies the left margin with an L, the right margin with an R, and preset tab stops with exclamation points. Each hyphen represents a typing space between tab stops and margins. You can type a character at any position on the line.

Each time you issue a ruler line command, you get the **Onscreen Menu.** That is because all of the ruler line commands begin with ^O, and that is the command to get the Onscreen Menu. So, when you are at help levels 2 or 3, you get the menu whether you want it or not.

The default settings for the ruler line are:

Left margin—column 1
Right margin—column 65
Tab stops—every 5 positions (from 6 to 56)

If you want the *left margin* in another position, type **^Ol,** followed by the position number. (To do this, type the letter O while holding down the Control key. Then, with both of those keys released, type a lowercase L. Then type the position number.) To set the *right margin,* enter **^Or** and the position number. For example, if you want the margins at 8 and 55, enter ^Ol8 and then enter ^Or55. When you press the Enter key each time, notice the ruler line change.

To reset the *tab stops,* first delete the ones you do not want to use. Enter **^On.** You are then prompted to identify the ones to be deleted. If you want to delete selected ones, enter the position number (such as 21). If you want to delete them all, enter an a in response to the prompt— **^Ona.**

To set tab stops at other positions, type **^Oi** and then enter the position number. After each position, press Enter. For example, if you wanted stops at 21 and 31, you would enter ^Oi21 an then enter ^Oi31.

Tab stops can be used to indent paragraphs and to arrange data in columns. You move the cursor to the tab stop with the Tab key. The Tab key is located in the upper left part of the keyboard, and has double arrows on it—one aiming left and one aiming right.

You can remove the ruler line from the screen and obtain an extra line for displaying text by typing **^Ot.** This is a toggle switch that switches from on to off, or off to on, each time you press it. To add the ruler line, type **^Ot** when the switch is off.

Exercise 3
Ruler Line

If you terminated your session at the end of the previous exercise, or if the Opening Menu is on the screen, change the logged drive if necessary and open a file named Letter to get the Main Menu. Follow this procedure on all exercises that start with the Main Menu, when that menu is not already on the screen.

1. Type **^Jr** to obtain the ruler line message. Change the default ruler line as follows.

2. Enter **^Ol5** to set the left margin at position 5. Notice that when you type the ^O, you get the Onscreen Menu.

3. Enter **^Or75** to set the right margin at position 75.

4. Enter **^Ona** to remove all of the tab stops.

5. Enter **^Oil0** to set one tab stop at position 10.

Figure 14.5   The Effect of Insertion on Keyboard Functions

Key	Insertion On	Insertion Off
Backspace key	Spaces over characters	Spaces over characters
Left and right arrow keys	Space over characters	Space over characters
Del key	Deletes character left of cursor	Deletes character left of cursor
Ins key	Turns insertion on and off	Turns insertion on and off
Space bar	Inserts a space	Blanks out cursor position
Character key	Inserts the character	Replaces the character

6. Set another tab stop at position 20.

7. Obtain a printed copy of the Main Menu with the revised ruler line.

The Status Line

The line at the top of the screen is called the **status line.** It identifies the logged drive, the name of the file that you have opened, the page number that you are on, as well as the cursor position (the line and column of the page). You will also notice the message "INSERT ON." As you use WordStar, other cues will appear on the status line. For example, as WordStar performs a complex task, it will signal "WAIT."

The Insertion Feature

WordStar has a special feature that makes it easy to add letters, words, sentences, and even paragraphs to existing text. The feature is called **insertion.**

Normally, you first type an entire document, then edit or correct it. The insertion feature is designed to make the editing job easier.

Insertion is turned on when you begin your WordStar session. That is the default setting. You turn it off by typing ^V or by pressing the Ins key (a toggle key). You turn it back on again the same way—with ^V or Ins. With the feature turned off, the keyboard operates rather like a typewriter with a correction tape: if you make a mistake in keying in data, you backspace to erase the error and then retype.

With insertion turned on, the keyboard functions as it does when the Ins and Del keys are used to correct errors in a BASIC program. Characters to the right of the cursor are moved to the left as you delete, and bumped to the right when you insert. This mode is preferred by users who have mastered the art of deletion and insertion.

Some of the keys function one way with insertion on, and another way with it off. Figure 14.5 summarizes the differences. The first four keys listed (Backspace, arrow, Del, and Ins) function the same in either mode. Only the last two keys (space bar and character keys) function differently. With insertion on, the space bar and character keys cause either a blank space or a character to be inserted at the cursor location, and all characters to the right of the cursor are shifted one position to the right. With insertion off, the space bar and character keys simply cause the character at the cursor location to be replaced with a space or a character. The characters to the right of the cursor are unaffected.

Exercise 4
The Insertion Feature

1. With the Main Menu on the screen, look at the right of the status line to see whether insertion is on. (It should be on, as that is the default option if you haven't turned it off.)

2. Turn insertion off by pressing the Ins key. Note that the message "INSERT ON" disappears.

3. Set the left margin at 1 and the right margin at 80. Remove all tab stops.

4. Type the following:

   The quick fix jumped over the fence.

5. If you type the wrong letter, use the left arrow key or the Backspace key to position the cursor on the error character and retype.

6. Position the cursor on the "i" in fix, and type an **o**.

7. Position the cursor over the period, using the arrow keys, and press the space bar. Then type **and ran away**.

8. Turn insertion on.

9. Position the cursor over the space between quick and fox, and type **, brown**.

10. Move the cursor to the space following the word fence, and delete the words "the fence" using the Del key.

11. With the cursor in the space following the word "over" type **the wall**.

12. Use the Backspace key to move the cursor to the space to the right of "fox." Use the delete key to delete the word "fox."

13. Type **rabbit**. The sentence should read: "The quick, brown rabbit jumped over the wall and ran away."

14. Obtain a printed copy of your editing efforts.

15. Type **^Kq** to abandon your file and return to the Opening Menu.

Let's review what you accomplished with the exercise. You learned how to turn the insertion feature on and off. You corrected typographical errors with insertion off. Each time you typed, only the character at the cursor position changed. Then, with insertion on, you deleted and inserted words. The characters to the right of the cursor shifted to the left on a deletion, and to the right on an insertion. You used the left arrow and the Backspace key to move the cursor to the left. You moved the cursor to the right with the right arrow key. You deleted characters with the Del key. You inserted characters by typing them at the appropriate position with insertion on.

The ability to edit your copy is also a key to using WordStar efficiently. If you feel that you need more practice, type another one-line sentence and make changes to it with insertion both on and off.

The WordStar Page

You have already seen that WordStar assumes certain margins and tab stops. These are default options; unless you specify otherwise, they will be in effect. There are some other default options that define the size and format of the page and are stored with WordStar until you change them:

* Single-spacing (6 lines per inch)
* 10 characters per inch (pica typewriter size)
* 55 lines per page

If you want double-spacing, type ^O, and the Onscreen Menu appears. It prompts you concerning the basic characteristics of the WordStar page—tabs, margins, justification, spacing, and so on. You notice that you type the letter S to set the spacing. Then type the number 2 for double-spacing. If you want triple-spacing, you type a 3. WordStar will accept any number between 1 and 9. Type ^Os1 to return to single-spacing.

The typing density of 10 characters per inch is a good one for business documents, so we will not change that option. The 55 lines per page is based on a standard typing page (8½ × 11 inches). At 6 lines per inch, you would get 66 lines on the page with no top or bottom margins. But, WordStar uses a top margin of 3 lines and a bottom margin of 8 lines, leaving 55 for typing. These are good margins for business work, and we will leave them as is.

After you type the 55th line, you will see a line of hyphens across the page with a letter P at the right end. This is the **page break line**. It doesn't print when you print the document; it only appears on the screen so that you can distinguish between pages.

Other Onscreen Indicators (Flags)

In the rightmost column of the screen, WordStar displays single characters that have special meanings. For an explanation of these flags, type **^Jf** to get the flags message. Although there are nine different flags, only four are of immediate interest— the blank space, the period, the "less than" sign, and the letter P.

A *blank space* means that your line has "wrapped around," and WordStar automatically continues on the next line. This is a basic difference between using WordStar and using a typewriter. You do not press the carriage return (Enter) key when you reach the end of the line. WordStar handles that for you. When the right margin is reached, the last word that fits within the margin is displayed, and the next word appears on the line below. This is called **word wrap**.

With WordStar, you can either justify the right margin, or not. **Justification** means that the right margin is made straight by adding spaces between words just as you see in many books. When you begin a WordStar session, the justification feature is on. You can turn it off by typing ^Oj. To turn it back on, type ^Oj again— it is a toggle command.

If you are uncertain whether the justification feature is on, call up the Onscreen Menu. It will tell you.

As a general rule, you keep justification on for business reports, and turn it off for correspondence. The reasoning is that with justification off, the letter or memo looks as if it had been typed rather than printed by a computer. Managers usually like to create this personal image, whether corresponding to someone within the company or outside. As word processing gets better established, this preference for a ragged right margin may fade.

With justification on, word wrap aligns the right margin when the last word on the line is displayed. With justification off, word wrap does not adjust the spacing on the line to achieve margin alignment.

Some printers print a certain number of characters per inch. The IBM Graphics Printer is an example. It prints 10 characters per inch. Other printers print a varying number of characters per inch, depending on the characters. An m occupies more space than an i, for example. These printers are called **proportional spacing printers** or **incremental printers**. With an incremental printer, the spacing of the words on a line to achieve right justification is very precise with the same space inserted betweeen each word. With a **nonincremental printer**, such as the IBM Graphics Printer, the spacing is only in multiples of the character widths—one-tenth of an inch. This means that some words on the line might be separated by one space, and other words by two. A nonincremental printer does not produce the same high-quality copy as can be obtained with an incremental printer.

You often hear the term **letter quality printer**. The term implies that the copy is as good as that prepared on an electric typewriter with a carbon ribbon. A dot matrix printer usually does not produce letter quality. Rather, a different printing technology such as a daisy wheel or ink jet is required. As a rule, a letter quality printer is more expensive than a matrix printer.

Let's continue with a discussion of the onscreen indicators in the right column. In addition to blank, you will see a *period*. The period means that you haven't yet reached that line in entering data. WordStar uses the period to mark the end of your document. As you enter data on a line, its period disappears.

Another flag is the **"less than"** sign (<). This represents a "hard" carriage return. A **hard return** is one that you insert by pressing the Enter key. Even though WordStar may later reform (modify) your text to fit changed specifications (maybe you will select narrower margins), it will not change the hard return. A hard return prevents anything from printing on the remainder of the line. Successive hard returns produce permanent blank lines, such as those between paragraphs. Users generally insert hard returns at the end of paragraphs, but you should understand that WordStar will not alter them as it reforms your text. You can later delete them if you wish, but WordStar cannot. To delete the > flag, position the cursor at the end of the line and type ^G.

The fourth flag that concerns us is the letter *P* that defines the page break line.

When WordStar performs word wrap, it records **soft returns**. WordStar can change these to produce changed page formats. Remember, hard returns are permanent; soft returns are temporary.

**Exercise 5
Word Wrap
and Flags**

1. Obtain the Main Menu by opening a file.

2. Move the margins in to 15 and 60 so that you can give word wrap a better workout.

3. Turn justification off by typing ^Oj, and turn insertion off by typing ^V.

4. Type several sentences that fill 3 or 4 lines. Make up your own sentences. Do not press Enter at the end of the line; just continue typing.

5. Notice that the period flag is replaced with a space as word wrap executes a soft return.

6. After you have typed several sentences, press Enter to record a hard return. Notice the "less than" flag in the margin.

7. Press Enter again to insert a blank line (with the < flag). This is the way to insert blank lines between paragraphs.

8. Turn justification on by typing ^Oj.

9. Repeat step 4. Notice the right margin. Is it different with justification on? Notice that some of the words are separated by a single space, and some by two. This is a characteristic of a nonincremental printer.

10. Obtain a hard copy of your two paragraphs.

11. Abandon your file and return to the Opening Menu.

Saving Your Document File

The cardinal rule is "Save often." This gives you a backup file that can be updated with a minimum of work, should anything happen to your file in primary storage.

There are three "file save" commands:

1. ^Ks saves the file by copying it on the diskette and returns the cursor to the beginning of the file. Use this when you want to save before you edit, or every few pages as you type a lengthy document.

2. ^Kd saves the file and returns you to the Opening Menu. This exits you from the file you have been creating. Use this when you want to save an edited file and then work on another file.

3. ^Kx saves the file and returns you to DOS. Use this when you want to exit WordStar and use another software package.

Exercise 6 A Letter

1. With the Opening Menu on the screen, change the logged drive to b: (if it hasn't been done previously), and open a document file named Bates.

2. Make certain that justification and insertion are both off.

3. Type the letter using the margins from Exercise 5 (15 and 60). Do not correct errors as they are made; correct them later.

(Today's date)
(Two blank lines)
Mr. Alan Bates, President
Bates Pharmaceuticals
P.O. Box 12381
Chicago, IL 60606
(Blank line)
Dear Mr. Bates,
(Blank line)
Thank you for your offer to join your firm. As you know, I have tremendous respect for Bates Pharmaceuticals. I regret, however, that I must refuse. I am heavily committed to government work at the present time and feel that I must stay where I am.
(Blank line)
I look forward to seeing you again, and recalling the good times we had together. Good luck to you and your firm. And, thank you again for your offer. I'm flattered, and also disappointed, that I cannot accept.
(Blank line)

Sincerely yours,
(Four blank lines)
(Your name)
(Your street address)
(Your city, state)
(Your area code and telephone number)

4. Type **^Kd** if you plan to continue with the next exercise. Type **^Kx** if you want to terminate your session.

Your File Directory

WordStar maintains a directory of your files on the diskette in the logged drive. The directory appears on the Opening Menu. The files are listed alphabetically, and the names do not include an extension.

You do not add a file to the directory simply by opening it. You must save it with a ^Ks, ^Kd, or ^Kx command. For that reason, you should have only one WordStar document file in your directory—the Bates file that you saved in Exercise 6.

Backup Files

The normal practice is to save your file immediately after creating it. We did this with the Bates file. Then, you edit it and correct errors. Then, you save again.

When you do this, WordStar automatically saves the old version of the file as a backup file. The old version is given the extension .BAK to distinguish it from the new version.

WordStar will save only one old version—the one previous to the current version. If you continue to save revised versions, the old .BAK file is deleted as the new .BAK file is added.

If something happens to the most recent version, you can use the .BAK file. However, it must be renamed before you can work with it. You rename a .BAK file by typing E with the Opening Menu displayed. You will be asked to identify the file to be renamed. Include the .BAK extension. Then, provide a new name that has no .BAK extension. You will be able to use the file with the new name.

If you want to save a backup copy of your new file on another diskette, perform two successive file save operations. The first saves your new file. Remove your document diskette and insert another formatted diskette. Perform the save operation again. This one saves the .BAK file (identical to the new one) on the second diskette. Reinsert the original document file diskette and proceed.

Deleting Unneeded Files

To delete unneeded files from your diskette (including .BAK files), type a Y with the Opening Menu on the screen. You will be asked to name the file to be deleted.

Editing Your Copy

You edit your copy by moving the cursor to the error location and making the correction.

Scrolling

Since you probably cannot display all of your document on the screen at one time (21 lines is usually the maximum), you will need to scroll your document up and down for viewing. Think of the screen as a movable window, and the document as stationary. To scroll up, type ^W. To scroll down, type ^Z. These commands move one line at a time.

To scroll continuously, insert a Q (for quick) before the W or Z. ^Qw and ^Qz provide continuous scrolling. Stop scrolling by pressing any key.

Sometimes you will want to scroll rapidly, and other times slowly. WordStar lets you control the speed. After you key in ^Qw or ^Qz, type a digit 1–9. The 1 is fastest; the 9 is slowest. If you don't add the digit, the default speed is 3. Once you set a speed, scrolling occurs at that rate until you change it again.

Moving the Cursor

The easiest way to move the cursor is with the arrow keys. The left and right arrows function as you would expect, but the up and down arrows do not. When you move up or down, the cursor will not move any farther right on a line than it has already been. This problem can be solved by *always moving up or down first, and then left or right.* For example, assume that your copy is double-spaced, and the cursor is at position 12 on row 4. There is an error at position 12 on row 6. When you press the down arrow key, the cursor doesn't move to position 12 on row 5 because row 5 is blank. The cursor moves to the first position on row 5. Press the down arrow key again and the cursor moves to position 1 on row 6. Then use the right arrow key to move the cursor to position 12.

The best way to sharpen your WordStar skills is to develop speed in moving the cursor. For short moves, use the arrow keys. But, for long moves learn how to do it most rapidly. Use these commands or keys whenever possible:

F9	moves you to the beginning of the file.
F10	moves you to the end of the file.
Home key	returns you to the screen's upper left-hand corner.
End key	moves you to the lowest line on the screen.
^Qs	moves you to the beginning of the line.
^Qd	moves you to the end of the line.
^A	moves you from right to left, one word at a time.
^F	moves you from left to right, one word at a time.
^E	moves you up one line (same as up arrow key).
^X	moves you down one line (same as down arrow key).
^S	moves you one character to the left (same as left arrow key).
^D	moves you one character to the right (same as right arrow key).

At first, this might seem to be too much to remember. It will take some practice, but there is a pattern that will help you learn quickly. The pattern is the arrangement of keyboard keys operated by your left hand. The pattern is illustrated in Figure 14.5. You recall that dBASE II uses the same general pattern. The A and S keys move the cursor to the left, and the D and F keys move it to the right. Insert a Q in front of the S and the cursor moves to the beginning of the line; put a Q in front of the D and the cursor moves to the end of the line.

Figure 14.6 Pattern of Cursor Moving Keys

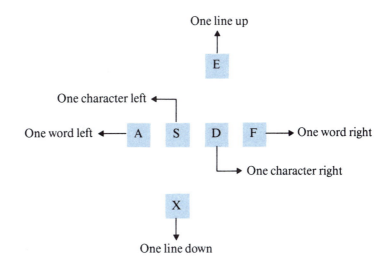

Correcting Errors

Once the cursor has been positioned, use these keys and commands to delete:

Del   removes the character to the *left* of the cursor; characters to the right shift to the left one position.

^G   removes the character *at* the cursor position; characters to the right shift to the left one position.

^T   removes the *word* at the *right*.

^Y   removes the *entire line.*

^Q Delete removes everything from the *beginning* of the line *to* the cursor position.

^Qy   removes everything *including* the cursor position to the *end* of the line.

**Exercise 7
Editing**

1. With the Opening Menu on the screen, type **D** to open a file, and then respond with **Bates** as the file name. The file name should appear in your file directory.

2. The Bates letter should be displayed on the screen, with the cursor at the beginning.

3. Look for errors, and when you find them move the cursor to that location. Use the commands that move the cursor as quickly as possible.

4. If the error can be corrected by replacing one character with another, do so with insertion off.

5. If the error requires extra characters to be added, have insertion on.

6. If the error requires deletion of extra characters, use the Del key. Insertion can be on or off.

7. After you have corrected all of the errors, experiment with the following cursor movement keys and commands:

F9	Move to beginning of file
F10	Move to end of file
Home	Move to top of screen
End	Move to bottom of screen
^Qw1	Scroll up fast
^Qz9	Scroll down slowly
^Qs	Move to beginning of line
^Qd	Move to end of line
^A	Move left, one word
^F	Move right, one word

8. Save your edited file with ^Kd and get the Opening Menu.

9. Your directory should list both the BATES and the BATES.BAK files.

10. Try to load the BATES.BAK file by typing **D**, followed by the file name.

11. Rename the BATES.BAK file by typing an **E** and supplying a new name.

12. Load the file with the new name.

13. Exit WordStar with ^Kx.

Reforming Your Copy

In our discussion of WordStar thus far, the only feature that sets it apart from conventional typing, as a DSS tool, is the ability to make corrections to the copy quickly and easily. This, in itself, is a big advantage, but there are additional features that we will identify as our discussion unfolds. One such feature is the ability to change the format, or **reform**, your copy by changing the margins and tab stops, changing the line spacing, changing from or to a justified right margin, and hyphenating words.

The procedure is to position the cursor at the beginning of the copy, decide on the specifications for the new format, communicate those specifications to WordStar, and type ^**B**. WordStar will reform your copy, a paragraph at a time. For each paragraph, you type ^B. The reforming is terminated when the first hard return is reached.

Changing Margins and Tab Stops

With the cursor at the beginning of the file repeat the same procedure described earlier for setting the margins and tab stops. Use ^Ol, ^Or, ^On, and ^Oi. Do this before you type ^B.

Changing Line Spacing

Repeat the procedure described earlier for setting the line spacing, using the ^Os command. Simply typing the ^Os command will not change the spacing on existing text immediately. The change is accomplished when you reform with ^B.

Changing Justification

Use the same procedure to change the right justification that was explained earlier. Type ^Oj, then reform.

Hyphenating Copy

The word wrap function doesn't hyphenate words. It simply moves an entire word to the next line if the entire word cannot fit on the line being typed. This means that, even though the right margin is justified, there may be unattractive gaps between the words. This situation can be improved through hyphenation.

When you type ^B, WordStar scans the paragraph looking for words that can be hyphenated at the end of the line. When it finds one, the cursor stops and flashes. It is asking you if you want to hyphenate at that location. If so, press the hyphen key.

Sometimes WordStar will try to hyphenate a word in the wrong place. If this happens, you can move the cursor to the right or left with the arrow keys to the correct position and press the hyphen key. In using the right arrow, do not go past the right margin, or the entire word will be moved to the next line with a **hard hyphen** inserted. As with the hard return, the hard hyphen is permanent. **Hyphen-help** is the term given to the hyphenation assistance that WordStar provides.

The hyphens that WordStar inserts during hyphen-help are **soft hyphens**. The soft hyphens, as well as the hard hyphens, print when you print your document. The soft hyphens are at the end of the line. However, if you reform your copy several times with different margins, you will notice words in the middle of the line with soft hyphens. WordStar doesn't remove a soft hyphen during subsequent reforming, but any soft hyphens in the middle of the line do not print.

You have to look closely at the screen to detect a difference between a hard and a soft hyphen. The soft one is not quite as distinct—it appears a little thinner.

**Exercise 8
Reforming**

1. Load the Bates letter that you edited in the previous exercise.

2. Change the margins to 8 and 63.

3. Type **^B** at the beginning of each paragraph. There are several single lines in the letter with a hard return flag; you will have to type ^B for each.

4. Save the reformed file with the proper ^K command, depending on whether you wish to terminate your session or continue.

Printing

You can use either the print screen or the print switch toggle technique to print whatever is displayed on the screen. However, you print a document with the PRINT command.

When you signal that you have finished editing your document (with ^Kd), you see the Opening Menu display. Type **P**. WordStar asks for the file name. If you can't remember, look at the displayed file directory. This directory can be turned on and off by typing F when the Opening Menu is displayed. If you make a mistake while typing the file name, backspace and retype.

After you type the file name, press Esc (Escape)—*not Enter*. Printing will begin immediately. If you accidentally press Enter, you will be asked a series of questions. Press Escape and printing will begin.

If you wish to stop printing before the file is complete, type P. This is the interrupt command for the printer. If you want to return to the Opening Menu, type Y. If you do not want to return to the menu, but want to resume printing, type N.

This procedure assumes that your system configuration includes the IBM Graphics Printer or one that is compatible, such as the Epson MX-100 or FX-80. If such is not the case, you press Enter rather than Esc and respond to the questions. Your instructor (or the person who sold you your printer) will tell you how to respond.

Exercise 9
Printing

1. Make certain that the printer is on. Align the paper in the carriage so that it is positioned properly.

2. Load your Bates file from the diskette.

3. With the Opening Menu on the screen, type **P**.

4. Type the file name. Press Esc to initiate printing.

5. When the printing is completed, switch the printer off line, and use the Form Feed key to eject the paper so that the letter can be removed.

6. Exit WordStar.

Summary

WordStar consists of many commands. The software helps you to initiate the appropriate command by displaying a set of menus. The menus are arranged in a hierarchy, with the Opening Menu at the top. This is the menu that you first see when you bring up WordStar. The Opening Menu enables you to change the logged drive, set the help level, open a document file, and print a file. The Opening Menu also includes a directory of the files from the diskette in the logged drive. You return to the Opening Menu with ^Kq or ^Kd.

The next menu in the hierarchy is the Main Menu. This menu is on the screen when you type your document file. Just below the menu is the ruler line.

From the Main Menu, you can call up five lower level menus by holding down the Control key and typing a letter: (J) Help Menu, (Q) Quick Menu, (O) Onscreen Menu, (K) Block Menu, and (P) Print Menu. You return to the Main Menu by pressing the space bar. From the Help Menu you can call up ten help messages. Most of the messages are short, but some require two or more screen displays. You step from one display to the next with the space bar, and, at the end of the message, use the space bar to return to the Main Menu. You can interrupt lengthy messages with the interrupt command—^U.

If you do not like the WordStar default options for the margins, tabs, and spacing, you can change them from the Onscreen Menu.

As you type your copy, you can have the insertion feature on or off. When off, the keyboard resembles that of an ordinary typewriter. When on, characters to the right of the cursor move to the right when additional characters are added, and move to the left when characters are deleted. Flags at the right of the screen identify untyped lines (period), hard returns (< sign), word wrap (blank), and the end of a page (P). Word wrap automatically starts a new line when a full word will not fit on the line being typed.

Typically, letters have a ragged right margin so that they will communicate a more personal, custom-typed image. Reports, on the other hand, feature a justified right margin.

When you save your file on the diskette you have the option of returning to the same file (^Ks), returning to the Opening Menu (^Kd), or exiting WordStar (^Kx). WordStar maintains a directory of your files on the Opening Menu, and automatically saves a backup (.BAK) file.

You edit text by scrolling and moving the cursor. The key to quick and efficient editing is a knowledge of the scrolling, cursor movement, and delete commands. After the errors have been corrected, you can reform the text, changing the margins, tab stops, justification, and spacing. As you reform, hyphen-help suggests places for hyphenation.

With this introduction to WordStar, you can prepare business correspondence such as letters, memos, and simple reports. In the next chapter, the formatting techniques that are useful in preparing management reports are described.

Key Terms

Opening Menu	Justification
Main Menu	Proportional spacing printer
Interrupt command	Incremental printer
Help levels	Nonincremental printer
Help Menu	Hard return
Ruler line	Soft return
Onscreen Menu	Reform
Status line	Hard hyphen
Insertion	Hyphen-help
Page break line	Soft hyphen
Word wrap	

Questions

(Do not fill in blanks in the book. Write answers on a separate piece of paper.)

1. The designers of WordStar intended to make it user-friendly through the use of _____.

2. There are _____ level(s) of menus in WordStar, plus _____ level(s) of help messages.

3. The first menu that you see when you run WordStar is the _____ Menu.

4. You change the logged drive by typing a(n) _____ with the Opening Menu on the screen.

5. You open a document file by typing a(n) _____ followed by the _____.

6. After you open a document file, you see the _____ Menu.

7. In WordStar, the _____ represents the Ctrl key.

8. The interrupt command is _____.

9. When you want to abandon a file without making changes to the diskette, you return to the Opening Menu by typing _____.

10. The four help levels range from _____ for expert to _____ for novice.

11. The device displayed on the screen that illustrates where the margins and tab stops are located is called the _____.

12. You can turn the insertion feature on by _____ or _____.

13. The dotted line that sometimes appears across the screen is the _____.

14. In the flag position at the right of the screen, _____ means that the line has not yet been typed, _____ means that the line has been wrapped around, _____ indicates that a hard return has been inserted, and _____ means that it is the page break.

15. To save your file and exit WordStar, you would type _____.

16. WordStar will save the most _____ version of your backup file.

17. When you type a digit to specify the scrolling speed, _____ means fastest, and _____ means slowest.

18. When you move the cursor, always move it _____ first, then _____.

19. You can delete an entire line by typing _____.

20. When WordStar reforms your copy, you position the cursor at the beginning of a _____ and type _____.

Assignment 1
Request for
Proposal (RFP)

You are Anthony Scarmodo, president of Maple Leaf Industries, Ltd., a small Canadian battery manufacturer. You have recently seen a demonstration of the dBASE II data base management system (DBMS) using the IBM Personal Computer. You have a PC installed and would like to learn what would be necessary to implement a DBMS in your firm.

After inquiring around, you learn that one of the top data base consultants is Helen McGregor, Partner, Electronic Auditing, Inc., P.O. Box 11709; Palo Alto, CA 94303.

Prepare a letter to Ms. McGregor explaining your interest in DBMS, and asking her to propose a series of steps that your firm should take in implementing a DBMS. It is not necessary that Ms. McGregor quote a fee; that can be worked out later.

Edit, save, and print the letter.

Assignment 2
Proposal Letter
and Attachment

Now you are Helen McGregor. Write a letter to Mr. Scarmodo (his address is Ottawa Technology Center, Ottawa, Canada I1S5B6) accepting his invitation to bid. Then, prepare an attachment that lists the steps that he has requested, and the persons responsible. The material for the attachment follows. Use tab stops to format the attachment. Edit, save, and print the proposal. If your line is too long and you get a wrap-around, move the right margin a few spaces to the left.

ATTACHMENT

Step	Persons Responsible
1. Achieve top management support	Top management
2. Identify major DBMS objectives	Top management Data base consultant
3. Hire a data base administrator (DBA)	Top management Data base consultant
4. Analyze firm's data needs	DBA
5. Request DBMS vendor proposals	DBA
6. Evaluate DBMS proposals	DBA
7. Recommend a DBMS	DBA
8. Approve DBMS for implementation	Top management
9. Convert data to DBMS format	Computer operations
10. Educate DBMS Users	DBA Systems analysts
11. Implement DBMS	DBA Systems analysts Management Computer operations
12. Review DBMS performance	Data base consultant

15 WordStar Part 2

Only a few basic capabilities set WordStar apart from ordinary typing methods and make it a valuable DSS tool. We discussed some of these capabilities in the previous chapter—easy correction/revision of copy, right margin justification, easy reformatting, and help with hyphenation. Several additional capabilities, perhaps more significant in terms of their DSS impact, are the subject of this chapter. You will learn how to underline characters and use boldface type, how to insert additional copy such as sentences or even paragraphs, and how to prepare tables. In addition, you will learn how to perform tasks that are very difficult without word processing—finding and changing words, and manipulating blocks of text.

After studying this chapter and working the exercises and assignments, you should be able to prepare business reports that feature special printing techniques that contribute to an increased communication ability. Additionally, you should be able to make major changes to the report copy in order to tailor it to the special characteristics of a particular audience. All of these capabilities make WordStar a powerful DSS tool, and mastery of the tool should contribute to your effectiveness as a communicator and as a manager.

Inserting Additional Text

In the previous chapter when you learned basic editing, you were only concerned with correcting the original copy. That operation can be performed with the insertion feature on or off, depending on the type of changes to be made. If you are only replacing one character with another, insertion should be turned off. On the other hand, if you are removing unwanted characters or adding extra ones, insertion should be on. The insertion feature causes characters to the right of the cursor to be moved to the right as new characters are inserted and moved to the left as old characters are deleted.

There is no limit to the amount of new material that can be inserted. This means that whole new blocks can be inserted into existing copy. Perhaps you would like to add a paragraph. You can do this without retyping the entire document. Just turn insertion on by pressing the Ins key, move the cursor to the point where the new material is to be inserted, and start typing. After everything has been entered, move the cursor to the top line of the paragraph and reform with ^B.

Exercise 1
Text Insertion

1. Load the Bates file from the previous chapter into primary storage.

2. Move the cursor to the end of the second sentence "...Bates Pharmaceuticals."

3. Make certain that insertion is on and that justification is off.

4. Type the following sentence:

   Bates has not only made a reputation for being a very efficiently managed operation, but an ethical one as well.

5. Insert the following paragraph between the two paragraphs in the original letter. Move the cursor to the end of the first paragraph and insert two hard returns. The cursor should be positioned properly for the second paragraph.

You can rest assured, however, that as I follow the progress of your firm as it reaches greater heights, I will be your most avid supporter. I'm sure that I will always have a special respect for you and your company.

6. Edit the revised copy, correcting any errors.

7. Reform the entire letter, using the default options for the margins.

8. Save the file on your diskette.

9. Prepare a printed copy.

Special Printing Techniques

The ability to emphasize certain words or groups of words can enhance the ability of a written document to communicate. WordStar offers two special printing techniques that identify important words or points. These techniques are **boldface printing** and **underlining**. **Boldface printing** is used in this book to highlight key terms. Underlining can accomplish the same purpose. In addition, underlining is commonly used to identify publications in a bibliography.

Boldface Print

You can obtain boldface print by pressing the F6 key before and after the word or words to be printed in darker-than-usual type. Actually, the print head strikes each letter twice. When you press the F6 key, ^B is inserted in your copy as a marker. The marker is inserted just to the left of the cursor. Therefore, position the cursor on the first letter of the (first) word to be printed in boldface and press the F6 key. Then, position the cursor on the position to the right of the last boldface character and press F6 again. When the markers are inserted, the characters on the line to the right of the markers are pushed to the right. It will look like the right margin was exceeded, but it was not. When the copy is printed, the markers are removed and the right margin is okay.

Make certain that the insertion feature is on when you add the markers. Otherwise, the markers will erase characters previously in those positions.

It's not possible to display the copy on the screen with selected words in boldface. The markers are the only way to identify the boldface words on the screen. The boldface print only appears when the copy is printed.

The addition of the markers might make it difficult to visually edit your copy on the screen. The markers can be removed from the screen display by using ^Od, the **print control display toggle switch.** Type ^Od and inspect your copy. Then type ^Od again to reinstate the markers.

When you want to permanently delete the markers, position the cursor to the right of each marker and strike the Del key once.

Exercise 2
Boldface Print

You have a file on your WordStar diskette named CUTOVER. It is on the diskette in the a: drive. We will use it for several exercises in this chapter.

1. With the Opening Menu on the screen, change the logged drive to the a: drive if that is necessary.

2. Open the CUTOVER file and print it so that you can have a record of its original contents.

3. The printed copy includes the title "Basic Approaches to Cutover" and three numbered paragraphs: 1. Immediate, 2. Phased, and 3. Parallel. Set the title and three paragraph names in boldface.

4. Scroll your copy with ^Qz1 and ^Qw1. See the effects of adding the markers. Notice how the ^B markers push the lines past the right margin. Type ^Od to remove the markers. Scroll the document to see the effect on the right margin. Type ^Od again to reinstate the markers.

5. Print out the copy with the boldface print.

6. Permanently remove the boldface markers with the Del key. Be sure to remove both beginning and ending markers.

Underlining

You underline words in basically the same way that you set them in boldface print. The only difference is that you use a different function key: F5. This time the marker is ^S. It also bumps characters past the right margin and can be removed from the screen display with ^Od.

Exercise 3
Underlining

1. With your CUTOVER file on the screen, underline the same words that you set in boldface in Exercise 2.

2. Print the file.

3. Replace the underline markers with boldface print markers.

4. Save the file with ^Kd.

5. Get a printout to ensure that the boldface print is reinstated, since you will use this file again later.

Indented Margins

Another technique for increasing the readability of copy is indented margins. This technique is frequently used in outline-style procedures such as job descriptions and policy manuals, where subsidiary sections are successively indented. As an example, a portion of a job description might appear as:

1. Daily duties
 1.1 Order processing
  1.11 Order entry
   1.11.1 Log in order
   1.11.2 Check for missing data
   1.11.3 Check credit
  1.12 Inventory
   1.12.1 Check balance on hand
   1.12.2 Update balance on hand
   1.12.3 Check reorder point
   1.12.4 Update quantity on order
 1.2 Receivables processing

This type of outline format is preferable for procedures, since it clearly specifies what is to be done.

If the lines are short and there is no word wrap, such as in the outline example, you simply set the tab stops at the correct positions and press the Tab key the correct number of times before typing each line. Use a hard return to go from one line to the next.

Exercise 4
One-Line indention

1. Open a file named Hardware on your document diskette.

2. Use the default options for the margins and set tab stops at positions 7, 12, and 17.

3. Specify double-spacing.

4. Enter the following copy. Align the major categories on the left margin. Use the Tab key to indent to the appropriate tab stops for the subsidiary categories. Use a hard return to go from one line to the next.

> **Central processing unit**
>> **Control unit**
>> **Arithmetic and logic unit**
>> **Primary storage**
> **Secondary storage**
>> **Sequential storage**
>>> **Magnetic tape**
>>> **Magnetic disk**
>> **Direct storage**
>>> **Magnetic disk**
>>> **Magnetic drum**
>>> **Metal oxide semiconductor**
> **Input devices**
>> **Terminal**
>> **Card reader**
>> **MICR unit**
>> **OCR unit**
>> **Speech recognition unit**
> **Output devices**
>> **Printers**
>>> **Impact printers**
>>>> **Chain printer**
>>>> **Drum printer**
>>> **Nonimpact printers**
>>>> **Xerographic printer**
>>>> **Ink jet printer**
>>>> **Laser printer**

5. Print the outline.

Multiple-Line Outline Entries

When the entries in the outline occupy more than one line, the process becomes more complex. You can't rely on word wrap, since it will cause the second and successive lines in the entry to be aligned on the left margin. For example, copy would appear as:

1. Central processing unit
     A. Control unit—this is the unit that causes the computer to execute the instructions in the proper sequence.

This problem can be solved by instructing word wrap to *not* return to the left margin, but to return to an inner margin identified by a tab stop. A function key, F2, is used to communicate this instruction. Let's set up some sample copy, and see how the F2 key is used. The numbers above the first line identify the tab stops.

1. Central processing unit
     A. Control unit—this is the unit that causes the computer to execute the instructions in the proper sequence.
         (1) Instruction register—this is the special storage unit that contains the instruction to be executed.

         (2) Instruction address register—this is the special storage unit that identifies the next instruction to be executed.

The major category (line 1) will be aligned on the left margin. When the cursor is at the left margin, we will press F2 one time to move the margin to tab stop 4, two times to move to tab stop 9, and three times to move to tab stop 14. The main difference between this example and the previous one is that you are using F2 for tabbing, not the Tab key. This approach is necessary so you can use word wrap on the multiline entries. Perform the following steps:

1. Type the **1**. Press the F2 key. This moves the left margin to the first tab stop in position 4. If you look at the ruler line, you will notice that the portion of the line up to the first tab stop is highlighted more than the rest of the line. This is WordStar's way of showing you where the new left margin is. Each time you press F2, the portion of the ruler line up to the next tab stop is displayed with bright light.

2. Type **Central processing unit** and press Enter. This records a hard return and *voids our previous F2 indentions*. The left margin is back to position 1. You use the hard return to get to the second line because you did not fill the first line.

3. Press F2. This moves the left margin to the first tab stop in position 4. Type **A.** and press F2. This moves the left margin to the second tab stop, at position 9. Type the "**Control unit—**" sentence. After you fill the line, word wrap starts the next line at the proper margin (position 9). After typing the sentence, press Enter to move to the next line.

4. Press F2 two times to move the margin to the second tab stop in position 9. Type **(1)** and then press F2. Type the "**Instruction register—**" sentence. When you finish the sentence, insert a hard return.

5. Repeat the previous step to type "**(2) Instruction**...."

This procedure might seem overly complex. But, as you have seen with the other software systems in this text, the material can be mastered with practice. After using the F2 indention technique a few times, it will not appear so complex. And, with repeated use, it will become second nature to you.

Before giving you an opportunity to use the F2 technique in an exercise, we should comment on reforming a multiline outline. You cannot simply position the cursor at the beginning of each paragraph and type ^B. If you do, everything will be realigned at the left margin. All of your effort in setting up the proper indentions will be lost.

When you position the cursor at the beginning of one or more lines to be reformed, you must use F2 to move the left margin to the proper position, *then* press ^B. For example, if you want to reform the indented copy with a different right margin, you would:

1. Change the right margin on the ruler line.

2. Position the cursor at the beginning of the first line and type ^B. Only the first line will be reformed, since it ends with a hard return.

3. With the cursor on the second line, move it to tab stop 9 with the right arrow key. Then, move the left margin to tab stop 9 by pressing F2 twice. Then type ^B. *When you reform indented copy, the cursor and the left margin must be on the same position.*

4. With the cursor on the line with "(1) Instruction register—" move the cursor to tab stop 14 using the right arrow key. Press F2 three times, and type ^B.

5. With the cursor on the line with "(2) Instruction address—" repeat the previous step.

Exercise 5
Multiline Indention

1. Open a file named OUTLINE1.

2. Type the following outline, using F2. Set the margins at 1 and 65 and set tab stops at 10 and 20.

Management Information Systems

Data processing systems. These systems process the firm's accounting data. There is very little management information generated, but the data base of accounting data provides the raw material for management information.

Decision support systems. These systems are designed primarily to suport the managers in decision making. The emphasis is on solution of semistructured problems.

Office automation systems. These systems speed the flow of information both inside the firm and between the firm and its environment. Examples of office automation are:

Teleconferencing. This is the use of television-type equipment to transmit visual images of activity between persons in various geographic locations.

Electronic mail. This is the use of computing equipment to store correspondence and then display it on a video screen at the request of the person to whom it has been sent.

Document transmission. This is the use of both copying and communication equipment to transmit an image to a distant point using some type of communication link.

Image storage and retrieval. This is the use of computer storage media to electronically store the image of a document and then make that image available for display on a video screen when requested.

3. When you have finished typing the copy, save *two* backup files on the same diskette by typing ˆ**Ks** and then ˆ**Kd**. When you save the second time, the first saved file becomes the .BAK file.

4. Prepare a printed copy.

5. Reform the outline, moving the right margin to position 75. Use the right arrow key and the F2 key as described above to maintain the indents as you reform. If you make a mistake, abandon the file and reopen your saved OUTLINE1 file. If something happens to the OUTLINE1 file, rename the OUTLINE1.BAK file and use it.

6. Prepare a printed copy of the reformed outline.

Bibliographies

There are many different formats for typing bibliographies. In most, the title of the publication is underlined or set in italics. In some, the volume number of a periodical is set in boldface type. Also, the first line of an entry very often has a different left margin than the succeeding lines. An example of a bibliographic entry using all three special printing techniques we have discussed in this chapter is:

[23]   Zald, M., & Berger, M.A. "Social movements in organizations." American Journal of Sociology **84**, 1978, 823–61.

Exercise 6
Bibliography

1. Type the following bibliograpy, using the same format (boldface print, underlining, and indents) as shown.

Bortner, R. W., and Rosenman, R. H. (1967). "The measurement of pattern A behavior". Journal of Chronic Disease **20**, 525–33.

Burke, R. J.; Weir, T.; and DuWors, R. E. (1979). "Type A behavior of administrators and wives' reports of marital satisfaction and well-being." Journal of Applied Psychology **64**, 57–65.

Caplan, R. D.; Cobb, S.; and French, J. R. P. (1975). Job Demands and Workers' Health. Washington, DC: U.S. Department of Health, Education and Welfare Publication No. (NIOSH) 75–160. U.S. Government Printing Office.

Cooper, C. L., and Davidson, M. J. (1981). "The pressures of working women: what can be done." Bulletin of British Psychological Society **34**, 357–60.

Cooper, C. L; and Davidson M. J. (1982). High Pressure: The Working Lives of Women Managers. London: Fontana.

Cooper, C. L., and Lewis, B. (1979). "The femanager boom." Management Today, July, 46–47.

Cooper, C. L., and Marshal, J. (1978). Understanding Executive Stress. London: Macmillan.

Cooper, C. L., and Melhuish, A. (1980). "Occupational stress and managers." Journal of Occupational Medicine **22**, 9, 588–92.

Davidson, M. J., and Cooper, C. L. (1980). "The extra pressures on women executives." Personnel Management **12**, 6, 48–51.

Printing Tables

Very frequently, business reports will contain tables of data. The tables are interspersed throughout the narrative. You set up the page format for the narrative, and begin typing. Then, you reach the point where a table is to be inserted. It would be helpful if you could create a special **midtext ruler line** to use in entering the table data. WordStar enables you to do this. Just start with an exclamation mark in the position where the leftmost data column should print, and locate additional exclamation marks at the leftmost positions of the other columns. Type hyphens between the exclamation marks. It is not necessary to include an exclamation mark at the right end of the line. Such a midtext ruler line has the appearance:

! _ _ _ _ _ _ _ _ _ _ _ ! _ _ _ _ _ _ _ _ _ _ _ ! _ _ _ _ _ _ _ _ _

Position the cursor anywhere on the line and type ^Of. This command resets the margins and tab stops to conform to the midtext ruler line.

Now type the table heading. With the cursor on the heading line, center it by typing ^Oc. Then insert one or more hard returns and begin to enter the column data. Enter the first data item (to be printed in the leftmost column), press the Tab key, enter the next item, Tab, and so on until the data item for the rightmost column has been typed in. Enter the rightmost item with the Tab key. This action returns the cursor to the leftmost tab stop on the next line. Using this approach, you enter all of the data with the Tab key—you never use the Enter key.

When all of the data has been entered into the table, insert hard returns for blank lines and then reinstate the text ruler line following the same procedure that you used initially— ^Ol, ^Or, and ^Oi.

With the table on the screen, you can center the column headings by deleting or inserting blank spaces. For example, after you enter the table data, the format might appear as:

EMPLOYEE NO.	NAME	DEPARTMENT
12763	JONES, JAMES	20
40792	SMITH, EDNA	12
51616	WHITE, FLOYD	20
70482	GARZA, ANDY	13
91981	CHANG, WAYNE	29

After shifting the column headings, the format is:

EMPLOYEE NO.	NAME	DEPARTMENT
12763	JONES, JAMES	20
40792	SMITH, EDNA	12
51616	WHITE, FLOYD	20
70482	GARZA, ANDY	13
91981	CHANG, WAYNE	29

The only problem with the midtext ruler line is that it will print. Before printing (as you edit your document), remove it by positioning the cursor on the line and entering ^Y (the line delete command).

Exercise 7
Printing a Table

1. Open a file named TABLE1.

2. Set the regular margins at 1 and 79.

3. Create a midtext ruler line with exclamation points at positions 1, 35, and 55. As you type the hyphens, watch the column indicator at the top of the screen to ensure that you use the correct positions. Extend the hyphens through position 79.

4. Type ^Of to implement the midtext ruler line.

5. Type and center the following table heading:

Table T–3
Marketing Information System
Product Subsystem
Product Deletion Model Subtasks

6. Insert two blank lines.

7. Enter the following column headings, with the first characters aligned at the tab stops (left justification):

        Subtask   **Responsibility**   **Time (Days)**

8. Leave one blank line.

9. Enter the following data (single-spaced):

1. **Identify deletion criteria**	**Product manager**	**7**
2. **Identify output requirements**	**Product manager**	**5**
3. **Identify input requirements**	**Systems analyst**	**4**
4. **Prepare pseudocode**	**Programmer**	**5**
5. **Code program**	**Programmer**	**15**
6. **Test program**	**Programmer**	**10**
7. **Approve program performance**	**Product manager**	**7**
8. **Implement model**	**Operations staff**	**7**

10. Position the cursor at the beginning of the column heading and press the space bar until the heading "Subtask" is centered over the column. (The right part of the heading line will go off the screen.) Then, position the cursor to the right of "Subtask" and press the Del key until the heading "Responsibility" is centered over its column. Then, with the cursor to the right of "Responsibility," use the Del key to center the heading "Time (Days)" over its column.

11. Print the table.

Finding and
Replacing Words

Have you ever typed a report and then realized that you misspelled a certain word or used the wrong word? You have to read the entire document and correct the errors as you find them. WordStar performs this time-consuming function for you.

You initiate this find and replace operation by typing ^Qa. WordStar asks which word is to be changed by displaying "FIND?" You type the word, such as MIS, then press Enter. Then WordStar asks which new word to use by displaying "REPLACE WITH?" You respond by typing the word, such as DSS, and pressing Enter again.

There are four options that WordStar can use in searching and replacing. After you provide the two words, WordStar will ask for the options by displaying "OPTIONS?" The four options are:

G   Search the *entire file*
N   Make the replacement *without* asking for your *approval*
W   Make the replacement for *whole words* only
U   Make the change regardless of whether the word is *upper- or lowercase.*

For example, if you respond to the "OPTIONS?" prompt with GNWU (or any combination of the four letters, such as WGNU), WordStar will search the entire file looking for a whole word, in either upper- or lowercase. When each occurrence of the word is found, it is automatically replaced.

If you don't supply the G option, WordStar will only search until it finds the first occurrence of the word. If you don't supply the N option, WordStar will ask your approval before each change is made. The cursor will flash at the location of the word, and the question "REPLACE (Y/N):" appears in the upper right-hand corner of the screen on the status line. If you respond Y, WordStar makes the replacement and either searches for another occurrence, or terminates the search, depending on whether the G option is in effect. If you respond with any character other than Y, WordStar does not make the change, and proceeds. If you don't supply the W option, WordStar will replace words within words, such as "form" within "information." And, if you don't supply the U option, WordStar will pass over "Management" looking for "management."

As a general rule, two options are those for a manager to use in finding and replacing words in business documents:

GNWU   Make changes *without approval*
GWU   Make changes *with approval*

All searches would involve the entire file, whole words, and words in both upper- and lowercase.

When one word is replaced with another word with the same number of characters (for example, replace MIS with DSS), you do not have to reform the copy after the replacement. But, reforming is necessary if the words are different sizes.

The maximum number of characters in the find and change words is 30. It is possible to use multiple words, such as replace "marketing manager" with "sales manager." The only problem is the spacing between the words. As you know, word wrap will add blank spaces between words to achieve right margin justification. So, there may be more than a single space between words. For example, the text might include the term "marketing manager," but there are two spaces between the words. In this case, WordStar will not detect a match. It is best to only search for single words. However, you can replace a single word with multiple words. You can, for example, replace "programmer" with "information specialist."

Exercise 8
Find and Replace

1. Open a file named SEARCH.

2. Turn justification off.

3. Type the following, using the default ruler line:

   The person responsible for the MIS operation is the vice president of information systems. He reports to a higher level executive, such as the executive vice president. The vice president of information systems is an executive in his own right. In every respect, he performs in an executive-like manner. He is responsible for valuable personnel and equipment resources and participates in the formulation of policy and procedures. He usually serves on various committees, such as the MIS Committee, Long-Range Planning Committee, and Executive Committee. All of the personnel in the MIS area report to the vice president of information systems, including systems analysts, programmers, operations personnel, and data base administrators.

4. Position the cursor at the beginning of the file.

5. Type ^**Qa**.

6. Your firm has decided to use the name "information services" rather than "information systems" for the computer department. Modify the paragraph above by instructing:

   FIND? **systems**   REPLACE WITH? **services**
   OPTIONS? **gwu**

   Approve the change(s) where appropriate.

7. Reform the text and make a printed copy.

8. Your firm has decided to use the term IS (for information systems) rather than MIS. Modify the paragraph by instructing:

   FIND? **MIS**   REPLACE WITH? **IS**
   OPTIONS? **gwnu**

   Be certain to type IS in uppercase letters, or the replacement will be in lowercase.

9. Reform the text and make a printed copy.

10. Your firm has decided to change the title of the executive vice president to senior vice president. Modify the paragraph by instructing:

    FIND? **executive**   REPLACE WITH? **senior**
    OPTIONS? **gu**

    Approve the change(s) where appropriate.

11. Reform the text and make a printed copy.

Manipulating Blocks of Text

When you prepare business correspondence, there is frequently a need to rearrange the sequence of sentences, paragraphs, or even groups of paragraphs. WordStar facilitates this manipulation through the use of **block commands**. A block can be of any size—from one sentence to several pages.

In order to manipulate blocks, they must be marked. Move the cursor to the beginning of the block and press the F7 key. As you do this, the cursor should be positioned on the first character of the block. The symbol <B> appears on the screen and bumps the material to the right three spaces. Then, move the cursor to the end of the block (to the right of the last character) and press F8. You have marked the block, and two things happen: (1) the beginning block marker disappears, and (2) the block is highlighted in low-intensity light. If you like, you can mark the end of the block first. Press F8 and get the <K> marker. Then mark the beginning. The order doesn't matter. Either way, when the second marker is entered the first disappears and the block is highlighted.

If you are not going to handle the marked block right away, you can "hide" it by typing ^Kh. This restores the display to regular intensity. ^Kh is a toggle command that is also used to restore the display to low intensity.

Normally, you mark a block and then handle it immediately. You can mark only one block at a time. As soon as you mark a block, the markers for an earlier marked block are erased.

To *move* a marked block, position the cursor at the spot to where the block is to be moved. Then type ^Kv. A block can be moved to a location between existing paragraphs or within a paragraph. If you move to a spot within a paragraph you will have to reform the paragraph after the move.

If you want to duplicate, or *copy*, a block you follow the same procedure as above, but type ^Kc. After a copy, the block exists at both the source and destination locations.

To *erase* a block, mark the beginning and end, and type ^Ky.

The ability to move, copy, and erase blocks makes it easy to rearrange text. This in itself is a useful capability. But the block concept facilitates the preparation of business correspondence and reports by permitting the storage (on your diskette) of blocks of copy, and their retrieval when needed. Such blocks, which are used over and over, are called **boilerplate**. Perhaps you compose a letter to a past-due customer simply by assembling prewritten paragraphs. Or you prepare a sales proposal that consists primarily of prewritten sections: product descriptions, company history, and so on.

To implement this data base of text material, each block must be stored on the diskette as a separate file. To store a block, use the block write command, **^Kw**. First mark the block and then store it. When you type ^Kw you will be asked to identify the name of the file to be stored. If there is already a file by that name, you will be asked to verify the store operation since it will erase what is already stored.

After you have stored the blocks, they are retrieved with the block read command, **^Kr**. Just position the cursor at the point where the block should be inserted and type the read command. You will be prompted to provide the name of the file to be read. If you can't remember the name, get a directory of the logged diskette by typing ^F in response to the "NAME OF FILE TO READ?" prompt. Then, type the file name.

When you hide a block, it is protected against accidental handling by certain block commands. With a hidden block, you get an error mesage when you try to use the block copy, move, write, or erase commands.

There is a special **Block Menu** that you can call up (at help levels 2 and 3) when you enter ^K. Since these are the first characters of the file and block commands, you get the menu every time you initiate a file or block operation at help level 2 or 3.

In this exercise, you will experiment with rearranging paragraphs in a report.

1. Open a file named REPORT2.

2. Type the following portion of a report:

IMPLEMENTATION PROCEDURE

To prepare for the implementation of a computer, it is necessary to accomplish the following steps:

   1. Prepare the physical facilities. Perhaps a new room must be built to house the computer. Or, an existing room must be remodeled.

   2. Educate users. All persons who will use the computer output must understand how to interpret that output.

   3. Select the computer. The proposals from the various hardware vendors must be evaluated, and the one selected that best enables the firm to meet its objectives.

   4. Plan the implementation. A schedule must be prepared, showing what is to be done, who is to do it, and when it is to be done.

3. Center the heading and set the print in boldface.

4. Set the section numbers and titles in boldface.

5. Rearrange the sections in the following sequence: 4, 3, 1, 2. Use the block move commands. Insert blank lines between the paragraphs after they are moved, if necessary. To insert a blank line, move the cursor to the end of the upper paragraph and press Enter.

6. Renumber the sections so that the numbers are in the order: 1, 2, 3, 4.

7. Hide the last block marked.

8. Print the rearranged report section.

1. Open a file named PARA.

2. Turn justification off.

3. Type the following:

We value your patronage and wish to retain you as a customer. If there is any assistance that we can provide in helping you bring your account up to date, please let us know.

We know that sometimes your finances get in such a situation that it is difficult to make your monthly payments. But, you must not let this damage your credit rating. Please bring your account up to date so that you will retain your excellent payment record.

We have no recourse but to turn your account over to a collection agency. This is an action that we regret as it most certainly will damage your credit rating. Unless we receive payment within ten days, we will cease to grant any future credit purchases.

4. Mark the first paragraph and perform a block write command. Name the block PARA30.

5. Mark and save the second paragraph as PARA60.

6. Mark and save the third paragraph as PARA90.

7. Abandon the PARA file with **^Kq**.

1. Open a file named PASTDUE.

2. Make certain that justification is off.

3. Type the following:

> **Mr. Earl Walker**
> **Route 3, Box 148**
> **Antlers, OK   74523**
>
> **Dear Mr. Walker,**
>
> **We have not received your payment that was due May 1.**

4. Enter two hard returns.

5. Type **^Kr** and read the block named PARA30.

6. Enter two hard returns.

7. Type:

> **Sincerely,**
> (4 hard returns)
> **Alice Lofton,**
> **Credit Manager**

8. Print the letter. This is the letter that is sent to customers who are 30 days past due in making their installment payments.

9. Assume that Mr. Walker is 60 days past due. Delete the second paragraph and replace it with PARA60. Print the letter.

10. Assume that Mr. Walker is 90 days past due. Delete the second paragraph and replace it with PARA90. Print the letter.

Remembering the
WordStar Commands

There are many WordStar commands, and even though we have not studied them all, it is difficult to remember what they do. In some cases, there is a logic to the selection of the codes and for the various commands. The block markers are a good example. The word *block* starts with a *B* and ends with a *K*, so those letters are logical choices for the block markers. Other command mnemonics are not quite so easy to understand; ^Oi to set the tab stops, for example.

All of the commands that you have studied are included in the following list, grouped by function. Seeing them in this grouping should help you review them and remember what they do. The letters in boldface print seem to explain why certain command codes were selected. You will have to provide your own memory aids for the others.

Main Menu

D	Open a **D**ocument file
H	Set the **H**elp level
L	Change the **L**ogged drive

P   Print a file

Help Menu

^J   Display the Help Menu

Onscreen Menu

^O	Display the Onscreen Menu
^Oc	Center a title
^Od	Delete print control characters from the screen
^Of	Set the margins and tab stops for the table ruler
^Oi	Set a tab stop
^Oj	Justification toggle
^Ol	Set the Left margin
^On	Remove tab stop(s)
^Or	Set the Right margin
^Os	Change the line Spacing
^Ot	Ruler line Toggle

Scroll

^W	Scroll up
^Z	Scroll down
^Qw	Continuous scroll up
^Qz	Continuous scroll down

Cursor movement

^E	Move up one line
^X	Move down one line
^S	Move left one character
^D	Move right one character
^A	Move left one word
^F	Move right one word
^Qs	Move to the beginning of the line
^Qd	Move to the end of the line

Deletion

^G	Delete the character at the cursor position
^T	Delete the word to the right of the cursor
^Y	Delete the line
^QDel	Delete all to the left of the cursor
^Qy	Delete cursor position to the end of the line

Find and replace

^Qa   Find a word and replace it with another word

Block manipulation

^K	Display the blocK menu
^Kc	Copy a block
^Kh	Hide a block
^Kr	Read a block
^Kv	MoVe a block
^Kw	Write a block
^Ky	Erase a block

Reform

^B   Reform to next hard return

Storage

^Kd   Store and work on a **D**ifferent file
^Kq   **Q**uit the file without storing
^Ks   Store and resume work on the **S**ame file
^Kx   Store and e**X**it WordStar

Interrupt

^P   Interrupt the **P**rinter
^U   Interrupt all other commands

In addition, you have used the function keys as shortcuts to entering WordStar commands. The keys that you have used are:

F2   Indent the following lines
F5   Underline marker
F6   Boldface marker
F7   Mark the beginning of a block
F8   Mark the ending of a block
F9   Move the cursor to the begining of the file
F10   Move the cursor to the end of the file

The task of learning the WordStar commands is greater than for most word processing systems. Most other systems have fewer commands, but they also have less power as a DSS tool. Learning to use the WordStar commands is a small price to pay for the benefits you will receive.

Summary

WordStar offers a number of advantages over conventional typing. These advantages contribute to WordStar's value as a DSS tool. In the previous chapter, you learned that it is easy to make corrections to a document and to reform the copy with new margins, tab stops, justification, and hyphenation.

In this chapter you became acquainted with processes for inserting blocks of material into existing copy, use of boldface print and underlining to lend emphasis to words and points, arranging copy in an outline form such as that found in procedures and bibliographies, printing tables, searching for words and replacing them, rearranging blocks of text, and storing blocks on the diskette for selective retrieval for preparation of business documents.

You set words in boldface print by inserting a beginning and ending marker using the F6 key. You underline words by following the same procedure with the F5 key. If you want to remove the markers from the screen to facilitate visual editing, use the ^Od print control display toggle switch.

Margins can be indented using either the Tab key or the F2 key. If entries contain only single lines, you use the Tab key to move the cursor to the appropriate tab stop, and start typing. When finished, you press Enter to move to the next line. When entries consist of multiple lines, you move the left margin with the F2 key, and let word wrap move to successively lower lines. Multiline, indented entries present problems when they are to be reformed; it is necessary to position the cursor and the left margin properly before typing ^B at the beginning of each entry.

You can intersperse tables throughout your copy by creating a special midtext ruler line for use in entering the table data. After the data has been entered, the column headings can be centered and the ruler line can be removed so that it does not print.

The ability to quickly and accurately find and replace words gives the manager a newly found ability that did not exist before word processing. You can specify that the entire file be scanned (option g), that replacement be made automatically (option n), that only whole words be sought (option w), and that the search disregard upper- or lowercase (option u). In most cases, options g, w, and u seem appropriate. The only significant choice is whether to let WordStar make the changes automatically.

The block manipulation commands also offer new opportunities to improve the communicating ability of messages and reports by rearranging their sequence with the block move (^Kv) and block copy (^Kc) commands. The added advantage of writing blocks on the diskette (^Kw) and retrieving the blocks (^Kr) when they are needed makes it possible to assemble communications largely from prewritten sections. These abilities did not exist before word processing.

This concludes our detailed discussion of DSS tools for the IBM PC: BASIC, dBASE II, VisiCalc, and WordStar. A manager who understands how to apply these tools in decision support has a great deal of power at her or his disposal. The tools do not guarantee that the best decisions will be made. But, the tools enable the manager to make the decisions using the most complete, accurate, and up-to-date information available. That is the decision support concept.

The next, concluding chapter summarizes the broad selection of software support that has been created for the IBM Personal Computer. To many PC users, this software resource is the primary reason for selecting the PC over other computers that often feature better performance, lower price, or both.

Key Terms

Boldface printing
Underlining
Print control display toggle switch
Midtext ruler line

Block command
Boilerplate
Block Menu

Questions   (Do not fill in blanks in the book. Write answers on a separate piece of paper.)

1. To insert a paragraph in an existing text, the _____ feature should be turned on.

2. You use the _____ function key to mark the material to be underlined.

3. You use the _____ function key to mark the material to be printed in boldface.

4. To indent multiple line entries in an outline format, you move the left margin in with the _____ function key.

5. The _____ key cancels an indent and returns the left margin to its original position.

6. When you reform indented copy, both the _____ and the left margin must be on the same position.

7. To use a midtext ruler line, position the cursor anywhere on the ruler line and type _____.

8. You initiate a find and replace operation by typing _____.

9. If you wanted to search an entire file for whole words in either upper- or lowercase, but wanted to approve each change yourself, you would respond to the "OPTIONS?" prompt with _____.

10. You use the _____ function key to mark the beginning of a block and the _____ key to mark the end.

11. After you mark a block, you move it by positioning the cursor at the location where the block should be moved and type _____.

12. Blocks of copy that are used over and over in business reports are called _____.

13. You write a marked block onto the diskette by typing _____, and you read it from the diskette by typing _____.

14. Compared with most other word processing systems, the WordStar commands are more _____ to learn but WordStar offers more _____ as a DSS tool.

15. With WordStar you are able to mark _____ block(s) at a time.

16. You _____ a block by typing ^Kh.

17. When you want to write or read a block you must specify a(n) _____.

18. You can duplicate a block by typing _____.

19. The midtext ruler line has a(n) _____ in the left-hand position.

20. You can remove the underline and boldface markers from the screen by typing _____.

Assignment 1

Moving Blocks;
Using Find
and Replace

1. Open the CUTOVER file (on drive a:).

2. Set the margins at 5 and 65.

3. Rearrange the numbered sections so that they are in the reverse order: 3, 2, 1.

4. Hide the last block marked.

5. Renumber the sections: 1, 2, 3.

6. Center the title.

7. Use the find and replace technique to search the entire file for the word "approach" and replace it with **strategy**. Let WordStar make the replacements without your approval. The search should be for whole words only, either upper- or lowercase.

8. Repeat step 7, replacing "approaches" with **strategies**. Look at the copy after the find and replace process is complete. Did WordStar make all of the changes? Do you know why not? The word "approaches" on the first line has a colon immediately following. Try again, and omit the whole word option.

9. Replace the word "MIS" with **DSS**. Search the entire file for whole words, uppercase only. You should approve each replacement.

10. Replace the word "system" with **DSS**. Search the entire file for both upper- and lowercase words. Do not specify whole words, but do approve all replacements.

11. Repeat step 10, replacing the word "firm" with **company**. This search should also enable you to replace "firm's" with **company's**.

12. Proofread the revised copy, correcting any words that seem to you to be inappropriate.

13. Print the document.

Module 7
Overview of
Software
for the PC

16 Survey of Existing DSS Software for the IBM PC

The IBM PC is the most popular computer in history. More PCs have been sold than any other model. Since its introduction in 1981, the PC has gained approximately 28 percent of the microcomputer market. The entry of IBM in this market not only created new opportunities for its own products, but for products of other companies as well. The IBM name lent legitimacy to the small-system market, and opened the eyes of many businesspersons to the potential of using small computers.

But, the PC represented a distinct departure from traditional IBM marketing policies. First, IBM elected not to be the sole distribution source, but to distribute the PC through other firms such as traditional retail outlets and computer stores. You can even buy a PC by mail order if you choose. Second, IBM elected not to develop the software itself, but to encourage the contributions of other firms. The result is a very wide range of programs for the PC—available from many sources. This situation has resulted in the largest selection of software ever assembled for a single computer. This software resource is the main reason that many firms have selected the PC, since it reduces or perhaps eliminates the need for custom programming.

This chapter identifies the major software categories and provides an idea of both the number and variety of offerings in each category. It will not attempt to identify all of the sources, nor is there an attempt to evaluate the various packages. There is, however, a suggested procedure for you to follow in learning what is available and selecting the set of packages that best fits your needs.

Software Categories

The four software categories that we have used in this book provide an effective means of segregating PC software by task. These categories are:

- Procedural languages
- Data processing software
- Decision support system software
- Office automation software

Chapter 4 reviewed the major *procedural languages* such as COBOL, FORTRAN, and BASIC. These are the languages that include a set of instructions enabling a programmer to tailor a computer to a specific application. The procedural languages are used to write programs to process the firm's data. The *data processing software* handles the firm's accounting transactions and maintains a data base describing largely historical data. *Decision support system software* uses data from the data base and from the environment to supply the manager with information for decision making, in the form of periodic and special reports and modeling results. *Office automation software* facilitates the flow of mainly informal information within the firm, and between the firm and its environment.

272   **Module 7
Overview of Software
for the PC**

Figure 16.1   Procedural Languages for the PC

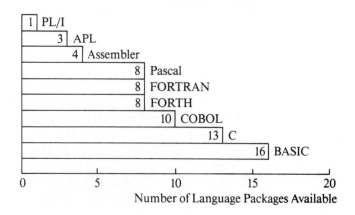

Number of Language Packages Available

Procedural Languages

In most respects, PC users come up short when their resources and benefits are compared with those of mainframe users. The mainframe users have the more powerful hardware and software. There is one exception, however, and that is in the area of procedural languages. Practically all of the mainframe procedural languages have been made available to the PC user. And, most of the languages can be obtained from several sources. Figure 16.1 illustrates the relative availability of procedural language processors.

The PC is unique in this respect. Before the PC came on the scene, selection of the language automatically carried with it selection of the source. There was only one version of each language available for each computer, and that version was usually obtained from the computer manufacturer. If you had an IBM System/360, for example, and decided to use PL/I, then you used the IBM PL/I.

The reason that the situation is different for the PC is IBM's decision to encourage software development by other firms. For the first time in history, a software vendor did not have to compete with IBM for the software market. And, the immediate success of the PC attracted the software vendors in droves.

This wide selection of languages is good for the PC user, since it increases the likelihood that the language best suited to the processing needs of the user is available. But, the wide selection also makes the language decision more difficult. Not only does the PC user have to decide which language to use, but also where to get it.

Figure 16.1 does not reflect the usage of the languages, only the availability. Most experts agree that BASIC is the most popular, followed by COBOL, FORTRAN, and Pascal, in that order. And, one would intuitively expect assemblers and PL/I to rank last because of the time required to learn them, and APL to have light use because of the mathematical skills it requires. So, in terms of these languages, there appears to be a direct relationship between the number of language versions available and their use. This is also what one would expect: the vendors concentrate their efforts on the best markets.

Two languages in Figure 16.1 do not reflect this relationship between availability and business use: FORTH and C. We discussed C in Chapter 4, and saw that its coding is too succinct to permit self-documentation. For that reason, it has not appealed to business firms. FORTH is in the same category. Introduced in the mid-1970s as a language to control realtime processes such as robots in factories, FORTH has never been accepted as a business language. Therefore, the firms producing the FORTH and C language processors are not aiming at the business market. Users of those languages are elsewhere. In the case of FORTH, the users are mainly in the area of computerized process control and robotics. In the case of C, the users are mainly in the area of scientific computation.

The other languages in Figure 16.1 represent the menu from which a PC user can select. There are a few others, such as LISP, Ada, Logo, and Thread, but their use is very specialized and they have not received much attention in business.

Which Language to Use?

With so many languages from which to choose, how does one pick the right one(s)? Several factors should be considered:

- *Characteristics of the job.* Each language has features that fit certain types of jobs. COBOL is good for preparing reports, and FORTRAN and APL are good for modeling. COBOL and PL/I are good at handling data files, but Pascal is not. Pascal cannot handle files that must be addressed directly. BASIC, Pascal, and assembler do not excel in any one area, but perform well on most all types of jobs. All three could be used for modeling as well as reporting.

- *Existing programming skills.* If your firm has programmers skilled in particular languages, then those languages should be used unless they are obviously inappropriate. Most programmers know more than a single language, but usually prefer one. New languages can be learned, but it takes time and money. It is not easy to change the orientation of a programming staff from one language to another.

- *Availability of additional programming skills.* Can new programmers be hired who have certain language skills? Some skills, such as APL, PL/I, and assembler, are more rare than others, such as BASIC and FORTRAN. Are there people within the firm who can be trained for particular languages? Is time available for the training? Some languages take longer to learn than others. BASIC and FORTRAN can be learned in days; assembler, COBOL, and PL/I take weeks.

- *Importance of program maintenance.* Will the programs have a long life cycle, and will there be many changes? If so, then a self-documenting language such as COBOL, Pascal, and PL/I should be used. These three languages have an added advantage in that they lend themselves to structured programming, which facilitates maintenance. Pascal was designed with structured programming in mind.

- *Importance of computer efficiency.* If the programs are to be executed frequently, a language should be selected that makes efficient use of storage and performs arithmetic operations quickly. Assembler excels in this area, as do FORTRAN and Pascal. BASIC probably has the poorest job performance times. If jobs are not to be executed frequently, then more emphasis should be given to ease of development.

- *Available program development time.* How much time is available to get the system up and running? Some languages take longer to code than others. COBOL is notorious for its lengthy style. BASIC, on the other hand, features succinct code, as do FORTRAN and APL. Structured programming also speeds up the development process, so Pascal, COBOL, and PL/I should receive good marks in that regard. All three permit several programmers to work on different parts of the same program at one time.

Figure 16.2   Typical Data Processing Subsystems

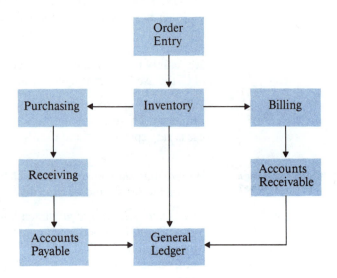

These are some of the more important factors that should be considered in selecting a language. Much depends on the situation of the firm. Some firms are "locked in" to particular languages due to existing staff and time constraints. Other firms, such as those getting their first computer, can start with a clean slate and pick the language(s) that best suit(s) their needs.

Language selection is an important and complex task, and should receive attention during the planning period. This is an area where professional help from a computer consultant is helpful if language evaluation skills do not exist within the firm.

Data Processing Software

A firm's data processing systems will vary, depending on the industry. Any company that sells something (a retailer, wholesaler, or manufacturer) will have the subsystems pictured in Figure 16.2. The process begins with the screening of sales orders by the order entry subsystem, and data flows from one subsystem to another, as indicated by the arrows. The various subsystems generate data that is ultimately processed by the general ledger system to prepare the firm's income statement, balance sheet, and so on.

You will find many of these subsystems, (accounts receivable, purchasing, receiving, accounts payable, and general ledger) in practically all types of firms. In some firms you will find subsystems unique to that particular industry. In banks, for example, you find subsystems with names like demand deposit and lock box. In insurance companies, you find underwriting and claims.

The computer programs that process all of this data, regardless of industry, can be either programmed by the firm (the "make" option described in Chapter 4) or purchased in a prewritten, packaged form (the "buy" option).

In just the few years since the introduction of the PC, considerable prewritten data processing support has become available. A PC user can buy prewritten software from software firms or directly from IBM. As we have seen, IBM initially elected not to produce its own software. Instead, IBM contracted with software firms such as Microsoft, Peachtree, BPI, and SofTech Microsystems (UCSD) to produce the packages that IBM sells. There is an indication that this philosophy is changing. On May 16, 1984, IBM announced eight software systems for the PC that it had developed.[1] And the price was considerably lower than the industry standard. Observers concluded that the time had come for IBM to begin seriously competing for the PC software business. If this is the case, expect IBM to offer good packages, since that has been its reputation with its other systems. If IBM enters the market, it should have the effect of stimulating competitors to continue to work to improve their products. Some marginal firms will not be able to compete, but the overall effect for the PC user should be even better software support.

In the following two sections, there are some examples of software that perform the standard accounting applications and meet the unique data processing needs of certain industries.

Accounting Packages

The data processing packages that you get from IBM were developed either by Peachtree or BPI.[2] The subsystems include:

	IBM/Peachtree	IBM/BPI
Inventory	X	X
Accounts Receivable	X	X
Accounts Payable	X	
Payroll	X	X
General Ledger	X	X
Job Cost		X

The Peachtree systems permit either online or batch input, but BPI is limited to batch. Both vendors include software checks to ensure data accuracy; they both provide for recovery from diskette failure. All of the Peachtree systems are integrated (the arrows in Figure 16.2) with the exception of inventory. All of the BPI systems are integrated, and the job-cost system has special appeal to a manufacturing firm.

These same types of packages can also be obtained from other software firms, either in a set or separately.[3] Software Laboratories, for example, markets a set of four programs—accounts payable, accounts receivable, payroll, and general ledger. Another firm, State of the Art, offers general ledger, inventory control, accounts payable, accounts receivable, budget and financial reporting, and sales invoicing.

Of the basic application areas, the one recieving the most attention is inventory. This is not surprising, since the inventory area is the best one for showing a financial benefit from computer processing. A number of packages are available, one of which is Infotory, from SSR Corporation. As many as 65,000 items can be carried

1. Dennis Kneale, "IBM Unveils PC Software for $149 or Less; Move May Trigger Fierce Industry Battle," *The Wall Street Journal* (May 16, 1984): 2.

2. More detailed descriptions of these Peachtree and BPI programs can be found in Chris DeVoney, *IBM's Personal Computer* (Indianapolis, Que Corporation, 1983), pp. 224–238.

3. For additional information on the non-IBM software, see Robert P. Wells, Sandra Rochowansky, and Michael F. Mellin, *The Book of IBM Software 1984* (Los Angeles, The Book Company), pp. 185–223.

in inventory, with 36 predefined fields for each. Each field has maximum sizes, but they seem adequate. For example, the item number can be as many as 15 alphanumeric positions. Decimal positions are important in an inventory package, since some firm's values can be very large. Infotory will handle a price up to $1,000,000.00, and year-to-date totals up to $100,000,000.00. These are more than adequate. Four standard reports are produced, and a feature called ANYREPORT enables the preparation of special reports.

A close study of any accounting package from any source is called for before you make a purchase. The packages are general in nature and usually do not exactly fit the practices and needs of specific firms. They usually constrain the user in certain ways—the maximum number of records that can be handled, data fields per record, field size, and so on. The packages least susceptible to these constraints are accounts payable and receivable and general ledger. The package most susceptible is payroll. Of all the accounting packages, payroll is the most difficult to generalize because of the unique nature of most firms' payroll systems.

The area of accounting applications is the one that usually determines whether a small firm uses a microcomputer. The firm should evaluate the accounting software before it takes the micro plunge. There might not be the prewritten systems available to do the job. In that case, custom programming is in order. And, many firms don't have the financial or personnel resources to get involved with programming.

Industry Packages

Industry packages are those that have been designed for particular fields such as trucking, construction, and medicine. The packages are aimed at a narrow market and address the data processing tasks that are unique to that market. The support here us very spotty, with the real estate area receiving excellent support, and the medical profession close behind. After that, the support drops off and there may not be any packages available to certain industries.

To understand that spotty support, you have to appreciate that the packages are aimed at industries in which there are a large number of PC computers used as data processors. This approach means that industries such as banking and insurance are unsupported, since their data processing is being handled by mainframe systems.

Of all the software support areas, this is the one with the most potential for improvement. Many industries remain good targets for specialized software. For example, there is hardly any support for manufacturers. True, many manufacturers are the giants of industry with mainframe systems. But, there are thousands of small manufacturers, either using a PC or who could use one, that have little manufacturing software from which to select. Likewise, much more attention can be given to retailing, independent insurance agents, farmers and ranchers, city and local governments, and so forth.

Several industry packages are briefly described in the following paragraphs. Along with each description is an indication of the quantity of packages available for that particular industry.[4]

Loancomp is a loan calculations program for investors, bankers, and mortgage loan firms. It handles mortgage loans with various types of monthly payment

---

4. These descriptions are based on those found in the *PC World Annual Software Review* (1983/1984), pp. 324ff. That annual describes other industry packages, as well as identifying their sources.

schedules and handles installment loans with a choice of interest rate calculations. Reports can be produced that show monthly balances, and year-end interest and principal amount totals. This is one of very few such packages.

Stockplot can be used by stock brokers to track the performance of stocks. A history is maintained of each stock, and graphs can be prepared showing the movement of the price over time. High, low, and closing prices can be given for each stock. Very few packages are available to perform this type of computation.

Tax Master is used by tax accountants to prepare clients' income tax returns. In addition to printing several tax schedules (1040, Schedules A through G, and so on), it selects the most beneficial tax method and maintains a year-to-year record for each client. There are a number of such packages from which the accountant can choose. This area is well-supported.

MRP-II enables a small manufacturer to plan raw material needs, control shop floor operations, and accomplish job-cost reporting. This is one of only a few such packages. Much more support is needed in this area.

Builder is used by a building contractor to first estimate the cost of a job for bidding purposes, and then track the actual costs of the job against the estimates. There are a wide variety of packages available to the construction industry.

MUNIS (Municipal Information System) is an accounting system for city and local governments that handles the standard record keeping chores (payables, receivables, tax billing, and so on) plus voter registration lists and utility billing. There is not a wide variety of this type of software for the PC.

Dental Office Management PC handles the bookkeeping for a dental office with up to ten dentists. It maintains appointment records, and identifies patients due for a check-up. It also processes claims and prints several reports indicating the profitability and productivity of the office. This area is well-supported.

Question-Writer can be used by marketing researchers to design questionnaires and then use the questionnaire for computer-aided telephone interviewing. Very few such programs exist as this is a function normally handled in the past by the large marketing research firms. Such software enables a firm to do its own surveying, assuming that the firm has the necessary personnel resources.

Comsen's Trucking System for Truckload can be used by any type of trucking firm to perform dispatching, rating, billing, and sales analysis. It can also prepare special fuel and mileage reports by state, as well as keep truck maintenance records up-to-date. Comsen, Inc. also has three other packages tailored to truckers hauling gasoline, fuel oil, and liquid propane. This industry area is well-supported.

Property Management keeps track of security deposits and rent payments for up to 1000 units. It also maintains records of maintenance costs, and prepares monthly bills and mailing labels. Real estate is the best-supported industry, with a wide variety of programs to address the investment, management, appraisal, cash flow, and portfolio tasks. There are two reasons for the abundance of these packages. First, the applications are financial in nature, and lend themselves to computing. Second, the real estate firms are excellent prospects for a microcomputer.

Retail Point of Sale System enables a retailer to handle cash and charge account transactions, and update inventory and customer records at the time the transactions are processed. Very little support is available in this area, probably because the large retailers use networks of terminals connected to a central mainframe computer. More support is needed for small retailers, but the PC would not be acceptable to all small stores, since it is limited to a single keyboard. Many small stores have multiple checkout or cash register areas and need a keyboard for each. The PC would fit only retailers with a single checkout area, but there are many of those.

Putting Data Processing Software in Perspective

The data processing software itself plays an indirect role in the DSS by processing transactions and entering the data in the data base. The manager can then use other software to transform the data into information. Some data processing software also produces output information and helps the manager make decisions, but those examples are rare.

Although the data processing software does not play a direct role, it is essential to a DSS. Usually, a firm implements a DSS in a two-step fashion. First, the accounting applications are installed, and then the accounting data provides the foundation upon which to build the DSS.

Decision Support System Software

This is an area where the manager is likely to personally use the software himself or herself. That situation is unlikely with the procedural languages and data processing software. The reason for direct involvement is the user friendliness of the DSS software.

As we have seen earlier, the manager obtains decision support information from periodic and special reports and from modeling. The areas in which the software firms have selected to focus their attention, however, are not these three output forms. Rather the support is aimed at data base management, electronic spreadsheets, statistical packages, support for management functions, and graphics. Figure 16.3 illustrates how these areas interrelate. As you can see, modeling has received the most attention, although the data base management systems are good for preparing special reports. The software suppliers have left periodic reports to the procedural languages. There is no software such as Report Program Generator (RPG) for mainframe systems that is designed specifically to prepare periodic reports.

Data Base Management Systems

The data base provides an interface between the data processing systems and the DSS. Special data file management and data base management software enables the user to perform data maintenance tasks without special programming.

We described one of the most popular systems, dBASE II, in Chapters 8 and 9 and will not describe other examples here. Most of the other entries in this market offer less capability than dBASE II. Many are designed to handle only mailing lists.[5] The systems with less capability are also easier to operate. And not all users need all of the capabilities of dBASE II.

Electronic Spreadsheets

The success of VisiCalc encouraged many other firms to produce electronic spreadsheet packages. The market is now saturated with spreadsheet packages

---

5. Brief descriptions of over 100 data base and file management systems can be found in George Tate (founder of Ashton-Tate, manufacturer of dBASE II), "Data Management," *PC World Annual Software Review* (1983/1984), pp. 164 ff. Seventeen DBMS and 19 file management systems are described in *The Book of IBM Software 1984,* pp. 87–136.

Figure 16.3   DSS Software Areas

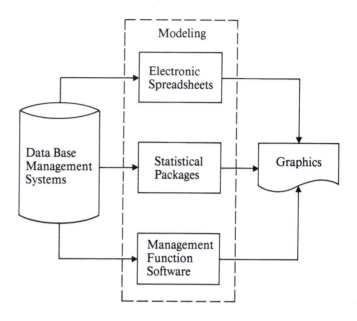

such as Multiplan, SuperCalc, Scratchpad, CalcStar, and so on.[6] Since you learned about VisiCalc in Chapters 11 and 12, we will only devote attention to one other spreadsheet package here: IFPS.

IFPS (Interactive Financial Planning System) is regarded as the premiere spreadsheet package, developed initially for mainframe systems. It does much more than VisiCalc and the other micro-designed speadsheets. IFPS permits the easy use of probabilities and also includes an optimizing capability. It is now available for the IBM PC with 256 KB of random access memory. It includes the modeling feature in addition to graphic output, report writing, and the ability to communicate with the corporate data base. It is aimed at Fortune 1000 firms who wish to "distribute" the success that they have enjoyed with the mainframe version.

Statistical Packages

Software packages have been available for performing basic statistical analyses such as regression, analysis of variance, discriminant analysis, and factor analysis since the beginning of the computer age. These packages, designed to run on mainframe systems, are used by persons with strong mathematical and statistical skills. Examples of mainframe statistical packages are SAS, SPSS, and BMD.

Now, similar examples are available to micro users. At least 10 packages can be used with the PC. All accept data from the keyboard, and some also permit use of dBASE II files. Figure 16.4 summarizes the statistical routines handled by

6. See Malcolm L. Stiefel and David R. Simpson, "Minicomputer Spreadsheets Take Advantage of Hardware Capabilities," *Mini-Micro Systems* XVI (September 1983): 172–76, 178 for a listing of spreadsheet suppliers. Forty-six packages, including those for non-IBM systems, are listed.

Figure 16.4   Table of Statistical Packages for the PC

	Regression		Analysis of Variance (No. of Ways)	Discriminant Analysis	Factor Analysis
	Simple	Multiple			
ABSAT	Yes	Yes	2	No	No
A-Stat	Yes	Yes	2	No	No
Introstat	Yes	No	2	No	No
Microstat	Yes	Yes	2	No	No
Micro-TSP	Yes	Yes	No	No	No
Number-Cruncher	Yes	Yes	4	No	Yes
NWA Statpak	Yes	Yes	3	No	No
SAM	Yes	Yes	10	Yes	Yes
SPS	Yes	Yes	1	No	No
STATGRAPHICS	Yes	Yes	12	Yes	Yes
SYSTAT	Yes	Yes	30	Yes	Yes
Wallonick Statpac	Yes	Yes	2	No	No

these packages.[7] The regression routines are of special value to top-level managers in forecasting the future activity of the firm. Analysis of variance, discriminant analysis, and factor analysis are tools of the marketing researcher in studying customer attitudes, buying habits, and so on.

A good example of a statistical package is STATGRAPHICS, marketed by Statistical Graphics Corporation. STATGRAPHICS was originally developed for IBM mainframes, and includes over 350 statistical functions. The functions can be called from menus and the results displayed in graphical form on the screen. Figure 16.5 illustrates the screen output that can be displayed in color. The graphs are displayed simply by pressing function keys and can be printed on a graphics printer or a plotter.

The availability of such statistical software for the PC does much to legitimatize the PC as a DSS tool, although the software is not likely to be used by the manager herself or himself. Rather, the situation that has existed in the mainframe area of hiring management scientists or operations researchers to use the software should persist. A manager, unskilled in statistics, would not be able to derive the full power of the packages.

Graphics   STATGRAPHICS is a statistical tool with a graphical output ability. There are other packages that concentrate on the graphics and do little or no processing. These packages take output data from other software systems and display it in a graphical form.

An example of a graphics package is BPS Business Graphics. It accepts English-like commands and can produce full or partial pie charts, horizontal and vertical bar charts, line graphs, and scatter diagrams. It will accept data from VisiCalc, SuperCalc, or Multiplan files, as well as from the keyboard. In addition, it includes

7. Most of these comparisons are based on data provided by James Carpenter, Dennis Deloria, and David Morganstein in "Statistical Software for Microcomputers," *Byte* 9 (April 1984): 234ff.

Figure 16.5   Graphical Output

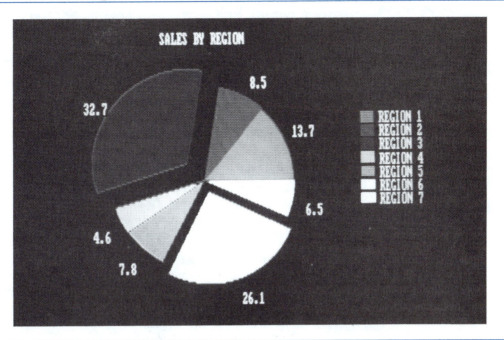

a built-in ability to perform several basic computations such as moving average, exponential smoothing, mean, and variance.[8]

Computer graphics have been around for a number of years, but they have been expensive. The availability of the PC, with its color monitor, graphics printer and/or plotter, and graphics software packages make the PC an excellent DSS graphic system.

Support for Management Functions

Software writers have zeroed in on several key managerial functions, such as forecasting, planning, project management, and control and have produced software to support those functions. A big area is project management, and a number of packages use Gantt chart, PERT, and CPM techniques. An example of a simple project management package is Project Manager, which displays tasks on the screen showing the duration, whether the task is on schedule, and who is responsible. Forwork is more elaborate, handling up to 4,096 projects for more than 255 managers on 16 levels. It uses the PERT technique of considering optimistic, most likely, and pessimistic estimates of activity times.

Some packages offer blanket coverage of multiple business problems. For example, Executive Package offers solutions to 40 ordinary business problems such as those of planning, budgeting, and scheduling. Another, Decision-Analyst, can assist the manager in quantitatively evaluating multiple solution alternatives.

Considerably more DSS support could be provided by addressing a wider variety of problems faced by the manager. At present, the support provided by prewritten DSS software is modest.[9]

8. The BPS Business Graphics package is compared with the Graphics Generator and the Chartmaster packages by Jack Bishop in "Three Generations of Charts for the IBM PC," *Byte* 8 (November 1983): 352ff.

9. Joe L. Miller describes 40 software packages tailored to managerial activities in the *PC Annual Software Review* (1983/1984): 368ff.

The Trend toward
Integrated DSS
Software

As recently as 1982, there was virtually no software specifically intended for decision support. VisiCalc was the most notable exception. Even data base management systems, which had been developed to support data processing, were in their infancy at the microcomputer level. Hardly any graphics packages had been announced, and statistical packages were nonexistent.

All of this changed almost overnight. VisiCalc was probably the stimulant. Software suppliers saw that managers would buy and use software if it addressed their problems and was easy to learn. Today, no one has to apologize for micro-based DSS software. There are many examples, and much is of high quality.

But, one basic problem has plagued most of the packages—they cannot be easily integrated. In an earlier chapter, we saw that you can create files with both dBASE II and VisiCalc that can be used with WordStar. But, such capabilities do not exist for all small-system software. And, when such integration is possible, much is left to the user in learning how to make it work; each software vendor explains its own product assuming it will be used in a standalone manner.

Only a handful of packages have been marketed that are intended to work together. VisiCorp, as an example, designed its VisiFile file management system to transfer data to VisiCalc or the VisiTrend/Plot graphics package. This is an example of a **product family**, and the user can mix the product offerings of the single vendor to meet specific needs.

A refinement of the product family concept is the **all-in-one applications package**, usually consisting of a spreadsheet, a data base management system, a word processor, and a graphics package that are designed to work together. All come from the same vendor, but the system is not "open ended"—the user must accept the predetermined software mix and cannot delete and add. Examples of this approach are the currently popular Lotus 1-2-3, Symphony, Context MBA, and Framework by Ashton-Tate. Lotus includes a spreadsheet, a file management system, and a graphics package, but no word processor. MBA integrates the same three applications as Lotus, plus telecommunications and word processing.

A third approach to integration is that of the **operating environment**. A single operating environment program is provided to which applications are added. This is the approach taken in the new Visi/ON package from VisiCorp, and DesQ from Quarterdeck. The advantage of this approach is that it enables you to integrate offerings from several vendors. For example, with DesQ you can integrate dBASE II, WordStar, and VisiCalc.

Industry experts are in agreement that the trend in DSS software is toward integrated systems. However, it is still too early to tell whether the all-in-one applications package or the operating environment will be the way to go.[10]

Putting DSS Software
in Perspective

DSS software is at the heart of the DSS concept. It is the software that provides information to the manager for decision making. Data processing software precedes this phase by processing the data and putting it into the data base. Office automation software is subsequent to the decision-making phase, it communicates the decision to the rest of the firm and to the environment.

DSS software is unique in that it is designed with the primary purpose of meeting the needs of the *manager*. The same cannot be said for data processing and office

---

10. A good discussion of the topic of integrated software can be found in Michael J. Brown, "The Complete Information-Management System," *Byte* 8 (December 1983): 199ff.

automation software. There, it is easy to see that the designers were catering to the needs of administrative employees. It has been left to the managers and their information specialists to integrate data processing and office automation into the DSS, as we have done in this book.

Office Automation Software

Most office automation software performs word processing. This area is flooded by excellent packages: PeachText 5000, PFS:WRITE, Volkswriter, and Word Perfect to name a few.[11] We will not describe any of these systems since we covered WordStar in Chapters 14 and 15. WordStar was the first high-quality package to emerge, and it quickly became the favorite. It provides a benchmark against which to compare the newer packages.

In addition to word processors, there are other software packages that perform more specialized functions such as checking spelling, editing copy for errors, printing and maintaining mailing lists, indexing records for retrieval, and so on. MicroPro offers an optional package that can be used with WordStar for handling mailing lists. It is called MailMerge, and can be accessed from the Opening Menu. The key point is that word processing and mailing applications are well-supported. The support in the other office automation areas will probably come from hardware, rather than software, innovations. For example, document transmission, document storage and retrieval, and teleconferencing all appear to be hardware-based.

The key to the office of the future will be the development of a **universal workstation** that can combine all of the data- and document-handling tasks. Hardware (and software) should appear within the next few years that will permit a clerical employee to completely process a transaction from a single workstation. The result will be faster information flow and improved efficiency. The effect that the workstation will have on the DSS is uncertain. Personal computers and terminals will probably continue as the means for the manager to interact directly with the DSS.

Putting Office Automation Software in Perspective

Office automation serves as one of the vehicles for transmitting the manager's directives to the firm once the decision has been made. This is the simplest way to think of office automation in a DSS context, and we illustrated that idea in Figure 3.2. In Chapter 13, we addressed the role of word processing in the DSS and illustrated in Figure 13.3 how the manager uses word processing to transmit information to the environment as well as internally. These figures explain the contribution that word processing makes as a communicator of information after a decision has been made.

In a broader context, office automation can also contribute to the decision-making process by transmitting information to the manager *before* the decision is made. This information can come from both within the firm and from its environment, and it can come in the form of letters, memos, teleconferencing, document transmission, and document retrieval.

---

11. Word processing products of more than 50 vendors are compared in a tabular format in "Buyers' Guide to Word Processors," *The Office* 98 (November 1983): 159ff. Another means of comparing the different products is provided in the form of a 100-point checklist in Arthur Naiman, "Evaluating Word-Processing Programs," *Byte* 9 (February 1984): 243–46.

Office automation plays an important role in the DSS by handling much of the informal information flow, leaving the formal information flow to the data processing and DSS systems.

The Selection Dilemma

Earlier in the chapter, we addressed some of the factors influencing the selection of a procedural language. While that task is difficult enough, it is only a part of a larger selection dilemma. Not only must procedural languages be selected should the firm elect to make its own software, but packaged data processing, DSS, and office automation software will likely be selected as well. And, the dilemma doesn't stop with software; it can include hardware. There are a number of computers on the market that claim to be **PC compatible**. These systems are described in the Appendix. A firm might get swept up in small-system computing because of the popularity of the IBM PC, and then find itself having to decide between a PC and a COMPAQ, a Panasonic Senior Partner, and a Seequa Chameleon.

Just how do you go about selecting a micro and its software? Listed below are several major steps, arranged in a logical order. Perhaps you will not follow them in exactly this sequence, or you will skip or add steps. But, this can serve as a guideline. This list is based on over 25 years of experience that larger firms have accumulated in selecting mainframe hardware and software. The experiences of the larger firms can benefit firms implementing smaller systems.[12]

1. *Learn about computers.* Read newspapers, magazine articles, and books. Visit computer stores and observe demonstrations, talk with salespersons and anyone else who appears knowledgeable. Ask questions. Enroll in courses. Consider evening classes at the local college, as well as short seminars offered by computer stores. There are many two- or three-day seminars offered by various organizations that are geared especially for managers. Some are general and some specific; some are introductory and some are advanced. The American Management Association offers a number of such courses.

2. *Define the computer applications in general terms.* Assuming that you are a business manager, just what job will the computer do? Will it solve some problems that have been bothering you, or will you use it to improve an already good organization, or both? The basic decision is the application area—will it be data processing, DSS, or office automation? Don't bite off too much at first. Take the key applications first, such as inventory. Doing that job well will save you money and it will give you the stimulus to tackle other, perhaps more difficult, applications. Don't waste valuable time on applications just because they are easy; meet your challenges head-on.

3. *Set objectives.* What must the computer do to satisfy you? If it is inventory, for example, how much must the investment be reduced, or how much must the service level be increased?

4. *Establish constraints.* How much can you spend? What resources, such as personnel time, can you dedicate to the computer project? This will define the hardware and software market for you to consider.

5. *Define the computer applications in specific terms.* Talk with other people in your organization. Sound them out on your plan. Ask for input. Think about how the computer will be used. Be as specific as you can in an effort

---

12. For a more detailed description of the implementation process, see Raymond McLeod, Jr., *Management Information Systems,* 2d Ed., Science Research Associates, 1983, pp. 511–614.

to fully understand the job to be done. If you haven't enlisted the help of an expert by now, this might be a good time. A computer consultant or a computer specialist in your accounting firm can do a lot in just a short time. They may appear to be expensive, but not as expensive as a misdirected, ill-defined computer project that ultimately leads to failure.

6. *Survey the software market.* What packages meet your needs? Which are close? Ask the people at the computer store for advice. Look at the books and magazines on their shelves, and buy the ones that appear helpful. Go to the local college library and look through back issues of the computer magazines such as *Byte, Mini-Micro Systems, PC World,* and *PC Magazine.* After you feel you understand the software picture, use the factors that we identified earlier as a guideline to selecting procedural languages. Apply the same logic in evaluating the data processing and DSS software: first define your needs and then measure how well the packages satisfy them. If this activity gets to be too much for you, call in an expert who can help you focus on the essentials.

7. *Verify the software performance.* See a demonstration of the software. Use the actual package with your own sample data—not a demo diskette. Think about your job in detail and try to think of problems you might encounter and how they can be solved. Find out whether the software can be modified, and if so, how and the cost.

8. *Identify and evaluate the hardware.* More likely than not, the software will run on more than one piece of equipment. Consider not only price, but the support that the manufacturer and the retailer can provide. Will they be there when you need them? Can you purchase a maintenance contract? If so, what is the cost, and who will do the work?

9. *Identify other resources needed.* Are you going to rely entirely on off-the-shelf software, or will you be doing some programming yourself? Should you hire one or more computer professionals—systems analysts, programmers, operations personnel? Look at your plan in a long-range sense. What people do you need? Where do they come from? Can you get them? What do they cost? In addition to personnel, think about facilities, space, supplies, user education, and all areas where the computer will likely impact the firm. What should you do to get the system on the air?

10. *Select the hardware and software, and prepare for implementation.* Assuming that your analysis hasn't discouraged you, make the decision of what computer and software to buy. Then, get your data in a form that will be acceptable to the computer. This might be a big task. Prepare the physical facilities and educate the users. Set a date for conversion and stick with it. Give thought to backup should the system fail.

11. *Implement the system.* Cut over one application at a time until the entire system is functioning.

12. *Evaluate the performance.* Set a date for a post-implementation review, such as 90 days after conversion is complete. Give the system time to settle down. Is it meeting the objectives set in step 3? This is a good time to call in an unbiased third party, a person who has not previously been involved in the implementation project. Even your consultant, who has helped you over the rough spots, might be inclined to assure you that "everything is rosy" when it is not. You should expect an accurate appraisal from someone who does not have a vested interest in the system.

286   Module 7
Overview of Software
for the PC

The implementation of a computer system (even a small one) is no easy task. It takes time and resources. But, it can be a rewarding experience when performed the right way. There is no guarantee of success. But, the best insurance policy is thorough planning and a realistic understanding of what a computer can and cannot do. Getting this far in this book is a good way to start.

Summary

In this concluding chapter we have viewed the broad area of DSS software and have given examples of various types available. In only a short time, the volume and quality of PC software has increased dramatically. To be sure, not all of the packages are of the same high quality, and there is much duplication in the areas of spreadsheets, word processing, and financial applications. But, the volume is likely to continue to grow. Whether the growth will continue at the present rate is unknown. Perhaps not. Much of the "cream" has been skimmed off of the software market with the easier applications—financial reporting, real estate, and so on. There are many applications remaining, but they tend to lie within the more difficult areas—manufacturing, marketing, engineering, and personnel. These plums will not be so easy to pick.

Probably the greatest single factor that will influence the future path that PC software development will take will be the posture of IBM to the market. A move by IBM into that market can only benefit the PC user in the long run.

IBM is one of the true success stories in American and world industry. A review of IBM success in the computer field recognizes the key roles played by a few computer models. During the first computer generation it was the 650, during the second it was the 1401, and during the third it was the 360. These have all been successes, but none has impacted society as a whole to the extent of the PC.

PC users benefit from its wide acceptance. The software support is excellent, and the cost is affordable by even the smallest organization. Today, a computerized DSS is within the reach of any manager. The hardware is there. The software is there. The necessary ingredient that must be applied is the ingenuity of the manager in harnessing these powerful DSS tools. There is no substitute for user involvement in the selection and implementation process. You know your needs better than anyone else ever will. Get involved, and then it will be *your DSS*.

Key Terms

Product family
All-in-one applications package
Operating environment

Universal workstation
PC compatible

Questions

(Do not fill in blanks in the book. Write answers on a separate piece of paper.)

1. IBM introduced the PC in _____.

2. IBM elected to follow a different approach than was used for other IBM systems in distributing the PC _____.

3. IBM also followed a new approach in developing the software by _____.

4. The four major software categories are _____, _____, _____, and _____.

5. _____ software handles a firm's accounting transactions.

6. In terms of having a wider selection from which to choose, PC users have an advantage over mainframe users in the area of _____.

7. Two procedural languages that are popular with nonbusiness users but that have not been widely accepted by business users are _____ and _____.

8. A factor limiting the appeal of Pascal to business application is its difficulty in handling _____.

9. Three languages that lend themselves to program maintenance are _____, _____, and _____.

10. Of all the languages, _____ is the most efficient in terms of conserving storage space and maximizing processing speed.

11. The data processing packages offered by IBM were developed by _____ and _____.

12. Two "industries" that have well-supported PC software are _____ and _____.

13. One factor limiting the use of the PC in retailing is _____.

14. Many firms follow a two-step approach in implementing a DSS by first implementing a _____.

15. Of the four basic software categories, the one in which the manager is most likely to use the software himself or herself is _____.

16. Originally developed for mainframes, _____ is generally regarded as the premier spreadsheet package.

17. Another software package originally developed for mainframes that outputs the results of statistical analyses in graphical form is _____.

18. The three approaches to achieving integration of software systems are _____, _____, and _____.

19. Lotus Symphony is an example of the _____ integration approach.

20. DSS software is unique among the four basic categories in that it was developed to meet the needs of the _____.

Appendix   IBM PC Compatible Systems

Compatibility between hardware systems has always been important to computer users. During the early years, there was none. A company would code programs for its computer, see the computer become obsoleted by improving technology, obtain a more modern computer, and reprogram everything again. Software was not portable, since it was coded in machine-oriented assembly languages. One of the factors stimulating the development of FORTRAN and, to a greater extent, COBOL was the need to overcome hardware dependence.

Today's mainframe computer users enjoy a high degree of compatibility through software. A COBOL program written for a Burroughs mainframe can, for example, be executed on an NCR mainframe with very minor modification. Similar compatibility is also enjoyed with FORTRAN, PL/I, and Pascal.

Small-scale computer users have not enjoyed this same compatibility through software. The main reason is that the most popular language, BASIC, has never been standardized. When you try to run a program written in BASIC for one system, such as a Radio Shack TRS-80, on another system, such as the Apple IIe, it will not work. The program has to be modified. This lack of software compatibility presents a problem for small-system users.

How Real Is PC Compatibility?

When IBM entered the personal computer market in August of 1981 with the PC, some industry experts felt that IBM was too late. As it worked out, the timing was just right. The market had settled down, and IBM could build on the foundation laid by other pioneering firms such as Apple and Radio Shack. The rest is history. Other computer manufacturers have been quick to recognize the wide acceptance of the PC, and have responded with hardware systems that are described as "PC compatible."

The prospective buyer assumes that you can buy a PC compatible and run any software that you can run on the PC. The fact of the matter is that, as of this writing, *no computer is considered to be one hundred percent compatible with the PC.* A few come close, but others leave much to be desired.

The purpose of this Appendix is to explain what facilitates compatibility. Armed with this information, you can evaluate the systems yourself to determine the extent to which they live up to their claims.

How Is Compatibility Achieved?

There has been some confusion concerning just what produces PC compatibility. There are three essential ingredients:

- The microprocessor
- The operating system
- The ROM Basic Input/Output System

IBM uses the Intel 8088 microprocessor chip as the CPU. Since this chip is commercially available to anyone, it has found its way into many competitive units. Figure A.1 lists 18 personal computers that have, in one way or another, been identified as a PC compatible. You can see that they all use either the Intel 8088 or an improved version, the Intel 80186.

Figure A.1   Table of Some of the "PC Compatibles"[1]

Computer	Use 8088?	Use MS-DOS?	Process PC Diskettes?	Run PC Programs?	Portable?
Columbia VP	Yes	Yes	Yes	Most	Yes
COMPAQ	Yes	Yes	Yes	Most	Yes
Corona PC	Yes	Yes	Yes	Most	No
Docutel Olivetti M21 and M24	Yes	Yes	Yes	Most	See Note 2
Eagle PC Spirit	Yes	Yes	Yes	Some	Yes
Bytec Hyperion	Yes	Yes	Yes	Most	Yes
Panasonic Senior Partner	Yes	Yes	Yes	Most	Yes
Seequa Chameleon and XT	Yes	Yes	Yes	Most	Yes
Sharp PC-5000	Yes	Yes	Yes	Some	Yes
Sperry PC	Yes	Yes	Yes	Most	No
Strategic Technologies PC Traveler	See Note 3	Yes	Yes	Most	Yes
Tandy TRS-80 Model 2000	See Note 3	Yes	Yes	Many	No
TeleVideo TS 1605	Yes	See Note 4	Yes	Some	No
TI Professional Portable	Yes	Yes	Yes	None	Yes
Visual Computer Commuter	Yes	Yes	Yes	Most	Yes
Wang PC	Yes	Yes	Yes	Many	No
Zenith Z-150 PC	Yes	Yes	Yes	Most	No

Notes: 1. Descriptions of most of these systems can be found in "Hardware Review," *Computer Buyer's Guide and Handbook* (July 1984): pp. 36ff.
2. The M21 is portable; the M24 is a desk-top model.
3. Uses the Intel 80186.
4. Uses TeleDOS, claimed to be compatible with PC-DOS.

IBM has contracted with Microsoft to supply the PC operating system, PC-DOS. Microsoft also markets the same operating system as MS-DOS, so it is easily available to IBM competitors. As Figure A.1 shows, there are many personal computers on the market using the same operating system as the PC. So, the first two ingredients of compatibility, the 8088 and MS-DOS, are easy to come by.

Does the use of the 8088 and MS-DOS ensure compatibility? The answer is no. There is another link in the chain that connects the applications software to the hardware. This chain is illustrated in Figure A.2. The important link is the RIOS (ROM Basic Input/Output System). RIOS is software that is stored in the ROM. It takes the commands issued by the operating system and converts them into a form that causes the units connected to the system unit to perform the tasks of the application program. A type of chain reaction occurs. The application program communicates to the operating system; the operating system communicates to RIOS; and RIOS communicates to the system unit.

So, a computer can offer the same chip and operating system as the PC, but, if it does not have something similar to RIOS, some instructions cannot be executed. Since IBM has copyrighted RIOS, the other companies must produce a RIOS that does the same things, but does not violate the copyright.

In early 1984, IBM brought suit against manufacturers of both the Corona and the Eagle personal computers, claiming copyright infringement. Both manufacturers were enjoined from selling their RIOS after a certain date, and were instructed to destroy any remaining copies.[1]

1. Erik Larson, "Meaning of 'IBM Compatible' Varies in Personal Computers," *The Wall Street Journal* (February 3, 1984): 25; and "IBM Obtains Injunction," *The Wall Street Journal* (February 22, 1984): 16.

Figure A.2   The Software/Hardware Link

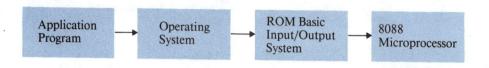

| Application Program | → | Operating System | → | ROM Basic Input/Output System | → | 8088 Microprocessor |

The main objective of using the 8088 as the CPU, using MS-DOS, and achieving a PC-like RIOS is to achieve a system that can read and write PC diskettes and run PC programs. All of the units listed in Figure A.1 have achieved compatibility in terms of the diskettes, but the proportion of PC programs that can be run varies from none to most. The TI Professional is a good example of a system that can handle the diskettes but not the programs. Although it has been erroneously identified as a PC compatible, TI did not intend it as such. The intent was to achieve a system superior to the PC, and in attempting to do so, compatibility in terms of program execution was lost.

The firm that has apparently been the most successful to date in emulating the PC is COMPAQ Computer Corporation. COMPAQ's sales literature claims that its portable runs "all the popular programs written for the IBM Personal Computer . . . and they run right off the shelf, without any modification."

The COMPAQ has been in the field long enough for its claims of PC compatibility to be backed up. The same can be said for the Columbia, Corona, and Hyperion systems. Other computers are just now emerging on the market that still must pass the use test. These newer computers include Docutel Olivetti, Panasonic, Seequa, Sperry, Strategic Technologies, Visual Computer, and Zenith.

Compatibility and Portability

The share of the personal computer market held by the PC and the PC compatibles is significant. It is estimated that the PC accounts for about 28 percent of the sales, and the compatibles for another 10 percent or so.[2]

The firms that have been most successful in competing against IBM with PC compatibles have packaged their units in such a way that they are portable. All of the units (CPU, diskette drives, and screen) are enclosed in a single, briefcase-sized cabinet, and the keyboard serves as a detachable lid. The photograph of the COMPAQ in Figure A.3 illustrates this design concept. Two-thirds of the units listed in Figure A.1 are portable.

The logic of this strategy is clear. It is difficult for IBM competitors to compete based on price—to market a lower-priced unit. Since IBM manufactures in such large quantities it can take advantage of the low costs of mass production. Some competitive units are lower priced, but there are also some that are more expensive. During the first two and one-half years of the PC's popularity, the portability feature was one that competitors could exploit in an effort to gain a competitive edge. And, exploit it they did. However, that edge may have been dulled considerably in early 1984 when IBM announced its own portable version of the PC.[3] Shipments

COMPAQ Computer Corp.

**Figure A.3
The COMPAQ Portable Computer**

---

2. Dennis Kneale and Alan Freeman, "Commodore Unit Signs License Accord Over IBM-Compatible Computer Gear," *The Wall Street Journal* (March 1, 1984): 10.

3. Richard A. Shaffer, "IBM Will Sell Portable Version of its PC Model," *The Wall Street Journal* (February 17, 1984): 2.

began in March of the 30-pound unit with a 9-inch amber screen, 256 KB of RAM, and a single diskette drive. The price was set at $2795, slightly lower than the leading portables on the market at that time—the COMPAQ, Columbia, and Eagle units. This price was reduced to $2595 on June 8, 1984, when IBM announced an across-the-board price reduction on all its PC models.[4]

Future Trends

The announcement of the IBM portable has not kept other firms from entering the PC market. The market is too lucrative. In February 1984, Zenith unveiled five new micros that are reputed to be PC compatible—three desktop units and two portables. The next month, Olivetti, an Italian company, introduced a portable and a desktop model that it will market in the U.S. through Docutel. The portable has a 9-inch screen and weighs 30 pounds—exactly the same as the IBM portable. Also in the spring of 1984, Matsushita began delivery of its Panasonic Senior Partner portable.

The competition for the PC market will not be restricted to the U.S. It will be worldwide. Firms such as Olivetti and Matsushita will be strong competitors for IBM, as will other U.S. firms seeing the international market as more attractive than the one at home. ITT Corp., for example, announced a PC compatible that it planned to market in Europe beginning in late 1984.

The battle for the personal computer market stacks up as very competitive. The prospective buyer, attracted to that market by the huge volume of PC software, will have a variety of hardware systems from which to choose. Assuming that all of the hardware measures up to the high quality standards that IBM has maintained for the PC, it will be a good situation for the prospecive buyer who likes to shop around.

**Look Before
You Leap**

How can you be certain that a PC compatible can process the programs that you plan to use? Do not base a purchase decision on the data listed in Figure A.1 or on the claims of the manufacturers. Go ahead and buy those programs that you intend to use and take them with you to a computer store for a demonstration. If the salesperson can get the programs to run with no special effort, then it is safe to assume that you can expect similar success.

If you aren't certain which programs you will be using, there are two that can be used as a benchmark—Lotus 1-2-3 and the Microsoft Flight Simulator. These programs are designed to give the PC a real workout, and they would do the same for a compatible. Even if they run on the non-IBM unit without a hitch, you are not guaranteed one hundred percent compatibility. But, you should have reason to feel that the compatibility is close.

If you check out the compatibles and their claims and you are still undecided, don't overlook the computer that will run *all* of the PC programs with no modification—the IBM PC.

4. John Marcom, Jr., "IBM Cuts Prices of Personal Computers Up to 23% and Changes Basic Models," *The Wall Street Journal* (June 8, 1984): 3.

Glossary

a: drive: the left-hand diskette drive located in the system unit of the IBM PC.

Absolute value: the value of a number without regard to its sign. For example, a minus five has the same absolute value as a plus five.

All-in-one application package: an approach for integrating various types of microcomputer software in which the types are offered as a single package. A package may offer data base management, spreadsheet, and graphics capabilities. Lotus 1-2-3, Symphony, and Context MBA are examples.

Alphanumeric: data that can take any form—numeric, alphabetic, or special characters.

APL (A Programming Language): a problem-oriented procedural language developed by Kenneth E. Iverson in 1962 that is used primarily to solve mathematical problems. It is unique in that it uses a large number of special characters, making the code succinct but difficult to maintain.

Application program: a program that processes a firm's text or data, as opposed to a system program that causes the computer to perform fundamental, computer-related routines. Examples are payroll, inventory, mathematical models, and statistical packages.

Argument: (VisiCalc) a subsidiary part of an IF function that specifies (1) the condition, (2) the action to be taken when the condition is true, and (3) the action to be taken when the condition is false. Each IF function has three arguments.

Arithmetic and logic unit (ALU): the part of the CPU that performs the mathematical and logical functions called for in a program.

Arithmetic operator: the symbol that specifies a mathematical operation to be performed, such as addition (+), subtraction (−), multiplication (*), or division (/). The symbols link the constants and variables in a mathematical expression.

Array: a one-dimensional arrangement of data, such as a column or a row. It is also called a *list*.

Assembler: a procedural language that transforms source code into object code on an instruction-for-instruction basis. It is "machine dependent" in that it is usually offered by a computer manufacturer for use on only that manufacturer's equipment. It is very efficient in processing speed and conservation of primary storage.

Assembly program: the system program that transforms a source program written in assembler language into machine language.

Attribute value: in modeling, a value that changes during the simulation (state variable); also, a value that does not change (parameter).

b: drive: the right-hand diskette drive located in the system unit of the IBM PC.

Backspace key: the key in the upper right of the PC keyboard that causes the cursor to move one space to the left each time it is pressed. If you hold the backspace key down, the cursor moves multiple spaces quickly to the left. The key has a left-hand arrow on it.

Backup file: a duplicate copy of a file that can be used if the original copy becomes damaged or lost.

Backward reference: (VisiCalc) a reference made by a formula to other coordinates that are located to the left or above the entry where the formula is stored.

BASIC (Beginner's All-purpose Symbolic Instruction Code): the most popular procedural language for small computers. Developed at Dartmouth University to enable students to use the computer from terminals, BASIC was quickly accepted because it is so easy to learn. The original version has been expanded to provide most of the capabilities of other popular procedural languages. The main disadvantage of BASIC is its lack of standardization from one computer system to another.

BASIC function: the BASIC computer language includes a number of special functions, such as one to compute a square root. The functions enable programmers to carry out processes that require considerable computation by coding only a single instruction.

BASIC prompt: the screen display of the word OK with a flashing underline mark beneath it; it indicates that the user can enter a BASIC instruction or command.

Batch processing: one of the two basic ways to process data (the other is online) that is characterized by grouping transactions so that they may be handled all at one time. It is the most efficient way to use computing equipment; but its main disadvantage is that it does not keep files up to date as the transactions occur.

Bidirectional printer: a printer with a print head that can print while moving in either a left-to-right or a right-to-left direction. Such a printer is faster than one printing in only a left-to-right direction since no time is lost in returning the print head to the opposite margin at the end of a line.

Binary coding system: a code composed of only two values. The digit zero is usually used to represent an "off" condition, and the digit one is usually used to represent an "on" condition. The off and on conditions are especially adaptable to electronic devices such as computers. All characters can be represented by a combination of zeros and ones.

Block command: (WordStar) a command that handles a block of text at a time. The block can be moved, copied, or deleted within a document, and can also be written onto a diskette as a separate file and read into text from a diskette file.

Boldface print: (WordStar) the darker appearance of characters than regular text. On a computer printer this is usually achieved when the print head strikes a character more than one time.

Booting the system: a process in which the system prepares itself for processing. With the IBM PC, the user boots the system by holding down the Ctrl and Alt keys with the left hand, and striking the Del key with the right. This action causes the operating system to assume control.

C: a procedural language characterized by its succinct code. It is especially appealing to programmers writing system programs because of its portability, but thus far has not been widely accepted as a business language.

Cash flow model: a mathematical model that simulates the volume and rate of cash flowing into and out of a business organization.

Cassette BASIC: the most fundamental version of BASIC offered on the IBM PC, it was originally intended for storage on a cassette tape. It is stored in ROM and can be used without a diskette.

Cell: a location in a table or a matrix where data or instructions can be stored. In a VisiCalc spreadsheet it is called an *entry* and is identified by the row and column coordinates.

Central processing unit (CPU): the main part of a computer system housing the arithmetic and logic unit, control unit, and primary storage unit. In the IBM PC it is incorporated into the system unit.

Circular reference: (VisiCalc) a reference made by a formula to itself. For example, coordinate A3 contains the formula +A3−A4.

Clean compile: a slang term meaning that a computer has compiled a program without identifying any syntax errors.

Closed-loop system: a system with a feedback loop.

COBOL (Common Business Oriented Language): the most popular procedural language used on mainframe systems for business applications. Its wordiness makes coding very time-consuming, but program maintenance is facilitated by the English-like structure.

Color monitor: the name given to the cathode ray tube that can be attached to the IBM PC to display output in the same colors as a color TV set.

Columnwise recalculation: (VisiCalc) the pattern followed in recalculating formulas when the user changes the value of a variable. The formulas are recalculated column-by-column, starting with the left-hand column.

Command: a name given to a high-level order issued to the computer. A command is more powerful than a program instruction and causes the computer to perform a fundamental task. While you are using BASIC you can initiate commands to cause the computer to LIST or RUN programs; with dBASE II you can cause the computer to CREATE or DISPLAY files; with VisiCalc you can cause the computer to MOVE rows and STORE spreadsheets; with WordStar you can cause the computer to REFORM text and to SEARCH AND FIND. All of these operations are commands.

Compiler: a system program that transforms a source program written in a problem-oriented language into an object program in machine language.

Computer schematic: the diagram showing the basic parts of a computer system—input units(s), central processing unit, output unit(s), and secondary storage. It applies to any computer system.

Conceptual system: the representation of a physical system. A good example is the MIS, which represents certain physical properties of the organization. The representation is accomplished by the storage of data reflecting conditions such as the status of inventory and reflecting activities such as the work flow.

Constant: a value in a program that does not change. For example, if a payroll program computes overtime hours by subtracting 40 hours from the number of hours worked, 40 is a constant.

Control unit: the part of the CPU that makes all of the units within the computer system work together.

Data base: in the broadest sense, all of the data existing within an organization. However the term has a narrower focus—that data residing in computer storage.

Data base concept: a new way of thinking about an organization's data resource that originated during early 1970s. Previous to that time files were considered to be separate entities, but the data base concept regards all files as a large reservoir of information. Files continue to exist separately but are integrated logically. This means that contents from several files can be brought together quickly and easily as needed.

Data base management system (DBMS): the system software that logically integrates data within a data base.

Data dictionary: a listing of all the data items or elements in a program or a data base. In a BASIC program the data dictionary usually appears first and lists each variable name (such as N$) and its description (such as Customer Name).

Data element: the smallest unit of data such as age, sex, name, and so on. Also called a *data item* and *field.*

Data item: *see* Data element.

Data processing: operations on data that transform it into a more usable form such as sorted data, summarized data, or stored data. The term is often used to describe accounting applications for the computer as opposed to those of a decision support nature. Some people use the term *information processing* to distinguish the decision support applications.

Decision Support System (DSS): a concept originating in the early 1970s that emphasizes solution of single problems, usually of a semistructured nature and which does not attempt to meet all of the manager's information needs. Many people consider the use of an online device such as a keyboard terminal or a small computer to be a requirement.

Deterministic model: a mathematical model that does not make use of probabilities.

Direct access: the ability to send an access mechanism directly to the location where data is stored and retrieve the data or write updated data in that location. Magnetic disk storage is an example of a direct access storage device (DASD).

Direct access storage device (DASD): *see* Direct access.

Directory: a list of files on the diskette. A directory can be displayed while a user runs any of the software systems described in this book. While in DOS the directory is displayed by entering DIR; in dBASE II a command like LIST FILES ON A: LIKE *.* is used; in VisiCalc the user enters /SL and presses the right arrow key; in WordStar the user returns to the Opening Menu.

Disk operating system (DOS): the version of the IBM PC operating system that resides on a diskette.

Disk pack: a removable stack of metal disks. This technology is no longer popular, since the capacities have increased to the point where swapping disk packs is no longer necessary.

Disk stack: a vertical arrangement of metal disks that share the same rotating shaft; the stack is permanently mounted in a cabinet.

Diskette: a flexible plastic disk that provides the secondary storage for small computers. Also called a *floppy*. The first diskettes were 8 inches in diameter, but the 5¼-inch size has been most widely adopted for use on the popular personal computers such as the IBM PC.

Diskette drive: the hardware unit that rotates the diskette and writes data onto it or reads data from it. Either one or two diskette drives are housed at the front of the system unit of the IBM PC.

DOS disk: the diskette containing the disk operating system.

DOS prompt: an uppercase A with a greater than sign after it (A>) appearing at the left-hand side of the screen. It tells you that you are in the operating system mode and that you must specify what DOS process (such as copying a file) or software system (such as WordStar) to initiate next.

Dot matrix printer: a printer that prints characters as a pattern of dots within a matrix. The IBM Graphics Printer uses a matrix of nine rows of six dots each. A dot matrix printer is fast and inexpensive, but does not produce letter quality printing. *See* Letter quality printer.

Double-density drive: a diskette drive that can write and read twice the normal number of bits within a given area. This doubles the diskette writing and reading speed.

Double-sided drive: a diskette drive that can write and read data recorded on both sides of a diskette.

Dummy end-of-file record: a special record placed at the end of a sequential file so that the computer can detect the end of the file. Some languages, such as COBOL, do not require such a record; other languages, such as BASIC, do.

Dynamic model: a mathematical model that includes time as a variable; it simulates activity over time.

Edit: (dBASE II) a command that is used to correct or change data in a data base.

Edit cue: (VisiCalc) a box appearing on the edit line that is used to highlight the position being edited. It can be moved using the arrow keys.

Edit line: (VisiCalc) the third line from the top of the screen that displays the characters as you enter them.

Editing: this term has at least three different uses in computing: (1) the data clean-up by an operator before the data is stored; (2) computer checking of data for errors after the data has been stored; and (3) the insertion of special characters such as dollar signs and commas into output data to enhance its appearance.

Electronic spreadsheet: a slang term describing the matrix of labels, values, and formulas that is handled by a software system such as VisiCalc, Multiplan, or Symphony.

Ellipsis: (VisiCalc) the three dots that appear on the edit line when you press the period key while keying in certain commands such as MOVE or REPLICATE.

Empty PRINT statement: (BASIC) an instruction containing only a line number and the word PRINT or LPRINT to produce a blank line on the screen or paper.

End-of-file routine: a series of program instructions executed after the last record has been processed. For example, a final total after processing a file of transaction records is printed during an end-of-file routine.

End-of-job routine: a series of program instructions executed just before the program is terminated. For example, to compute an arithmetic mean of a series of numbers, after the last number had been added to the total your routine would compute the mean.

Enter key: the key at the right of the PC keyboard marked with ↵ that is used to enter data into primary storage.

Entity: a modeling term that describes the phenomenon being modeled. For example, to simulate the behavior of an inventory item such as a brand of soap, the soap is the entity.

Entry contents line: (VisiCalc) the top line of the screen that identifies (1) the coordinate where the cursor is located, (2) whether the contents are a label or a value, and (3) the actual contents.

Error routine: a series of program instructions that are executed when an error condition is detected.

Exception report: an application of the principle of management by exception to the preparation of reports. A report is prepared that calls the manager's attention to only the exceptional situations—variations above or below acceptable limits.

File: a group of data records all relating to a particular subject. For example, a payroll file includes a payroll record for each employee

File maintenance: the process of keeping a file up-to-date by adding, deleting, and modifying records.

Floppy disk: a slang term for a diskette. *See* Diskette.

Form Feed key: the key located on some printers such as the IBM Graphics Printer and the Epson FX-80 that is used to advance the paper to a new page.

Formal information: information coming to the manager from a formal source or system; examples are reports received from the computer and scheduled meetings.

Formal system: a system producing information for a manager that is described by a procedure.

Formatting: the process of preparing a diskette for use. The operating system initializes the diskette to an acceptable recording format, checks each track for defects, and initializes the directory. The command file can also be copied onto the diskette so that you can boot the system with only that diskette.

Formula: (VisiCalc) an arithmetic expression stored at an entry that contains combinations of coordinates, constants, and/or function names, linked by arithmetic operators.

FORTRAN (FORmula TRANslator): the first widely adopted problem-oriented procedural language, released by IBM in 1957. FORTRAN has always been highly regarded as a powerful language for use in solving mathematical and scientific problems.

Forward reference: (VisiCalc) a reference made by a formula to other coordinates that are located to the right or below the entry where the formula is stored.

Function key: one of the set of ten keys at the left of the IBM PC keyboard labeled F1 through F10. These keys have special meanings depending on the software system in use. For example, in BASIC the F2 key is used to RUN the program, but in WordStar it is used to indent the left margin.

Function name: (BASIC, VisiCalc) the name of one of the built-in functions such as SQR (BASIC) or SQRT (VisiCalc).

General format: (VisiCalc) the standard format (right-justification for values and left justification for labels) that is in effect unless special formatting is specified with the FORMAT command.

Global: (VisiCalc) the command used to define specifications for the entire spreadsheet, such as the column width. The term has general applicability throughout the field of computing to mean that something "applies to everything."

Global descriptor: (dBASE II) a shorthand method of including in a command many file names, records, etc. For example, to display a directory by entering LIST FILES ON A: LIKE *.*, you use the asterisks as global descriptors. They say in effect to list all file names with all extensions.

GO TO key: (VisiCalc) the "greater than" key that is used along with the coordinate to specify where the cursor is to be moved. This is the fastest way to move the cursor more than a few entries when you know the address of the target entry.

Hard disk: a magnetic recording disk or stack of disks made of metal.

Hard hyphen: (WordStar) a hyphen that is entered in your copy by pressing the hyphen key; it prints whether or not it appears at the end of a line.

Hard information: information coming from a formal source or system such as the computer.

Hard return: (WordStar) use of the Enter key to cause the cursor to return to the left margin on the next line. A "less than" sign is recorded as the flag at the right margin.

Hard-sectored diskette: a diskette with multiple timing holes. This is not the type used with the IBM PC.

Hard copy: a slang term meaning a paper document.

Hardware: probably the most widely used computer term that refers to the equipment comprising the computer system. The computer units are the hardware.

Hierarchy diagram: a name given to a drawing of system parts that looks like an organization chart. It is used in top-down design to show the levels of subsystems within a system. Also called a *structure chart.*

Hyphen-help: (WordStar) the hyphenation of words usually used to reform right-justified text to achieve the best appearance of the right margin and minimize spaces between words.

IBM Graphics Printer: the printer marketed by IBM that can print graphs in addition to alphanumeric data.

IFPS: Interactive Financial Planning System. The premier electronic spreadsheet developed initially for mainframe systems but now available for the IBM PC.

Incremental printer: a printer that does not print all characters using the same width, but that allows a narrow space for some (like the letter "i") and a wider space for others (like the letter "m"). Such a printer does the best job of justifying the right margin because there are fewer unattractive gaps separating the words. Also called a *proportional spacing printer.*

Index: (dBASE II) a file of sort keys used to make records available for processing in a certain sequence without physically rearranging them in primary storage.

Index variable: (BASIC) the variable used in a FOR instruction to control the number of times the loop is executed. In the instruction FOR L = 1 TO 20, L is the index variable.

Informal information: information coming to the manager from an informal source or system.

Informal system: a system providing information to the manager that is not described by a procedure. Examples are memos, telephone calls, unscheduled meetings, and business meals.

Information System (IS): a term sometimes used to mean the same thing as MIS. It is also used to mean a system that has broader application than an MIS—one providing information not only to managers but to other employees and to the environment as well.

Initial value: (BASIC) the variable used in a FOR instruction to identify the starting point for counting the number of times a loop is executed. In the instruction FOR L = 1 to 20, 1 is the initial value.

Initialization: the process of preparing the computer by setting certain storage locations to zero or other predetermined values. A slang term is "housekeeping."

Input unit: a device for entering data or instructions into the CPU. On the IBM PC the keyboard serves as the input unit.

Instruction: a line of code in a program. The term *statement* is frequently used. An instruction or a statement is on a lower hierarchical level than a command in terms of the power of the process initiated. *See* Command.

Integer: a whole number such as 1; 25; or 1,250; contrasted to a number with decimal positions such as 1.75.

Intermediate sort key: when data records are sorted using more than two keys, the keys in the hierarchy between the major and minor keys are intermediate keys. For example, to sort by salesperson number within a sales region within a state, the sales region is the intermediate sort key.

Inventory management: an application program that manages the firm's inventory when the objectives are to minimize the investment yet maximize the level of service offered.

Kilobyte (KB): one thousand bytes. Actually there are 1024 bytes, computed by raising 2 (the basis of the computer's binary coding system) to the 10th power.

Label: (VisiCalc) the name of a data item or several items. For example, the description over a column of data in a report is considered to be the label.

Left-justified: *See* Justification.

Letter quality printer: a printer capable of producing a quality as good as that of an electric typewriter. The technology of the print mechanism is the determining factor. A printer using a daisy wheel can produce letter quality text, but a printer using a dot matrix cannot. The quality is normally achieved with a loss of speed and an increase in cost.

Line Feed key: a key on the printer that causes the paper to move up one space each time it is pressed.

Line number: (BASIC) a number that precedes each instruction in a BASIC program that tells the computer the sequence to follow in executing the instructions. Most other procedural languages do not require a number for each line.

Linear programming: a mathematical technique that determines the optimal mix of ingredients or routing of resources to achieve a particular objective within certain constraints. Called *LP*.

List: another name for an array. *See* Array. Also, a command used in BASIC to display a program on the screen, and a command used in dBASE II to display records on the screen or print them out on the printer.

Logged drive: the diskette drive being used at the time. The a: drive is the logged drive when you boot the system. You switch to the b: drive by specifying b: after the DOS prompt or by using a b: prefix with a file name after a prompt in dBASE II, WordStar, or VisiCalc.

Logical error: an error made by the user, systems analyst, or programmer in stating the solution to a problem incorrectly, such as adding a quantity discount to a price instead of subtracting it. The computer cannot detect a logical error, since it doesn't know the intent of the program.

Logical operators: the characters used in a logical IF statement to represent an equal (=), greater than (>), or less than (<) condition.

Machine language: the language that is understood by the computer; it consists of only zeros and ones. It is necessary to convert a program written in a problem-oriented language such as COBOL or BASIC into machine language by a compile process or, if the program is written in an assembler language, by an assembly process.

Machine-oriented language: a language that is intended for use on a particular computer. An assembler language is machine-oriented, whereas a language such as BASIC, C, or APL is problem-oriented.

Magnetic disk: a type of secondary storage in which data is recorded in tracks on the surfaces of rotating disks. Magnetic disk storage facilitates direct access to the data.

Magnetic tape: a type of secondary storage in which data is recorded on reels of magnetic tape similar to the way sound is recorded on sound tape. Records on magnetic tape must be processed in the same sequence as they appear on the tape; direct access is not possible.

Main memory: another name for the primary storage of the computer housed in the CPU.

Mainframe: the slang term used to describe larger computers. Originally the term meant the main part of the computer system, or the CPU, but with the advent of the minicomputer the term came to identify that group of computers larger than the minis.

Major sort key: the most important key involved in a sort. When you sort using two keys, such as salesperson number within sales region, the sales region is the major key.

Management Information System (MIS): a system that provides the manager with information for decision making. Originally the term was used to distinguish such a computer application from the traditional accounting jobs. Over the years it has come to describe the firm's overall computer operation. Recently the term *decision* *support system (DSS)* has gained popularity in describing the information-producing applications. Some people believe that DSS replaced MIS. Others feel that DSS is a part of MIS.

Managerial functions: the basic tasks that a manager performs—to plan, organize, staff, direct, and control. This classification scheme was developed by Henri Fayol in 1916, along with several other fundamental ideas that became the foundation for classical management theory.

Mask: a slang term describing a pattern used to influence the appearance of data. In BASIC the term is used in conjunction with the PRINT USING instruction to describe the pattern of special characters that causes a dollar sign, commas, or a decimal point to be inserted into a data item for printing.

Master file: a file containing data of a fairly permanent nature. Master files are typically maintained for a firm's customers, personnel, inventory, and so on. They form the most important part of the data base.

Matrix: a group of data items assembled in rows and columns forming two or more dimensions. We are most familiar with two-dimensional matrices, called *tables*. The computer can handle matrices with as many as three or more dimensions.

Microcomputer: classification of the smallest computers—smaller than a minicomputer.

Microprocessor: the central processing unit of a computer housed on a single metal-oxide-semiconductor (MOS) chip. It forms a major portion of the circuitry of a microcomputer and accounts for its small size.

Midtext ruler line: (WordStar) the special ruler line that can be created during the middle of a text for use in arranging data in columns.

Minicomputer: the class of smaller computers that became popular during the early 1970s. Some minis are more powerful than larger mainframes and are called super minis.

Minor sort key: the least important sort key when two or more keys are used. For example, if you are sorting records by salesperson number within sales region, the salesperson number is the minor sort key.

Mnemonic name: a name used to identify data or computer operations that is more meaningful to the programmer than is the machine language name. Mnemonic names form the basis of assembler language. For example a mnemonic name HOURS is used to identify the storage location where the number of hours worked is located, and the name MPY is used to identify a multiplication operation.

Model: a simulation or representation of a situation. Various types of models exist—physical, graphic, narrative, and mathematical. The mathematical model forms the basis for management science applications (those involving use of advanced mathematics to solve business problems) and is an integral part of an MIS or DSS.

Monochrome display: the name given to the cathode ray tube (CRT) attached to an IBM PC that displays data using only one color such as green or amber on a black background.

MS-DOS: the version of the disk operating system marketed by Microsoft.

Nested loop: a loop within a loop. Usually nested loops are used to perform operations on a matrix of data.

Nested parentheses: pairs of parentheses contained within pairs of outer parentheses. Nested parentheses are found in arithmetic statements to control the sequence of the processes. The processes within the inner parentheses are performed first.

Networking: the interconnection of two or more computers using some type of data communication lines. Very often networks consist of small computers linked to a mainframe computer. This arrangement enables the small computer users to have access to the data base or the processing power of the larger computer.

Networks: the configurations of multiple computers interconnected by data communications lines. *See* Networking.

No-change coordinate: (VisiCalc) a coordinate in a formula that is not to be changed as that formula is replicated.

Nonincremental printer: a printer that prints all characters with the same width. For example, even though the letter "i" is narrower than the letter "m," both occupy the same space on the line. Regular typewriters are examples of nonincremental printers, as are dot matrix printers.

Nonoptimizing model: a mathematical model that does not produce only the best answer; it produces an answer and it is left to the user to determine whether it is the best one or not. Most models are nonoptimizing, and the manager uses them by playing the what-if game.

Numeric coprocessor: the metal-oxide-semiconductor chip contained within the IBM PC that is used as the arithmetic and logic unit.

Numeric keypad: the set of ten keys at the right of the IBM PC keyboard that are used to enter numeric data. The user can perform calculations using only the right hand, speeding the entry of numeric data.

Object program: the machine language program produced by a compiler or an assembler.

Off-the-shelf software: *see* Prewritten software.

Online key: the toggle key on the printer that switches the printer from an offline to an online condition and back again. The printer must be online to print, but must be offline to load the paper or to manually space down to a lower line using the Line Feed key or advance to the next page using the Form Feed key.

Online light: the light on the printer that tells you whether the printer is online (the light is on) or offline (the light is off). *See* Online key.

Online processing: the name given to one of two basic ways of processing data. The most traditional way is batch processing. Online processing requires the computer configuration to include some type of keyboard to enter transactions as they occur, plus direct access storage. The term *transaction processing* is often used synonymously, but transaction processing also can mean accounting applications. When online processing includes a feedback loop enabling the computer system to effect changes in the physical system, the computer is said to be operating in real time.

Open-loop system: a system without a feedback loop.

Operating budget: often called simply "the budget," it is the financial plan for a firm or a subunit within the firm identifying the amounts of money that can be spent during a certain period, such as a year.

Operating environment integration: one of three methods for achieving integration of software systems in which a special program enables separately designed packages to work together. For example, dBASE II can furnish data to WordStar. Visi/ON and DesQ provide such an environment.

Operating system: the master program that controls the computer. You cannot use the computer without complying with the instructions from the operating system. Early computers did not have operating systems and many system tasks had to be done by the operator. The IBM System/360, announced in 1964, was the first computer to offer an operating system furnished by the vendor.

Optimizing model: a mathematical model that identifies the best answer in terms of achieving the model's objective. Usually the objective is to minimize something, such as costs, or to maximize something, such as profit. Linear programming is an example of an optimizing model.

Output unit: the part of the computer system that produces the output, such as a printed document. The IBM PC has two output units—the printer and the screen.

Overflow: the term used to describe the condition when a computed answer is too large to fit within the assigned storage space. For example, if a multiplication produces an answer 123.75 but only four spaces are reserved to store the digits, the leftmost or "high-order" position is lost. The storage location would contain 23.75.

Page break line: (WordStar) the dotted line that appears on the screen to separate one page from the next.

Parameter: an attribute value of a mathematical model that does not change during a simulation. For example, if you use a model to simulate the effect of a price of $35 for a year's operations, 35 is a parameter.

Pascal: the procedural language developed by Niklaus Wirth that facilitates the use of structured programming, but has not been widely adopted in business because of its inability to handle direct access files.

PC compatible: a computer that can read data from a diskette produced by an IBM PC, write a diskette to be used with a PC, and execute most (but not necessarily all) programs written for the PC.

PC-DOS: the version of the disk operating system for the PC marketed by IBM. It was developed by Microsoft for IBM and is compatible with MS-DOS.

Periodic report: a report prepared on a certain schedule, such as monthly. Also called a *repetitive report*.

Personal computer: a computer used by an individual rather than an entire organization. One used in the home or by only one person in an office are examples.

Physical system of the firm: the integration of resources existing physically such as personnel, machines, materials, and money that comprise the business firm. Managers and computers are also a part of the physical system, but they both have properties enabling them to function as a conceptual system representing the physical system.

PL/I (Programming Language I): the procedural language developed by IBM to contain the best features of COBOL and FORTRAN. Although not as popular as COBOL, it is used by many mainframe programmers because of its ability to handle files and to facilitate structured programming.

Portable: the ability to execute a program on a variety of computers. An example is a VisiCalc program that can be executed on both IBM and TI personal computers.

Pre-data base approach: the technique for designing computer-based systems where files are treated separately. The advent of data base management systems permitted many users to logically integrate multiple files to form a data base. However, many firms are still following the pre-data base approach.

Prewritten software: software purchased from a vendor, as opposed to software that a firm's programmers produce. The terms *off-the-shelf software* and *packaged software* are synonymous.

Pricing model: a mathematical model that is used to assist the manager in determining what price to charge for a product or service.

Primary storage: the storage contained within the CPU.

Print switch toggle technique: (dBASE II) a method for causing the printer to print file contents as they are displayed on the screen.

Probabilistic model: a mathematical model that incorporates probabilities.

Problem avoider: a manager who dislikes problems and will not attempt to solve them even when they are called to his or her attention.

Problem seeker: a manager who enjoys the challenge of solving problems and will seek them out.

Problem solver: a manager who will not make a special effort to uncover problems to be solved, but will not back away from them when they become evident.

Problem-oriented language: the term given to languages such as FORTRAN and COBOL to distinguish them from assembler languages. A problem-oriented language is designed to solve a certain class of problems rather than to be used on a certain machine.

Procedural language: a programming language that enables the programmer to solve a problem by instructing the computer to follow a certain procedure. The language includes a set of instructions that perform a wide variety of operations, and the programmer uses them in the proper sequence. Such a language is adaptable to a very wide variety of problems.

Product family integration: a means of integrating multiple software systems by developing them so that they work together. A good example is the family of systems developed by VisiCorp that includes VisiCalc, VisiTrend, and VisiPlot.

Profit model: the basic business equation $P = R - C$, where P is profit, R is revenue, and C is cost.

Program: the sequence of instructions, written using a procedural language, that causes a computer to perform the desired operations. The term *software* is commonly used to describe programs.

Program flowchart: a schematic diagram using symbols of different shapes to illustrate the logical structure of a program.

Program maintenance: the activity of keeping a program current by incorporating changes and improvements.

Programmer: the person who prepares programs.

Programming process: the procedure followed by a programmer in developing a program.

Prompt: a cue that appears on the screen, telling the user that an action is required. For example, the DOS prompt tells the user that a command must be entered to cause DOS to perform a function, such as copying a file, or to call up a program such as WordStar.

Prompt line: (VisiCalc) the second line from the top of the screen that tells the user which type of data is being entered—label or value.

Proportional spacing printer: *see* Incremental printer.

Prt Sc technique: (DBASE II) the method used to print what is displayed on the screen by holding down the Shift key and pressing the Print Screen key (labeled Prt Sc).

Pseudocode: a narrative description of a program that looks like a computer language, but isn't. It is a means of describing a program in a structured manner as an alternative to using a program flowchart. It is usually used in conjunction with other documentation tools such as data flow diagrams and data dictionaries.

Query: a request for information entered into a computer system. In most cases the computer configuration includes a keyboard terminal used to enter the query and a direct access storage device to provide the information with very little delay.

Query language: a special language that exists alone or as a subset of a data base management system that enables the user to easily make a query.

Random access memory (RAM): computer storage that enables direct access to any location without the need for sequential search. The storage permits writing of data as well as reading. The RAM is used to store programs and data.

Read-only memory (ROM): a type of primary storage that enables the user to only read data or instructions that have been recorded there by the manufacturer. The user cannot alter the contents of ROM. In the IBM PC, cassette BASIC is stored in ROM. Some people use the term *firmware* to describe such software stored in a hardware form.

Record: a collection of data items that all relate to a certain subject. For example, a payroll record describes all payroll-related data for an employee. Multiple records make up a file.

Reform: (WordStar) the changing of the format of a paragraph by placing the cursor on the top line and typing ^B. The format of the paragraph is changed to comply to the line spacing, ruler line, and justification mode then in effect. The process is stopped when the first hard return is detected.

Relational operator: (dBASE II) the name given to one of the special characters used in a LIST or DISPLAY command to show logical relationships between data items. For example, in the command LIST FOR SALES > 10000, the > is a relational operator. The term *logical operator* is used in other software systems.

Relative coordinate: (VisiCalc) a coordinate in a formula that is to be changed as that formula is replicated.

Right-justified: *See* Justification.

RIOS: the ROM Basic Input/Output System of the IBM PC that converts operating system commands into a form that causes units connected to the CPU to carry out tasks specified by a program.

Rowwise recalculaton: (VisiCalc) the pattern followed in recalculating formulas when the user changes the value of a variable. The formulas are recalculated row-by-row, starting with the upper one.

Ruler line: (WordStar) the line that appears as a part of the Main Menu and shows the left and right margins as well as the tab stops.

Scenario: the attribute values entered into a mathematical model that "set the stage" for the simulation. The values specify the conditions within which the phenomenon will be simulated.

Screen: a slang term describing the cathode ray tube (CRT) that is used to display computer output.

Scrolling: the process of losing a line at the top of the screen as one is added at the bottom, or vice versa. It occurs because there are too many lines to display on the screen at one time.

Search argument: a term used in a table lookup operation to describe the value for which you are searching. When found, the number in the table is called the *table argument*. Table lookup therefore is a process of searching a table to find a table argument that will match the search argument.

Secondary storage: storage that is online to the computer but is not a part of the CPU. Magnetic disk and magnetic tape units are examples.

Sector: a section of a disk or diskette surface that is shaped like a slice of pie. When a diskette is formatted on an IBM PC using a 2.0 or later version of DOS, each side of the diskette is divided into 9 sectors. Within each sector there are 40 track segments, each with a capacity of 512 bytes.

Self-documenting language: a procedural language that produces understandable documentation as an automatic byproduct of the coding process. COBOL is the best example because of its English-like instructions. Examples of languages that have little self-documentary features are APL and C.

Semistructured problem: a problem that includes some variables that are identifiable and their compositon and relationships are understood. This is the type of problem at which the DSS concept is aimed. Some people argue that no problem is completely unstructured, and that therefore even the most difficult problem is a semistructured one.

Sequential processing: the type of processing in which one record is processed after another. In most cases the sequence is determined by the order in which the records appear in storage. For example, on magnetic tape the first record is processed first, the second record is processed second, and so on. This term is often mistakenly used to mean the same thing as batch processing. Most batch processing is performed in a sequential manner, but it is not absolutely necessary.

Sight verification: an error-checking process that involves the visual comparison of data entered into the computer (such as that displayed on the screen) with the data on the source documents.

Simulate: to represent something with a model.

Simulation: the process of using a model to represent some real phenomenon.

Simulator: the mechanism performing the simulation. If a computer is used, the computer and its software are the simulator.

Single-density drive: a diskette drive that does not achieve any special efficiencies in use of the storage space as double-density drives do by packing the data bits closer together. The drives on the IBM PC have never been this type. PC drives are double-density—the bits are recorded at twice the density as on a single-density drive.

Single-sided drive: a diskette drive that writes or reads data recorded on only one side of the diskette. Early IBM PC drives were of this type, but recently manufactured ones are double-sided.

Small business system: the name given to a small computer, usually a micro, that is used by a business organization. Most IBM PC systems are used in this manner.

Soft hyphen: (WordStar) the hyphen added to text as it is being reformed. This hyphen will print only when it is the last character on the line.

Soft information: information coming from an informal source or system, such as personal conversation, memos, and letters.

Soft return: (WordStar) the automatic return of the cursor to the left margin when the line becomes full. It does not become a permanent part of the text and can be changed by reforming the text with different margin settings.

Soft-sectored diskette: a diskette such as the one used by the IBM PC that has a single timing hole.

Software: the slang term used to describe computer programs.

Sort key: the data item used as the basis for rearranging the sequence of records in a file. For example, if you are sorting the records into sequence based on customer number, the customer number is the sort key.

Source diskette: the diskette that you are copying from in a DISKCOPY operation.

Source program: the program that the programmer writes, using a problem-oriented language or an assembler language.

Special report: a report prepared in response to a special request or event as opposed to one prepared on a regular schedule.

Spreadsheet: a large sheet with many rows and columns used in manual accounting systems.

State variable: an attribute value of a mathematical model that changes during the course of the simulation. As an example, in an inventory model the ending balance changes each day; hence it is a state variable. The variable reflects the "state" of the model at a point in time.

Static model: a model reflecting the condition of the phenomenon being modeled at a single point in time. It is analogous to a snapshot.

Status line: (WordStar) the line at the top of the screen above the Main Menu that identifies the file being used, the page, line, and column number where the cursor is located, whether the insert feature is on, and the line spacing.

String constant: a term used to describe a "string" of alphanumeric characters that usually forms some type of descriptor or message, such as a customer's name or the words "final total."

Structure chart: *see* Hierarchy diagram.

Structured problem: a problem consisting of variables that are all identified and their relationships understood. The decision of how much of an item to order (the economic order quantity) is an example.

Structured programming: the currently popular approach to programming that is very rigid in terms of the types of modules used, what is contained within each module, and how the modules are interconnected.

Subscripted variable: a value in a list or a table that must be identified by attaching a subscript to the name. The subscript can be a number, a variable name, or an arithmetic expression.

Syntax error: a mistake made in a program line that violates the rules of the language being used, for example, if you include a left parenthesis in a LET instruction with no accompanying right parenthesis. The computer can detect this type of programming error.

System: an integration of elements designed to accomplish some objective.

System flowchart: a schematic diagram of a system using specially shaped symbols.

System unit: the part of the IBM PC housing the CPU and the diskette drive(s).

Systems analyst: the person having the responsibility of interfacing with the user and then designing a system that meets the user's needs.

System program: a program designed to perform some function that is useful to all or nearly all of the users of that computer. For example, most users of the IBM PC would need an operating system and a procedural language compiler. Any type of organization could use these system programs; they are not unique to any business application.

Tab key: the key in the upper left part of the PC keyboard that causes the cursor to move eight spaces at a time while in BASIC and five spaces at a time while in WordStar. It has both a left and a right arrow on it.

Target disk: the diskette that you are copying to when executing a DISKCOPY operation.

Terminal value: (BASIC) the portion of a FOR instruction that specifies the maximum value of the index variable. As an example, in the instruction FOR L = 1 TO 20, the 20 is the terminal value.

Timesharing: the use of a computer by multiple users.

Toggle key: a key that switches the computer between two modes of operation. An example is the Caps Lock key: each time it is depressed the keyboard shifts from lower case to upper case or vice versa.

Top-down design: the approach followed in designing a solution to a problem by starting with the overall picture and gradually making it more refined and detailed.

Track: a circular area on a disk or diskette surface on which data bits are recorded. The diskette used by the IBM PC has 40 tracks on each surface.

Transaction file: a file containing descriptions of transactions, such as product sales, that are used to update a master file.

Truncation: the loss of one or more digits when the space devoted to their storage, display, or printing is not large enough. For example, if you try to print the value 12.785 with only two spaces available for the decimal digits, the 5 will be lost due to truncation, and the value will print as 12.78.

Universal workstation: a keyboard unit that provides the operator with all of the media needed to perform a task. The unit displays contents of computer records as well as images of documents.

Value: (VisiCalc) a numeric data item stored at an entry.

Variable: an element in an arithmetic formula that can take on different values. The variable is given a name, and the name rather than the value is used in a computer program. This enables the same program to be used with many different values assigned to the variables.

What-if game: a use of a nonoptimizing model to try out various decision strategies.

Winchester disk: a hard disk enclosed in a contamination-free container.

Window: (VisiCalc) a portion of the screen devoted to displaying a part of the spreadsheet. As many as two windows can be used—side by side, or one on top of the other.

Word wrap: (WordStar) the name given to the automatic return of the cursor to the next line when a line becomes full. If a word will not fit at the end of the line it is not hyphenated but is placed at the beginning of the next line.

Wrap-around: a computer feature in which data is not lost when it exceeds the allowed space, but appears at the opposite end of the space. An example is the manner in which variables are printed in zones by a BASIC program. If there are too many variables to print on one line, they will be printed in sequence from left to right on successive lines. The printer operates in the same manner while in the VisiCalc mode.

Write protect notch: the notch at the edge of a diskette that can prevent accidental erasure when it is covered with an adhesive sticker. It is impossible to execute a write operation when the diskette is write protected.

Index